Alice Munro's Miraculous Art

Alice Munro's Miraculous Art

Critical Essays

Edited by
Janice Fiamengo and Gerald Lynch

Reappraisals: Canadian Writers
University of Ottawa Press 2017

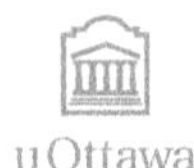

The University of Ottawa Press gratefully acknowledges the support extended to its publishing list by Heritage Canada through the Canada Book Fund and by the Canada Council for the Arts. This book has been published with the help of a grant from the Federation for the Humanities and Social Sciences, through the Awards to Scholarly Publications Program, using funds provided by the Social Sciences and Humanities Research Council of Canada.

Copy editing: Michael Waldin
Proofreading: Robbie McCaw
Typesetting: CS
Cover illustration and design: Bartosz Walczak

Library and Archives Canada Cataloguing in Publication

Alice Munro's miraculous art : critical essays / edited by Janice Fiamengo and Gerald Lynch.

(Reappraisals : Canadian writers ; 38)
Includes bibliographical references and index.
Issued in print and electronic formats.
ISBN 978-0-7766-2433-4 (softcover).--ISBN 978-0-7766-2434-1 (PDF).--
ISBN 978-0-7766-2435-8 (EPUB).--ISBN 978-0-7766-2436-5 (Kindle)

1. Munro, Alice, 1931- --Criticism and interpretation. I. Fiamengo, Janice Anne, 1964-, editor II. Lynch, Gerald, 1953-, editor III. Title: Miraculous art. IV. Series: Reappraisals, Canadian writers ; 38

PS8576.U57Z52 2017 C813'.54 C2017-900570-7
C2017-900571-5

Canada

for
Alice Munro,
with gratitude

Table of Contents

Acknowledgements

We are grateful to many people and a number of institutions for contributing generously of their time, expertise, and funds, and consequently for helping to make possible the success initially of the Alice Munro Symposium in spring 2014 and subsequently of the present volume of select essays.

Sandra MacPherson's abundant energy and unflappable good spirits were instrumental in organizing the large symposium and ensuring its unqualified success. As well, throughout the process we have been encouraged by the support of our Department of English at the University of Ottawa, our colleagues and fellow Canadianists.

Robert Thacker was a wise guide in matters Munro from the inception of this project to its completion, and Tracy Ware was as unstinting with helpful advice.

We continue grateful to the panel of writers and publishing professionals who presented at the symposium but do not appear in the book: Munro's long-time American editors, Ann Close and Daniel Menaker, her equally long-time Canadian editor, Douglas Gibson, and her agent, Virginia Barber. And we similarly thank Canadian writers Stephen Heighton, Robert McGill, Lisa Moore, and Aritha Van Herk for sharing their appreciations of Munro and thoughts on her influence in their writing lives.

University of Ottawa Press has been the loyal publisher of the Reappraisals: Canadian Writers series since its inception, in 1972. We thank the current personnel of UOP, particularly Dominike Thomas and Elizabeth Schwaiger, as well as the anonymous external readers of our manuscript and its copyeditors, all of whose exemplary professional work made for a better book at every turn.

It is highly doubtful that this project, both symposium and book, would ever have been realized—and assuredly not as successfully—without the financial support of the Social Sciences and Humanities Research Council of Canada, the Faculty of Arts Research and Publications Committee of the University of Ottawa, and the University of Ottawa Research Fund.

Finally, our greatest debt is of course to the contributors to this volume. The edifying quality of their critical insights remains primary. But their patient endurance of the editors' requests and questions over some two years can be explained only by our shared admiration of Alice Munro's miraculous art and their own kindly dispositions.

Thank you all.

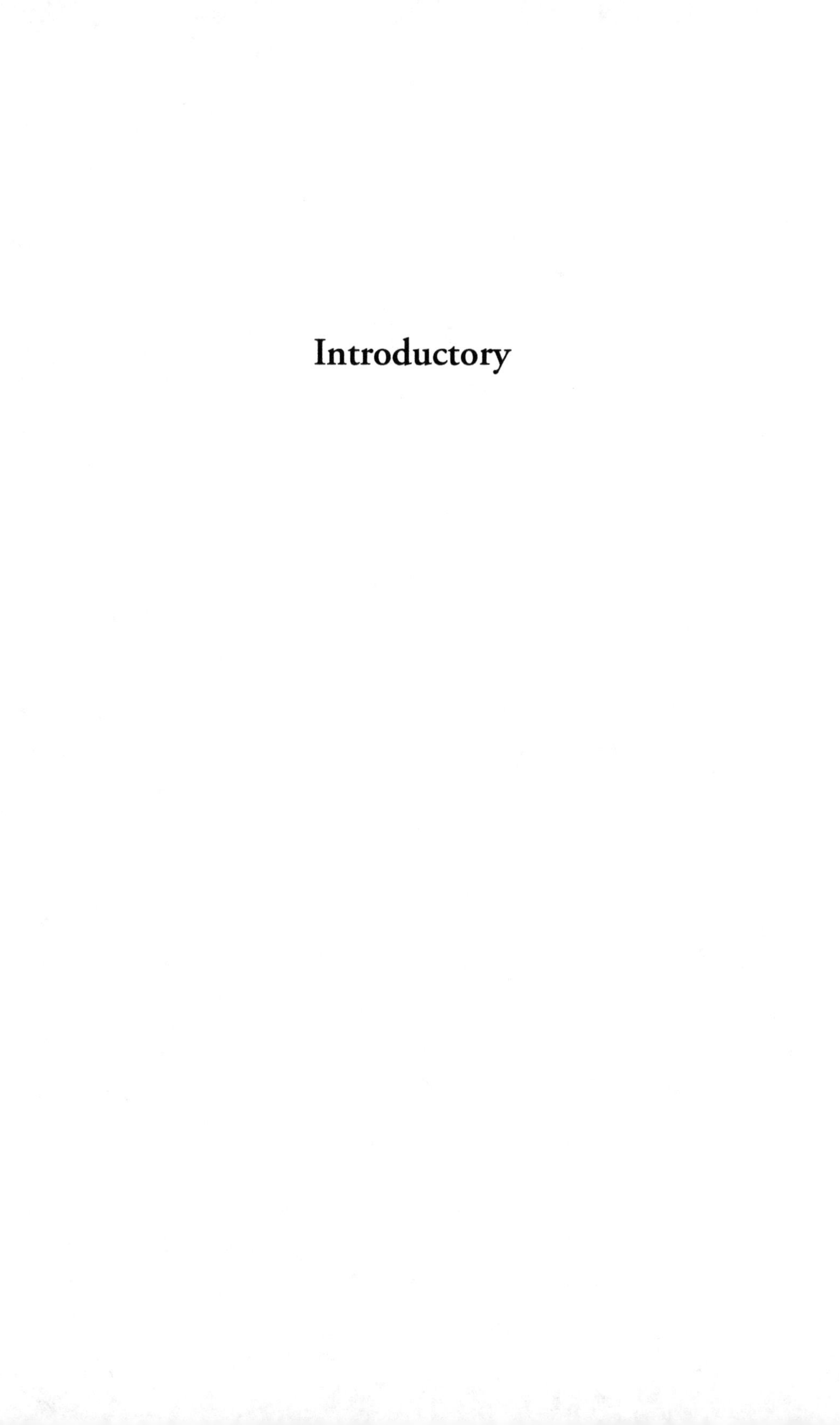

Introductory

Alice Munro's Miraculous Art

JANICE FIAMENGO AND GERALD LYNCH

Canadians and lovers of the short story were delighted, if perhaps surprised, when the Nobel committee awarded the literature prize to Alice Munro in October 2013, praising her cultivation of the story form "almost to perfection" ("Canadian" n.p.). At last, a Canadian had been recognized—and not only a Canadian, but "our Alice," humble bard of the bush farms and unglamorous lives of her southern-Ontario people, crafter of weird and wonderful tales. And perhaps, like various Munro characters who feel disappointed or bitter when they know they should feel glad, or for whom the taint of the disreputable attaches to recognition, there may even have been some few who were ambivalent at the news, accustomed as they were to keeping Munro to themselves.

In the wake of the Nobel, plaudits from contemporary writers and critics poured in, with commentators reaching for superlatives and applying broad-brush summations to convey the nature of Munro's achievement. A note struck more than once was the extraordinary compassion of Munro's vision, often with comparison to Chekhov. Writing for the *New York Times*, for example, Michiko Kakutani spoke of the "emotional amplitude" and "psychological density" of the stories: "Mrs. Munro has given us prismatic portraits of ordinary people [. . .] delivered with the sort of 'unsparing unsentimental love' harbored by a close friend or family member." Kakutani commended the stories for having "the swoop and density of big, intimate novels, mapping the crevices of characters' hearts with clear-eyed Chekhovian empathy and wisdom." The Mail Online concurred, calling Munro "a thorough but forgiving documenter of the human spirit" and "a modern Chekhov for her warmth, insight, and compassion, and for capturing a wide range of lives and personalities without passing judgement on her characters" ("Canadian" n.p.).

Some might find this a striking, not to say counter-intuitive, summation of an author whose storytellers seem so often motivated not by compassion and warmth but by unforgiveness or downright malice, who betray friends or family members seemingly on a whim, who use memories in an attempt to "get rid" of a long-dead mother ("The Ottawa Valley" 215), or who record without apology their long-smouldering resentments, jealousies, and ill-wishing. Such an emphasis seems to have influenced Margaret Atwood, who, when asked to comment on Munro's work for the *New Yorker*, highlighted the viciousness and depravity of Munro's created worlds, her "wallowing in the seamier and meaner and more vengeful undersides of human nature, the telling of erotic secrets, the nostalgia for vanished miseries" as well as, it must be said, her "rejoicing in the fullness and variety of life" ("Writers on Munro" n.p.). Lorrie Moore, quoted alongside Atwood, also commented on Munro's relationship to her characters, in this case stressing her dispassionate neutrality: "She does not overtly judge—especially human cruelty—but allows human encounters to speak for themselves. She honours mysteriousness and is a neutral beholder before the unpredictable." Jeffrey Eugenides had a foot in both camps when he claimed in the *Washington Post* that "She's the most savage writer I've ever read, also the most tender, the most honest" ("Reactions" n.p.).

When critics commented on Munro's content and form, there were again some notable differences of emphasis. The *Guardian* quoted Colm Tóibín on her "sentences of the most ordinary kind [...] constructed with slow Chekhovian care" (Higgins n.p.). In the *New Yorker*, Jhumpa Lahiri emphasized the revolutionary nature of the stories, how Munro "turned the form on its head" ("Writers" n.p.). Anne Enright in the *Guardian* stressed the ordinariness of Munro's tales, arguing that her characters "are like you, actually—or a heightened, more perceptive version of you . . ." (Higgins n.p.). In contrast, one reader in the comments section following the Mail Online article found Munro's characters like no people he could imagine or understand, describing "Beautifully detailed stories of people who interact in ways that leave me baffled—What was that all about? Where was the point? Colour-blindness must be much the same" ("Canadian" n.p.). For this reader, far from revealing the secrets of the human heart, Munro's stories would appear to offer a "sealed-off country" (*Lives* 57).

Even from these few comments, one can glean something of the complexity of summing up Munro's fiction, and such differences have been at the heart of responses to her work over the decades. Is her fiction compassionate or dispassionate, realistic or metafictional, domestic or grotesque? Is Munro a writer's writer, or is she a popular writer of ordinary lives—who yet tells us that there *are* no ordinary lives (Richards xiv)? Is she a classic short-story writer in the tradition of Chekhov, or a revolutionary one who turns the form on its head? Munro herself, a master of the paradox, often creates stories out of self-cancelling strings of modifiers ("dull, simple, amazing, and unfathomable [*Lives* 236]), or even out of whole scenes drastically undercut ("I don't think so. I don't think I really saw all this" ["Miles City, Montana" 80]). Bewildering shifts in time or perspective, a sudden undermining of previously definitive judgements, jarring revelations, a confessional emphasis on the tricks and provisionality of the story being told—all encourage readers to recognize how experience, and its recounting, are never clear or singular. Readers are tasked, like many of Munro's narrators, to come to terms with "everything that is contradictory and persistent and unaccommodating about life" ("Bardon Bus" 128).

From the earliest stories (one thinks of the narrator in "Walker Brothers Cowboy," who senses her father's life "darkening and turning strange, like a landscape that has an enchantment on it" [18]). Munro has been par excellence the writer of the unfathomable, the "something you will never know" (18), with stories so rich and strange that we feel we can never get to the bottom of them. Coral Ann Howells, perhaps taking her cue from Del Jordan's description of her Uncle Benny's world "lying alongside our world [. . .] like a troubling distorted reflection" (*Lives* 26), uses the metaphor of "two worlds at once" to describe the persistent doubleness of Munro's vision:

> To read Munro's stories is to discover the delights of seeing two worlds at once: an ordinary everyday world and the shadowy map of another imaginary or secret world laid over the real one, so that in reading we slip from one world into the other in an unassuming domestic sort of way.

The experience of reading Munro can indeed leave one with the sense that the characters and events of the world as we know it, or as we thought we knew it, are but projections in a Plato's cave. Reality, unknowable directly, is glimpsed only in her fiction's assuredly tentative "translation." And as one of her characters thinks about the art of representation, "translation is dubious. Dangerous, as well" ("Who Do You Think You Are?" 206).

It is a commonplace to say that Munro is a chronicler of the lives of girls and women, a storyteller of the "open secrets" of the domestic, those "deep caves paved with kitchen linoleum" (*Lives* 236). Many of her characters are "wrecked survivors of the female life, with stories to tell" (*Lives* 39). Her particular genius has been, perhaps, her matter-of-fact portrayal of the realities of sex and the body: sexual initiation, the adulterous desires, shocking inclinations, betrayal of maternal impulse, animalistic obsessions, and remorseless necessities of female desire. Never flattering feminine sensibilities or pandering to sentimental (or radical feminist) conceptions of female (or childhood) innocence, she has returned repeatedly to the conflict between small-town sexual mores and carnal compulsions, often to unsettling effect. Here are women who betray their husbands without regret, who abandon their children for a romantic fantasy ("The Children Stay") and learn to live with the pain. She has also, as a determinedly secular writer, occasionally provided an unsparing examination of religious practices and beliefs, their continuing power as a bulwark against despair, their fascination and failure.

Although the word "ordinary" often comes up in relation to Munro's fictional characters and their locales, her stories have always been preoccupied by the gothic and the grotesque, the uncanny and the unnatural: rat poison in the kitchen cupboard, a hand held down on a stove burner, a severed head in the hallway. Over the length of her career, this aspect seemed to intensify such that the stories' focus on murder, perversion, deformity, betrayal, and hideous accident has come ever more insistently to the fore. Notwithstanding many critics' avowal that Munro reveals the heart of her characters and shows us human nature in all its variety—which at one level is undeniable—there is also in her stories the overriding emphasis on the inexplicable, on characters whose behaviour is obscure even to themselves (and certainly to the reader), who seem to operate outside the bounds of psychological believability. A college-age girl sits before a middle-aged man, a relative stranger, and reads poetry, stark naked—and seems to triumph in the event ("Wenlock Edge" 80–81). A good woman who has dedicated her life to serving the indigent sick decides to marry a man who may be a murderer ("The Love of a Good Woman" 64). A grotesque decapitation at a piano factory brings romance into the life of a woman who years before had carried on an epistolary romance with the dead man ("Carried Away"). In such stories it often seems that psychological plausibility is less the point than some larger vision of the strange, perhaps random, patternings of human life. The stories' emphasis on the passage of time and how it estranges us from our own memories often deepen one's sense of inscrutability, of the "puzzles you can't resist or solve" ("The Progress of Love" 13). In the highly complex "The Progress of Love," for example, conflicting memories of key events in the history of a family are layered one upon the other as inextricably as the old home's layered wallpaper that, if peeled, damages the earlier versions. Reading and appreciating such stories can require a good measure of Keatsian negative capability.

In her earlier stories Munro displayed a fondness for concluding paragraphs offering insights—often employing overt contradiction ("abusive and forlorn" ["Thanks for the Ride" 53], "undefeated, unrequited love" [*Lives* 133])—to bring her stories to a satisfying though often ambiguous (sometimes jolting) resolution. One thinks of Del's "tender remorse, which has on its other side a brutal, unblemished satisfaction" (*Lives* 60). These earlier stories had a tightness of structure that balanced their often lavish, hyper/realist detail: the abundant, excessive lists, the compulsive cataloguing of objects. Later stories drew back from what Munro had begun to feel was a too-mannered style. The stories became longer, and though always carefully patterned, made the reader work harder to discern the patterns. The refusal of resolution became more pronounced. Often there was more than one narrative strand going on, with the relationship between them left unclear for much of the story (magisterially in, for example, "The Love of a Good Woman," "Miles City, Montana," and "Friend of My Youth"). Switches in time and place became bolder, more disorienting; often the story would begin somewhere *in medias res* and then move backward and forward in time with dazzling ease. Shifts in narrative perspective and a blurring of reality and fantasy also became more frequent. At the same time, the overtly metafictional elements of such stories as "Epilogue: The Photographer" (in *Lives*), "Images," and "Simon's Luck" receded, though never entirely (for example, see the later "Fiction"). In Munro's most recent stories, there has been a return to a more linear narrative structure and a simpler plot, though the inexplicability of characters' behaviour remains a hallmark of her vision (for instance, a man returning home from war suddenly jumps from the train into a new life, then makes as radical a change again ["Train"]).

The question of the autobiographical has always coloured readings of Munro's fiction. So many of the stories return to the same material—the dying mother, the guilt of the daughter, the loved but estranged father, women who need men, men in changing times, women who don't want to need men, marriages heading toward divorce. The repetition strongly suggests an autobiographical element, an excavating and working through of bedrock personal material. And yet the very repetition with variations confuses the precise delineations of autobiographical parallel. Munro's own comments, as various of the authors in the present volume suggest, both gesture toward and resist autobiographical readings. She has claimed that the emotion of her stories, but not the facts, is true. Yet as attentive readers of Munro know, the one thing that is most unreliable in any recounting of experience is the exact emotion. Often her stories are about characters who aren't sure what they felt about an event—or whose feelings have changed over time—and readers are left unsure also. "How hard it is to believe that I made that up," confesses the narrator of "The Progress of Love." "It seems so much the truth it is the truth; it's what I believe about them" (29). One of the insights of Munro's oeuvre, preoccupied from first to last with narrators who seek to tell their stories, is how difficult it is to remember exactly what something was *like*, how difficult to be true to the moment, which recedes with every remembrance and every telling.

Another significant feature of Munro's work is her representation of place, her ability to provide readers with the pungent flavour of (mostly) small-town and rural landscapes, from the dilapidated shacks and broken-down farms that we encounter at the end of the Flats Road in *Lives of Girls and Women* to the outlaw landscape of such a story as "Vandals." Here are characters who live on the edge, or well beyond the boundary, of respectability—a rich variety of eccentrics, loners, losers, drunkards, religious fanatics, and obsessives—as well as those more consciously virtuous types who observe and report on their neighbours while concealing their own craven secrets. In earlier stories, there was often a detailed visual portrait of such places; in later writing, while the visual emphasis does not entirely drop out, it diminishes. Always, though, there is a strong sense of social geography, of a felt environment.

At times the narrator is an outsider. Sometimes an upper-middle-class milieu is described from the perspective of one who may or may not accept the values of the inhabitants (many of the early stories set in Vancouver establish this relation) but who is always aware of herself as someone who must perform her role to avoid social embarrassment. At other times, the observer knows her milieu intimately; one thinks of the narrator in "Miles City, Montana" helping her father on his turkey farm just before she is to join her husband in Vancouver. Here, the narrator's deeply felt recognition of her home is heightened by her awareness that she is getting out. Escape is both necessary and regretted. Paradoxically (of course) return is also at times necessary for the sake of self-recuperation (as with Rose in *Who Do You Think You Are?*). Sometimes, the social environment is such a given that anything else—especially perhaps the more cosmopolitan environment and academic setting in which such stories are read and interpreted—seems shallow and alien.

In speaking of "Alice Munro country," we are speaking not only of southwestern Ontario but also of created worlds in which layers of meaning and feeling are evoked by a language at once direct and elusive, familiar and estranging, full of nuances and flashes of apprehension, fantastical visions or insights glimpsed out the corner of one's eye ("something not startling until you think of trying to tell it" ["Open Secrets" 160]). Without resorting to stylistic vagueness or gimmicks, Munro has mastered the ability to capture with vivid clarity experiences that cannot finally be seen whole, that seem always in the process of changing, shedding the obvious, accruing radiance. No matter what the stories do and where they take us—how formally daring or bizarre in content, how they mystify or shock us with revelation—there is about them the authority and inevitability of great art. As Elizabeth Strout said in the *Washington Post* of Munro's genius, "she goes wherever she wants, and I go with her."

* * *

The essays in this volume were originally presented at the Alice Munro Symposium, May 9–11, 2014, at the University of Ottawa, part of the annual Canadian Literature Symposium series hosted by the Department of English. We began planning the symposium in the spring of 2013, well before Munro received the Nobel committee's imprimatur, and the program of distinguished international scholars, critics, publishers, writers, and editors was already determined when the good news was announced. In addition to our complement of teachers and students of Munro, we were fortunate to secure the participation of a wide range of non-academic commentators and colleagues, including a panel of creative writers—Steven Heighton, Robert McGill, Lisa Moore, and Aritha Van Herk—and a panel of those in the publishing business who could claim responsibility for bringing Munro's work before the public: Knopf U.S. editor Ann Close, literary agent Virginia Barber, and Canadian and American editors Douglas Gibson and Daniel Menaker. Their presentations were an integral part of the symposium's success.

The essays selected for this volume represent the scholarly critical work on Munro's writings, offering a range of approaches and interpretive strategies, and covering the Munro corpus from her first stories as an undergraduate at the University of Western Ontario in the early 1950s to what would appear to be her final books, *The View from Castle Rock* and *Dear Life*. We begin with a substantial critical overview by Munro biographer Robert Thacker, who charts three significant literary moments in Munro's career in order to address representative elements of her art: the tension between personal-sociological record and creative artifact; the continual reworking of the mother-daughter relation; and the explicitly autobiographical impulse of her last books. Following this introductory survey, the collection is organized into a three-part division.

The essays in the first section address Munro's handling of literary forms. In "Living in the Story," Charles May develops his theory of the short story as a distinctive genre, markedly different—especially in the hands of a master like Munro—from the novel. May defines the particular view of the world and of human nature that Munro's stories allow, a view in which flashes of insight rather than linear development, tightly unified patterning rather than mimetic representation, and allegory rather than realism sustain interest and meaning. In "From Munro's *Lives* to Shields's 'Scenes,'" Laurie Kruk makes the case for Munro's creation of a particularly female *Bildungsroman* in her story-cycle *Lives of Girls and Women*, a form later adapted in miniature by Carol Shields in her story "Scenes." Focusing on the protagonist's journey to become both reader and storyteller, Kruk explores those elements of female inheritance, synecdoche, self-reflexivity, and resistance to traditional literary innovation that link Munro's and Shields' works as accounts of female artistic maturation.

In "'The stuff they put in the old readers': Remembered and Recited Poetry in the Stories of Alice Munro," Sara Jamieson shows how poetry makes a significant appearance in Munro's stories through their representation of the once-common practice of memorizing and reciting verse. Placing the practice in the context of pedagogical discussion of the utility of memorization, Jamieson explores how recited verse may work to bind generations together or to provide emotional and intellectual sustenance in Munro's fiction, but may also keep generational and class grievances alive or affirm a melancholy sense of loss and insufficiency. Letters also make frequent and diverse appearances in Munro's stories. In "Carried Away by Letters," Maria Löschnigg discusses the functions of epistolarity in Munro's fiction, including the creation of multiple perspectives and dramatic irony, the foregrounding of questions of interpretation, and the construction of elaborate imaginary worlds to contrast with narrative reality. In "Bridging the Gaps through Story Cycle," Tina Trigg investigates the efficacy of the story-cycle form in creating and conveying autobiographical truth. The gaps of a story cycle foreground discontinuities and recurrence in narrative, enabling Munro to negotiate the indeterminacies and mysteries of telling one's own family story with its blend of documented fact and invention. Trigg postulates that the story cycle is well suited for the autobiographer who wishes to tell her story while simultaneously acknowledging the unknown.

The second section of the volume explores Munro's characteristic themes and subject matter: social unease, illicit desire, failures in love, sexual betrayal, sexual threat, mother-daughter relations, and religious faith. In "The Short Stories of Alice Laidlaw," D. M. R. Bentley analyzes the three stories Munro published as an undergraduate student at the University of Western Ontario in order to examine her early influences and interests. The stories reveal Munro's apprenticeship debt to James Joyce and D. H. Lawrence, and they pursue Jungian and Freudian psychoanalytic themes of repression, sublimation, the shadow self, and psychic disintegration. In "Momentous Shifts and Unimagined Changes in 'Jakarta,'" Tracy Ware focuses on Munro's depiction of the struggle of the sexes, arguing that her oft-noted repetition of subject matter suggests a strategy for intertextual interpretation. He examines "Jakarta" as a revision of the earlier "Mischief," also about the breakdown of a marriage, finding that the latter story includes a more complex awareness of male subjectivity as well as explicit commentary on the gender dynamics in Katherine Mansfield and Lawrence.

The mother-infant bond is the focus of Ailsa Cox's "First and Last," which analyzes two stories, one fictional and one declaredly autobiographical, in which the narrator recounts events from her own early infancy that she is unable to recollect consciously. Cox shows how the stories use the infant's point of view to troubling and creative effect, employing temporal and spatial fluidity, and shifts between memory, perception, and fantasy to explore the overlapping and merging identities of mother and baby daughter.

In "Invasion Narratives," Carol Beran compares the treatment of a woman under threat in Alice Munro's "Free Radicals" and Joyce Carol Oates's "Where Are You Going, Where Have You Been?" to examine how a standard Gothic motif—the lone woman confronting a male invader in her home—is handled to different ends by the two authors. She finds that while both stories are indebted to folk narratives and highlight the complex relationships between fiction and reality, Oates's focus on the question of innocence and Munro's on the theme of survival suggest the differing cultural preoccupations of their respective national traditions. In "Religion in Alice Munro's *Lives of Girls and Women* and *Who Do You Think You Are*," Josephene Kealey shows the seriousness with which Munro treats Christianity in two early works; she argues that for Munro, religion is a source of meaning and consolation that must be rejected by her protagonists and replaced by art and sexual experience as more authentic sources of identity. Yet as Kealey shows, religious concepts of faith and truth remain essential to Munro's protagonists.

The third and final section of the volume is concerned with the effects achieved in Munro's stories, their distinctive textures and pleasures. For David Jarraway in "'Something': The 'Dark Sides' of Alice Munro's Story-Telling in its American Context," a central feature of Munro's later stories—their deliberate vagueness, their stress on alternative realities—is highlighted through comparison with American modernist writers and painters. He pays particular attention to an ineffable "something" at the heart of the stories, a counter-factual narrative reality that cannot be explicitly told but toward which the stories repeatedly gesture. In "Desire and Deferral," Ian Dennis provides a reading of Munro's "Royal Beatings" to examine how the deferral of readerly desire works as one of the primary techniques by which Munro achieves her much-commented-upon fictional complexity. Drawing on Girardian notions of the primacy of the sign over the referent, aesthetic contemplation over plot consumption, Dennis shows how Munro's practice of deferral marks one distinction between melodrama and high art.

The mobilization of readers' shame is at issue in Linda Morra's "Don't Take Her Word For It," an exploration of how Munro's most overtly autobiographical book, *The View from Castle Rock*, works at the intersection of readerly greed and authorial circumspection. By exploiting and refusing readers' desire for personal factual information, Munro engages in a "deliberate and strategic ambiguity" about the real that may lead readers to ponder the ethics of their longing to know. Munro's distinctive handling of narrative temporality is the subject of E. D. Blodgett's "Once Upon a Time," which looks in detail at Munro's preference for interrupting and derailing her story-telling and her creation of moments of time without a transcendent perspective. His analysis seeks to demonstrate both the insufficiency of realism as a framework for assessing Munro's achievement and the challenge of classifying her narrative technique, which is neither classical nor postmodern.

The volume concludes with Magdalene Redekop's "On Sitting Down to Read 'Lichen' Once Again," which proposes an interpretative strategy based on multiple rereadings over time and attention to intertextual echoes and allusions. From its punning title through its *ekphrastic* citations and references, "Lichen" is shown to be parable-like in its invitation to a multilayered figurative reading.

As editors, we trust that this book provides many new perspectives and studies that will enhance the reading, teaching, and appreciation of Munro's remarkable body of work. It has been a pleasure shepherding it to publication.

Works Cited

"Canadian Author Alice Munro Wins the Nobel Prize For Literature." Mail Online, 10 October 2013. http://www.dailymail.co.uk/news/article-2453140/Canadian-author-Alice-Munro-wins-Nobel-Prize-literature.html.

Howells, Coral Ann. *Alice Munro.* Manchester, UK: Manchester UP, 1998.

Munro, Alice. "Bardon Bus." *The Moons of Jupiter.* Toronto: Macmillan, 1982. 110–28.

———. "Carried Away." *Open Secrets.* Toronto: McClelland & Stewart, 1994. 3–51.

———. "The Children Stay." *The Love of a Good Woman.* 1998. Toronto: Penguin, 2007. 153–180.

———. *Dear Life.* Toronto: McClelland & Stewart, 2012.

———. "Fiction." *Too Much Happiness.* 2009. Toronto: Penguin, 2012. 28–53.

———. "Friend of My Youth." *Friend of My Youth.* Toronto: McClelland & Stewart, 1990. 3–26.

———. "Images." *Dance of the Happy Shades.* 1968. Toronto: Penguin, 2005. 29–40.

———. "The Love of a Good Woman." *The Love of a Good Woman.* 1998. Toronto: Penguin, 2007. 3–66.

———. *Lives of Girls and Women.* 1971. Toronto: Penguin, 2006.

———. "Miles City, Montana." *The Progress of Love.* 1986. Toronto: Penguin, 2006. 80–100.

———. "The Ottawa Valley." *Something I've Been Meaning to Tell You.* 1974. Toronto: Penguin, 2006. 199–215.

———. "The Progress of Love." *The Progress of Love.* 1986. Toronto: Penguin, 2006. 3–29.

———. “Simon’s Luck.” *Who Do You Think You Are?* Toronto: Macmillan, 1978. 152–73.

———. “Thanks for the Ride.” *Dance of the Happy Shades.* 1968. Toronto: Penguin, 2005. 41–53.

———. *Too Much Happiness.* Toronto: McClelland & Stewart, 2009.

———. “Train.” *Dear Life.* Toronto: McClelland & Stewart, 2012. 175–16.

———. “Vandals.” *Open Secrets.* Toronto: McClelland & Stewart, 1994. 261–294.

———. “Walker Brothers Cowboy.” *Dance of the Happy Shades.* 1968. Toronto: Penguin, 2005. 3–18.

———. “Who Do You Think You Are?” *Who* 189–206.

———. *Who Do You Think You Are?* Toronto: Macmillan, 1978.

Higgins, Charlotte. “Alice Munro Wins Nobel Prize in Literature.” *The Guardian* [UK], 10 October 2013. http://www.theguardian.com/books/2013/oct/10/alice-munro-wins-nobel-prize-in-literature.

Kakutani, Michiko. “Master of the Intricacies of the Human Heart.” *New York Times*, 10 October 2013. http://www.nytimes.com/2013/10/11/books/alice-munro-mining-the-inner-lives-of-girls-andwomen.html?action=click&contentCollection=Books&module=RelatedCoverage®ion=Marginalia&pgtype=article.

“Canadian Author Alice Munro Wins the Nobel Prize For Literature.” Mail Online, 10 October 2013. http://www.dailymail.co.uk/news/article-2453140/Canadian-author-Alice-Munro-wins-Nobel-Prize-literature.html.

“Writers on Munro.” *New Yorker*, 10 October 2013. http://www.newyorker.com/books/page-turner/writers-on-munro.

“Reactions to Alice Munro’s Nobel Prize.” *Washington Post*, 10 October 2013. http://www.washingtonpost.com/entertainment/books/reactions-to-alice-munros-nobel-prize/2013/10/10/32e7bd66-31ba-11e3-9c68-1cf643210300_story.html.

Richards, David Adams. “Introduction.” *Something I’ve Been Meaning to Tell You.* Alice Munro. Toronto: Penguin, 2006. ix–xv.

“Reactions to Alice Munro’s Nobel Prize.” *Washington Post*, 10 October 2013. http://www.washingtonpost.com/entertainment/books/reactions-to-alice-munros-nobel-prize/2013/10/10/32e7bd66-31ba-11e3-9c68-1cf643210300_story.html.

“Writers on Munro.” *New Yorker*, 10 October 2013. http://www.newyorker.com/books/page-turner/writers-on-munro.

"This is Not a Story, Only Life": Wondering with Alice Munro

ROBERT THACKER

How much does this count for in your life, these views, lights, skies? How much can be expected [?] do you wear them out?

—Alice Munro (Draft of "Dulse" 1980, 38.11.7)

But when you do have to let go [of the version of your story you believe] there's something unexpected, a lightness which isn't just relief. There's a queer kind of pleasure, not malicious, not personal, in recognizing how the design doesn't fit, in taking into account just what you can see of contradictions and turnarounds and general unmanageability of life.

—Alice Munro (Draft of "Bardon Bus" 1982, 38.8.5.6)

Nothing is ever as perfect as it seems. I don't on purpose follow any true story, but they're in there from time to time, but not a full story, but they're in there.

—Alice Munro (Thacker, interview September 6, 2013)

INTRODUCTION: "EVOCATIVE AND LUMINOUS"

"Walker Brothers Cowboy" (1968) was probably many readers' first Alice Munro story. It was one of three she produced during 1967–68 at the behest of her editor at the Ryerson Press, Audrey Coffin, to round out *Dance of the Happy Shades* (1968). It is the first story in that collection, a book that was a long time coming and launched Munro's writing career in Canada. More than that, "Walker Brothers Cowboy" is notable as the opening story: it introduces the detail and character of what some have called "Alice Munro country," beginning as it does with the narrator's meditation on Lake Huron and its geological past ("The tiny share we have of time appalls me . . . "). It offers a contrasting view of the narrator's parents, the father easygoing, philosophical, kind; the mother a bit pretentious, keen; she is "a *lady* shopping" (3). Most of all, "Walker Brothers Cowboy" offers a tour of Huron County during "the nineteen-thirties." Describing their afternoon, when her father is still selling his Walker Brothers wares—that is, before he breaks off to visit his old girlfriend Nora and her mother—the narrator recalls that day in detail:

> How much this kind of farmhouse, this kind of afternoon, seem to me to belong to that one decade in time, just as my father's hat does, his bright flared tie, our car with its wide running board (an Essex, and long past its prime). Cars somewhat like it, none dustier, sit in the farmyards. (8)

The father introduces his children to Nora and her mother, and then regales them with tales of his Walker Brothers company adventures; he takes a drink but refuses a dance with Nora after she has changed her dress for the occasion. So Nora dances with the narrator. For her part, the narrator sees for the first time that her father had another life before her mother, that during that earlier time he was friends with this woman, this Catholic, this person who "*digs with the wrong foot*" (14), and that there is space between how her mother sees her father and how he reveals himself to the narrator that day. As they leave, the likelihood of any reciprocal visit nonexistent, Nora does not repeat the directions to their house after the father invites her to stop by. Instead, Munro presents a sharp, clear image: as we last see Nora, she "stands close to the car in her soft, brilliant dress. She touches the fender, making an unintelligible mark in the dust there" (17).

The image encapsulates this moment's pathos; it is followed by a break in the text. Munro then describes the trio heading back to Tuppertown, the father "fresh out of songs," the narrator wondering still over all she has seen that day, the brother watching for rabbits. She then also offers one of those single-sentence penultimate paragraphs that Munro makes, one capturing the narrator's wonderings, one that concludes the action, and one that asserts the story's whole affect. Munro writes:

> So my father drives and my brother watches the road for rabbits and I feel my father's life flowing back from our car in the last of the afternoon, darkening and turning strange, like a landscape that has an enchantment on it, making it kindly, ordinary and familiar while

> you are looking at it, but changing it, once your back is turned, into something that you will never know, with all kinds of weathers, and distances you cannot imagine. (18)

When Alice Munro wrote "Walker Brothers Cowboy," she had been away from Ontario for more than fifteen years, in British Columbia, remembering her "Places at Home" from there (that was a working title for the story that became "The Peace of Utrecht" [1960]). *Dance of the Happy Shades*, containing as it does stories written between 1953 and 1968, amply surveys these years and Munro's rememberings, and so any one of a number of stories from that book might be taken up as significant for Munro and for Canadian literature. "Thanks for the Ride," for instance, first appeared in the second issue of the *Tamarack Review*, in the winter of 1957, along with an interview with Mordecai Richler and pieces by Phyllis Gottlieb, Douglas Grant, George Johnston, A. J. M. Smith, and others; that issue's editorial observes that "the dream of a distinctively Canadian culture still possesses us. It is an idle dream" (3). Another important story, "The Peace of Utrecht," followed "Thanks for the Ride" in the *Tamarack Review* in the spring of 1960; that story, an elegy for Munro's mother, Anne Chamney Laidlaw, who had died in February 1959 after an almost twenty-year struggle with Parkinson's disease, was immediately followed there by Irving Layton's elegy for his mother. "The Peace of Utrecht," Munro has told interviewers, "was the story where I first tackled personal material. It was the first story I absolutely had to write." It was her "first really painful autobiographical story . . . the first time I wrote a story that tore me up" (Struthers 21; Metcalf 58).

I have begun with *Dance of the Happy Shades* because with that book Munro really began herself: the breadth of its survey—in time, imagination, approach, technique, and biographical space—lends itself to a long view of her art. The three stories mentioned so far—"Walker Brothers Cowboy," "Thanks for the Ride," and "The Peace of Utrecht"—are indicative of their author's approach to fiction, to what she called in 1973 the "approach and recognition" involved in the fictional act (Gardiner 178). "Walker Brothers Cowboy" is mostly imaginative, a fictional recreation from afar of Munro's memories from those "nineteen-thirties" she highlights. While the father's geniality there doubtless owes to Robert E. Laidlaw (to whom the book is dedicated), and while he certainly drove Alice and her brother Bill about Huron County's back roads in an old car, probably an Essex, during the 1930s and '40s in just the way we see, there is nothing especially biographical here beyond a mention of a failed fox farm.

The mother there is another matter, however: the figure in "Walker Brothers Cowboy" is Anne Chamney Laidlaw before the onset of her Parkinson's disease about 1943, when she was about forty-five. And there she is the same figure we see again in the "Finale" section of *Dear Life* (2012). There she infuses "The Eye," and is a strong, felt presence in two of its three other pieces. She is the mother in "Voices," who takes her ten-year-old daughter to a house dance and then, almost at once, takes her home—having discovered that a local madam is in attendance, garishly dressed, and dancing. (The geography in "Voices" is still that of "The Flats Road," or Lower Wingham, a place Munro once described as being inhabited by "casual thieves, dedicated brawlers, occasional prostitutes" ["Working for a Living," 38.10.39 f1]). "Thanks for the Ride," Munro's first really accomplished, really made story, is wholly imagined. As she has said, she got its situation whole cloth from a friend of Jim Munro who visited them in Vancouver (Simpson).

Nora's slight "unintelligible mark" in the car's dust in "Walker Brother's Cowboy" is one of those images that have always leapt out from Munro's stories. In 1952 Joyce Marshall, a reader for *Canadian Short Stories* at the CBC, called them "evocative and luminous" phrases. They are just that. And they are still there. Another is in "Thanks for the Ride" when Dick recalls the moments just after he and Lois emerge from the barn where they have had sex, he for the first time; another is in "The Peace of Utrecht" when the narrator looks into the hall mirror at home and notes the visible changes in her own appearance (*Dance* 56–57, 197–98). "Evocative and luminous" phrases: such phrases, such images, such moments multiply in Munro.

The stories collected in *Dance of the Happy Shades* are apt as a beginning to any overview of Alice Munro's art. Their gestation and their provenance show where Munro started out and how she proceeded: shaped from away through memory, the fifteen stories comprise a catalogue of her early career. All of the stories are quite evidently made things—she has long said that, had she the chance, she would revise those endings, and years ago she sometimes did so in readings. Some of them are clearly apprentice pieces ("The Time of Death" [1956], "Day of the Butterfly" [1956], "A Trip to the Coast" [1961], "The Shining Houses" [1962]), while others ("The Peace of Utrecht" [1960], "Boys and Girls" [1964], "Red Dress–1946" [1965], "Walker Brothers Cowboy," "Images" [1968]), are more accomplished, more personal. They show where Munro was going. Following their direction, Munro burst out in 1970: she wrote the whole of *Lives of Girls and Woman* (1971) in that single year. Her long apprenticeship, the tentativeness of the 1950s and early '60s, was over. She moved back to Ontario in 1973, and her third book, *Something I've Been Meaning to Tell You* (1974), a pastiche volume made up of reshaped older material and new stories, came together relatively quickly. While the ongoing disintegration of her marriage contributed to the need for this productivity, it is also quite clear that throughout these books Munro was making herself into an altogether different sort of artist as she moved back home. But the real shock, the real transformation, was to come when she moved back to Huron County, to Clinton, to live with Gerald Fremlin in August 1975.

Once there, she again tried out the title "Places at Home," but then it did not title a story. It was to be a manuscript of descriptive vignettes to accompany a series of photographs of Ontario scenes by Peter D'Angelo and to be published by Macmillan of Canada. Munro's vision did not match the photographer's and the book never appeared, but many of her vignettes ("Airship Over Michigan," "Clues," and "Nosebleed," for instance) were incorporated into *Who Do You Think You Are* (1978) (*The Beggar Maid*, 1979; see n1 below). Seen another way, "Places at Home"—a reasonably complete manuscript that can be found in the Alice Munro Fonds at the University of Calgary—is a stark and pointed record of what Munro noticed when she first returned home to Huron County (see Thacker, *Alice* 294–301). Looking back at herself then, she has explained that

> When I came home I was interested in something different about the country. When I was in British Columbia, writing about home, it was just an enchanted land of your childhood. It was very odd to say that Lower Town was the enchanted land, but it was. It was sort of out of time and place. And when I came back I saw this was all happening in a sociological way, and I saw the memories I had as being, in a way, much harsher, though they never were very gentle actually. (Thacker, interview April 23, 2004)

Such an assessment is autobiographical, of course. Many critics, less concerned with facts than with their narrative rendering, deprecate this approach. Yet as most of *The View from Castle Rock* (2006)—another book with a long gestation—and the "Finale" section that closes *Dear Life* have asserted again and most emphatically, the autobiographical is never very far in Munro. As Karl Miller—who wrote a biography of her ancestor, James Hogg, and who sees her as the better artist of the two—wrote while reviewing *The View from Castle Rock*, "But then the whole corpus of Munro's stories is a memoir, the novel of her life." Or as Tessa Hadley, while reviewing the same book, maintains, "Without ever losing her focus on these other, past lives, she also seems to be giving us a magical account of her own life in writing, tracing a history for her imagination" (17).

In the periodical version of "Dolly" (2012)—the story which appears just before the "Finale" section in *Dear Life*—Munro has the narrator calling herself "a perfectly ordinary and savage woman" (*Tin House* 80). This characterization drops away in the book version, and does so because Munro thought it "too clever," but even so it is one that might well be kept in mind (Thacker, interview September 6, 2013). Another relevant comment is in "What Do You Want to Know For?" (1994): "There are always puzzles" (*View* 325).

In what follows, I wish to highlight three points in Munro's career that seem especially to resonate. Seen within its span of more than sixty years, these instances are moments. But using them as stepping stones, I want to present them through the textual and biographical evidence they have left. They offer key moments in Munro's career that, to some degree, explain the enormous aesthetic effects this writer has had through the powerful and humane stories she has published since her first appearance in print in the University of Western Ontario's literary magazine, *Folio*, in the spring of 1950.

1973–80: "A Moving, Complicated, Work of Fiction"

There are now only a few Munro stories that were published in periodicals but have not, as yet, been included in a book. The most recent of these is "Axis," which appeared in the *New Yorker* on January 31, 2011. Focused on three characters and set mostly during Munro's university years, the story details their personal involvements and telescopes their whole lives. But it also invokes, as central allusions, two of the most important physiographic features of Ontario. There, a character named Royce hitchhikes back from a farm where he had an altercation with a university girlfriend, Grace, and her mother during a visit to their home (he and Grace are caught in bed by the mother; Royce leaves immediately, never to see Grace again). On this return trip he pauses and notices the Niagara Escarpment. This experience moves him to shift his career focus from philosophy to geology. Years and whole lifetimes later, he meets the widowed Avie, their third friend from university years, on the train to Montreal. Royce had longed for Avie when he spotted her by chance on his way to visit Grace all those years ago. When the train to Montreal passes evidence of the Frontenac Axis, he makes a point of showing it to her, and a point of explaining it. Thus the story's title. The Niagara Escarpment and the Frontenac Axis: Munro's geological sense yet again.

In writing "Axis," Munro dramatizes an experience she herself had. Coming back to Ontario in 1973, finding Fremlin there and so moving to Clinton and back to Huron County in 1975, Munro began writing about Ontario in ways she had never done before. As she said in 2004, she shifted from memory and imagining to "a more sociological way." Thus the analytical vignettes of the photo text version of "Places at Home" were ultimately revising the "enchanted land," "The Flats Road" of *Lives*, into the gritty realities of Flo and Rose's West Hanratty in *Who Do You Think You Are?* (*The Beggar Maid*). "'Until she came along,'" as James Reaney has written of Munro, "'southwestern Ontario had no voice—she gave it a voice and that has made such a difference. I don't know what we'd have done without her'" (qtd. in Thacker, *Alice* 570). Together, "Axis," Munro's biography, her own sense of what happened then, and Reaney's self-deprecating comment point to the first moment I wish to describe: the textual effects of Munro's return to Huron County.

Certainly among the most celebrated episodes in Canadian publishing history was Munro's decision during the fall of 1978 to take *Who Do You Think You Are?*, then in production, off the press and restructure it. Helen Hoy has detailed this reshaping and made the case that Munro's decision owed, at least in part, to her ongoing work with Sherry Huber, an editor at W. W. Norton in New York, who was pushing Munro to shape her material into a more conventional novel (see Hoy; Thacker *Alice* 336–52). Production of the earlier version of the book had got so far at Macmillan that bound proofs were sent out and, in two instances, reviewed; one of these proof copies is held in the Metcalf collection at McGill, so just how the book was reshaped is readily discernable.[1]

Given the extraordinary events preceding the publication of *Who Do You Think You Are?* that fall, most of the scholarship on its reshaping has focused on the book that Macmillan actually published. That is fair enough, but here I would like to define my first moment by considering Janet, the first-person narrator whose stories were ultimately left out of the book. In turn, these stories became key to *The Moons of Jupiter* (1982), arguably also one of *the* critical collections in Munro's oeuvre.[2]

As the "Rose and Janet" version of the book was first structured, there was to be a revelation that Rose was a character written by Janet. And Janet, for her part, is the narrator of the three stories that were dropped from *Who Do You Think You Are?*: "Chaddeleys and Flemings:

1. Connection," (1978), "Chaddeleys and Flemings: 2. The Stone in the Field" (1979), and "The Moons of Jupiter" (1978).[3] Looking back now, knowing just how *Who Do You Think You Are?* (*The Beggar Maid*) and *The Moons of Jupiter* were published, Munro's decision to drop Janet makes sense. Rose bears some evident relation to Munro's biographical beginnings—West Hanratty is another version of "The Flats Roads," and her life trajectory is not unlike Munro's—but as mentioned, Flo is almost wholly an imagined character. Janet the writer could well have created them. In fact, Janet did. But Janet's name was Alice Munro.

What I mean by this is not as baldly autobiographical as it might first sound. Two factors here are key. First, by having Janet a writer writing these three stories—and for simplicity's sake I will stay with these three, although other stories that did appear in the published *Who Do You Think You Are?* began as first-person Janet stories—Munro was extending a meditation on the role and function of the writer that she had begun with Del Jordan in *Lives* (see Thacker, *Alice* 341–42). This meditation was overtly extended through "Material" (1973) and through her metafictional experiments in "Home" and "The Ottawa Valley" (both 1974). And once Janet's presence in *Who Do You Think You Are?* was sorted out, Munro continued the meditation on the writer's essential egotism through her biographical analysis of Willa Cather in "Dulse" (1980). Second, the Janet stories held out of *Who Do You Think You Are?* personalize Munro's use of her sociological rediscovery of Huron County in ways that the Rose and Flo stories do not. Theirs are imagined and outward focused, sociological analyses of West Hanratty as home place, and of Flo as Rose's mother. During this time, too, Munro has Janet the narrator of the first-person story version of "Working for a Living."[4]

The *New Yorker* bought "The Moons of Jupiter"; it was Munro's third appearance there. But they rejected "Chaddeleys and Flemings"—they saw the long, two-part version, not yet separated (at Doug Gibson's suggestion) into the two stories we now know. When they rejected it, Charles McGrath both delivered and demurred from the decision, making it clear that the editor, William Shawn, had overruled the fiction editors. Shawn felt that the piece "read more like straight reminiscence than a story," McGrath wrote to Munro, and he continued, "I don't know whether it's autobiographical or not, but it's my feeling that you've taken the material of reminiscence and turned it into something much stronger—a moving, complicated work of fiction" (November 1, 1977). McGrath's comment here encapsulates just where Munro was in the later 1970s and the early 1980s; her imaginative struggle between reminiscence and fiction, borne directly from her return to first Ontario and then Huron County, was everywhere evident. Her metafictional forays—"Home" and "The Ottawa Valley"—reveal misgivings about what Robert McGill has called "the ethics of writing back," the use of personal history in fiction, and they combine with her meditations on the writer's role in "Material" and in "Dulse."

But it is more than that. In a rejected passage in the supplanted version of *Who Do You Think You Are?* Janet writes of herself at home, visiting her father and going with him to the Canadian Legion, saying that "I was not very comfortable about being identified as a writer in the midst of what was, so to speak, my material"; and she continues, "I knew that some of my inventions must seem puzzling and indecent" (Advance 229). Munro knew *just* what she was doing here, but as she settled back deeper into Huron County, becoming once again more comfortable with its immediacies—its scenes, presences, ways, and culture—using its detail in ways new for her was something she *had* to do.

Munro's father, Bob Laidlaw (as everyone called him), was key to all this. In 1974 he provided her with specific factual information that became the basis for "Everything Here is Touchable and Mysterious" (1974), arguably among Munro's most important critical statements (Laidlaw to Munro, February 10, 1974, 38.1.65). In return, she gave him some of the money she received for its publication. His presence and decline are key to "Home." The boyhood reminiscences he published in his later years, and especially his *The McGregors* (1979), a historical novel based on the pioneering of Huron, involved Munro: she edited and saw to the book's publication by Macmillan after his death in August 1976. His death allowed her the freedom to write "Royal Beatings," since its central beating was based on those he had administered; but it also led to "The Moons of Jupiter," an elegy for him and a tribute to his spirit, his inquisitive humor, and to his life of hard physical work.[5] Laidlaw's death led as well to "Working for a Living" (1981), her profound memoir of her parents that began as a short story and was connected as well to "The Turkey Season" (1980) in that form. After his fur farm failed, Laidlaw worked at the Wingham foundry and also raised and sold turkeys.

Munro knew all this and respected Laidlaw deeply for his work. She also saw her connection to him as key. That is clear when the father and the turkeys appear in "Miles City, Montana" (1985) when the just-married narrator and her father rescue turkeys from drowning, a danger caused by a heavy rain, and she writes, "I was happy to be working with my father. I felt close to the hard, repetitive, appalling work, in which the body is finally worn out, the mind sunk . . . and I was homesick in advance for this life and for this place" (Progress 94). And when Munro was writing and reshaping "Working for a Living" into a memoir in late 1979, she was also still meditating, in "Dulse," on the ethics of writing and reshaping "The Turkey Season." It was then too that she first mentioned her idea for the "family book," which ultimately became *The View from Castle Rock* (see Thacker, *Alice* 366–70).

When Munro came to write "Soon" (2004), the middle story and masterpiece of what has been called her "Juliet Triptych," she wrote as the story's penultimate paragraph, "Because it's what happens at home that you try and protect, as best you can, for as long as you can" (*Runaway* 125). The reference here is to Juliet's own circumstance in the story and to her understanding of the meaning of the word "home," but even so this passage resonates throughout the whole of Munro's oeuvre, most especially in her work from 1975 into the early 1980s. Returned then to Huron County, living there again, probing its culture and details, discovering things about it she never knew, confronting its inbred prejudices through her political role in the 1978 book-banning controversies, Alice Munro rediscovered her real home there and, in so doing, reshaped, deepened, and confirmed the effects her stories were able to have. Whether seen as fiction or as memoir, the works Munro produced then are autobiographically rooted in, as she said in 2004, the "sociological." That fact—in its range, precision, and variety—has been the grounding of Munro's writing ever since, from *Who Do You Think You Are?* onward.

The Juliet Triptych: "Personal Fate was Not the Point, Anyway"

Munro's seventy-first birthday, July 10, 2002, saw the dedication in Wingham of the Alice Munro Literary Garden—an appropriate, though somewhat bittersweet, recognition of the town's most famous native. Munro was feted and celebrated; friends and colleagues spoke. Describing this gala celebration, Munro has said that "all was wonderful and happy," but in the midst of the gaiety, she was approached by a woman. She continues:

> I was signing books and a woman, an old woman, came up to me and said, did you know your mother got out of the hospital? She began to talk to me and then other people interrupted and she just stayed until she could get me, and she told me the whole story of how my mother

> got out in the snow barefoot, got out some back door. [Knowing where this woman, a nurse, lived,] she went and knocked on the door in her hospital gown and told her she had to get out of there and she had to go home. (Thacker, interview June 20, 2003)

While Munro had long known about her mother's escape from the hospital in early 1959—"The Peace of Utrecht" makes that clear—she had never heard its details until that day in 2002 when she was approached in the midst of her great personal celebration by this persistent, remembering woman. Her father had never told Alice these details, nor even about the escape itself; she learned of it from others.

In 1993 Munro told Jeanne McCulloch and Mona Simpson that the "material about my mother is my central material in life, and it always comes the most readily to me. If I just relax, that's what will come up" (237). Looking at her stories sequentially, Munro's point is readily confirmed: beyond "The Peace of Utrecht," Anne Chamney Laidlaw, in the throes of her struggles with Parkinson's disease, figures in "Home," "The Ottawa Valley," "Chaddeleys and Flemings: 1. Connection," "Working for a Living," "The Progress of Love" (1985), "Friend of My Youth" (1990), "Lying Under the Apple Tree" (2002), and, most recently, "Soon" and "Dear Life" (2011).

But beyond Anne Chamney Laidlaw's presence and centrality in the stories and memoirs just named, there is what seems the deeper consideration: just as Bob Laidlaw's literal presence in Wingham on Munro's return to Huron County figured in her sociological rediscovery of home, so too her mother's palpable absence has resonated then and since throughout Munro's imaginary. Judging from "Dear Life" and the "Finale" section of the book *Dear Life* generally, it does still. Intellectually knowing about her mother's absence while still in British Columbia was one thing, but coming home in 1973 to see and feel that absence as patent fact is another. Returned home, her father still living in the Lower Town house with his second wife, Munro was very much aware of Anne Laidlaw's ongoing presence (or her present absence). As she re-acclimated herself then, she dealt most directly with that absence in her writing—in "Home," in "Winter Wind," and especially in "The Ottawa Valley."[6]

The three stories that comprise the Juliet Triptych—"Chance," "Soon," and "Silence"—were first published together as the bulk of the summer fiction issue of the *New Yorker* in June 2004. Though not unheard of, the *New Yorker* has seldom published more than one piece by any single author in a single issue; clearly, the Juliet Triptych was major treatment, a visible acknowledgement of Munro as one of its most significant writers.

This recognition makes the Juliet Triptych an apt second moment, through its first presentation, certainly, but more than that by its imaginative compass. Taken together, the three stories imagine and detail the whole of Juliet's most urgent circumstance: finding her partner, Eric; her relations with her mother, Sara; and those with her daughter, Penelope. Set side by side in their presentation in the *New Yorker* and in *Runaway*, they echo Munro's method in both *Lives of Girls and Women* and in *Who Do You Think You Are?* (*The Beggar Maid*), and Juliet herself echoes Rose as mother and on-air interviewer. But such parallels acknowledged, there is also in the Juliet Triptych a sharper, deeper, and more historically implicated construction of human relations and, indeed, of meaning itself. Though not caustic, Munro's shaping of Juliet's circumstances contains both an unrelenting harshness and considerable wonder. With Juliet and Munro we wonder at the vagaries of being, at what happens, and at how we understand those occurrences. That is, we wonder at the very randomness of existence.

Earlier I mentioned a line Munro wrote, published, and then excised from "Dolly": her narrator refers to herself, as the story's action wends toward its end, as "a perfectly ordinary and savage woman."[7] Such a phrasing is "evocative and luminous" in Munro's writing, and even worth pointing to despite its having been deleted as too clever, too prone to call attention to itself, because it captures what she has been most often about in her best recent stories. I would certainly put the Juliet Triptych in this group, and most especially "Soon."

In "Chance," Munro once more uses her 1950s and '60s transcontinental train travel to good effect. She sets twenty-one-year old Juliet, a PhD candidate in classics, on the train to Vancouver from Toronto. Sharing outlines of Munro's own childhood background, Juliet has travelled west during December 1964 or January 1965, taught a term as a replacement Latin teacher, and reconnected with Eric, a British Columbia fisherman she met on the train coming out. Munro juxtaposes two moments in Juliet's life by framing the first meeting on the train with the subsequent reconnection. On the train, looking out the window at Northern Ontario winter scenes, Juliet thinks "*Taiga*" and wonders if that is the right word: the word for the subarctic forests of Eurasia and North America; she thinks further of the landscape she is seeing in relation to a Russian novel, where she would go "out into an unfamiliar, terrifying and exhilarating landscape where the wolves would howl at night and where she would meet her fate." But, Juliet thinks still further, "Personal fate was not the point, anyway. What drew her in—enchanted her, actually—was the very indifference, the repetition, the carelessness and contempt for harmony, to be found on the scrambled surface of the Precambrian shield." With this, we see another instance of Munro's geological awareness, presenting offering yet another major Ontario physiographic region. At the same time, Munro makes it clear that, as Juliet is thinking these thoughts, she is rereading E. R. Dodds's *The Greeks and the Irrational* (1951). Just as Juliet concludes this meditation on the *taiga* and the "scrambled surface" of the Precambrian Shield, a "shadow appeared in the corner of her eye. Then a trousered leg, moving in" (*Runaway* 54). Juliet, who has has been taught to "be accommodating to anybody who wants to suck you dry, even if they know nothing about who you are," does not want to talk to this man, who is desperate and looking for someone to be friendly with. He is not trying, she knows, to pick her up. Gathering herself, having decided for the first time to rebuff such an entreaty, Juliet "looked straight at this man and did not smile. He saw her resolve, there was a twitch of alarm in his face." He asked, "'Good book you got there? What's it about?'" (*Runaway* 56). Rather than reply to his question, she gets up and leaves him, saying that she does want to read. So rebuffed, this man then takes advantage of the train's stopping shortly after, walks ahead on the tracks and, once the train has started up again, afterward, throws himself in front of it—an act of suicide that allows Juliet to connect with Eric.

A British reviewer of Munro's *New Selected Stories* (2011), Ruth Scurr, begins her review with this scene, and reads Munro's use of Dodds's book to very good effect, noting that he begins his book with a quotation from William James: "'The recesses of feeling, the darker, blinder states of character, are the only places in the world in which we catch real fact in the making.'" Munro, she says, "centres her fiction on catching real fact in the making in precisely this Jamesian sense." Scurr titles her review, significantly, "The Darkness of Alice Munro."

The application of James's phrase, "real fact in the making," to Munro's more recent stories is particularly acute. Her use of Dodds and *The Greeks and the Irrational* points us in that direction. By rebuffing the man on the train, Juliet achieved "the first victory of this sort that she had ever managed, and it was against the most pitiable, the saddest opponent" (*Runaway* 57). She thinks this before the man kills himself. Once he does, she seeks out Eric—who assisted the train crew with the recovery of the remains—to see if the suicide was the man she had spoken to.

Juliet, in turn, is rebuffed herself, though later Eric recants and they connect. Discussing her actions with Eric, later, she speaks of her guilt, asking, "You think feeling guilty is just an indulgence?"; he replies, "I think that this is minor. Things will happen in your life—things will probably happen in your life—that will make this seem minor. Other things you'll be able to feel guilty about" (*Runaway* 68). Playing Eric's comments forward, he seems to anticipate something Munro would later write in "Face" (2008): "Something happened here. In your life there are a few places, or maybe only the one place, where something happened, and then there are all the other places" (*Too Much* 162).

Juliet certainly does ultimately have things to feel guilty about, just as Eric foresees. Having cut the man who approached her on the train sufficiently to drive him to suicide, she continues on in "Soon"—at home in Ontario visiting her dying mother Sara—to discover her parents' conventional shame, in 1969, over her living with Eric and having a child by him out of wedlock, and that her father resigned his long-time teaching job over that fact. And after a needless argument over God and religious belief with her mother's minister, Don (one that Munro handles sharply and with a revelation at its core), Sara tells her that her own faith is "'a—wonderful—*something*. When it gets really bad for me—when it gets so bad I—you know what I think then? I think, all right. I think—Soon. *Soon I'll see Juliet.*'" Just after this Munro inserts a letter Juliet had written from Ontario to Eric after this incident, one she discovers "years later," probably after his death; reading it then,

> Juliet winced, as anybody does on discovering the preserved and disconcerting voice of some past fabricated self. She wondered at the sprightly cover-up, contrasting with the pain of her memories. Then she thought that some shift had taken place, at that time, which she had not remembered. Some shift concerning where home was. Not at Whale Bay with Eric but back where it had been before, all her life before.

Munro follows this with another characteristic single-sentence penultimate paragraph, already quoted: "Because it's what happens at home that you try to protect, as best you can, for as long as you can" (*Runaway* 125).[8]

What is striking about "Soon" are the myriad ways it replicates so much from Munro's life and work. It is a retelling of "The Peace of Utrecht." Sam and Sara—Juliet's parents—while not exactly so, nevertheless echo Munro's. Sara's debilitating illness echoes Anne Chamney Laidlaw's, and with the image of "half-drunk" cups of tea, recalls "Friend of My Youth." After Juliet steps off the train in a nearby town, one not her own, and is being driven home, she notes that

> It was full summer—a season which never arrived, as far as Juliet could see, on the west coast. The hardwood trees were humped over the far edge of the fields, making blue-black caves of shade, and the crops and the meadows in front of them, under the hard sunlight, were gold and green. Vigorous young wheat and barley and corn and beans—fairly blistering your eyes. (*Runaway* 95)

This passage reminds of another, in Munro's own voice and from "Home": "Such unremarkable scenes, in this part of the country, are what I have always thought would be the last thing I would care to see in my life" (*View* 286). Juliet had given her parents a print of Chagall's *I and the Village*—the same image Munro liked and owned in Vancouver, and where Jim Munro would not allow her to hang it in the living room (Thacker, *Alice* 225–26). Juliet finds hers similarly banished, though for different reasons. There is also the suggestion of the danger of a baby scalded by boiling water—"The Time of Death"—and Irene's family background in the story recalls the Lower Town School Munro attended and used in "Privilege." Speaking of Irene, Sam tells Juliet that "She restored my faith in women" (*Runaway* 113)—just what Bob Laidlaw said about his second wife, a fact Munro records in "Home" (*View* 314).

Again, let me go back to the ending of "Soon":

> Because it's what happens at home that you try to protect, as best you can, for as long as you can.
>
> But she had not protected Sara. When Sara had said, *soon I'll see Juliet*, Juliet had found no reply. Could it have been managed? Why should it have been so difficult? Just to say *Yes*. To Sara it would have meant so much–to herself, surely, so little. But she had turned away, she had carried the tray to the kitchen, and there she washed and dried the cups and also the glass that had held grape soda. She had put everything away. (*Runaway* 125)

As Magdalene Redekop has observed (7), Anne Chamney Laidlaw said the same thing while she was dying—"Soon I will see Alice"—about her daughter out in Vancouver, when she would escape barefoot into the snow from the hospital in early 1959. In "Soon," as well, Sara tells Juliet something about her father "with a sudden change of tone, a wavering edge of viciousness, a weak chuckle." So too Juliet, withholding herself from her dying mother, "put everything away." She, like Munro her creator, understands herself as a "perfectly ordinary and savage woman" though she, unlike her creator, did attend her mother's funeral. "The Darkness of Alice Munro" indeed.

Yet Juliet's withholding of herself from her mother Sara pales beside Penelope's withholding of herself and her post-early-twenties life from Juliet in "Silence." The whole of that story elaborates Penelope's withholding, and with step-by-step, excruciating detail. After years of awaiting and hoping for some contact, Juliet thinks, "Penelope was not a phantom, she was safe, as far as anybody is safe, and she was probably as happy as anybody is happy." Withholding herself from Juliet "*is just a way that* [Penelope] *found to manage her life*" (*Runaway* 157; italics in original). Still awaiting "a word from Penelope," Munro writes as "Silence" ends, Juliet "hopes as people who know better hope for undeserved blessings, spontaneous remissions, things of that sort" (*Runaway* 158). With these words the Juliet Triptych ends, and by their very acknowledgement of the commonplace quality of Juliet's hope—"things of that sort"—Munro sharply focuses once more on a quotidian "real fact in the making." (Another is found in "Nettles" [2000] when she describes a character's running over his three-year-old son, killing him: "It could happen to anybody" [*Hateship* 182].) The darkness of Alice Munro, again.

"Not a Story, Only Life": *Dear Life*, Its "Finale," and Wondering with Alice Munro

Munro's use of Dodds's *The Greeks and the Irrational* in the Juliet Triptych leads back, in a somewhat inchoate way, to the image of Nora's finger in the car's 1930s dust in "Walker Brothers Cowboy." The early Munro pointed to such moments in life as revelatory or epiphanic—moments of being when possibility and understanding converge, revealing their meaning by the construction of the narrative contexts about them—but in recent years Munro seems sometimes to point toward a specific, larger gloss, as with the Dodds. In "Face," it is the poetry of Walter de la Mare; in "Wenlock Edge" (2005)—which offers in that narrator another "perfectly ordinary and savage woman"—it is the poetry and implied perspective of another classicist, A. E. Housman.[9] She has done this before, with her probings of Willa Cather as model writer in "Dulse," but there, as mentioned, it was related directly to Munro's own uncertainties about her writing. The glosses we have seen since are broader, more philosophical and complexly intertextual, and they seem to have been derived from Alice Munro's own wonderings over being.

Used in stories, they are, as Scurr wrote, focused on "real facts in the making," and they participate actively in cultural inheritances.

Dear Life, Munro's most recent book, is replete with such considerations. It is my third moment. If it proves to be her last book, as Munro has said it will be, it is an aptly final one. First, a small step back: *Too Much Happiness* contained a revised and expanded "Wood," a story first written along with "Dulse," "The Turkey Season," and "Working for a Living," and first published in the *New Yorker*, in 1980. After that, it was passed over repeatedly as collections were being assembled. I am told this was because the man who inspired it was still alive, and that it was almost passed over again when *Too Much Happiness* was being assembled. In *The View from Castle Rock*, other pieces long withheld from collections—"Home," "Working for a Living," "Hired Girl" (1994)—were included. In that book too there is "The Ticket," which includes Munro's memories of passages from a 1951 story called "The Yellow Afternoon," broadcast on the CBC in 1955 but never published (see Thacker, *Alice* 542–44). What all this suggests is that after completing *Runaway*, Munro turned her attentions back in time—that is certainly true of "The View from Castle Rock." But literal ancestors and earlier versions of herself to one side, Munro was also then looking back to material she worked with—and lived—before *Dance of the Happy Shades* and just after. *Dear Life* suggests this throughout. Take, for instance, "Train" (2012). It begins with Jackson returning home from World War Two and jumping off the train before it reaches his hometown—and so missing the life he expected to have there and finding another. Then, after years he jumps again and has another, and as the story ends he is embarked on yet another train on yet another phase of his life. During the 1960s and through the 1970s Munro worked, repeatedly, on a story in which a soldier returns from the war and gets off the train too soon in another town; in "Places at Home," there is a vignette, "The Boy Murderer," that begins "Franklin jumped off the train at Goldenrod, where he didn't need to" (37.13.10).[10]

Most of the stories in *Dear Life* are set in the 1950s and '60s and draw, variously though not especially significantly before the "Finale," on Munro's life. The columnist whom the poet-narrator meets at the Vancouver literary party in "To Reach Japan" is based on the first professional writer Munro ever knew; the town in "Leaving Maverley" owes much to Wingham (as do other towns there, of course, and to Goderich too in "Pride"); and "evocative and luminous" phrases appear which are clearly autobiographical ("Devotion to anything, if you were female, could make you ridiculous" ["Haven," *Dear Life* 128]). Largely, though, *Dear Life* recreates Munro's early times as context for character, although with "Corrie" and "In Sight of the Lake" she works toward mysteries and a reversal. There is yet another poet in Franklin in "Dolly." That story sharply shapes a vision of an unmarried pair moving into old age, contemplating the end. If only vaguely, it echoes Munro's relation to Gerry Fremlin. It was during this time, too, that Munro wrote and published "Axis"; there Royce is drawn to the Niagara Escarpment—the subject, as it happened, of Fremlin's 1958 MA thesis.

Some of these stories are punctuated—again and ever—by central images that resonate in the imaginations of both characters and readers. The Mennonite boys on a cart going by on their way to church, singing, in "Train"; they are seen the morning after Jackson jumps off the train, and they are recalled again in a dream just as the story ends, when he is sleeping on another train on his way to Kapuskasing (180, 216). Or, and most especially, the image that ends "Pride": a birdbath "full of birds. Black-and-white, dashing up a storm. Not birds. Something larger than robins, smaller than crows . . . . 'Skunks. Little skunks. More white in them than black.'" Amazed, Munro's characters looked on:

> While we watched, they lifted themselves up one by one and left the water and proceeded to walk across the yard, swiftly but in a straight diagonal line. As if they were proud of themselves but discreet. Five of them.

Oneida, the woman looking on here, offers a face that "looked dazzled." She and the narrator "were as glad as we could be" (*Dear Life* 153). Such images simply are in Munro's stories: they are not explained, just marveled over, as here. Quotidian. As Munro wrote in "A Real Life" (1992): "The walnuts drop, the muskrats swim in the creek" (*Open Secrets* 80). Wondering with Alice Munro.

But the great fact of *Dear Life* is its "Finale." Introducing the "final four works" it contains, saying that they "are not quite stories," Munro calls them "a separate unit, one that is autobiographical in feeling, though not, sometimes, entirely so in fact. I believe they are the first and last—and the closest—things I have to say about my own life." Asked about the episodes they present, Munro has said that they all happened pretty much as she offers them—"because this is not a story, only life," as she writes in one of them, "Dear Life" (Thacker, interview September 6, 2013, *Dear Life* 255, 307).

But factual bases apart, Munro offers these "not quite stories" as, in effect, images to wonder over, like Nora's "unintelligible mark in the dust," or like Juliet's meditation on "the contempt for harmony . . . on the scrambled surface of the Precambrian shield," or like the baby skunks in the birdbath at the end of "Pride." Throughout them, she is wondering herself, testing the veracity of her sixty-to-seventy-year-old memories. Placed side by side in the "separate unit" that is "Finale," they offer what may be Munro's final assertion of herself as a discovering child at home in Wingham with her father and, most especially, with her mother during "the nineteen-thirties" (*Dance* 3). In "The Eye," Munro begins with the changes brought to her life by the birth of her brother in 1936; no longer the celebrated only child, and just about five years old, she began seeing her mother differently. Before his arrival "the whole house was full of my mother, of her footsteps, her voice, her powdery yet ominous smell that inhabited all the rooms even when she wasn't in them." Munro sounds here and throughout "Finale" like herself speaking, wondering. She continues, "Why do I say ominous? I didn't feel frightened. It wasn't that my mother actually told me what I was to feel about things. She was an authority on that without having to question a thing" (*Dear Life* 257–58). Here, in "The Eye," and in "Voices" too, Munro presents the construction of Anne Chamney Laidlaw I began with from "Walker Brothers Cowboy," her mother imperious, forthright, overly grammatical, moral, wanting to get ahead socially—that is, her mother as she was before the onset of Parkinson's disease. Throughout "Finale" there are echoes of many other Munro stories besides.[11]

Her father figures significantly only in "Night," but there he is the Bob Laidlaw we have seen before in "Home" and "Working for a Living," sensible and giving good advice to fourteen-year-old Alice, who is not able to sleep. She is riven by thoughts of strangling her nine-year-old sister Catherine (by using this name, Munro replaced her actual sister Sheila's name with that of her own second child, Catherine, who was born and died the same day in 1955). Looking back, she realizes that telling her father of these events transformed her ("Now I could not unsay it, I could not go back to the person I had been before"). But "on that breaking morning he gave me just what I needed to hear and what I was even to forget about soon enough." But because she found her father that morning "in his better work clothes," Munro wonders yet: was he going to see a banker "to learn, not to his surprise, that there was no extension on his loan," so that "he had to find a new way of supporting us and paying off what we owed at the same time. Or he may have found out that there was a name for my mother's shakiness and that it was not going to stop." Both of those possibilities are familiar to us as readers of Munro, but she then moves toward a different wondering before ending:

"Or that he was in love with an impossible woman. Never mind. From then on I could sleep" (*Dear Life* 283, 284–85).

But it is the final piece in Munro's "Finale," "Dear Life," which both gives the book its title and returns her to what Munro called "my central material in life," "the material about my mother." That memoir once more defines the geography and imaginative separateness of the Laidlaw home and farm—at the western edge of Lower Town, above the pasture flats along the river (the Meneseteung/Maitland), its back to both Lower Wingham and to Wingham itself—and it tells the histories of each of her parents again, and of their fur farm. The mythical Roly Grain, whose place is the only one the Laidlaws can see to the west in the distance and is mentioned in "Working for a Living," appears again (*Dear Life* 307, *View* 147). But he "does not have any further part in what I'm writing now, in spite of his troll's name, because this is not a story, only life."

"Dear Life" focuses on a story Munro's mother told about Alice as a baby and Mrs. Netterfield, an apparently crazy neighbour who one day came to the Laidlaw house, looked in the windows, and frightened by her behaviour. Rather than posing a threat, as Anne Laidlaw thought at the time, she was only looking into the windows of the house she grew up in, as Munro discovered after her mother died. Having seen a letter in the Wingham *Advance-Times* from this woman's daughter, Munro deduced that Mrs. Netterfield was merely curious. She wondered. Munro thinks that she might have visited the author of the letter that allowed her to make this connection, "If I had not been so busy with my own young family and my own invariably unsatisfactory writing." "But the person I would really have liked to talk to then was my mother," she continues, "who was no longer available." With that, Munro shifts to her absence from her "mother's last illness or . . . her funeral," explaining her decision and taking responsibility for it. Still, she wonders, writing "We say of some things that they can't be forgiven, or that we will never forgive ourselves. But we do—we do it all the time" (*Dear Life* 319).[12]

When Robert Weaver and his colleague editors at the *Tamarack Review* wrote, in their second issue that included Munro's "Thanks For the Ride," that "the dream of a distinctly Canadian culture" is "an idle dream" (3), they meant that any vibrant literary culture is connected to every other one and is, in some sense, derived from being itself. That Alice Munro was present in that second issue of that most significant publication, and with a story which is her first really accomplished one, was just as it should be. Seen now, Alice Munro in 1957 was embarked on a literary career that has proved to be as unprovincial, as focused, as non-chauvinistic, and as accomplished as any. She has written her lives—drawing from the one she has lived herself and also from the lives of people she has known, heard about, read about, or imagined. In doing she has wondered over them, meditated over them, and shaped them into her own characters' lives. Alice Munro has had a "dear life," in fact, one that has captured and constructed the meanings, and the feelings, and the confusions of being human, of being alive. *Our* Alice Munro, writing Ontario, writing her own *Dear Life*, making her own dear life our own.

Notes

1. In this connection it is worth noting that, after it was published in Canada in November 1978, *Who Do You Think You Are?* continued on in 1979 to become *The Beggar Maid* in the United States (Knopf) and Britain (Allen Lane). Because Munro continued to reshape her stories, there are differences between the texts of these two versions of this book. Most of these are syntactical and stylistic, but some are substantive. "Providence," for instance, has a different ending in each book.
2. I see *The Moons of Jupiter* this way for several reasons. It is a collection that looks both ways in Munro's career. In the first instance, the three stories held out of *Who* were reshaped—owing to the additional time between books—in personal autobiographical fictions of especial pertinence and power. Timothy McIntyre has made this case persuasively regarding the title story. At the same time, and acknowledging the increased output in the late 1970s and early '80s, with the transformation of "Working for a Living" into a memoir, Munro was achieving a deeper synthesis of personal material with fictional. "Bardon Bus," one of two stories first published in the collection, is both metafictional and open-ended in its construction of a love affair; another full draft of it, which Munro produced after the published version, exists in the Calgary archives. And as I indicate here, "Dulse" is part of Munro's ongoing critique of the writer's position.
3. Because Munro used book proofs from the initial version of *Who* to revise these stories after the book's first publication, the case is clear. There remains a reference to Janet's name in the book version of "The Moons of Jupiter" as well; Ann Close pointed it out to Munro when they were working on *The Moons of Jupiter*, and Munro left it there (Moons 218).
4. While this is not the place to go into any real detail, during the late 1970s Munro established professional relations and friendships with three people that proved key to her career: her Canadian editor, Douglas Gibson; her New York agent, Virginia Barber; and Ann Close, her American editor at Knopf. In addition, there were also a succession of editors at the *New Yorker:* Charles McGrath, Daniel Menaker, Alice Quinn, Bill Buford, and

Deborah Treisman. Thus, during this period, Munro went from being a writer working largely in isolation, as she had throughout the 1950s and most of the 1960s, to a writer with a range of interested associates offering sustained and variegated professional feedback on her stories as she wrote them.

5. Given what she would later write in "Soon"—"Because it's what happens at home that you try and protect, as best you can, for as long as you can" (*Runaway* 125)—it is worth noting that Munro publicly protected her father in 1982 by taking exception to a description of him that accompanied a personality piece about her in the Toronto *Globe and Mail* (Munro "Distressing Impression"). In 1989, after she had received a copy of *The Longman Anthology of Literature by Women, 1875–1975* (1989), which contained her "The Found Boat," Munro wrote to her agent Virginia Barber asking that they take action to remove the characterization of her father in the biography, writing that "my father is described as a '*ne'er-do-well* who failed at fox-farming, *among other things*. I find this characterization of a defenceless dead person, a person whose only public notice this is, appalling. It is snide and cruel and untrue." Munro wrote "a blistering note" to the biography's author "and another to the editor-in-chief" (Munro to Barber, italics in original). Munro wanted to take the story out of any subsequent edition and to have Barber threaten them. Unfortunately, there was no subsequent edition.
6. Relevant here too is the fact that when Munro returned to Huron County to live with Fremlin, she began regularly visiting her great-aunt Maud Code Porterfield, who then lived in the Huron View nursing home. Along with her sister, Sadie Code Laidlaw (1876–1966), Munro's paternal grandmother, she had moved to Wingham after Anne Laidlaw had fallen ill and so was a fixture in Munro's teenage years. She was the model for one of the aunts in "The Peace of Utrecht," is a presence in *Lives of Girls and Women*, and figures in "Winter Wind" (1974). These visits produced some of the nursing-home details in "Royal Beatings" and "Spelling" in *Who Do You Think You Are?* (*The Beggar Maid*), and, likely, in "The Bear Came Over the Mountain" (1999–2000) in *Hateship, Friendship, Courtship, Loveship, Marriage*. Porterfield died at the age of ninety-seven in 1976. And along with Fremlin, Munro lived in Clinton with his mother, who at the time was in her eighties and frail, until her death.
7. The deleted paragraph ending with this in the *Tin House* version is the beginning of a wholly different ending found in *Dear Life*, and it was excised by March 2012. Presumably, the version published in *Tin House* was submitted to its editors before that and Munro, as is her practice, continued to revise stories as *Dear Life* was being assembled.
8. A version of "Soon," dated by Munro July 30, 2003, and submitted to the *New Yorker*, has this single-sentence paragraph as the very ending of

the story. The final version of the ending, with the added paragraph that concludes the published story, came in as a revision of the final two pages dated by Munro September 16, 2003.

9. These literary glosses are in need of further attention in Munro studies. K. P. Stich has written on Greek myths in "Meneseteung" (1988) and on the Grail quest. Ian Rae has detailed parallels between Juliet's background as a classicist and the poetry of Anne Carson (although, when asked about it, Munro seemed surprised that anyone saw Carson as a model for Juliet [Thacker, interview September 6, 2013]). In addition, I have noted them and, in an article on Willa Cather and A. E. Housman, noted also that Munro uses *A Shropshire Lad* in "Wenlock Edge" to connect our own times with that of the Romans ("Quartet" 375; "One Knows"). In August of 2001, when I first met Munro for purposes of the biography, she told me that she loves *A Shropshire Lad* and can recite great swatches of it from memory.
10. There are also notebook versions of this elsewhere in the Munro archive (for example 38.12.7). When asked about this correspondence, Munro recalled working on similar stories during the 1970s and said she was conscious of using the same motif when she was writing "Train" (Thacker, interview September 6, 2013).
11. I am not suggesting direct correspondences here, the sort that might suggest that Munro was consciously echoing herself. Rather, the parallels likely derive from her use of the same or similar personal memories. Even so, I read echoes in the "Finale" pieces, in the first instance, of "The Peace of Utrecht," "Boys and Girls," "Images," "Walker Brothers Cowboy," *Lives of Girls and Women*," "Home," "Winter Wind," *Who Do You Think You Are?*, "Working for a Living," and "Nettles." There are quite a few others.
12. In the *New Yorker* version of "Dear Life," which was published as "personal history," there is another paragraph after the one which now ends the book version:

    When my mother was dying, she got out of the hospital somehow, at night, and wandered around town until someone who didn't know her at all spotted her and took her in. If this were fiction, as I said, it would be too much, but it is true. (47)

    When asked about this paragraph and her decision to delete it, to end with the original penultimate *wondering*, Munro said she decided it was too late to add such a powerful and new consideration, and that the decision also had to do with the placing of "Dear Life," the personal history, within *Dear Life*, the book (Thacker, interview September 6, 2013).

Works Cited

Alice Munro Fonds. Special Collections. U of Calgary. Calgary, Alberta.

Editorial. *Tamarack Review* 2 (Winter 1957): 3, 5.

Gardiner, Jill Marjorie. Interview. Appendix. "The Early Short Stories of Alice Munro." MA Thesis. U of New Brunswick, 1973. 19–82.

Hadley, Tessa. "Dream Leaps." Review of *The View from Castle Rock*, by Alice Munro. *London Review of Books*, 25 January 2007: 17–18. http://www.lrb.co.uk/v29/n02/tessa-hadley/dream-leaps. Accessed 4 June 2013.

Hoy, Helen. "'Rose and Janet': Alice Munro's Metafiction." *Canadian Literature* 121 (1989): 59–83.

[Marshall, Joyce.] Reading of Alice Laidlaw's "The Shivaree" and "The Man From Melbury." Robert Weaver to Alice Munro. 3 October 1952. National Archives of Canada. Ottawa. MG 31 D 162.

McCulloch, Jeanne, and Mona Simpson. "Alice Munro: The Art of Fiction CXXXVII." Interview. *Paris Review* 131 (1994): 226–64.

McGill, Robert. "'Daringly Out in the Public Eye': Alice Munro and the Ethics of Writing Back." *University of Toronto Quarterly* 76 (2007): 874–89.

McGrath, Charles. Letter to Alice Munro. 1 November 1977. Alice Munro Fonds. U of Calgary Archives. 37.2.30.5.

McIntyre, Timothy. "'The Way the Stars Really Do Come Out at Night': The Trick of Representation in Alice Munro's 'The Moons of Jupiter.'" *Canadian Literature* 200 (2009): 73–88.

Metcalf, John. "A Conversation with Alice Munro." *Journal of Canadian Fiction* 1.4 (1972): 54–62.

Miller, Karl. "Lives and Letters: Humble Beginnings." Review of *The View from Castle Rock*, by Alice Munro. *Guardian Review*, 28 October 2006: 21.

Munro, Alice. Advance Proof of Supplanted Version of *Who Do You Think You Are?* (August 11, 1978). John and Myrna Metcalf Collection. Rare Books and Special Collections. McGill UP. Montreal, Quebec.

———. "Axis." *New Yorker*, 31 January 2011: 62–69.

———. *Dance of the Happy Shades*. Foreword by Hugh Garner. Toronto: Ryerson, 1968.

———. "Dear Life." *New Yorker*, 9 September 2011: 40–42, 44–47.

———. *Dear Life*. Toronto: McClelland & Stewart, 2012.

———. "Distressing Impression." Letter to the editor. *Globe and Mail*, 22 December 1982: 6.

———. "Dolly." *Tin House* 13.4 [Cover] Issue 52 [Contents page] (2012): 65–80.

———. *Hateship, Friendship, Courtship, Loveship, Marriage*. Toronto: McClelland & Stewart, 2001.

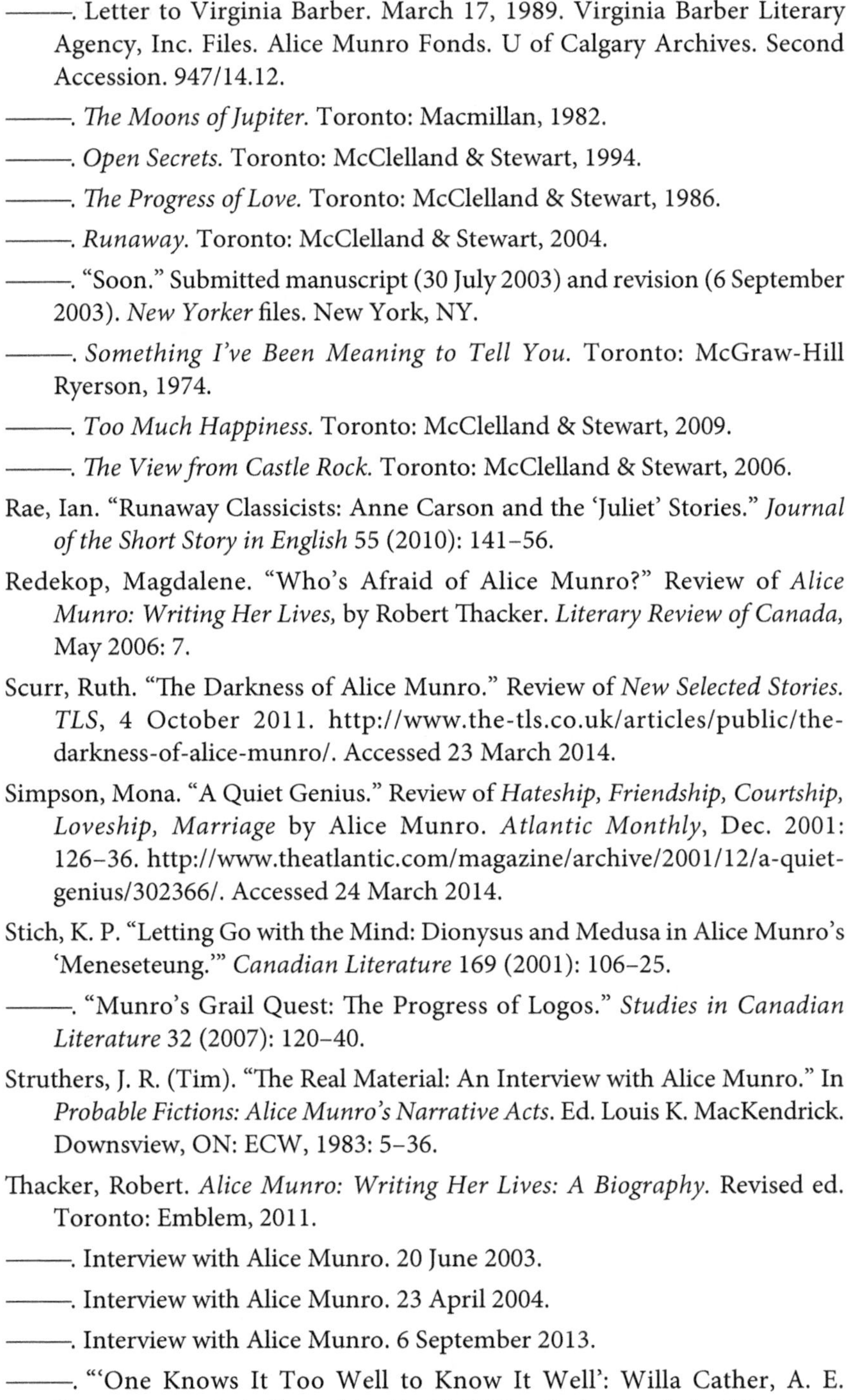

———. Letter to Virginia Barber. March 17, 1989. Virginia Barber Literary Agency, Inc. Files. Alice Munro Fonds. U of Calgary Archives. Second Accession. 947/14.12.

———. *The Moons of Jupiter.* Toronto: Macmillan, 1982.

———. *Open Secrets.* Toronto: McClelland & Stewart, 1994.

———. *The Progress of Love.* Toronto: McClelland & Stewart, 1986.

———. *Runaway.* Toronto: McClelland & Stewart, 2004.

———. "Soon." Submitted manuscript (30 July 2003) and revision (6 September 2003). *New Yorker* files. New York, NY.

———. *Something I've Been Meaning to Tell You.* Toronto: McGraw-Hill Ryerson, 1974.

———. *Too Much Happiness.* Toronto: McClelland & Stewart, 2009.

———. *The View from Castle Rock.* Toronto: McClelland & Stewart, 2006.

Rae, Ian. "Runaway Classicists: Anne Carson and the 'Juliet' Stories." *Journal of the Short Story in English* 55 (2010): 141–56.

Redekop, Magdalene. "Who's Afraid of Alice Munro?" Review of *Alice Munro: Writing Her Lives,* by Robert Thacker. *Literary Review of Canada,* May 2006: 7.

Scurr, Ruth. "The Darkness of Alice Munro." Review of *New Selected Stories. TLS,* 4 October 2011. http://www.the-tls.co.uk/articles/public/the-darkness-of-alice-munro/. Accessed 23 March 2014.

Simpson, Mona. "A Quiet Genius." Review of *Hateship, Friendship, Courtship, Loveship, Marriage* by Alice Munro. *Atlantic Monthly,* Dec. 2001: 126–36. http://www.theatlantic.com/magazine/archive/2001/12/a-quiet-genius/302366/. Accessed 24 March 2014.

Stich, K. P. "Letting Go with the Mind: Dionysus and Medusa in Alice Munro's 'Meneseteung.'" *Canadian Literature* 169 (2001): 106–25.

———. "Munro's Grail Quest: The Progress of Logos." *Studies in Canadian Literature* 32 (2007): 120–40.

Struthers, J. R. (Tim). "The Real Material: An Interview with Alice Munro." In *Probable Fictions: Alice Munro's Narrative Acts.* Ed. Louis K. MacKendrick. Downsview, ON: ECW, 1983: 5–36.

Thacker, Robert. *Alice Munro: Writing Her Lives: A Biography.* Revised ed. Toronto: Emblem, 2011.

———. Interview with Alice Munro. 20 June 2003.

———. Interview with Alice Munro. 23 April 2004.

———. Interview with Alice Munro. 6 September 2013.

———. "'One Knows It Too Well to Know It Well': Willa Cather, A. E. Housman, and *A Shropshire Lad.*" *Willa Cather and the Nineteenth*

Century. Cather Studies 10. Ed. Anne L. Kaufman and Richard Millington. Lincoln: U Nebraska P, 2015. 300–27.

———. "Quartet: Atwood, Gallant, Munro, Shields." *The Cambridge History of Canadian Literature.* Ed. Coral Ann Howells and Eva-Marie Kröller. Cambridge: Cambridge UP, 2009. 357–80.

I
Forms

Living in the Story: Fictional Reality in the Stories of Alice Munro

Charles E. May

Throughout her distinguished career, Alice Munro has frequently been asked by reviewers and interviewers, "Why do you write short stories?" behind which, of course, always lurked the reproach, "Why don't you write novels?" Although she is no longer nagged about her narrative choice of the much-maligned short story, reviewers and interviewers have shifted to a new tactic. Instead of chiding Munro for not writing novels, they now try to account for the success of her stories by claiming that they are *like* novels, not like short stories at all. How else to account for how great they are? Two or three such claims should be sufficient to underline the point:

> "No one else quite constructs short stories that have the slow, rich emotional depth of novels." (Lockerbie)
>
> "You get, in fact, all the complexity and nuance of a novel, concentrated within several dozen pages." (Springstubb)
>
> "Each story reads like a novel; each is a vast canvas of complicated characters, tangled events and quietly turbulent revelations." (Changnon)

Munro definitively answered the impertinent "Why do you write short stories?" question back in 1986, when she said that originally she planned to write a few stories to get some practice and then to write novels, but shrugged, "I got used to writing stories, so I saw my material that way, and now I don't think I'll ever write a novel" (Rothstein). And now everyone, even, I dare say, her agent and her publishers, are glad she never did.

Given my long-time interest in the genre, I have always been very gratified by Alice Munro's suggestion that there is a "short-story way" of seeing reality and delighted with her persistent denial that her stories are *like* novels. She has said she is not drawn to writing novels because she doesn't see that people develop and arrive anywhere, but rather that they live in flashes, from time to time (Hancock)—an image that echoes Nadine Gordimer's famous argument that the short story as a form may be better equipped than the novel to capture whatever can be grasped of human reality where contact is like the "flash of fireflies, in and out, now here, now there, in darkness" (180).

Munro has said, "I'm after the intensity of moments and layers of meaning that come from short stories. I want these moments to be bright and clear and also filled with density and mystery. I couldn't get that from the novel form . . . I don't understand where the excitement is supposed to come from in a novel, and I do in a short story" (Rothstein). On another occasion, she used a metaphor to describe this short-story excitement. "I can get a kind of tension when I'm writing a short story, like I'm pulling on a rope and I know where the rope is attached. With a novel, everything goes flabby" (Struthers).

Still, it seems that reviewers can find no other way to explain the complexity of Munro's works except by lumping them together with that "flabby," or, as Henry James once called it, "baggy," monster—the novel. Can we blame her then for not being able to resist a sly jab at short-story naysayers in a fairly recent story in *Too Much Happiness* entitled "Fiction"—in which the central character buys a book written by a woman she has met briefly at a party and is disappointed to find out it is a only collection of short stories, not a novel: "It seemed to diminish the book's importance, making the author seem like somebody who is just hanging on to the gates of Literature, rather than safely settled inside" (52).

Jonathan Franzen scolded critics and judges for the international neglect of Munro a few years ago by chiding, "The feeling in Stockholm is that too many Canadians and too many pure short-story writers have already been given the Nobel Prize." We are all happy now that Alice Munro is safely inside the Nobel gates of Literature—even if she does *only* write short stories. In one of her first interviews after winning the prize, she graciously said that the award was not only a wonderful thing for her, but a wonderful thing for the short story in general, and she hoped it would bring new readers to the form (Smith).

Despite critics' insistence on the "novelistic" nature of Munro's stories, the qualities of her work that are so compelling are actually the very qualities that have always made great short stories so powerful: for example, the short story's transformation of seemingly trivial and unrelated material into a tight, thematically significant pattern. Fellow short-story master Deborah Eisenberg has said that one of the joys of Munro's writing is "the apparently casual narrative that turns out to have led inexorably to some inescapable juncture" (129). And another fellow short-story writer, Lorrie Moore, noted, "The particular and careful ways Munro's themes are laid into her narrative trajectories cause them to sneak up on the reader" (41). As I have argued for many years, this has been one of the dominant characteristics of the short-story form since Gogol, Poe, Hawthorne, Maupassant, and Chekhov. Like the stories of her predecessors, Munro's fictions build toward a tightly unified thematic pattern, not the construction of a mirror in the roadway.

In the story "The Love of a Good Woman," which many reviewers have singled out as being novelistic, minor details, which in a novel would merely be part of characterization or verisimilitude, become elements of a dominant thematic/aesthetic configuration. For example, at the beginning of the story, the young boys talk about the time when one of their fathers was taken to the hospital with pneumonia and the wet sheets and towels in which he was wrapped all turned brown from the nicotine in him—traces of some secret stain manifesting itself externally. Later the boys shout at some girls passing by, "You got blood all over your arse" (24)—still another reference to the external traces of a hidden secret. This motif becomes central when the story shifts to Mrs. Quinn, whose kidneys are failing, causing a smell to come out through her skin that was "acrid and ominous." The stains of blood that mark a hidden secret culminate in the stain of the dead optometrist's blood on the floor and in Mrs. Quinn's clothes, whose burning smell marks the beginning of her illness.

The novel may create a verisimilar illusion of phenomenal reality, but the short story, concerned with universal thematic significance, requires more artifice and patterning. Poe, Chekhov, Carver—indeed all great short-story writers—knew this difference between the two forms well and, consequently, by means of tight control and tension, created a self-sustained moral and aesthetic universe in what Stephen Millhauser recently characterized as a grain of sand. So does Alice Munro. What she means by a short story being “alive” is not a mimetic depiction of so-called everyday reality, but what Chekhov meant when he once said that it is unified “compactness” that “makes short things *alive*” (*Letters*).

The complexity of Munro’s short stories is not the result of multiple characters, the passage of time, or the creation of an historical/social context—all traditional characteristics of the novel—but rather the result of seeing the world in a uniquely “short story way.” To my mind, Munro’s “specific kind of creative activity”—manifesting “tension,” “control,” “mood,” “emotion,” “mystery”—underlies the complexity of short stories in general and her short stories in particular.

Critics are often puzzled by the motivation of Munro’s characters. For example, in a *Los Angeles Times* review of *Open Secrets*, Susan Heeger wonders about the story “Carried Away”: Why, she asks, would a soldier engaged to a girl back home start a mail-order romance with a woman he’s never met? Why, after the war ends, would he not contact the woman again but instead haunt her workplace surreptitiously for the rest of his life? Edith Pearlman, another one of my favourite short-story writers, who says she has a “taste for the inexplicable” and is drawn to stories that dispense with that essential quality of realistic fiction—“motivation”—agrees with the poet Amy Clampitt, who asks, “who knows what makes any of us do what we do? ”—an insight Pearlman says writing workshops should keep in mind (419).

Although the novel may focus on cause-and-effect in time, the short story accepts that what makes characters do what they do is often quite mysterious. Munro’s short stories deal with moments when people act in such a way that even those closest to them cannot understand what drove them. My favourite recognition of this mystery of motivation is from Flannery O’Connor, who once said she lent some stories to a country lady who lived down the road from her, and when she returned them the woman said, “Well, them stories just gone and shown you how some folks *would* do.” O’Connor agreed that when you write stories you have to show how “some specific folks *will* do, *will* do in spite of everything” (90). The short story’s focus on mysteriously motivated, or seemingly unmotivated, behaviour is at least as old as Poe’s puzzling about the perverse in “The Tell-Tale Heart” and “The Black Cat” and as recent as Raymond Carver’s presentation of characters, who, scolded critic John W. Aldridge, are “impulsive and arbitrary,” sadly “lacking in realistic motivation”—a criticism which suggests that Aldridge just does not appreciate a central characteristic of the short story as a form (51–54).

When Geoff Hancock talked about this mystery of motivation with Munro and suggested that her stories "give voice to our secret life," she emphatically agreed: "That is absolutely what I think a short story can do" (76). Part of the reason for this sense of an elusive and mysterious "secret" life of the characters of short stories derives from its origins in the folk tale and the romance form. Whereas the focus of the novel is often on the social life of as-if people in the world, characters in short fiction seem somewhat like allegorical figures because of their obsessive focus on some single experience: Goodman Brown's journey into the forest, Old Phoenix's trip to get the healing medicine in Welty's "Worn Path," Bartleby's preference "not to," Nick Adam's fishing trip at Big, Two-Hearted River. Although in Joyce's "The Dead" Gabriel's mind wanders through a number of memories, thoughts, and tasks, there is an intensifying pattern to his preoccupations, or else the story would not end with that famous revelatory sense of transcendence and meaningful closure with snow all over Ireland, falling on the living and the dead.

The ambiguity and complexity of such early prototypes of the short story as Hawthorne's "Young Goodman Brown," Poe's "The Fall of the House of Usher," and Melville's "Bartleby, the Scrivener" result from the fact that in these stories allegorical characters in a code-bound pattern uneasily interrelate with realistic characters in the verisimilitude of a real world. Our sense that something "unnatural" motivates Goodman Brown, Roderick Usher, and Bartleby results from the fact that they are like allegorical figures who seem to have stepped into an "as-if-real" world.

Angus Fletcher provides a suggestion about the effect created by such a juxtaposition in his book on allegory, arguing that because the allegorical figure is bound to its single role in the story in which it plays a part, if placed in the real world, the character would act like an obsessed person. For example, a character named "Faith" would act as if she were obsessed with faith and thus could not "think" of anything else. And indeed, the characters in short fiction often seem motivated by something that they cannot articulate and that those around them cannot understand.

The hidden story of emotion and secret life, communicated by atmosphere, tone, and mood, so common to the short story, is always about something more unspeakable and more mysterious than the events engaged in by as-if-real characters in a time-bound world. The genius of Munro's stories is that whereas they *could* indeed be the seedbeds of novels, they do not communicate as novels do. And if we try to read them as if they were novels, they will never haunt us with their mystery. If "The Love of a Good Woman" were a novel, for example, it would be a psychological, literary "whodunit" that would explore the lives of two women who have become victims of the social assumptions and gender differences of a recognizable social world. However, like most great short stories, Munro's story is concerned with a much more abstract, universal, existential meaning of what it means to be human.

"The Love of a Good Woman" may begin like a novel, but instead of continuing to broaden out as it introduces new characters and seemingly new stories, it tightens up, slowly connecting what at first seemed disparate and unrelated. It is a classic example of Munro's most characteristic technique of creating a world that has all the illusion of external reality, while all the time pulling the reader deeper and deeper into what becomes an hallucinatory inner world of mystery, secrecy, and deception. Unlike a novel, which would be bound to develop some sort of satisfying closure, Munro's story reaches a moral impasse, an ambiguous open-end in which the reader suddenly realizes that instead of living in the world of apparent reality, he or she has been whirled, as if by a centrifugal force, to an almost unbearable central point of intensity.

The notion of a lonely secret life has a strong ancestry in the short-story form, beginning with Gogol and Poe, but it is quintessential in the stories of Chekhov. Although the theme of the secret self could be illustrated in any number of Chekhov's short fictions, the paradigmatic statement can be found in one of his most famous stories, "Lady with the Dog." Near the end of what seems to be merely an anecdotal tale of adultery, the central male character agonizes over the division he senses in himself:

> He had two lives: one, open, seen and known by all who cared to know, full of relative truth and of relative falsehood, exactly like the lives of his friends and acquaintances; and another life, running its course in secret. And through some strange, perhaps accidental, conjunction of circumstances, everything that was essential, of interest, and of value to him, everything in which he was sincere and did not deceive himself, everything that made the kernel of his life, was hidden from other people; and all that was false in him, the sheath in which he hid himself to conceal the truth—such, for instance, as his work in the bank, his discussions at the club, his "lower" race, his presence with his wife at anniversary festivities—that was open. (23)

This "secrecy" that makes it impossible for us to know anyone or for anyone to know us, is, of course, the basic human condition, and it is the source of the sense of loneliness that Frank O'Connor has said characterizes the short story as a form. O'Connor argues that the short story has always functioned in a quite different way from the novel, claiming we find in it at its most characteristic something we do not often find in the long form—"an intense awareness of human loneliness" (19).

I believe that what O'Connor has perceived about the central focus of the short story as a genre is the primordial story that constitutes human beings existentially—our basic sense of aloneness and yearning for union. As British theorist Roger Poole once pointed out, the problem is the enigma of the "other," for I can only see from the other's point of view what I would have seen if I were there in the same place as he or she. But my "here" and the other's "over there" are mutually exclusive. Since "There is no way of knowing what the other actually sees, feels, intends, *as if I were he* . . . we are born into solipsism" (130). As Mervyn Rothstein has said about Munro's stories, they "deal with the utter subjectivity of truth—our inability to see things through others' eyes."

Thus arises, says Martin Buber, the "melancholy of our fate" in the earliest history of both the race and the individual (27).This is, of course, the reality underlying the Judeo-Christian myth of the Fall. When Gogol's Akakey Akakievitch says, "I am your brother," or Melville's lawyer/narrator recognizes that he and Bartleby are "sons of Adam," the basic command to love the neighbour as the self, which Rudolph Bultmann says surpasses all other demands and knows no boundary or limit, is acknowledged (18); for to love the other as the self is the supreme fiction—the aspiration to enter the mind of the other so profoundly that the other becomes indistinct from the self. It is, I like to think, no accident that the romance Alice Munro has said had the most powerful influence on her youth, *Wuthering Heights*, dramatizes the paradigmatic proclamation of that longing when Cathy says to Nelly Deans, "I am Heathcliff."

This awareness of separation has recently been explored by cognitive psychologists as the human development of what is called "theory of mind"—also known as mind reading—that human ability to, if not know, at least to hypothesize theories about the minds of others—make assumptions about what others are thinking, speculating why they do what they do—an ability, psychologists suggest, developed by humans approximately in the third year of life.

Studies by Keith Oatley, Raymond Mar, and others at the University of Toronto indicate that readers of fiction perform better on theory-of-mind tests and thus understand and empathize with the mysterious "other" better than readers of nonfiction, who don't do well at mindreading at all. A recent study of theory of mind, done by David Comer Kidd and Emanuele Castano at the New School for Social Research, in New York, went further, suggesting that it is reading *literary* fiction that improves one's ability to understand the mental states of others, while reading popular fiction or nonfiction does not.

Cognitive psychology researchers David Miall and Don Kuiken of the University of Alberta suggest that literary fiction unsettles readers' expectations and engages the psychological processes needed to gain access to characters' subjective experiences. Kidd and Castano argue that literary fictions are writerly texts replete with complicated individuals whose inner lives are rarely easily discerned. Popular fictions, on the other hand, are readerly texts that tend to portray characters as internally consistent and predictable.

One of the stories Kidd and Castano used as an example of literary fiction that *did* improve readers' theory of mind was an Alice Munro story—"Corrie," as it appeared in the 2012 edition of *The O. Henry Prize Stories*. For popular fiction, they chose a romance story by Rosamunde Pilcher entitled "Lalla" from her book *Love Stories*. In an interesting bit of convergence, Pilcher has said the book that most influenced her in her youth, at least in teaching her about love stories, was *Wuthering Heights*, staying awake until five in the morning reading it. Munro once told an interviewer that she read *Wuthering Heights* seven or eight times, admitting, "this was maybe a bit unhealthy?" "It certainly doesn't prepare one for life" (Miller125).

Although I can readily believe that reading an Alice Munro story might engage one's theory of mind—might improve one's ability to leap across the divide that separates us from our fellow human beings—try to understand them, empathize with them, recognize we are all sons and daughters of Adam, and say "I/Thou" and "I am Your Brother"—I am not sure this is due to fictional characters in her stories simply replicating human beings in the world, like those who live down the street from us, making us privy to their subjectivity. Indeed, in many Munro stories, characters seem to have little or no subjectivity at all. Characters in short stories are less like people in the real world than they are like characters in fiction, the qualities of the reality of which are quite different.

Munro has always known this. Since her childhood, like many writers, she has found the world of books more real than the world around her. Munro has said she began making up stories when she started school and was planning novels when she was in high school. In her *Paris Review* interview in 1994, she said, "Reading was my life until I was thirty. I was living in books." And living in books, one might suspect, doesn't prepare one for life, although it indeed surely prepares one for transforming one's life into fiction.

Munro has often called Lucy Maud Montgomery's *Emily of New Moon*, about a girl who is obsessively driven to be a writer, a watershed book in her life. Emily experiences her most powerful sense of meaningful reality as "flashes" of awareness that life, like story, is mysterious. But she is an unchild-like child who others think talks queer and acts too old for her twelve years. She loves to live in a story world that she creates, and is fascinated by those people in the real world who talk and act like characters in stories.

In the collection Constance Rooke put together a few years ago as a fundraiser for PEN Canada, called *The Writing Life*, David MacFarlane says, "The world of the writer, writing—the only world in which the writer is entirely engaged—is largely unknown to most people, even to those who live with a writer, writing" (225). And in Eleanor Wachtel's collection of interviews *Writers and Company*, Munro said that she realized early on that her obsessive reading and writing was a cause for suspicion and knew that her "real life had to be hidden, had to be protected" (103). In her Nobel Prize interview, she said, "When you're a writer, you're never quite like other people—you're doing a job that other people don't know you're doing and you can't talk about it, really, and you're just always finding your way in the secret world and then you're doing something else in the 'normal' world."

American writer Jayne Anne Phillips has said, "The writing life is a secret life, whether we admit it or not. Writers focus perpetually on the half-seen, and we live in the dim or glorious shadows of partially apprehended shapes. We could bill ourselves as perceptually challenged—given that we live two lives at once, segueing from one to the other with some distress . . . . We occupy a kind of border country" (91). Munro agrees, telling an interviewer once that she lived two completely differently lives—"the real and absolutely solitary life and the life of appearances." "I've always worked both sides of the fence," Munro has said. "I feel that I'm an outsider; I go in disguise most of the time" (Rothstein).

A question we might ask is: If the story-world is more real to a writer like Alice Munro than the everyday world of so-called reality, then what kind of characters inhabit that world? Are they like people in real life, or is their complexity due to something else? Furthermore, we might ask: Is this especially true for the world of the short story, which Russian formalist B. M. Éjxenbaum has argued is a "fundamental, elementary, form" (81), indebted, as it is, to the romance—a form Northrop Frye has called the structural core of all fiction (*Secular*). As Frye pointed out, although the novel deals with personality, "with characters wearing their personae or social masks," the romancer does not attempt to create real people so much as "stylized figures" (*Anatomy* 304).

When E. M. Forster was asked about the process of turning a real person into a fictional one, he said a "likeness isn't aimed at and couldn't be obtained, because a man is only himself amidst the particular circumstances of his life and not amid other circumstances. . . . When all goes well, the original material soon disappears, and a character who belongs to the book and nowhere else emerges" (qtd. in Furbank and Haskell). Is it different to make a fictional character out of someone in a novel than it is to make a fictional character out of someone in a short story? I think so. In a novel you might transform a person into a character in order to say, "This is what happened to this person." It is not exactly what happened, nor is it exactly the person it happened to, but if you read this novel, you will recognize this person as a person in the world, or at least pretty much like a person in the world. However, in a short story, you may say, "Something happened to this person that means something." Because I am trying to discover what that meaning is and to make a meaningful fiction in which the person seems to live, that world may seem less like the real world than like a pattern constructed for a thematic purpose. In the seemingly real world of the novel, the fictional person may seem to move in a linear line until the line stops—either arbitrarily or phenomenologically. But in a short story, when the story ends, one seems to be thrown back to the beginning in order for the reader to construct or reconstruct the meaning that the author is trying to discover. Thus, the short story may seem more artifice than the novel.

Perhaps short-story writers recognize, as Thomas Mann once pointed out, that life is a "mingling of the individual elements and the formal stock in trade; a mingling in which the individual, as it were, only lifts his head above the formal and impersonal elements" (411–28). Perhaps short-story writers consequently recognize, as critic Robert Langbaum notes, at that level of experience, when events fall into a formal pattern, they are "an objectification of your deepest will, since they make you do things other than you consciously intend; so that in responding like a marionette to the necessities of the story, you actually find out what you really want and who you really are" (175–77).

I suggest that one possible answer to the question—Why do characters in Alice Munro's stories do the strange and mysterious things they do?—is that they are enthralled by the formal demands of the story, bound to the thematic pattern of the basically mysterious human motivation that emerges in the process of the writing of the story. Munro once said, "What I like is not to really know what the story is all about. And for me to keep trying to find out." What makes a story interesting, she says, is the "thing that I don't know and that I will discover as I go along" (Hancock). Munro would agree with Randall Jarrell who once said, "In fiction to understand everything is to get nowhere" (43).

If a fictional character acts on the principles of story and discourse, that is, acts as if he were indeed a fictional character rather than an "as if" real character in the world, acts according to the demands of story and of metaphor, but does so within the simultaneous similitude of a real world, the character becomes transformed into metaphor in the process of the story, becomes a character caught in the discourse of his own obsessive metaphoric making. When we try to understand a fictional character in a novel as if he or she were a real person, we approach the character in terms of the context of the similitude of a real world the story presents—that is, what we know about life. When we try to understand a character in a short story, we must discover the latent structure of the thematic pattern, the schema or code that governs the character by virtue of the position he or she holds in the story itself—that is, what we know about story. The realistic response is individual and subjective; the formal response is traditional and schematic.

This approach to character as determined by theme, form, and pattern is critically well established, although anathema to novelists and other realists who favour readerly texts that focus on the *territory* of social context rather than writerly texts that focus on the *map* of language that creates an artifice of reality. In what Roland Barthes called readerly works, we assume that when we are talking about the work (which is after all a map of some assumed real "territory") we are indeed talking about the territory itself. In "writerly" works, the reader is made to focus on the "literariness" of the work, that is, its existence as a map made up of differences rather than reality made up of some hypothetical essential actuality.

Of course, Barthes argued that even so-called realistic works are actually not realistic at all, but rather drawn from artistic and cultural conventions and codes which, in fact, constitute their very being as art works. As William H. Gass has said, the so-called life one finds in fiction is nothing like actual life at all. He illustrates how absurd it is to think of fiction as a window onto, or a mirror held up to, life by asking us to think of a painting by Picasso which depicts a pitcher, a candle, and a blue enamel pot. "They are siting unadorned, upon the barest table. Would we wonder what was cooking in that pot?" (38)

What often determines the behaviour of many of Alice Munro's characters are not the slings and arrows of everyday life but rather the thematic demands of her story world, which often include role playing, storytelling, gossiping, pretending, getting lost in reading, being obsessed by writing, acting like characters in fiction. Munro's characters are always losing themselves in stories, making up scenarios, creating fictions in which they try to live, or in which they trick others to live.

For example, in the story "Jesse and Meribeth," a teenage girl tries to impress her best friend by inventing a story about an affair with a married man. In "Hateship, Friendship, Courtship, Loveship, Marriage," a girl invents a scenario to deceive a lonely woman. In "The Children Stay," a young woman abruptly leaves her husband and two children for a lover, thinking it is something that Anna Karenina had done and what Madame Bovary wanted to do. Characters in Munro's stories, like the woman in the story "Material," are guilty of trying to make life interesting by converting people into fictional characters. For Munro's characters, imaginative reality is superior to the merely real, and the storied past trumps the simple present. Always in Munro's work, there is the theme of storytelling, as in "The Ottawa Valley" and "Royal Beating"; the theme of fantasy vs. reality, as in "Wild Swans" and "Chadderly and Fleming"; the theme of a fairy tale world, as in "Images" and "Beggar Maid"; the theme of acting and the theatrical, as in "Something I've Been Meaning to Tell You" and "Simon's Luck." Ken Adachi, in his *Toronto Star* review of *Moons of Jupiter*, has it just right, noting that her stories "carve out an image of an amphibious being which lives, with mysterious simultaneity, both on the hard, dry land of everyday reality and in the fluid realm of artifice and imagination."

Munro sees people in real life as if they were fictional characters, creating their own stories in which to live. The answer to the question that readers often ask about Munro's characters—Why do they do the things they do?—cannot be found by thinking of them as if they were real people. The question must be answered by reading them as fictional characters governed by the demands of the story in which, and only in which, they live. Here are a few examples from her latest stories in *Dear Life* (2012):

The questions—Why does Vivien agree to marry Dr. Fox in the story "Amundsen," and why does Fox decide at the last minute not to marry her—cannot be answered by appealing to any simple psychology of the two characters as if they were particular people in the world, but rather by referring to what Henry James once said about Nathaniel Hawthorne's concern with a "deeper psychology." Vivien's attraction to Fox can be attributed to her romantic, fiction-based fascination with his mysteriousness maleness. His decision not to marry her derives from his desire to maintain his own fictional concept of maleness inviolate from any female involvement.

In the story "Gravel," the narrator feels caught between stability and instability, between things that exist solidly in the world and things that are so unstable that they just disappear, a theme reinforced by the motif of "roleplaying." The mother's leaving her husband for an amateur actor because she wants to *really* live rather than imagine living reflects the ambiguity in Munro's fiction of what is "real life" and what is "play or pretend life." The narrator wonders about her mother's motivation for leaving, thinking ironically that perhaps she would live now, not just read.

Although it could not have occurred to us on the first reading of Munro's "Leaving Maverly," a second reading may lead us to ask why Munro opens her story with a movie theater and its owner, since neither play a significant role in the remainder of the story. It seems to ignore Poe's injunction: "In the whole composition there should be no word written, of which the tendency, direct or indirect, is not to the one pre-established design." It seems to ignore Chekhov's famous advice: "If you say in the first chapter that there is a rifle hanging on the wall, in the second or third chapter it absolutely must go off." It seems, in other words, mere novelistic verisimilitude.

However, neither Poe nor Chekhov meant to suggest that every detail in the story must contribute to the plot or events of the story, for neither believed that plot was the most important element; both were more concerned with thematic design or pattern. If we assume that "Leaving Maverly" is built around a spatial thematic pattern rather than a temporal plot, the opening description of the theatre and its owner can be seen a kind of introit to a story about the mystery of how we "try out" the roles that define our place in the world. "Leaving Maverly" is about people making decisions based on their experience with fictional depictions or impressions of life—the fictions of literature, movies, religion—the stories we make up about those around us whose lives are secret.

My favourite Munro story about a character being governed by fiction is "Wenlock Edge" in *Too Much Happiness*. When I posted a discussion of this story on my blog a few years ago, many of my readers were puzzled about the motivation of the central character—why would this young woman agree to take off her clothes in front of a strange older man and read an A. E. Houseman poem to him? The answer is because she is a bookworm who primarily lives in what she reads, believing that one who studies literature should see reality differently than others. The other characters in the story believe that you have to get a footing somewhere, that reading literature is only a game. The narrator thinks that those who do not read have no pegs on which to hang anything. When she reads Housman's "Wenlock Edge," she feels comfortable, at peace with the familiar rhythms of the poem, living in language more easily than in phenomenal reality.

The narrator realizes that she is wicked in the way that all writers of fiction are wicked—creating fictional characters, pretending they are real, and then manipulating them mercilessly as merely fictional characters. One of Munro's most powerful stories about the wickedness of the writer may well be "Family Furnishings," from *Hateship, Friendship*, which Catherine Lockerbie in the *Ottawa Citizen*, describes as a "potent and cautionary tale about the ways in which fiction appropriates life" and which Lorrie Moore calls a powerful story about the "willing trade of the human for art."

I would like to conclude with a few comments about the story "Corrie," which, as I noted earlier, cognitive psychologists have juxtaposed with Rosamunde Pilcher's story "Lalla" to suggest that reading literary fiction better improves the human ability to understand what motivates others than popular fiction does.

Pilcher's story is simple and transparent. As told by the beautiful titular character's more ordinary younger sister, it is a coming-of-age piece with a satisfying twist at the end, in which Lalla suddenly realizes she has made a "ghastly mistake" in pursuing the good life with a wealthy young man and recognizes that she really loves the boy who may not be able to buy her things, but with whom she can share her thoughts—a decision that the young narrator knows will be good for everyone. Although the story is short, it is novelistic in the transparency of its language and the surface level of its reassuring and simplistic plot turn.

"Corrie," on the other hand, *is* a mystery. I have discussed it several times on my blog, where it has received more reader attention than any story I have talked about there. The very fact that "Corrie" covers a time period of over twenty years is one of those characteristics of a Munro story that cause reviewers to assume that it is novelistic. However, I suggest that "Corrie" is a classic short story with all the virtues of that form subtly displayed. In this story there is no development over time, and that fact lies at the heart of what the story is about. If "Corrie" were a novel about a real-life situation, then we might ask the following questions:

Why does Corrie stay with her lover Ritchie for so long? What kind of experience do they have together? Why doesn't Corrie find herself a good man? Why is Ritchie such a exploiting bounder? But the story is not about such issues. Corrie is not a real person; she is a paradigm of a woman having an affair. The story, like Chekhov's "Lady with a Dog," is about an affair as a universal, classic, even literary, phenomenon. Ritchie is not a real person; we know very little about him, about what he thinks, and it is futile to guess. He is a paradigmatic married man having an affair. The complexity of Munro's short story is nothing like the complexity of a novel. In a novel, we make judgments about particular people in a particular situation at a particular time and place. But "Corrie" does not lead us to make such judgments, but rather to contemplate the quintessential meaning of "affair." And "affair" is about secrecy, sacrifice, selfishness, retribution, stasis.

This story does not embody a novelistic complexity about the evolution of experience over time, but rather a short-story complexity about the revelation of a secret that has sustained a situation for which someone has to pay. We do not get inside the mind of Corrie in the last section of the story any more than we get inside the mind of Ritchie in the first section. We have no particular information about her feelings. We only know she is trying to adjust to the realization she has come to and that she feels a sense of emptiness—"a cavity everywhere, most notably in her chest." She knows that Ritchie may never know of Sadie's death since he has no connection with her and no connection with the family she has worked for. He will therefore expect things to go on just as they have—with Corrie giving him the money twice a year and him pocketing it. Corrie could say something, but she knows that their relationship demands payment, and she is the one who can afford to pay. And so, she will continue to pay, for what difference does it make if the money goes to Sadie or to Ritchie? She goes downstairs, as "if gingerly, making everything fit into a proper place."

And indeed, making everything fit into its proper place, a characteristic of the short story, understood by short-story writers since Poe first formulated it, is central to embodying the mystery of human motivation in that form. Flannery O'Connor knew that the short-story writer's "kind of fiction will always be pushing its own limits outward toward the limits of mystery," that the meaning of a "story does not begin except at a depth where adequate motivation and adequate psychology and the various determinations have been exhausted. Such a writer," says O'Connor, will be interested in "what we don't understand rather than in what we do" (41).

Alice Munro is such a writer. Her stories do not improve the reader's ability to understand the minds of others by creating characters like people in real life. Rather, her stories, by putting everything in its proper place, challenge us to understand the patterns that govern the basic human condition of separation and mystery.

In *Such Stuff as Dreams*, Keith Oatley reports on a study that revealed when readers read Munro's story "The Office" and had to pick up the writer's indirect suggestions via the first-person narrator, they understood the narrator better than when direct information about the narrator was added to the story. This seems to suggest that it may not be projection of the inner secret mind of the character that improves theory of mind when reading literary fiction, but rather the interpretive activity that the literary fiction demands. The very fact that short stories provide little information and demand interpretation to put everything in its proper place may be what improves the reader's theory of mind.

Characters in short fiction simultaneously give the reader the illusion of existential reality and the sense that they are representative figures in the service of the story. The question that interests me is: What happens if a fiction is occupied by a character who is more artifice than real, but in a world that seems as-if real, inhabited by other characters who seem more real than artifice? Put another way, what happens in a fiction when one character acts according to the conventional rules of art—that is, acts like a fictional character—and other characters act as if they were real? The question for me is: Are the laws of short stories different than the laws of novels? And if so, do short stories create a sense of character, and thus character motivation, radically different than in novels?

According to Walter Benjamin, whereas realistic narrative forms such as the novel focus on the relatively limited areas of human experience that indeed can be encompassed by information, characters in stories encounter those most basic mysteries of human experience that cannot be explained by rational means. When stories come to us through information, they are already loaded down with explanation, says Benjamin; it is half the art of storytelling to be free from information.

Like all great short stories, Alice Munro's stories are infused with uneasy magic, mysterious motivation, and confounding inevitability. In all great short stories, there is mystery and not a little menace—secrets so tangled and inexplicable that efforts to explain them with the language of psychology or sociology are futile. Munro's stories create that scary, sacred sense that what happens is not as important as what it signifies, and the shock of recognition that those you thought you knew you don't really know at all. Munro invents characters who sound authentic, even though they are highly stylized, and tells stories of messy reality, even as they are tightly controlled artifices. Like all great short stories, Alice Munro's are complex and powerful not so much because of what seems to actually happen in them, but because of what happens in the mysterious literary imagination.

Works Cited

Adachi, Ken. Review of *Moons of Jupiter*, by Alice Munro. *Toronto Star*, 21 September 1986.

Aldridge, John W. *Talents and Technicians.* New York: Scribner, 1992.

Barthes, Roland. *S/Z.* Trans. by Richard Miller. New York: Hill and Wang, 1975.

Benjamin, Walter. "The Storyteller: Reflections on the Works of Nikolai Leskov." *Illuminations:* Trans. Harry Zohn. London: Jonathan Cape, 1970. 93–109.

Bultmann, Rudolph. *Theology of the New Testament.* Vol. 1. Trans. Kendrick Grobel. London: SCM, 1952.

Buber, Martin. *I and Thou.* 2nd ed. Trans. Ronald Gregor Smith. New York: Charles Scribner's Sons, 1958.

Changnon, Greg. Review of *The Love of a Good Woman*, by Alice Munro. *Atlanta Journal and Constitution*, 25 April 1999.

Chekhov, Anton. "Lady With the Dog." *Selected Tales of Chekhov.* Trans. Constance Garnett. London: Chatto & Windus, 1927. 1–26.

———. *Letters on the Short Story the Drama and Other Literary Topics.* Ed. Louis S. Friedland, 2nd ed. New York: Dover, 1966.

Eisenberg, Deborah. Review of *The View from Castle Rock,* by Alice Munro. *Atlantic,* December 2006. 128–29.

Éjxenbaum, B. M. "O. Henry and The Theory of the Short Story." *New Short Story Theories.* Ed. Charles E. May. Athens: Ohio UP, 1994. 81–88.

Fletcher, Angus. *Allegory.* Cornell UP, 1964.

Franzen, Jonathan. "*Runaway:* Alice's Wonderland." *New York Times Book Review,* 14 November 2004: 1.

Frye, Northrop. *Anatomy of Criticism.* Princeton UP, 1957.

———. *The Secular Scripture: A Study of the Structure of Romance.* Cambridge, MA: Harvard UP, 1978.

Furbank, P. N., and J. H. Haskell. Interviews. "E. M. Forster, The Art of Fiction No. 1." *Paris Review* 1 (Spring 1953). http://www.theparisreview.org/interviews/5219/the-art-of-fiction-no-1-e-m-forster. Accessed 15 August 2015.

Gass, William H. *Fiction and the Figures of Life.* New York: Knopf, 1970.

Gordimer, Nadine. "The Flash of Fireflies." *Short Story Theories.* Ed. Charles E. May. Athens: Ohio UP, 1976. 178–81.

Hancock, Geoff. "Interview with Alice Munro." *Canadian Fiction Magazine* 43 (1983): 74–114.

Heeger, Susan. Review of *Open Secrets,* by Alice Munro. *Los Angeles Times,* 30 October 1994.

Jarrell, Randall. "Stories." *Short Story Theories.* Ed. Charles E. May. Athens: Ohio UP, 1976. 32–44.

Kidd, David Comer, and Emanuele Castano. "Reading Literary Fiction Improves Theory of Mind." *Science,* 18 October 2013: 377–80.

Langbaum, Robert. *The Modern Spirit.* Oxford UP, 1970.

Lockerbie, Catherine. "The Loving Literature of Alice Munro." *Ottawa Citizen,* 30 September 2001: C11.

Lukács, Georg. *Soul and Form.* Trans. Anna Bostock. London: Merlin Press, 1974.

MacFarlane, David. "On Not Going to a Party for Ian McEwan." *Writing Life.* Ed. Constance Rooke. Toronto: McClelland & Stewart, 2006. 281–27.

Mann, Thomas. *Essays of Three Decades.* Trans. H. T. Lowe-Porter. NY: Knopf, 1947.

Miall, David S., and Don Kuiken. "Beyond Text Theory: Understanding Literary Response." *Discourse Process* 17 (1994): 337–52.

Miller, Judith, ed. *The Art of Alice Munro: Saying the Unsayable.* U Waterloo P, 1984.

Millhauser, Steven. "The Ambition of the Short Story." *New York Times Book Review*, 3 October 2008.

Moore, Lorrie. "Artship." *New York Review of Books*, 17 January 2002: 41–42.

Munro, Alice. "Fiction." *Too Much Happiness*. New York: Alfred A. Knopf, 2009. 34–63.

———. "Corrie." *Dear Life*. New York: Knopf, 2012. 154–74.

———. "The Love of a Good Woman." *The Love of a Good Woman*. New York: Alfred A. Knopf, 1998: 3–78.

———. Nobel Prize Interview. http://www.nobelprize.org/nobel_prizes/literature/laureates/2013/munro-lecture_en.html.

———. "Wenlock Edge." *Too Much Happiness*. New York: Alfred A. Knopf, 2009. 64–94.

———. "What is Real?" *Making It New: Contemporary Canadian Stories*. Ed. John Metcalf, Toronto: Methuen, 1982: 223–26.

Oatley, Keith. *Such Stuff as Dreams*. New York: Wiley, 2011.

O'Connor, Flannery. *Mystery and Manners: Occasional Prose*. Eds. Sally and Robert Fitzgerald. New York: Farrar, Straus, and Giroux, 1961.

O'Connor, Frank. *The Lonely Voice: A Study of the Short Story*. Cleveland: World, 1963.

Pearlman, Edith. "Reading the O. Henry Prize Stories 2013." *The O. Henry Prize Stories 2013*. New York: Anchor, 2013. 418–20.

Phillips, Jayne Anne. "The Writer as Outlaw." *The Writing Life*. Ed. Marie Arana. New York: Public Affairs, 2003. 90–94.

Pilcher, Rosamunde. *Love Stories*. New York: St. Martins, 1992.

Poole, Roger. *Towards Deep Subjectivity*. New York: Harper & Row, 1972.

Rothstein, Mervyn. "Canada's Alice Munro Finds Excitement in Short-Story Form." *New York Times*, 10 November 1986: C17.

Smith, Adam. Telephone Interview with Alice Munro. 10 October 2013. http://www.nobelprize.org/nobel_prizes/literature/laureates/2013/munro-telephone.html.

Springstubb, Tricia. "Short Story Collection Shows Munro in Top Form." *Plain Dealer* [Cleveland], 22 November 1998.

Struthers, J. R. (Tim). "The Real Material: An Interview with Alice Munro." *Probable Fictions: Alice Munro's Narrative Acts*. Ed. Louis K. Mackendrick. Downsview, ON: ECW, 1983: 159–77.

Wachtel, Eleanor. *Writers & Company*. New York: Harcourt Brace, 1993.

From Munro's *Lives* to Shields's "Scenes": A Canadian Female *Bildungsroman* that "fit[s] into the hollow of her hand"

LAURIE KRUK

In 2013 Alice Munro made history as the first Canadian Nobel Prize Laureate for Literature, the thirteenth such woman, and one of the few recognized for work in the short story. I would like to propose a textual dialogue between two Canadian authors, Munro and Carol Shields, who were collaborators in the ongoing project of making women's voices central to our national literature, and who did so by means of the short story. I will compare key formal and thematic aspects of *Lives of Girls and Women* (1971), the work closest to a novel of Munro's sixteen-book oeuvre, and "Scenes," a story from Shields's first collection, *Various Miracles* (1985). While showing how Munro rewrites novelistic tradition from a Canadian as well as a feminine perspective, I will then propose that Shields reflects her sister writer's influential work by creating her own micro short-story cycle in response.[1]

Short stories remain a marginalized form in the twentieth/twenty-first century relative to the novel. *Lives of Girls and Women*, which Munro herself described in 2006 as "really just a collection of linked stories" (Allardice 6), has been popularly proclaimed her novel, for through eight stories it traces the coming-of-age of first-person narrator Del Jordan of Jubilee, Ontario.[2] Thus unified by character, perspective, and setting, *Lives* is best read sequentially—although it wasn't written that way, according to Besner (*Introducing* 32)[3]—and even ends with an "Epilogue: The Photographer." While Gerald Lynch has championed the short-story cycle as a "distinctly Canadian genre," in this instance he sides with those who call *Lives* a novel. Lynch excluded it from his own critical study because the stories had not been separately published, the work fits the novelistic *Bildungsroman* tradition, and the "thought of return . . . is but a projection whose meaning is wholly literary . . . as opposed to Jubilee figuring as the self-confirming site of the relation between place and identity that the Canadian short story cycle inscribes" (214–15, n2). However, whether reflecting a presumed Canadian "inferiority complex," or a feminine sense of difference, Munro's genius did not lend itself to writing novels, despite external and internal pressures to do so. In fact, as a young mother and beginning writer, Munro recalls falling into a depression as a result, telling Lisa Allardice, "I had simply lost hope, lost faith in myself. Maybe it was just something I had to go through. I guess it was because I still wanted to do something great—great the way men do." And Allardice comments, "By 'great' she means writing a novel" (5–6).

Putting aside Munro's 2006 authorial pronouncement, *Lives* has been viewed not just as a novel but as a "composite novel" and the more countercultural "narrative of community," as well as a short-story cycle.[4] Coral Ann Howells deems it a "*Bildungsroman* with a decentralised narrative structure," or a "'whole book story sequence' comparable to Joyce's *Dubliners* and constituting a distinctive genre in contemporary Canadian writing" (*Alice* 33). Whichever label is applied to it, however, it is clear that *Lives* is a brilliant blend of the discontinuous and the unified, the hybrid child of what Forrest L. Ingram originally called "the tension between the one and the many" (qtd. in Lynch 18). Ironically, it was perhaps Munro's "failure" to follow literary tradition that has led to her greatest *success:* the creation of a masterpiece, as I see it, in the form of the Canadian short-story cycle. For if we accept E. D. Blodgett's description of "The Flats Road" as the book's prologue, counter-balancing its official "Epilogue," then *Lives*, like other short story-cycles, demands special attention be paid to its opening and closing stories. According to Lynch, it is in the final "return" story that "patterns of recurrence and development initiated in the opening story come naturally to fullest expression" (25).[5] In its productive interplay between what Marjorie Garson calls "Parts and Wholes," *Lives*, like other cycles, inhabits a formal threshold familiar to many women writers, including Shields, who are interested in exploring what Barbara Godard deems a "female aesthetic." Janet Beer even suggests that with its interconnected short stories, *Lives* enacts formal resistance against the novelistic "romance plot." Since *Lives* has been the subject of numerous critical studies, I will restrict myself here to comparing Munro's fictional framework to Shields', and their shared project of sketching a female *Bildungsroman* as short-story cycle. As I will explain, in their opening and closing stories or "scenes," both Canadian women writers display a self-reflexive focus on the unique perceptions, and performative elements, of the female artist.

It is undeniable that *Lives* participates in the long tradition of the *Bildungsroman* as well as the *Künstlerroman*. The classic modernist instance is James Joyce's *A Portrait of the Artist as a Young Man* (1914), to which *Lives* has been frequently compared.[6] But the differences between Stephen and Del are of gender as well as generation and nationality. Del, a colonial like Stephen, must confront the added restrictions of being female in a post-WWII world. As prologue, "The Flats Road" situates the Jordans on their failing silver-fox farm in the country among "an assortment of drunks, bootleggers and idiots" (Macdconald 1). It also introduces Del to the need to develop a perceptive eye on a world where women and girls are more often objectified as texts, like Madeleine, "that madwoman!"(27), whose life is reconstructed, first in the letter designed to marry her off, written by her brother, and then in Flats Road folklore, both of which effectively silence her. Del is first drawn into the story of Madeleine in the role of her illiterate suitor's scribe. Del writes out Benny's "address"—*not* hers—in what Godard calls a "pastiche" of Stephen Dedalus's self-location, part of Munro's "double talk" as a woman writer marginalized within the Western tradition (65, 43). As Besner observes in "The Bodies of the Texts in *Lives of Girls and Women*," it is Del's lifelong habit as a *reader* which protects her from continued feminine marginalization, while preparing her to become author of her own vision. "The Flats Road" thus works "to initiate kinds of meaning and order that are developed in the rest of the book" (Blodgett 38). And unexpectedly, Uncle Benny is the first storyteller as teacher she encounters.

Illiterate Uncle Benny—an uncanny reflection of Uncle Craig as historian—provides an important example of "the other country" (Macdonald) that will fascinate Del, with his chaotic hoarder's home, his piles of tabloids greedily consumed by the pre-adolescent girl, and his own peculiar mixture of knowledge and ignorance, leading to his ill-fated marriage. He can navigate the legendary Grenoch Swamp, for instance, but loses his erstwhile wife and daughter in the wilds of Toronto, where he stubbornly pursues them without a map. As Del concludes, following his recitation to her family of his fruitless journey,

> So lying alongside our world was Uncle Benny's world like a troubling distorted reflection, the same but never at all the same. In that world

> people could go down in quicksand, be vanquished by ghosts or terrible ordinary cities; luck and wickedness were gigantic and unpredictable; nothing was deserved, anything might happen; defeats were met with crazy satisfaction. It was his triumph, that he couldn't know about, to make us see. (26)

Munro's own eye for paradox and oxymoron ("the same but never at all the same," "terrible ordinary cities,") is used here to underscore the insight that Benny's "other country" co-exists with her judgemental mother's world. Benny's visionary impact on Del, the allure of his world and its "crazy satisfaction," is revealed in the compelling multiple ironies of this concluding passage, providing Del's first artistic lesson. In Blodgett's view, Uncle Benny "is the impetus that prepares Del to see the world as textual material" (40). Ajay Heble writes in his chapter on *Lives*,

> Although various ways of 'getting at' people's lives will be chronicled throughout *Lives of Girls and Women*, it is Uncle Benny's world of vision and story, and his faith in the paradigmatic realm, which are perhaps most influential in paving the way for Del's development as a creative writer. (n.p.)

Preceding and, in a sense, pre-empting her mother Addie's rationalist views with his transcendent meaning, Benny prepares the way for that other "hoarder," Uncle Craig, another of Del's possible models. Benny will in turn be echoed or reflected in "The Epilogue" by Bobby Sheriff, the domestic madman of Del's house of fiction, who offers her a "valedictory performance" much more empowering than Art Chamberlain's (160).

For as "Epilogue: The Photographer" reveals, the book ends on the paradox of Del's both leaving and yet not leaving Jubilee. In keeping with both the *Bildungsroman* and *Künstlerroman* tradition, the book concludes with Del's growing expansion of self-awareness and intuition of life's "unstoryable" essence, the final challenge to the young writer.[7] Munro's "Epilogue," however, breaks the chronology expected of a chaptered work to return us to a slightly younger Del, before her regretful if definitive rejection of her lover, before her official academic failure. Yet we are already—have always been—in the presence of the older Del, the implied writer of our text. A space is opened, as Blodgett suggests, as so often with Munro's speakers, "between their former (narrated) and present (narrating) selves" (9). Further, Dieter Meindl points out, *Lives* "does not demonstrate how Del became an artist but provides the proof that she did. And the proof is as much in the parts as the whole of the book" (21). This is perhaps where the short-story cycle is in greatest conflict with a novelistic tradition, for its parts add up to more than the whole. Parts that we first encountered in "The Flats Road" include the setting of Jubilee, writing, Del's mother as voice of both resistance and convention, the Wawanash River, and madness. The "Epilogue" begins by citing three: "This town is rife with suicides, was one of the things my mother would say, and for a long time I carried this mysterious, dogmatic statement around with me . . ." (227). Del the writer then "reads" Jubilee through this Gothic lens, focusing on the mysterious second drowning (after Miss Farris) of Marion Sherriff, a girl just her age. Projecting onto Caroline's character her own "surrender . . . to the body" (204) still to come with Garnet French, Del creates a perverse parable of artistic revelation by means of the "Photographer," Caroline's mysterious lover, who disappears after impregnating her. Ailsa Cox observes that, in her projected fiction, "Del is both subject and object—both the photographer himself and his image, Caroline" (12). His grotesque art, including the prophetic portrait of doomed Caroline with white eyes, while "not real" is "true" in revealing the town's social hypocrisy and moral failings (231). The "realistic" detail that prepares for this Gothic re-telling, however, is found earlier in "Changes and Ceremonies," when a younger Del first notices the "brides in the Photographer's window" (110), a revealing substitution of part for whole, image for reality. Later in that chapter/story, she herself will become one of the Photographer's "subjects," as a dancer in the school operetta (129–30). Del's "picture," it seems, must now be hung together with Caroline's, for she is both artistic subject and feminine object of male desire.[8]

Garson has argued that in *Lives*, Munro uses synecdoche to communicate "the inscrutability of human experience" (424). This artistic mission obviously accords well with the short-story cycle and its deliberate creation of gaps as well as "overlaps," or "the [documentary] real" in dialogue with "the [artistic] true." In Garson's reading, there is indeed something dialogic in Munro's creation of Del's experiences, where mystery reigns and people cannot be comfortably reduced to characters like Caroline and the Photographer. This is the lesson of her failed novel about Jubilee and her final encounter with Bobby Sherriff, the last "madman" of the text.[9] Heble points out how Bobby's influence (retrospectively) balances that of her lover:

> As she learned from her plunge into the realm of experience with Garnet French that language was indeed inescapable, now, through Bobby, she makes a corollary discovery concerning both the limitations

of language and the importance, in fact, the necessity, of returning outward into the world of experience. (n.p.)

Encountered on Del's walk home from seeking her exam results after being "sabotaged by love," as she acknowledges (232), Bobby surprises her with his slightly mocking courtesy as he invites her onto his porch, then serves her lemonade, cake, and dietary advice, warning her about "rats and white flour" (236). As she sits on the porch with her lemonade and cake, realizing "*This was the Sheriff's house*" (234),[10] what Del discovers in Bobby is that "the two worlds [of documentary realism and Gothic fiction] need to be combined, and Bobby is the catalyst that suggests the combination" (Blodgett 60). In his very domestic ordinariness, Bobby decisively explodes the artistic frame she had put around the haunted Sherriffs. Cox suggests that he also reconciles the male and female identities that Del dramatically opposes in her stillborn novel (12). As Del, of past and present, reflects: "It is a shock, when you have dealt so cunningly, powerfully, with reality, to come back and find it still there. Would Bobby Sherriff give me a clue now, to madness?" (209). Perhaps this is also Del's (or Munro's?) realization of the need for a different *form* as well as a different mode of writing, an "anti-novel." Just as Bobby, in his house, undermines her writerly "authority" over the story based on his family history, causing her to lose "faith" in her first novel (234), so Del's fragmentary, circular stories will replace the unified narrative and its links to the (patriarchal) "history" of Uncle Craig, with its indifference to "the secret histories of unmarked places which have been lost behind official accounts" (Howells, *Alice* 39).

It is possible, in fact, to consider Bobby the hermaphroditic "monster" of Godard's utopian feminist analysis, as he, a failed law student turned asylum resident, combines male identity with feminine marginalization and domesticity.[11] In Magdalene Redekop's terms he also represents a "mock mother" who, after maternally nourishing and advising the young woman, rises clownishly "on his toes like a dancer, like a plump ballerina," and introduces her to "a letter, or a whole word, in an alphabet I did not know" (237).[12] According to James Carscallen's suggestive typology, Bobby as "Messenger" "is presenting reality itself as a way of presenting more"; he has "reached a greater life in which reality and truth are one" (496–97). And as Garson observes, Bobby's "gesture is a Munrovian synecdoche. That the whole of which it is a visible part will remain inaccessible is the very condition of its suggestive power" (434–45). Like Uncle Benny, then, Del is presented with a map, or a letter, she cannot read—yet. Nevertheless, Del ends by affirming this alternate vision, this "other country," and its synecdochical significance, with what some have seen as a Joycean "Yes."[13] By using the short-story cycle, a synecdochical form in itself, Munro "swerves from" masculine novelistic tradition in her own anxiety of influence, parodically revising common male traditions or genres, as Godard asserts (50). Munro also establishes a Canadian "map" of experience, situated in the familiar small-town setting and grounded in an embodied feminine perspective that blends the uncanny with the domestic: "deep caves paved with kitchen linoleum" (236).

Carol Shields has called Munro "our best writer" (Kruk *Voice* 203) and "'the divine Alice'" (Foster Stovel 268); strong evidence of Munro's influence may be found in Shields's own short stories. In 1985, Shields published her first of three collections, *Various Miracles*. As she explained to me in our 1990 interview, this was a deliberate experiment in fiction writing, setting a new direction for her career. These unconventional stories include the title piece's *mise en abyme*, the essayistic or episodic "Dolls, Dolls, Dolls, Dolls" and sonnetesque "Mrs. Turner Cutting the Grass."[14] Robert Thacker writes that "Shields's most spectacular narrative experiments are to be found in her short stories," while Howells summarizes Shields's body of short fiction as "the product of her disillusionment with the conventions of literary realism in the early 1980s" ("Quartet" 378; "Space" 41). Yet Shields did not reject realism so much as put "a slant" on its "truth," as her first collection's epigraph, taken from Emily Dickinson, suggested: "Tell all the truth but tell it slant" (n.p.). "Scenes," from *Various Miracles*, shows the inspiration of Munro's feminine *Künstlerroman*, with its self-reflexive treatment of gendered and artistic identity. Borrowing Munro's synecdochical strategy of offering parts for wholes, in "Scenes" Shields probes the nature of perception through an episodic, nine-page biography of Frances, an inquisitive, bookish woman whose maturation echoes Del's in many ways. Like Del, Frances has an early encounter with the body of a dead ancestor (her grandmother), the face of which Frances touches with the middle finger of her right hand, as Del longs to do, but does not.[15] As Shields's heroine reflects, "This touch, she knew, had not been an act of love at all, but only a kind of test" (82). Thus Frances is characterized as another fascinated observer of life's surfaces and depths, becoming even in girlhood a contravener of "so many natural laws" (82).

"Scenes" opens, however, *in medias res*, with adult Frances's brush with mortality in an emergency airplane landing—she is returning from giving a lecture, which implies an intellectual or literary career—

memorialized by the gift of her male seatmate's business card, a synecdochical signature in itself. This reminder of an unexpected intimacy (they had clung together in the crisis) is then kept tucked into the frame of her bedroom mirror, as if to "reflect on" the nature of a public, textual, and masculine identity. The mirror is an inheritance from the same deceased grandmother. We are told, "It is a beautiful mirror, a graceful rectangle in a pine frame, and very, very old. . . . The mirror is the first thing she remembers seeing, *really* seeing, as a child" (81).With the introduction of this "framing" specular image, both perception and reflection are highlighted in the "scenes" that follow.[16] Thus, it is possible to read the description of the bureau mirror as a mini-prologue or frame to Shields's artful story.

The traditional association of women with narcissistic self-objectification leads Grandmother, who observes the child's fascination with it, to will the mirror to her "vain little granddaughter" (81). We may here recall the specular scene of double awareness in which Del, grieving the end of her love affair, looks at her tear-stained face in the mirror, and comments with amazement, "I was watching, I was suffering" before performing Tennyson's line of poetry with "absolute sincerity, absolute irony" (225). Grandmother's mirror has a "beveled edge" that causes the effect of a bisected reflection (82), leading to teenage Frances's reflection, "Life is like looking into a beveled mirror" (82), an insight then rejected, in a self-critique, as "precious." But what initially draws the girl's gaze in this formative encounter is not so much self-presentation, as with the older Del, but the carved wooden frame that holds the glass, shaped into natural vegetation of "square pansies" and "rigid grapes," and described as "primitive" in workmanship (81). We are told that Frances is drawn "to those things that are incomplete or in some way flawed" (81) and need the artist's eye to render them whole, to translate or transform the part into the whole. If Del's legacy was Uncle Craig's mistaken "History," Frances's is the gift of self-reflection, which leads not to expected feminine self-absorption but to the artist's testing, or questioning, of boundaries.

In Simone Vauthier's narratological analysis, "Scenes" is a "narrative of substitutions, which vertically pile up a series of variations" on a theme, rather than building tension by conflict in a traditional plot (116). Reflecting on the writing process of *Various Miracles*, Shields says of "Scenes":

> The story "Scenes" . . . represents an attempt to dislocate the spine of a traditional story, that holy line of rising action that is supposed to

> lead somewhere important, somewhere inevitable, modelled perhaps on the orgasmic patterns of tumescence followed by detumescence, an endless predictable circle of desire, fulfilment, and quiescence. I was for some reason drawn to randomness and disorder, not circularity or narrative cohesion. ("Arriving Late" 248)

Shields's artistic "testing" leads to a stringing together of seemingly "random" events in what appears almost a "list" of the formative moments, or "Scenes," of Frances's life, from girlhood to marriage: "She thinks of them as scenes because they're much too fragmentary to be stories and far too immediate to be memories" (89). Like Del, Frances vacillates between image and reality, being absorbed by books and fascinated with the languages she will later study as an adult: "Learning to read was falling into a mystery deeper than the mystery of airwaves or the halo around the head of the baby Jesus" (84). She also has an attraction to "the other country," which includes life in the "back lane," behind her suburban home, where she is "roughly kissed a number of times" and learns to master basketball "free throws" (86). We are told by the urbane narrative voice, "the subject of childhood interests Frances, especially its prohibitions, so illogical and various" (83). She then recalls a scene or two with "bad girl" Pat Leonard, attracted by her knowledge of the grosser aspects of sexuality and physicality (somewhat like the young Naomi): "She had a boyfriend who went to the technical school, and several times she'd reached inside his pants and squeezed his thing until it went off like a squirt gun" (87). Frances's academic ambitions, however, like Del's, soon separate her from this friend from "the other country," as barely literate Pat is expelled from school, leaving Frances with a strange sense of loss, "even though she wouldn't have been seen dead walking down the hall with Pat Leonard" (87). Just as in *Lives*, female friendship provides a means to rebel, even if only temporarily, against the strictures of gender socialization.

I have suggested that "Scenes" could be called a "micro" short-story cycle in itself, sharing Munro's commitment to including "gaps" in this compressed *Bildungsroman* and to using "Scenes" as "parts" that stand for wholes in just the way that the short-story cycle juxtaposes stories distinct in time but linked by character or setting. Shields takes Munro's experimentation one step further, however, in reducing "reality" to "scenes" that

> seem to bloom out of nothing, out of the thin, uncolored air of defeats and pleasures. A curtain opens, a light appears, there are voices or music or sometimes a wide transparent stream of silence. Only rarely

> do they point to anything but themselves. They're difficult to talk about. They're useless, attached to nothing, can't be traded in or shaped into instruments to prise open the meaning of the universe. (89–90)

One feature of the short-story cycle that separates it from the collection is some form of "return," circling back to the work's opening themes or concepts. As *Lives* ends with an "Epilogue" on the challenge of artistic creation, juxtaposing Del's unsatisfying construction with Jubilee's elusive reality, "Scenes" also returns the middle-aged woman to a self-conscious reflection on her reconstruction of these scenes by circling back to a childhood memory. Vauthier, speaking of Shields's experiments with "closural strategies," observes, "Scenes" ends on "four attempts to define these so-called scenes through comparisons and memories" (123, 116). Frances begins with the theatrical title image, moves to foundational "English paving stones" that neatly fit together, substitutes "keys on a chain that open nothing," and finally, to "the Easter eggs her mother used to bring out every year," which were real hens' eggs, blown out and painted by mother and daughter, the best ones saved from year to year. The young Frances is fascinated by this craft, always finding a special one, meditating, in the final line, on "this one little thing, this little egg that was round like the world, beautiful in color and satin to the touch, and that fit into the hollow of her hand as though it were made for that very purpose" (90).[17]

In this spring ritual, we see a woman's art that is a legacy from mother to daughter. Their "best" art is preserved and displayed, just before Easter, on "the same little pewter cake stand," in keeping with domesticized tradition. According to Vauthier,

> The story ends, then, on an image of totality pregnant with all sorts of potentialities: a perfect symbol of closure, the egg, nevertheless, figures the return to and of the beginning (an archetypal signification of the egg strengthened here by the fact that this, after all, is an Easter egg). The egg is the story and the world. (128)

Yet the young artist not only paints the eggs, she also "frames" each finished one, holding it with her hand and her attentive gaze. There is a return here of Grandmother's mirror, which "frames" its captured images within a simulated natural border, made of wood *and* depicting plants of the wood. The female artist thereby frames, or completes, the world in art. In its evocation of female fertility, as well, the egg meditated upon by the young girl represents the union of mind and body, the hope of the female artist or intellectual in a female *Bildungsroman* (or *Künstlerroman*). It is, of course, as the old chicken-and-egg joke indicates, another essential instance of using parts for wholes, as the short-story cycle does so well: even a micro short-story cycle.

Both Munro and Shields take a distinctive Canadian genre, the short-story cycle, in a feminine, if not feminist, direction. Howells' description of Munro's fiction could easily be applied to that of Munro's friend and colleague Carol Shields:

> [L]ike gossip, these stories have a positive function as women's counter-discourse, suggesting alternative maps for women's destinies beyond traditional patterns of male authority and gender stereotyping, sketching new ways to represent women's differences—not only from men but also from one another across gaps of generation, class and education. (*Alice* 4)

Del's refusal, as *Lives* ends, either to follow the marriage plot or to deny her embodied female self, is answered by Frances's own "mainly . . . happy" marriage, enriched by "scenes," on her scholarly travels, of suggestively erotic "alternate endings" involving men. Yet the line between reality and fantasy, for these heroines, as well as for their writers, is continually challenged. Addressing Munro's work as a whole, Heble makes a point most of her critics and readers would acknowledge: "Despite Munro's realistic presentation of lives and events, despite her surface desire to provide a true-to-life picture of the world as it really is, her text is all the while engaged in a re-examination of the conventions of realism . . ." (n.p.). While never abandoning the pleasures of realism, both Munro and Shields enact a postmodernist scepticism toward mimesis, while refusing to give up the artistic quest for something "radiant, everlasting" (*Lives* 210), or the "*Various Miracles*" born out of a loving attention to the contemporary interplay between reality and textuality, between *Lives* and "Scenes."

Notes

1. For evidence of their mutual support, admiration, and interaction as Canadian writers, see Thacker's biography, 440–41.
2. The initial labelling of *Lives* as a novel was her McGraw-Hill Ryerson editor's idea. Thacker comments, "For his part, of course, a novel was what he wanted to sell. For hers, Munro knew that while it was not the conventional novel she had begun and later abandoned, the final result was in fact 'part-way between a novel and a series of long stories'" (*Alice Munro* 218).
3. See also Thacker, who records Munro's original plan in January 1970 of writing "'a regular novel' with the 'Princess Ida' section of the finished book. Munro kept at the material in this way until sometime in March, when,

during a lunch with a group of other women, she realized that the structure of a regular novel was 'all wrong' for what she was doing, so she went home and started to break the material into sections" (*Alice Munro* 210).

4. See Dunn and Morris on the "composite novel," Roxanne Harde and Sandra Zagarell on the nineteenth-century's "narrative of community" (updated as "women's story books" by Harde), and Susan Garland Mann on *Lives* as "short story cycle."
5. See, for instance, *Sunshine Sketches of a Little Town*, where Mariposa is introduced in the first four or five pages of "The Hostelry of Mr. Smith," and then recalled, retrospectively, in "L'Envoi: the Train to Mariposa." Similarly, in *A Bird in the House*, we are memorably introduced to Grandfather Connor's "Brick House," as "the one which, more than any other, I carry with me" (11) in "The Sound of the Singing," and returned to it once more, physically, at the closing of "Jericho's Brick Battlements."
6. See Martin, Meindl, McWilliams, and Garson. Barbara Godard sees *Lives* as a "Bildungsroman written *against* Joyce" (65, emphasis in original).
7. Thacker observes, about the much-debated "Epilogue," "Little wonder she struggled and worried over [it], for in it she encapsulated not only her own life's details—seen and imagined—but also the very sensibility that had made her the writer she had become" (*Alice Munro* 212–13).
8. Cf. the reflection, at the end of "Changes and Ceremonies," on Miss Farris's shocking death: "Though there is no plausible way of hanging these pictures [of Miss Farris] together—if the last one is true then must it not alter the others?—they are going to have to stay together now" (133).
9. Madness is of course a popular theme running throughout the book: from Madeleine in "The Flats Road" to the other "idiots" Del fears meeting there, to the mysterious, cursed Sherriff family, to Mr. Chamberlain's grotesque, self-gratifying display—even the family dog, Major, goes "mad" in his old age, kills sheep, and must be put down.
10. Cf. Munro's use of the house-as-story analogy: "Everybody knows what a house does, how it encloses space and makes connections between one enclosed space and another and presents what is outside in a new way. This is the nearest I can come to explaining what a story does for me, and what I want my stories to do for other people" ("What is Real?" qtd. in Howells, *Alice*, epigraph).
11. "Munro chooses eclectically from both mother and father, a combination that blurs boundaries. Body/language, female/male are joined in a totality which moves beyond differences but which in its refusal of categories proves disturbing" (Godard 45).
12. Del also has difficulty reading or recognizing Bobby's official gender: "I could smell his shaving lotion. Odd to think that he shaved, that he had hair on his face like other men, and a penis in its pants. I imagined it curled

upon itself, damp and tender" (235). Cf. her reading of Mr. Chamberlain's display, which most critics have seen as a feminist critique of a phallic aesthetic that subordinates or silences female desire.

13. Cf. Molly Bloom's "Yes" at the conclusion of *Ulysses:* Godard insists that Munro is echoing Joyce parodically: "The temptation to be Molly Bloom, to be an Earth Mother submerged in her body continually in search of a man, has been overcome when Del fights off Garnet in the water" (70).
14. See Thomas, "Stories like Sonnets," in Besner's *Carol Shields.*
15. "[Uncle Craig's] face was like a delicate mask of skin, varnished, and laid over the real face—or over nothing at all, ready to crack when you poked a finger into it. I did have this impulse, but at a level far, far removed from possibility, just as you might have an impulse to touch a live wire" (56).
16. Cf. "Mirrors" by Shields, in *Dressing Up for the Carnival* (2000).
17. There is an intriguing echo, also, of George Elliott's *The Kissing Man*, an important short-story cycle in Canadian literary history, and its story "The Listeners." There, seven-year-old Audie Seaton is taught by his mother to "blow the egg": "He remembered trying to blow out the egg and watching the last drip of yellow fall off the egg into a blue striped bowl. His mother took the blown egg from him, sealed the pin holes with jar wax and put it in the box on the top shelf of the sideboard in the best room. That was young Audie's memory of it" (30). After the mother dies, Audie presents his brothers with one of these carefully preserved eggs, a symbol of the defeated mother herself, Lynch suggests (149). Contrast this with the positive memory evoked by the ritual in Shields's later story.

Works Cited

Allardice, Lisa. "Nobel prizewinner Alice Munro: 'It's a wonderful thing for the short story.'" Interview. *The Guardian* [UK], 6 December 2013. https://www.theguardian.com/books/2013/dec/06/alice-munro-interview-nobel-prize-short-story-literature.

Beer, Janet. "Short Fiction with Attitude: The Lives of Boys and Men in the *Lives of Girls and Women.*" *Yearbook of English Studies* (2001). *Literature Resource Center.* 12 August 2014.

Besner, Neil. "The Bodies of the Texts in *Lives of Girls and Women:* Del Jordan's Reading." *Multiple Voices: Recent Canadian Fiction.* Ed. Jeanne Delbaere. Sydney: Dangaroo Press, 1990. 131–44.

———. *Introducing Alice Munro's Lives of Girls and Women: A Reader's Guide.* Toronto: ECW, 1990.

Blodgett, E. D. *Alice Munro.* Boston: Twayne, 1988.

Carscallen, James. *The Other Country: Patterns in the Writing of Alice Munro.* Toronto: ECW, 1993.

Cox, Ailsa. *Alice Munro.* Writers and Their Work. Tavistock, UK: Northcote House, 2004.

Dunn, Maggie and Ann R. Morris. *The Composite Novel: The Short Story Cycle in Transition.* New York: Twayne, 1995.

Elliott, George. *The Kissing Man.* Toronto: Macmillan, 1962.

Foster Stovel, Nora. "'Excursions into the Sublime': A Personal Reminiscence of Carol Shields." *Studies in Canadian Literature* 38.1 (2013): 267–80.

Garland Mann, Susan. *The Short Story Cycle: A Genre Companion and Reference Guide.* New York: Greenwood, 1989.

Garson, Marjorie. "Synecdoche and the Munrovian Sublime: Parts and Wholes in *Lives of Girls and Women.*" *English Studies in Canada* 20.4 (1994): 413–29.

Godard, Barbara. "'Heirs of the Living Body': Alice Munro and the Question of a Female Aesthetic." *The Art of Alice Munro: Saying the Unsayable.* Ed. Judith Miller. Waterloo, ON: U Waterloo P, 1984. 43–71.

Harde, Roxanne. "Teaching Women's Story Books: Genre and Gender Politics in *Lives of Girls and Women.*" *Eureka Studies in Teaching Short Fiction* 6.2 (Spring 2006): 54–61.

Heble, Ajay. *The Tumble of Reason: Alice Munro's Discourse of Absence.* Toronto: U Toronto P, 1994. 12 August 2014. ProQuest ebrary.

Howells, Coral Ann. *Alice Munro.* Contemporary World Writers. Manchester/New York: Manchester UP, 1998.

———. "Space for Strangeness: Carol Shields's Short Stories." *Open Letter* 13.2 (Spring 2007): 40–51.

Joyce, James. *A Portrait of the Artist as a Young Man.* 1916. Toronto: Penguin, 2003.

Kruk, Laurie. *The Voice is the Story: Conversations with Canadian Writers of Short Fiction.* Oakville ON: Mosaic, 2003.

Laurence, Margaret. *A Bird in the House.* 1970. Rpt. Toronto: McClelland & Stewart, 1994.

Leacock, Stephen. *Sunshine Sketches of a Little Town.* 1912. Rpt. Ed. D. M. R. Bentley. New York/London: Norton, 2006.

Lynch, Gerald. *The One and the Many: English-Canadian Short Story Cycles.* Toronto: U Toronto P, 2001.

Macdonald, Rae McCarthy. "Structure and Detail in *Lives of Girls and Women*" *Studies in Canadian Literature* 3.2 (1978): 199–210.

McWilliams, Ellen. "Alice Munro's *Lives of Girls and Women:* A Case Study of Literary Influence." *Eureka Studies in Teaching Short Fiction* 6.2 (Spring 2006): 150–54.

Martin, W. R. *Alice Munro: Paradox and Parallel.* Edmonton: U Alberta P, 1987.

Meindl, Dieter. "Modernism and the English Canadian Short Story Cycle." *RANAM* 20 (1987): 17–22.

Munro, Alice. *Lives of Girls and Women.* 1971. Rpt. Toronto: Penguin, 1990.

Redekop, Magdalene. *Mothers and Other Clowns: The Stories of Alice Munro.* London and New York: Routledge, 1992.

Shields, Carol. "Arriving Late: Starting Over." *How Stories Mean.* Ed. John Metcalf and J. R. (Tim) Struthers. Erin, ON: Porcupine's Quill, 1993. 244–51.

———. "Mirrors." *Dressing Up for the Carnival.* Toronto: Random House, 2000. 65–71.

———. "Scenes." *Various Miracles.* Toronto: Stoddart, 1985. 81–90.

Thacker, Robert. *Alice Munro: Writing Her Lives, A Biography.* Toronto: Emblem/McClelland & Stewart, 2005, 2011.

———. "Quartet: Atwood, Gallant, Munro, Shields." *The Cambridge History of Canadian Literature.* Ed. Coral Ann Howells and Eva-Marie Kröller. Cambridge: Cambridge UP, 2009. 357–80.

Thomas, Clara. "Stories Like Sonnets: 'Mrs. Turner Cutting the Grass.'" *Carol Shields: The Arts of a Writing Life.* Ed. Neil Besner. Winnipeg: Prairie Fire, 2003. 96–103.

Vauthier, Simone. *Reverberations: Explorations in the Canadian Short Story.* Concord, ON: Anansi, 1993.

Zagarell, Sandra A. "Narrative of Community: The Identification of a Genre." *Signs* 13.3 (Spring 1988): 498–527.

"The stuff they put in the old readers": Remembered and Recited Poetry in the Stories of Alice Munro

SARA JAMIESON

While Alice Munro is chiefly associated with the short story, several readers have drawn attention to how her work has consistently incorporated quotations of poetry, from "scandalous doggerel" to "best-loved verses" (Clark 50). Lorraine York, for example, has shown how *Lives of Girls and Women* represents tensions between mother and daughter by associating Addie and Del Jordan respectively with the conflicting sensibilities of Victorian "rival bards" Tennyson and Robert Browning (211). Magdalene Redekop explores Munro's engagement with the history of Scottish ballads in "Hold Me Fast, Don't Let Me Pass," and argues that the story's representation of an old woman's recitation "reinstates the figure of the ballad transmitter" occluded by male ballad collectors ("Alice Munro" 35). In this paper, I will be concerned with a different kind of orally transmitted poetry: the recitation of memorized poems that was a widespread pedagogical practice in North America from the last quarter of the nineteenth century to the middle of the twentieth. While several of Munro's stories depict the memorization of poetry as a routine aspect of school life in Ontario during the first half of the twentieth century, her fiction generally manifests less interest in recitation as a classroom exercise than in the ambiguous ways in which memorized poetry circulates in people's lives long after they have left school. Through this focus on the place of the memorized poem in daily life, Munro's fiction tests the claims that have been made on its behalf, both in the writings of the educators who introduced poetry recitation into Canadian classrooms, as well as in contemporary reminiscences of the practice.

This chapter is particularly concerned with the circulation of memorized poetry within families as a phenomenon that Munro returns to in stories that foreground situations in which children, grown or not, listen to their parents recite. When situated within the context of the contemporary conversation about "the lost art" of recitation, Munro's stories can express a powerful cultural desire that the memorized poem function as a site of familial connection and sympathy (Barber). At the same time, they also question the extent to which memorized poetry can possibly fulfill this desire: more often than not in Munro's stories, recitation fails to bring about the familial reconciliation that the characters often seem to want from it, or it functions in a manner ultimately rather peripheral to any affirmation of family bonds that does take place, or if it does define familial connection, it does so in ways not entirely benign. For all their probing of the powers ascribed to memorized poetry, these stories nonetheless imply that something was lost when the practice of recitation declined. As written representations of acts of oral recitation, these stories conduct a doubly ambivalent comparison of two very different ways of engaging with literature: hearing it spoken aloud versus reading it silently. While they can manifest a certain wariness of how the recitation of a text can potentially distort its meaning, they simultaneously acknowledge the extent to which vocal performances can also enhance a text's meaning in a way very difficult to represent in writing, thus exposing the limits of what Munro's own fiction can accomplish.

Thanks to increasing critical interest in matters related to the cultural history of reading, the practice of recitation has recently become the object of sustained scholarly inquiry. Catherine Robson's 2013 book *Heartbeats: Everyday Life and the Memorized Poem* intricately details its rise and fall in Great Britain and the United States. My own research into the history of recitation in Canada suggests that while the canon of poems may have been slightly different, many of the justifications were the same. The recitation of poetry committed to memory from the pages of school readers can be seen as one of several 19th-century "innovations in curricula, pedagogy, and school management [that] formed part of an internationally shared technology of elementary instruction" (Houston and Prentice 235). In its issue for February 1883, the *Canada Educational Monthly and School Chronicle* reprinted an article by Cincinnati school superintendent John B. Peaslee insisting that "the practice [. . .] of memorizing the choice thoughts of our best writers should be made a prominent feature of school work" (59).

Peaslee was careful to distinguish the kind of memorization exercise he advocated from the verbatim regurgitation of textbook contents that had held a longstanding and dubious position in the history of public education and was not limited to the study of English literature, or to American classrooms. In the middle decades of the nineteenth century, Ontario teachers often relied on "verbal memory work," whether out of a genuine commitment to the idea of memorization as a form of mental discipline, or as a way of coping with multiple grades in a single classroom (Houston and Prentice 254). Before the widespread professionalization of teaching, rote recitation could cover up a given teacher's lack of knowledge and pedagogical training, since having students "memorize the textbook could pass the time and placate the school trustees on examination day" (Houston and Prentice 239). While Peaslee condemned this reliance on memory work as a "stultifying process" that "kills the life of its subject," he made an exception for poetry, whose aesthetic properties allegedly render it easy and pleasurable for children to learn by heart within the classroom, and impossible for them to forget once they leave it: through the memorization of what Peaslee called "Gems of Literature," a

> store of beautiful imagery and glowing sentiment may be gathered up as the amusement of childhood, which in riper years may beguile the heavy hours of languor, solitude, and sorrow; may enforce sentiments of piety, humility, and tenderness; may soothe the soul to calmness, rouse it to honorable exertions, or fire it with virtuous indignation (60).[1]

This passage is an example of the ideas that would form a dominant thread in the discussion of verse recitation for several decades to come. As historian Joan Shelly Rubin has noted, the image of "the [child's] mind as a storehouse" to be filled with a hoard of incorruptible literary treasures was one that persisted well into the twentieth century, even as the memorized poem had begun to enter its decline as a regular feature of classroom life ("They Flash" 262).

Decades after the sound of recited poetry faded from the majority of classrooms, the turn of the twenty-first century has witnessed a flurry of public reminiscences about the memorized poem, which seems poised to enter a second, more profound, silencing, with the aging into old age of "the last generation" of people who experienced it as a customary part of their schooling (Muske-Dukes). A particularly rich source of contemporary attitudes toward memorized poetry is Rubin's description of the archive of letters she collected while conducting research for her book *Songs of Ourselves: The Uses of Poetry in America* (2007). In an "Author's Query" placed in the *New York Times Book Review*, Rubin asked people to "describe the poems they had recited in school between 1917 and 1950, as well as to comment on what the task meant to them at the time and later in life" ("They Flash" 264). Of the four hundred and seventy-nine people who responded, the majority remembered the practice with great enthusiasm as one that had left them in possession of an inner archive of poems that had in myriad ways enriched their lives.

This conviction as to the enduring value of memorizing poetry has fuelled recent efforts to revive the practice. In 2010, Canadian businessman and philanthropist Scott Griffin, in an effort to "restore poetry's place in the classroom and reintroduce the skill of recitation" to contemporary students, established Poetry In Voice, a recitation competition for Ontario high-school students that has since spread nationwide (Medley).[2] In press materials about the event, organizers repeatedly describe it as an "opportunity for students to have a lifelong and very intimate relationship" with particular poems (Medley). Such justifications sound remarkably similar to Peaslee's view of the memorized poem as something to "beguile" one's "riper years," though his association of memorized poetry with virtues like "piety" and "humility" is replaced by promises of intimacy and companionship, perhaps more appealing to contemporary students. Griffin attributes his own love of memorizing poetry not to his schooling but to his father, who "used it as a punishment. If we committed some misdemeanour, we had to memorize a poem and recite it in front of the family" (Berry). Griffin describes this ritual as characteristic of the "very competitive" atmosphere of his childhood home (Berry), inviting us to recognize the degree to which poetry recitation has long been bound up with the values of industrial capitalism: as Rubin comments, nineteenth-century educators who described poems using "tropes of jewels and riches" characterized memorization as the accumulation of symbolic wealth in a process intended to instill the self-discipline and self-confidence that could, theoretically at least, ensure one's success in a competitive marketplace ("They Flash" 262).

Griffin's characterization of the memorized poem as something that he inevitably associates, however agonistically, with his father, underscores the assertion, reiterated throughout contemporary reminiscences about poetry recitation, that the memorized poem is uniquely capable of speaking across generations and enhancing bonds between parents and children. Most of the respondents to Rubin's query were over sixty-five, and, thanks to the stability of the contents of many school readers between the 1890s and the 1930s, had been able, as children, to recite many of the same poems that their parents and grandparents could still recite themselves (Rubin, "They Flash" 260). The perception of poetry recitation as something that has the power to instill a sense of intergenerational connectedness through the shared knowledge of particular poems contributes to the note of lament that permeates contemporary discussions of the practice in North America, which are characteristically tinged with regret for the erosion of familial and communal bonds that its decline has allegedly hastened (Robson 2).

Munro's fiction often appears to participate in the contemporary enthusiasm for memorized poetry as a potent site of communal and familial bonding through collective memory, yet at the same time qualifies this position by inviting readers to recognize the limits of the communities that recitation brings into being. In "Mrs. Cross and Mrs. Kidd," a story about two women in their eighties living in a long-term-care facility, Munro engages playfully with the idea of the memorized poem as life-long companion by supplying Mrs. Kidd with the habit of "launch[ing] forth" into impromptu recitations (160). When she recites stanzas by Robert Browning and Bliss Carman, with a crowd of fellow residents eagerly signalling their recognition by calling out things like "Wasn't that in the Third Reader?," the scene is ambiguously focalized through a perspective seemingly aligned with Mrs. Cross, who does not appear to participate (160). The story goes on to detail the class difference that "separate[s]" the two women despite their friendship and the relative affluence of the retirement home, Mrs. Cross retaining the tastes and attitudes of her working-class background, and Mrs. Kidd subtly indicating her middle-class sense of superior refinement, despite, or perhaps because of, the fact that her grandchildren make less money than Mrs. Cross's. Robson has written extensively about the class politics of the memorized poem in the context of British grammar schools, arguing that poetry recitation can be seen as belonging to the "systems of individuation, regulation, competition, and self-advancement" that helped to characterize the school as "antithetical to the prevailing ethos of working-class life" (159). This dissonance was often masked by the "seemingly egalitarian" rhetoric in which the practice of recitation was grounded, and which characterized poem memorization as a process through which "great" literature could become "the property of rich and poor alike" (Robson 173). Munro's story challenges assumptions regarding the supposed classlessness of literature in its implication that, although both women attended the same school and were exposed to the same curriculum, the recitation of memorized poetry has been absorbed much more readily into Mrs. Kidd's white-collar existence.

In "Oh, What Avails," Munro explores in more detail the complicated relationship between social class and recited poetry, and the way in which the memorized poem enables certain people to affirm their belonging in a community that does not readily take in outsiders. The community in question here is the once-prosperous Fordyce family, a widow raising her two children, Morris and Joan, during the "sudden poverty" of the Depression (184). The mother "knows a lot of poetry, from school or somewhere," and weaves quotations into the daily life of the household in a way that creates a kind of secret family language described as "private" and "enclosed," and that speaks to her children of their distinction from other people in their small town (183):

> She will fix a couple of lines on somebody, summing them up in an absurd and unforgettable way. She looks out the window and says a bit of poetry and they [Morris and Joan] know who has gone by. Sometimes she comes out with it as she stirs the porridge they eat now and then for supper as well as for breakfast, because it is cheap. (183)

The juxtaposition of recited poetry with cheap porridge suppers suggests Mrs. Fordyce's commitment to the idea of poetry as a form of internalized wealth that cannot be tarnished by reduced economic circumstances. It is this conception of the separateness of poetry from issues of money and social status that enables her to use it in order to generate for her children a sense of family distinction that, she insists, has nothing to do with their former prosperity or their continuing prominence in the community as owners of the now-struggling lumberyard; elsewhere, however, the story implies that this sense of distinction rests at least as much on the material traces of the family's vanished wealth, items like the old evening dresses and the "picnic hamper with a silver flask" contained within their "large, cold, unmanageable house" (183).

Joan and Morris nonetheless appear to have internalized their mother's view of poetry as inhabiting a classless realm sealed off from the vicissitudes of the marketplace, and as adults they continue to rely on the memorized verses they associate with her to delineate a private familial bond. Despite having become a successful businessman cognizant of the "cash value" of everything, Morris has tellingly not sold his mother's bookcase along with other effects from her home (198). His evident belief in the separateness of literature from economic matters is reinforced at the end of the story when he and Joan visit their mother's grave in the company of Morris's bookkeeper, a woman named Ruth Ann. Morris is suddenly reminded of a poem his mother used to recite, "Rose Aylmer" by Walter Savage Landor, but neither he nor Joan can remember more than a few words. Ruth Ann comments that the words make her think of a "skin lotion" called "Rose Emulsion" (210). Morris and Joan signal their resistance to this connection of poetry to the world of commodities by simply ignoring it, continuing their effort to remember the rest of the poem as if Ruth Ann has not spoken at all (210). By having Ruth Ann speak her next words using improper grammar ("Of course, I don't know hardly any poems"), Munro invites readers to consider the extent to which Morris and Joan's access to the supposedly classless realm of literature is inextricably bound up with their position in the social hierarchy, and actually reinforces class difference (210).

Munro's exposure of the fault lines dividing the community that the memorized poem might appear to unite extends to the family itself, as the scenes in which Morris and Joan try to recall the poem in the cemetery, and later look it up in their mother's *Anthology of English Verse*, are interrupted with the information that Morris has cheated both women, Joan and Ruth Ann, out of money that is rightfully theirs. Oblivious of her brother's dishonesty toward her, Joan continues to see the poem as part of the atmosphere of "specialness" that their mother created in their childhood home, one calculated to teach them "a delicate, special regard for themselves, which made them go out and grab what they wanted, whether love or money" (215). Joan's ignorance of how her brother has profited from this lesson at her expense ironizes their satisfaction at retrieving the poem, and characterizes their joint recitation at the end of the story as offering only an illusion of familial harmony. Joan's lack of awareness is further underscored by the particular poem that Munro has chosen to include in this story: when Morris suddenly makes reference to "Rose Aylmer" in the graveyard, Joan initially thinks that he is reading a name off of one of the headstones. Behind this misperception is Munro's nod to the fact that this poem, an elegy to a young woman who died in India, is in fact carved in its entirety on a tablet affixed to her tombstone in the South Park Street Cemetery in Kolkata ("Rose Aylmer" 9). By gesturing to the wider world encompassed by this poem's particular history, a history that implicitly lies outside the characters' knowledge, the story articulates a critique of the value the Fordyce family finds in memorized poetry, implying that to fit poetry to one's own private uses certainly has its pleasures, but also suggesting that there is something troublingly self-absorbed about this mode of engaging with literature.

The ending of "Oh, What Avails," in which two grown children recollect a poem they remember being spoken by their mother, is not the first time that Munro has sought fictive closure through the foregrounding of parental acts of recitation. Memorized poetry appears at climactic moments in both "The Moons of Jupiter" and "The Ottawa Valley," two of her most deeply autobiographical stories, dealing respectively with her father's death and her mother's premature development of a debilitating terminal illness. Situating recited poetry in the emotionally charged context of a daughter's attempts to negotiate the legacy of her troubled relationships with both parents, these stories offer a particularly poignant articulation of the cultural longing that the memorized poem function as an affirmation of intergenerational connection; at the same time, however, both stories subject this notion to scrutiny, ultimately exposing the memorized poem as being not quite equal to the level of hope that has been invested in it by depicting familial relationships that are simply too complicated for acts of recitation to resolve.

Memorized poetry surfaces in "The Moons of Jupiter" when the narrator, a writer named Janet, visits her father in the hospital where he waits to undergo heart surgery. Her appearance in his room coincides with his sudden retrieval of a phrase from Joaquin Miller's "Columbus," a classroom recitation standard "once known to every schoolboy" (Martin 160): "'Behind him lay the gray Azores, / Behind the Gates of Hercules; / Before him not the ghost of shores, / Before him only shoreless seas'." (324). The father's mild amazement at how the phrase "shoreless seas" "popped into [his] head" just as his daughter came into the room would seem to imbue the memorized poem with an almost mystical ability to affirm familial bonds; in what follows, however, the poem itself is left behind, having opened the door to a conversation about the workings of memory and the existence of the soul, which leads in turn to the father's skeptical account of stories of near-death experiences that he has been reading from a pile of tabloid newspapers left behind by the previous occupant of his room. In the juxtaposition of recited poetry and tabloid "rubbish," I cannot help but hear an echo of the old conviction that memorizing poems ensures the cultivation of literary taste (325): in an 1884 essay titled "Hints on Teaching Literature to Junior Pupils," Alice Freeman, a teacher at Ryerson Public School in Toronto, insists that when "each nook and cranny of [a child's] mind" is "fill[ed] up" with poetry, he may survey "all the varied literature of the present day [. . .] and find no place for useless or vicious matter" (204). Although he has grown up into a person who will "read anything handy," the father nonetheless does not challenge the hierarchy that places poetry above tabloid journalism (he acknowledges that the newspapers contain mostly "tripe" [325]); the story nevertheless questions oft-iterated claims about what memorized poetry does and why it should be valued, by indicating that the narrator's appreciation of her similarity to her father, the "appalling rush of love and recognition" that she feels during their conversation, is grounded as much in their shared response to a tabloid paper as to a poem (325).

While it might seem like a bit of a stretch to listen for traces of nineteenth-century pedagogical theorizing in this narrator's recounting of her last hours with her father, the story in fact at several points foregrounds issues of schooling in ways that contribute to its demystification of the reverence in which memorized poetry came to be held. In a small but significant detail, we are told that the narrator's nephews, her sister's sons, attend a "private school that favored old-fashioned discipline and started calculus in Grade 5" (326). Leaving us to speculate about exactly what "old-fashioned discipline" might involve, the story curtails the temptation to feel too nostalgic toward similarly old-fashioned practices like poem memorization. When the narrator attends a planetarium show in an effort to calm her anxiety about her father's impending operation, she is one of the only adults in an audience composed mostly of schoolchildren on a field trip. Unnerved herself by the show, she wonders about the motivations of the educators who have organized this venture to expose children to the "horrible immensities" of the universe (330). As Redekop has already recognized, the "horrible immensities" of the planetarium show correspond to the "shoreless seas" of Miller's poem (*Mothers* 170); the connection invites readers to think critically about the processes that have turned both into pedagogical objects, as does the narrator's gratification at the "natural immunity" of children to the lessons that adults think are good for them (331).

I do not deny the pleasure that children can find in memorizing poems or visiting planetariums, or the possible reassurance that the narrator's father finds in Miller's lines as he faces the end of his life; at the end of the story, however, he participates in a last act of recitation that again suggests the limits of the powers attributed to the memorized poem. Returning to her father's bedside from the planetarium, the narrator engages him in a conversation about the solar system. While Karen Smythe hears something "childlike" in the narrator's imperative "Tell me the moons of Jupiter" (140), we can also detect something distinctly pedagogical, as it is the father who assumes the role of the reciting child, "gravely" repeating the lesson that "'the moons of Jupiter were the first heavenly bodies discovered with the telescope'" as if "he could see the sentence in an old book" (332). Earlier in the story, the narrator has admitted that she "[doesn't] care to think of [her father's] younger selves," since to do so makes the prospect of his death unbearably painful; here, however, the structure of the recitation exercise intervenes and enables her to acknowledge the child still present in the old man while facing his loss with greater equanimity than before. If this recitation does facilitate a final moment of reconciliation between father and daughter, it does so simply through the act of reciting itself, rather than through the consoling properties of poetry; by reminding us of the long pedagogical history of memory work that once encompassed far more than just poetry, Munro's story undermines the importance that came to be attributed to the memorized poem specifically. By raising questions about the uses of literature, this final recitation appropriately registers the narrator's anxieties about the success and purpose of her own writing, anxieties that her father, "in his mild way," was always adept at stirring up (327).

In its emphasis on the daughter's role as the one who hears her father's recitation, "The Moons of Jupiter" is typical of many of Munro's depictions of memorized poetry, which are often focalized through the perspective of the person who listens rather than the one who recites. As an activity that disturbs the prevailing "hierarchy of the senses" in which hearing customarily comes "a poor second" to vision, listening to recited poetry can be an unsettling experience for Munro's characters (Bull and Back 1). In "Mrs. Cross and Mrs. Kidd," for example, the memory of Mrs. Kidd's schoolgirl performances exists for Mrs. Cross in primarily visual terms: "[her] first picture of Mrs. Kidd is of her standing at the front of the class reciting some poem" (160). Developing the contrast between the dismissive anonymity of the phrase "some poem," and Mrs. Cross' retention of specific visual details like Mrs. Kidd's "dark, thick bangs" and her "pinafore sticking up in starched wings," Munro's emphasis on how Mrs. Cross's consciousness has seemingly failed to absorb the aural aspect of recitation is key to how the story delineates the difference between the two women in a way that places Mrs. Cross at a greater distance from the memorized poem than Mrs. Kidd (160).

By far the most extreme example of the perplexities arising from listening to recited poetry in Munro's work occurs in "Working For a Living," a memoir about her father, Robert Laidlaw. As a country boy who passes the entrance examination to high school in 1913, Laidlaw seems to be "on his way" toward some kind of professional career (127). During the first week, he hears the teacher read a poem:

Liza Greyman Ollie Minus
We can make Eliza blind.
Andy Parting, Lee Beehinus.
Foo Prince in the Sansa Time. (127–28)

This garbled rendition of a stanza from Longfellow's "A Psalm of Life" marks the moment when Laidlaw gains his first inkling of how the world of the high school threatens to alienate him not only from his family origins but also from the as yet only dimly imagined life he wants for himself. Angela Sorby comments that "A Psalm of Life," with its injunctions to "act" in emulation of the "lives of great men," couched in "conventional" tetrameter quatrains, is perhaps the preeminent articulation of the mixture of ambition and conformity that the public school system sought to cultivate in its pupils, and through which it seemed to groom them for lives of middle-class productivity (26–27). That Laidlaw mishears it so drastically indicates how utterly at odds is the public declamation of such a poem with "the family caution, the country wisdom" ingrained in him at home, according to which "stretching [oneself] to the limit" in any aspect of life could be seen as "unbecoming" (136). The poem makes sense to Laidlaw only once he sees it written on the blackboard; while he remains an avid reader throughout his life, his dropping out of school may signal his discomfort with what the recitation exercise in particular seems to be trying to teach him.

The classroom recitation of poetry is of course just one example of how written texts may be transferred into the acoustic realm. In her analysis of dramatic readings of literary works by authors and professional actors, Kata Gellen explores the extent to which such "text-based" events, in which the texts in question are not necessarily available to the audience at the time of performance, may "[leave] the listener disoriented, confused, or simply uneasy, perhaps because of the fleeting quality of spoken language" (109). In the recitations that Munro depicts, the listener's position is even further complicated by the fact that most of them are not staged performances that happen as part of the normal course of activity in classrooms or at school recitals, but rather erupt spontaneously in locales like porches and hospital rooms, exacerbating the problem of exactly how one is supposed to listen and respond. When Janet's father utters the phrase "*Shore*-less seas," her initial response is a confused "What?" (324). Her disorientation stands in marked contrast to how, throughout the story, she is able to anticipate with accuracy exactly what her father will say in the course of ordinary conversation. The unexpectedness of her father's recitation defamiliarizes her interactions with him and demands that she listen attentively. It makes her uncomfortably aware of how she has failed to listen to him in the past, and allows her to atone somewhat for her former "presumption" in thinking she understands everything about him (321). Far from trying to recuperate the memorized poem as a timeless signifier of intergenerational understanding, Munro instead exploits the unfamiliarity into which it has fallen in order to emphasize the father's otherness, and those aspects of his life that do not align with how his daughter has always wanted to see him.

In "The Ottawa Valley," Munro similarly evokes the uncertainties of listening to register the uncanny interplay of parental familiarity and strangeness. The antepenultimate scene, in which the narrator's mother refuses to provide assurance that her arm will ever "stop shaking," cuts immediately to a scene in which the mother, her cousin Dodie, and her brother James play a game of matching quotations remembered from their "old readers" (97, 98). As in "The Moons of Jupiter," the recitation has a silencing effect on the narrator, who simply presents the extracts of poetry with little comment except to indicate her childish embarrassment at the "tremor" that creeps into her mother's voice (98). Critics have disagreed as to how to interpret this tremor, with Redekop seeing it as representative of the mother's helplessness in the face of the disease that is overtaking her, and Tracy Ware attributing it to the mother's own embarrassment at flubbing her lines. Ware is referring here to how the mother appears to jumble together two entirely different poems, one by Charles Wolfe, the other by Tennyson, though, as Louis McKendrick notes, it is possible to read the Wolfe excerpt as being spoken by Dodie (Ware 133). The indeterminacies arising from this scene indicate both the distortion that can result when a written text is recited aloud (the tremor in the voice), and also the potential for confusion when recited texts are written down, with the possibility of distinguishing different voices lost. It is through this complex layering of print and orality that Munro records these losses, and assesses the degree to which her fiction can recuperate them.

Like "Working for a Living," "The Ottawa Valley" repeatedly foregrounds instances of listening that emphasize the potential for misprision that arises from hearing words spoken without having access to their written counterparts. One example occurs when Uncle James "unexpectedly [begins] to sing" while driving the family home from a

Saturday night in town (91). While the narrator at the time had listened with rapt attention, she has since forgotten most of the words, and her repeated attempts to remember them yield only fragments. Munro's emphasis on the ephemerality of the spoken word would seem to privilege the certainties of the written text, yet Uncle James's song is an example of an auditory experience that apparently exceeds her ability to represent it in writing. For Roland Barthes, the attempt to describe music reduces the writer to rely on "the poorest of linguistic categories: the adjective" (179). Munro's description of Uncle James's singing conveys something of this dilemma, since she not only relies on adjectives, but recycles the same adjectives over and over: "He had a fine voice, a *fine*, sad, lingering voice" (91, emphasis added). The word "sad" appears twice more in the passage, indicating the "sad-sounding" last line of the song, and the "tender sadness" of Uncle James's voice. Since there doesn't appear to be anything inherently sad about the words of the song that she can remember (which seem to be about the delights of alcohol), the sadness is rather a quality that she associates with the voice itself. It is this quality that the writer cannot quite catch, as indicated by how the effort to capture it more precisely keeps bringing her back to the same words.

Munro's emphasis on the sadness of lost voices also echoes throughout the recitation scene, where Aunt Dodie is struck by how many of the poems that she and the mother remember are about death: "Heavens, wasn't it all sad, the stuff they put in the old readers?" (98).[3] The last poem to be recited in the scene, William Wilfrid Campbell's elegiac "Indian Summer," is less overtly funereal than the selections that precede it; Dodie's comment that even it "has kind of a sad ring" evokes audibility in a way that draws attention to how Munro's transcription of the recited poems attempts to convey not simply the words, but the sound of the words and the voices saying them. The quotations themselves echo one another, not simply thematically in their preoccupation with death, but also literally in terms of their sound: Campbell's line "And all day long the blue jay calls," which is itself a description of a sound, echoes, at least partially, the sound of Tennyson's "And all day long the noise of battle rolled" (98). With such sonic effects, Munro emphasizes the "lost art" of recitation *as* lost, and characterizes the memorized poem as the reverberation of a sound whose original utterance is locked in the past. While the writer-narrator characterizes the recitation scene as her attempt to "bring back all I could" of the past, and specifically, of her mother, her invocation of memorized poetry ultimately stands for what is not recoverable, and complicates the idea of the remembered poem as a reassuring and consoling reminder of parental connection.

As in "The Moons of Jupiter," Munro's narrator turns to the memorized poem in an attempt to conjure the voice of a dead parent in a way that will, she hopes, be free of the impatience and bitterness that often characterized their verbal exchanges in life. Like the father in "The Moons of Jupiter," the mother in "The Ottawa Valley" is repeatedly characterized as irritatingly predictable in her everyday speech, and the narrator seems to hope that poetry recitation (as an instance where the mother speaks in words that are not her own) will have a kind of distancing effect that will "mark her off" and "get rid of her," enabling the narrator to remember her mother in a way that is appreciative and free of guilt (99). Of course, this does not happen, and the mother continues to "[loom] too close, just as she always did" (99). That memorized poetry fails to facilitate the kind of posthumous reconciliation that the narrator seems to desire is all the more significant if we consider what her own experience with poem memorization might be. A child during the Second World War, this narrator belongs to the same generation as other Munro characters, such as Del in *Lives of Girls and Women*, and Rose in *Who Do You Think You Are?*, who are both shown memorizing poems in school. While the narrator spends some time detailing her unsuccessful attempts to remember the words to Uncle James's song, no such struggle characterizes the recitation scene, where her apparently effortless recall suggests the possibility of her own familiarity with this particular canon of poems. While the story thus subtly acknowledges the educational history that may well have made memorized poetry into a site of shared knowledge between mother and daughter, it affords the opportunity to put contemporary nostalgia for poem recitation into perspective, since this shared knowledge cannot begin to overcome their differences.

The emphasis on the contrast between what people often expect memorized poetry to do and what it is realistically capable of doing culminates in what is probably its most disturbing appearance in Munro's fiction. "Before the Change" takes the form of a series of letters from the narrator to her ex-fiancé, composed while visiting the home of her father, a small-town doctor. During the visit, her father asks her to assist him as he performs an illegal abortion, since his usual attendant is indisposed. When the woman undergoing the procedure says something that is distorted by pain, what the narrator hears is a request that she recite something. The narrator's interpretation aligns with one of the more common uses that people claim to find in memorized poetry: several respondents to Rubin's query describe turning to the memorized poem as an "anesthetic or diversion" during painful medical or dental treatments ("They Flash" 269). The story does not fully affirm the usefulness of the recited poem in such circumstances: we do not know what effect it might be having on the woman who hears it since we are not given access to her perspective; her obvious physical suffering reminds the narrator of her own experience with childbirth, and a pain so annihilating as to make any relief that the recited poem might offer seem pathetically inadequate.

The poem in question here is Yeats' "The Song of Wandering Aengus," a poem that the narrator remembers not from school but from her ex-lover, a theology student named Robin. It was the narrator's unexpected pregnancy that ended their engagement, leading as it did to a bitter argument over her refusal to comply with Robin's insistence that she seek an abortion in order to preserve his reputation among his colleagues. The story thus offers a devastating inversion of the belief in the memorized poem's ability to affirm familial bonds, since its recitation takes place in the context of a family that was blasted apart before it ever came together, the engagement having been broken off, and the baby adopted. In this story, our attention is directed to the dark flipside of the optimistic rhetoric about the memorized poem as something that, once installed in your memory, stays with you for life; yes, Munro's fiction says, it does stay with you, but not in a way that is reliably comforting: it can function as a persistent reminder of loss, pain, separation, failure, and exclusion just as easily as a source of aesthetic pleasure, intellectual engagement, and familial connection. As one voice in the ongoing contemporary dialogue about the value of the memorized poem, Munro's stories suggest that we take what enjoyment we can from it, but with a warning not to idealize it by expecting more than it can realistically deliver. Surfacing in her stories in ways that are powerful, pleasurable, and troubling, the memorized poem is an important aspect of Munro's ongoing exploration of the complicated relationship between literature and life.

Notes

1. Peaslee's use of the phrase "Gems of Literature" is tied to the widespread use, in late-nineteenth-century classrooms, of books and pamphlets known as "memory gem" collections. According to Robson, "volumes with this title or versions thereof enjoyed a publishing boom between 1880 and 1910" (72). They typically contained "brief prose excerpts, abridgements

of long poems, and short verse," selections specifically intended to be memorized and recited by students (Rubin "They Flash" 262).

2. In its structure and aims, Poetry in Voice appears to be modeled on Poetry Out Loud, a recitation competition established in 2006 in the United States by the National Endowment for the Arts and the Poetry Foundation. In the United Kingdom, the Poetry Archive has initiated a similar competition, called Poetry By Heart.
3. Dodie's impression of the lugubrious content of the school readers she remembers is corroborated by Robson, who observes that the poetic selections in such texts were "habitually, rather than incidentally, marked with the stamp of death" (89).

Works Cited

Barthes, Roland. "The Grain of the Voice." *Image, Music, Text.* Ed. and trans. Stephen Heath. New York: Hill and Wang, 1977. 179–85.

Barber, John. "Scott Griffin launches school poetry-reading competition." *Globe and Mail,* 23 November 2010. 9 July 2014. http://www.theglobeandmail.com/arts/scott-griffin-launches-school-poetry-reading-competition/article1315130/.

Berry, David. "Scott Griffin: The rhyme and the reason." *National Post,* 15 May 2013. 9 July 2014. http://news.nationalpost.com/arts/books/scott-griffin.

Bull, Michael, and Les Back, eds. *The Auditory Culture Reader.* New York: Berg, 2003.

Clark, Miriam Marty. "Allegories of Reading in Alice Munro's 'Carried Away'." *Contemporary Literature* 37.1 (1996): 49–61.

Freeman, Alice. "Hints on Teaching Literature to Junior Pupils." *Canada Educational Monthly and School Chronicle* 6 (1884): 199–205. *Early Canadiana Online.* 9 July 2014.

Gellen, Kata. "Works Recited: Franz Kafka and the Art of Literary Recitation." *Germanic Review* 86 (2011): 93–113.

Houston, Susan E., and Alison Prentice. *Schooling and Scholars in Nineteenth-Century Ontario.* Toronto: U Toronto P, 1988.

Martin, W. R. *Alice Munro: Paradox and Parallel.* Edmonton: U Alberta P, 1987.

Medley, Mark. "Poetry gets cool for school: Scott Griffin launches Poetry in Voice." *National Post,* 23 November 2010. 9 July 2014. http://news.nationalpost.com/afterword/poetry-in-voice.

Munro, Alice. "Before the Change." *The Love of a Good Woman.* Toronto: McClelland & Stewart, 1998. 254–92.

———. "Mrs. Cross and Mrs. Kidd." *The Moons of Jupiter.* 1982. New York: Vintage, 1991. 160–80.

———. "Oh, What Avails." *Friend of My Youth.* 1990. Toronto: Penguin, 1995. 180–215.

———. "The Moons of Jupiter." *Selected Stories.* Toronto: Penguin, 1998. 316–33.

———. "The Ottawa Valley." *Selected Stories.* Toronto: Penguin, 1998. 82–99.

———. "Working For a Living." 1981. *The View from Castle Rock.* Toronto: McClelland & Stewart, 2006. 127–72.

Muske-Dukes, Carol. "A Lost Eloquence." *New York Times*, 29 December 2002. 9 July 2014. http://www.nytimes.com/2002/12/29/opinion/a-lost-eloquence.html.

Peaslee, John B. "Moral and Literary Training in Public Schools." *Canada Educational Monthly and School Chronicle* 5 (1883): 55–65. *Early Canadiana Online.* 9 July 2014.

Redekop, Magdalene. "Alice Munro and the Scottish Nostalgic Grotesque." *The Rest of the Story: Critical Essays on Alice Munro.* Ed. Robert Thacker. Toronto: ECW, 1999. 21–43.

———. *Mothers and Other Clowns: The Stories of Alice Munro.* New York: Routledge, 1992.

Robson, Catherine. *Heart Beats: Everyday Life and the Memorized Poem.* Princeton: Princeton UP, 2013.

"Rose Aylmer." *Dominion* (New Zealand) 31.645 (1909): 9. https://paperspast.natlib.govt.nz/newspapers/DOM19091023.2.58.4.

Rubin, Joan Shelley. *Songs of Ourselves: The Uses of Poetry in America.* Cambridge, MA: Belknap, 2007.

———. "'They Flash Upon That Inward Eye': Poetry Recitation and American

Readers." *Reading Acts: US Readers' Interaction with Literature 1800–1950.* Ed. Barbara Ryan and Amy Thomas. Knoxville: U Tennessee P, 2002. 258–80.

Smythe, Karen. *Figuring Grief: Gallant, Munro, and the Poetics of Elegy.* Montreal: McGill-Queen's UP, 1992.

Sorby, Angela. *Schoolroom Poets: Childhood, Performance, and the Place of American Poetry, 1865–1917.* Durham: U New Hampshire P, 2005.

Ware, Tracy. "Tricks with 'a Sad Ring': The Endings of Alice Munro's 'The Ottawa Valley'." *Studies in Canadian Literature* 31.2 (2006): 126–41.

York, Lorraine. "The Rival Bards: Alice Munro's *Lives of Girls and Women* and Victorian Poetry." *Canadian Literature* 112 (1987): 211–16.

Carried Away by Letters: Alice Munro and the Epistolary Mode

MARIA LÖSCHNIGG

"She went on expecting a letter every day and nothing came. Nothing came" (*Open Secrets* 18). Louisa in "Carried Away" is one of the many characters in Alice Munro's stories who expect, receive, and produce letters. The practically minded Johanna in "Hateship, Friendship, Courtship, Loveship, Marriage" unwittingly falls for the magic of (forged) romantic letters ("Well I must be losing my mind. Or else it is a sign of a letter coming"; *Hateship* 34), while Greta in "To Reach Japan" pours all her hopes and longings into the following lines to Harris: "Writing this letter is like putting a note in a bottle – / And hoping / It will reach Japan (*Dear Life* 14). About Dorrie in "A Real Life," we read that "after the first meeting the entire courtship appeared to have been conducted by letters" (*Open Secrets* 53), and Gail in "The Jack Randa Hotel" forges letters in an attempt to win back her ex-lover Will.

Munro's stories abound with letters. So far, of her 148 collected stories, twenty-two contain letters, and there are about a dozen more where letters or notes play an important role. If this is remarkable in itself, the striking diversity in Munro's exploration of the narrative potential of letters to multiply, defer, and condense meaning deserves proper attention. However, while such critics as Ailsa Cox (2004), Coral Ann Howells (2009), and Isla Duncan (2011) have pointed out the prominence of epistolary discourses in Munro's stories and have explored specific features of this narrative device in individual stories, there is no critical work to date that specifically and extensively addresses this aspect of Munro's writing. Here, I shall first identify narrative qualities that are intrinsic features of epistolary narrative and that therefore engender particular effects in the stories. I shall then focus on "Carried Away," "Hateship, Friendship, Courtship, Loveship, Marriage," and "Dimensions" in order to analyze one of the numerous functions that letters adopt in Munro's work, namely, their power to "carry away" the recipient emotionally. As to the great variety of other forms and functions of the epistolary in Munro's work, let it suffice here to mention briefly some of the shapes letters assume.

While some stories are entirely or almost entirely composed in the form of letters, as is the case with "A Wilderness Station," a multi-voiced story composed of letters by various correspondents, and "Before the Change," which provides only one side of an exchange, other stories feature letters or sometimes short but significant notes within the overall framework of third- or first-person narration. Sometimes the letters never reach the intended addressee, whether due to external manipulations or because they are never sent, as is the case in "Vandals," or because they are composed solely in the mind. In "Accident," we even find a "dreamed" letter, whose content is recounted by the first-person narrator. In some stories, epistolary discourse comes close to what Brian Richardson has referred to as the "autotelic form of second person narration" (30ff.); that is, the intradiegetic addressee becomes an agent in the story, which is in fact the case in "Before the Change," "Tell me Yes or No," and "The Spanish Lady." In these three stories the letters serve a therapeutic function, that is, they are a means of coming to terms with a broken relationship and are addressed to the protagonists' respective ex-lovers. In contrast to this, "Something I've Been Meaning to Tell You" type of letter, the letters in "The Jack Randa Hotel," "A Queer Streak," and "Hateship, Friendship, Courtship, Loveship, Marriage" are instrumentalized by the respective characters to play tricks on the addressees. Polyphony and the questioning of concepts of truth are clearly the most important effects of the letter mode in "A Wilderness Station," but also play a role in numerous other epistolary stories. In some stories the content and discursive make-up of letters are as important as the intradiegetic reaction to these letters, as can be observed in the stories "Deep Holes" and "Child's Play."

The letter's potential to "carry away" the recipient emotionally or to serve as a trigger for imaginary worlds was used by Munro as a narrative device in a very early story, "Postcard," collected in *Dance of the Happy Shades* (1968). In this story, Helen, the first-person narrator and protagonist, receives a short, typewritten letter from the man of her dreams, which reads as follows:

> *I usually hate to write a typewritten letter because it lacks the personal touch but I am so worn out tonight with all the unfamiliar pressures here that I hope you will forgive me. . . . I want you to know how grateful I am for all your sweetness and understanding.* (134, 135)

Even though Helen is later aware that "any fool [could] see" that this was a farewell letter, at the moment when she receives it she is completely overwhelmed: "Typewritten or not it used to be that just by looking at that letter I would get a feeling of love, if that is what you want to call it, strong enough to pretty nearly crumple me up and knock me over" (134). While Munro uses letters in this 1960s story as a trigger for exceptional feelings, she has, in her most recent stories, decisively extended and elaborated her technique of employing letters in order to make intradiegetic correspondents build up idealized imaginary worlds that often radically contrast with the reality they inhabit. It is this use of letters that I shall explore.

In "Carried Away" (*Open Secrets*, 1994) a woman falls in love, through letters, with a man she has never seen and, in fact, never gets to see; in the title story of *Hateship, Friendship, Courtship, Loveship, Marriage* (2001), a woman falls for the magic of (feigned) letters, while in "Dimensions" (*Too Much Happiness*, 2009), letters lure the protagonist into the distorted world of a psychopath from whom she is finally saved by an epiphanic moment. The question in each case is what role letters play in the narrative rendering of these themes. How is the special structural and communicative potential of these specifically grafted hypotexts employed by Munro to render these stories captivating and convincing despite their rather improbable plots?

* * *

The use of letters in stories represents a lacuna in narratological studies of the epistolary mode. Of the critical works exploring letter narratives, I have found Wulf Koepke's article "The Epistolary Fiction and Its Impact on Readers" and, above all, Janet G. Altman's lucid analysis of structural and communicative features of the letter in fiction a productive basis for an approach to Munro's experimentation with this narrative device. Contrary to Ruth Perry's claim that "epistolary fictions [are] transcribing uncensored streams of consciousness" (128), I would argue that letters are more than "thinking out loud" (128), as Perry has it; in fact, this definition would be more valid for the diary mode. Rather, what most significantly characterizes the epistolary is the fact that letters are composed with the addressee in mind and are thus marked in particular by a persuasive element (Koepke 263). "The letter writer," as Altman points out, "simultaneously seeks to affect his [sic] reader and is affected by him [sic]" (88).

We may conclude, accordingly, that it is above all the figure of the internal reader "whose presence alone distinguishes the letter from other first-person forms" (Altman 87). The specific effect of letters in fiction thus results to a significant extent from the "mise-en-abyme of the writer-reader relationship" (Altman 200) within the form itself. While Joe Bray is doubtlessly right when he says that the letter mode allows for "sophisticated ways of representing individual psychology" (Bray 2), we always have to be aware that this "individual psychology" takes shape against the backdrop of the envisioned recipient, a "determinant of the letter's message" (Altman 88), who demands to be decoded accordingly by the actual reader. In all three stories analyzed in this article, but especially in "Hateship, Friendship, Courtship, Loveship, Marriage" and "Dimensions," the narrativizing of the act of reading becomes indeed an important factor, encouraging the extra-textual reader to explicate/interpret the given letter from three different angles: from that of the internal recipient, from that of the internal writer, and, finally, from our own point of view, which in most cases equals that of a "super-reader" (cf. Altman 111, 94). Fictional letter reading frequently leads to situations of dramatic irony as, in contrast to the extra-textual reader, the internal characters usually have but a fragmented knowledge of the letters.

Two other essential features of epistolary narrative are, first, the spatial distance between correspondents, which prevents actual dialogic exchange (Koepke 265), and, second, the temporal displacement in the turn-taking-process, which (seemingly) prolongs the validity of the letter for the respective recipient. As far as the former is concerned, we can argue that letters draw their power from the fact that they exclude all non-verbal signals that usually go with a face-to-face encounter, and thus leave ample room for imaginary constructions, as can be observed, for example, with regard to Louisa in "Carried Away" and Johanna in "Hateship, Friendship, Courtship, Loveship, Marriage." The time lag, in turn, encourages the recipient of a letter to take something that is already past as present and to fix fluid entities as permanent. This feature is especially relevant with regard to the power of the letter to "carry away" the recipient, as it "makes the past persist into the present with all the illusion of reality, when no real present comes to reveal the past as past" (Altman 131).

These two features of temporal and spatial displacement contribute particularly strongly to the "larger-than-life dimension" created by epistolary communication, whose mechanisms are described by Wulf Koepke as follows:

> [O]rdinary figures, objects and situations are beautified and aggrandized and thus projected into a larger, more decorative, more elevated environment. Such beautification through elevation involves, by necessity, a dissolution of realistic details into mere suggestions and perception, a creation of "Leerstellen" which the readers are invited to fill with the processes of imagination. The reader can thus project personal wishes and fears into the sketchy picture, indeed, project the self and a vicarious life into such a text. (271 f.)

In Munro's stories, intradiegetic recipients of letters (and to a varying extent also the extra-textual reader) "[are] drawn into an inner world where projections create reality, where ordinary limitations don't seem to be valid, and where fact and fiction merge" (Koepke 273). In addition, the letters also suspend linearity and create multiple perspectives (Cox 85). In all three stories, "Carried Away," "Hateship, Friendship, Courtship, Loveship, Marriage," and "Dimensions," letters are used to incite emotional transformations and the construction of idealized imaginaries; they are embedded in or framed by a third-person discourse which oscillates between the recounting of events from an external perspective and internal perspectives provided by a number of focalizers. Within this framework, the letters can be seen as miniature stories within stories, as hypodiegetic narratives with their own meaningful present of narration i.e., that of the correspondents) rendering additional points of view. While "[l]ike tesserae, each individual letter enters into the composition of the whole without losing its identity as a separate unit with recognizable borders" (Altman 167), its full functional potential, as Munro's stories testify, can unfold only within the narrative space that frames it.

* * *

In "Carried Away," a young woman, Louisa, has just settled in the (fictitious) town of Carstairs, Ontario, where she has taken the position of librarian. In early January 1917, she receives a letter from a young local serving with the Canadian Expeditionary Force. He knows Louisa from his visits to the library. Lying in hospital overseas, he tells Louisa that he is trying to "get [his] mind off of all that [the war] by picturing things" (4). His apparent understatements ("*What has landed me here in hospital is not so serious,*" 4; "*I didn't join up right away when I was eighteen so you will not see me as a Brave Man,*" 5) match Louisa's image of herself in her reply: "*I am very glad that you appreciated what I did in the library though it was just the normal organization, nothing special*" (5). Both seem to emphasize the ordinary and the unexceptional while actually implying the opposite. Even though Louisa cannot recall the man, she draws on common denominators—his reference to himself as a "*lone wolf*" (4), for example, matches her reference to herself as "*an outsider*" (5). Also, they both emphasize their interest in literature. Jack and Louisa's construction of their respective selves and their search for a common ground, in fact, point to another intrinsic feature of the epistolary, which Altman describes as follows:

> The *I* of the epistolary discourse always situates himself vis-à-vis another; [. . .] To write a letter is to map one's coordinates—temporal, spatial, emotional, intellectual—in order to tell someone else where one is located at a particular time and how far one has travelled since the last writing. Reference points on that map are particular to the shared world of writer and addressee: underlying the epistolary dialogue are common memories and often common experiences that take place between the letters. (119)

As Robert Lecker has pointed out, the exchange of letters "offers the hypodiegetic authors the ability to invent themselves as they write, and to edit their creations by choosing to emphasize certain activities over others, or to omit emotions or events that detract from the persona that the letter writer wishes to construct" (107). While Jack "is textually invested in eroticizing" Louisa, his construction of himself, in turn, invites Louisa "to read him as enigmatic, invisible, and therefore powerful by virtue of his physical absence" (Lecker 111). Thus, they both create images of the other, with only Jack being able to found his images on actual memories of Louisa in the library:

> *One day when I got to the Library it was a Saturday afternoon and you had just unlocked the door and were putting the lights on as it was dark and raining out. You had been caught out with no hat or umbrella and your hair had gone wet. You took the pins out of it and let it come down. Is it too personal a thing to ask if you still have it long or have you cut it? You went over and stood by the radiator and shook your hair on it and the water sizzled like grease in the frying pan. I was sitting reading in the* London Illustrated News *about the War. We exchanged a smile. (I didn't mean to say your hair was greasy when I wrote that!)* (7)

The fact that Jack's increasingly eroticized image of Louisa also changes her own image of herself can be seen when she muses about how she would like to look in the photograph she sends to Jack upon his request: "And she would have liked to let her hair down. Or if it had to be up, she would have liked it piled very loosely and bound with a string of pearls" (10). Having ignored the war before their correspondence started, she now follows it almost obsessively. In his last letter Jack confesses that he loves her, because, as he says, he does not expect to survive anyway and so he thinks he can say anything he wants (119). When the war is over she waits for him, even keeping the library open during the Spanish flu epidemic so as not to miss him should he appear. After a long wait, she happens to see "a short notice of his marriage to a Miss Grace Horne" (17). A little later, she comes upon a scrap of paper on her library desk reading, "*I was engaged before I went overseas.*" (18) This line is repeated shortly later in the story, again in italics. Whereas in the first appearance the presentation in italics merely refers to the hypotextual nature of this statement, the italics in the repetition denote "[t]he impact of this disclosure, on narrator[, focalizer] and reader." (Duncan 24) Since in epistolary exchange the valid present is always linked to the last letter contact, Louisa's infatuation with this man she does not even know continues until she reads about his marriage and even more so until she comes upon his short note, "until a more immediate present effaces the past" (Altman 132).

While most critics tend to focus on Louisa as the victim of the thoughtless game of a soldier who, in the face of his war experience, is carried away by his idealized image of a woman, my reading of the story takes a somewhat different course. With regard to the *entire* story, which pursues Louisa's life until the mid-1950s, I do not see her as a victim. Nor do I subscribe to the interpretation that their correspondence has changed only Louisa's life—it has similarly affected Jack and may, in his case, even have led to more radical consequences, namely his fatal accident in Doud's sawmill. According to Robert Lecker, "Louisa never recovers from the knowledge that the man whom she has created as her lover will always remain unseen. Her tragedy is that she is condemned to fictionalize him forever" (166 f.). Of course, there is clear evidence that Louisa is indeed "haunted by Jack's absence," as Ajay Heble (186) puts it, but at the same time the story also suggests that the whole episode has not crushed her; on the contrary, it may even have endowed her with an additional, if imaginary, life parallel to her actual one (see also Cox 84; Howells 170).

In the last section of the story, which renders a visionary encounter between Louisa and Jack, this imaginary dimension gets the upper hand. In Virginia D. Pruitt's words, it represents "a counterpart reality as a source of fulfilment for emotional yearning" (10). This, in fact, corresponds with Munro's conviction "that life is not just made up of the facts, the things that happened . . . . But all the things that happen in fantasy, the things that might have happened, the kind of alternate life that can almost seem to be accompanying what we call our real lives" (Thacker 450). Pruitt even goes so far as to claim that "[a]lthough Louisa's correspondence with Jack was platonic, their passionate and candid correspondence freed to a considerable extent Louisa's repressed sexual nature" (8). She bases this statement on Jim Frarey's observation that Louisa "was looking better than she used to" (14), and also on the fact that she opens up sexually to Jim, who had only been a friend before that. As a consequence of Jack's accident, Louisa also becomes acquainted with Arthur Doud, the owner of Doud's factory, and later marries him. This is definitely not the story of a broken-hearted victim. One may even argue that Louisa, through her unconsummated epistolary romance, is spared the disillusionment that confronting the ideal can bring. She has lived her real life while also integrating into it an enriching imaginary alternative.

Letters are a perfect medium for "creating illusions and make-believe and wanting to transform an imperfect reality into wish-fulfilling perfection," as Koepke argues (266). While Louisa survives and even thrives because she manages to integrate these illusions into her reality, Jack does not manage to do so and dies—first, emotionally, and then physically. Readers will tend to focus on Louisa's suffering because she also functions as one of the focalizers in the story. As opposed to Louisa's story, rendered in detail and often from her point of view, we obtain only an external and highly fragmented account of what happens to Jack after the war. The sparse signals we do get, however, are worth following and are apt to change a reductive view of the young man as the one who "turned [Louisa] into a voyeur's fantasy" (Lecker 110), thereby ruining her life.

Unlike for Louisa, the only perspective we get of Jack is the one from his letters. Apart from these, as Ailsa Cox notes, "his subjectivity is withheld" (81). However, the information we are given about Jack implies that his life after his return from the war is not a happy one: we find that he steals into the library and secretly "carries away" some of its holdings, while his wife, Grace, has a strong aversion to books. We are given a closer look at Grace when Arthur Doud visits her after her husband's death: The episode is full of markers that indicate the "paucity of [her] attachment to Jack" (Pruitt 8). Jack's imaginary world was not compatible with his real life; rather, his was a split life, a fact which is symbolically (and eerily) rendered by the way he dies—his head being severed from his body by the circular saw. Was the accident really an accident? Jack survived the war, and there is no indication in the story that he was a careless or clumsy person. Why are we informed that "[i]t wasn't the machine grabbing him and pulling him in, like an animal. He made a wrong move or at any rate a careless move" (30). Why does the newspaper note say "He never spoke or uttered a cry" (25)? Jack was still attached to Louisa, to the library, to a world of the imagination, as we have reason to assume, but at the same time he was caught in a marriage he could not escape. It was not the machine grabbing him, as Arthur Doud tells Louisa. Could it have been that he let himself be caught by the saw, semi-intentionally, since he could no longer juggle the imaginary world he had built up and his drab reality? This reading is certainly possible from the textual evidence we have, which indicates that both Jack as well as Louisa were carried away by the power of letters. However, while Louisa has managed to gain from this imaginary potential, Jack has obviously failed to do so. Slightly modifying Coral Ann Howells' statement that all of Munro's characters "share the sense that life can be lived simultaneously in two different dimensions or experienced from two perspectives, with the result that her protagonists are not split subjects but pluralized subjects" (170), I would argue that this is true mainly for Munro's female characters, who live their fantasies *and* continue with their here-and-now realities. Munro's heroines may be carried away by letters, as the intricate epistolary make-up of these stories convincingly shows, but they still resist "becoming estranged from the material spaces of their everyday worlds" (Howells 170). This skill to reconcile fantasy with reality is one of many implicit feminist markers of Munro's writing, and it certainly also characterizes Johanna, the heroine of the story, which is the focus of the following section.

* * *

In "Hateship, Friendship, Courtship, Loveship, Marriage," Munro again exploits the idiosyncratic make-up of the letter in order to render the construction of fantasies visible. The first impression the reader gets of the story's heroine is that of the station agent in an Ontario small town, where Johanna is employed by an indifferent elderly gentleman to take care of his household and, above all, his granddaughter Sabitha. The reflections of the station agent whom Johanna commissions to send 'her' furniture to Gdynia, Saskatchewan, throw a rather negative light on the heroine: "The person she really reminded him of was a plainclothes nun he had seen on television . . ." (7). He also holds it against her that she looks at him "without a smile or any admission of her female foolishness" (6) and, taking a glimpse at her left hand, he is not surprised that she is not married. Introducing her as plain and pragmatic and lacking any sense of humour misleads the reader, similarly to the other characters in the story, into denying her the capacity to nourish dreams, to delve into romance. However, in the subsequent scene in which focalization shifts from the station agent to Johanna herself, the first indications of practical Johanna's other self emerges when she enters an extravagant shop in order to buy a dress for her encounter with her lover and future husband. In the shop, we follow her train of thought: "Even when she was younger she could never have contemplated such extravagance, not just in the matter of money but in expectations, in the preposterous hope of transformation, and bliss" (8). When "Milady herself" (8), the shopkeeper, finally finds a dress that suits Johanna, she *does* feel the magic of transformation, a sensation which makes the otherwise rather reserved woman reveal that she might get married in this dress, even though "marriage had not, in fact, been mentioned. Not even in the last letter" (12). The fact that she mentioned her marriage still bothers her when she walks home with her conspicuous Milady's box, and the reader is allowed to witness how she tries to weigh and balance the words written in the letter. The irony, of course, is that these two letters, which have aroused Johanna's romantic feelings and on the content of which she acts when she prepares to travel to Ken Boudreau, Sabitha's father, have not been written by Ken at all. Slowly the story moves backward, revealing Sabitha and her friend Edith's outrageous trick on the unwitting Johanna, which commences with the interception of Johanna's first letter to Ken: "*Dear Mr. Ken Boudreau,*" Johanna writes, "*I just thought I would write and send my thanks to you for the nice things you said about me in your letter to your daughter*" (29). After providing Ken with her sad biography, she signs the letter with "*Your friend, Johanna Parry*" (30). The monitoring of the girls' reception of this letter reveals not only Johanna's loneliness but also the girls' teenage mindset, that is, their ambivalent attitude toward love and romance, which, obviously, they regard as ridiculous and fascinating at the same time, the former in particular with regard to their conception of Johanna:

> Edith read Johanna's words aloud, in an imploring voice and with a woebegone expression....
>
> "Stop," said Sabitha. "I'm laughing so hard I'll be sick."...
>
> "She's in love with him," she [Edith] said.
>
> "Oh, puke-puke," said Sabitha, holding her stomach. "She can't be. Old Johanna." (30 f.)

Johanna's letter to Ken marks the starting point of the girls' own "fantasy script" (Howells 173). When Ken does not answer Johanna's letter, the girls invent a romance for Johanna with the intention to lead her into a trap. Both letters forged and sent to Johanna are rendered in two stages, the process of their sinister fabrication as well as in their completed form in which they reach Johanna.

While in "Dimensions," as well as in "Carried Away," Munro has largely cut off the address as well as the signature line, these elements, which, after all, characterize epistolary discourses, play a central role in "Hateship, Friendship, Courtship, Loveship, Marriage." In Johanna's two long letters to Ken (the first one actually reaching him and the second intercepted by the girls), she first addresses him with "*Dear Mr. Ken Boudreau*" (29) and then with "*Dear Friend*" (33), relating to the content and closing line of the girls' fake letter to her. In both closing lines Johanna uses "*Your friend, Johanna Parry*" (30; 34), thus giving away her longing for a friend, her longing for an escape route out of the indifference that surrounds her in her present circumstances. The girls, and Edith in particular, sense this "weakness" in her when they fully exploit the letter's potential to raise expectations and create imaginaries—culminating in the closing line: "*L-v-, Ken Boudreau*" (40).

One of the unique aspects in this letter story, as mentioned above, is the portrayal not just of the reading of and commenting on letters, but also of their fabricating by the two teenage conspirators, whose different personalities are revealed by the dialogic discourses which render these production and reception scenes. While "pretty" Sabitha just wants to have fun, the more intelligent Edith is more seriously drawn into the matter, showing much empathy in her forged letters, which seem at times like giveaways of her own hidden longing for magic transformation.

Like the reader, the girls are granted a privileged vantage point on the epistolary exchange in this story, but are suddenly and unknowingly deprived of their power as soon as Johanna starts to act autonomously and against the girls' expectations. Johanna's last brief letter to

Ken, which appears earlier in the text than all the other letters in the story and thus raises the reader's curiosity, is posted by Johanna herself. While Johanna's voice "is obliterated in the girls' malicious game" (Howells 177), the adventurous young woman unwittingly outwits the girls by refusing to step out of the fantasy script they have laid out for her. What was meant as a malicious joke turns out to be the overture to Johanna's independence and fulfilment, or, as Coral Ann Howells puts it, "Munro has deftly turned romance on its head, translating the dynamics of fantasy into real life while subverting the traditional gendered power relationship into celebration of a woman's managerial capacities and a man's gratitude for being rescued" (177). Again, we have a female character who is able to straddle romantic fantasy and pragmatic reality. When Johanna arrives in Gdynia, a derelict town, and finds a sick and feverish Ken in his rundown hotel, she almost heroically refuses to regard this as the end of her imaginary script of desire but rather actively tries to rearrange what she finds in order for it to fit into this script. Without the exchange of letters, we may well argue, this magic transformation, which endows the protagonist with active agency, would not have happened. Similarly, it is Munro's skilful use of the manifold potential of epistolary discourse that renders Johanna's story convincing. Love letters in particular, as Ailsa Cox notes, show their "power to transform lives through romance . . . [L]ove letters are at least as exciting as actual experience, and perhaps even more so, since they are predicated on anticipation, rather than satisfaction. They demonstrate the power of discourse to construct a subjective reality" (80).

* * *

In "Dimensions" the letters go in only one direction. Written by the protagonist's former husband, the murderer of her children, they threaten to carry away the recipient against her better knowledge. "Dimensions" is one of those Munro stories that are not easy to digest. Doree, a sixteen-year-old girl, falls in love with Lloyd, one of the orderlies at the hospital where her mother is treated. When her mother suddenly dies, Doree decides to move in with Lloyd; she becomes pregnant, marries him, and becomes completely dependent on him. The narrative, however, starts only seven years later, when we find the twenty-three-year-old Doree working as a chamber maid, taking the bus to London and seeing a therapist on a regular basis. The story is interspersed with allusions to some dark event in her past. Moving back and forth between Doree's sessions with Mrs. Sands, the therapist, and her former life with Lloyd, the reader is finally acquainted with the fanatical sides of Lloyd, who controls everything his wife does, says, or thinks, and who is similarly possessive of their three children. When they have one of their frequent quarrels, this time over a dent in a spaghetti tin, with Lloyd accusing her of having tried to poison the family, Doree walks over to a neighbour, Maggie, because she needs a "breathing space," as she later tells Lloyd. Early the next morning, Maggie drives Doree home and the young mother finds all three children killed by her husband. Lloyd is declared criminally insane and locked up in an institution in London. Doree tries to blot out her old life, changes her hair, her name and her address, and the only people she now seems to be in contact with are her therapist—and Lloyd.

This is the part of the story where the letters come in: Doree seems to visit Lloyd on a regular basis, even though, when they actually meet, they have nothing much to say to each other. This changes, however, when Lloyd sends her two long letters, both highly manipulative. The first comes in the guise of spiritual reflections indicating that he, Lloyd, has acquired some kind of superior insight during his confinement. He sets himself off from ordinary people whose lives are determined by superficial material concerns, while he has risen to another dimension: "*Peace. I arrived at peace and am still sane. . . . What I do is Know Myself*" (22). The other strategy he uses is a rhetorical downplaying of his crime by comparing it to even greater monstrosities, such as mass murder:

> *I am judged by the world as a Monster and I have no quarrel with that, even though I might say in passing that people who rain down bombs or burn cities or starve and murder hundreds of people are not generally considered Monsters but are showered with medals and honours, only acts against small numbers being considered as shocking and evil.* (23)

The third strategy employed by the murderer is the allusion to a secret he would like to share with Doree, but which, as he claims in the letter, he could not write down. Doree swallows the bait and visits Lloyd in the hope of some revelation, yet "when she [sees] him again he behave[s] as if he had never written to her at all" (24). Face-to-face with Doree, he "can't talk anymore." "I want to," he says, "but I just dry up talking" (24). Even though he claims in his first letter that he cannot write the secret down, he realizes in the end that letters, besides giving him the chance to exploit their potential for rhetoric, are the medium to bind Doree irreversibly to him. In a letter he tells his wife that he has actually seen and talked to their children, that "*after such suffering and solitude there is Grace that has seen the way to giving me this reward*" (25).

While before the letters reach her, Doree has moments when she manages to "deconstruct" her husband as a person ("But maybe it was better that she had gone on, and seen him so strange and wasted. Not a person worth blaming for anything. Not a person. He was like a character in a dream" [18]), Lloyd reconstructs his self via his meticulously shaped letters. He invents himself as the chosen one with additional powers, as the one who has been transformed: "*I was crazy at one time but believe me I have shed all my old craziness like the bear that sheds his coat. Or maybe I should say the snake that sheds its skin*" (26). He elevates himself to a position from which he can provide Doree with "*the Truth*" (26). Even though Doree is aware that her therapist would regard this letter as "dangerous nonsense" (26), and even though she makes a conscious effort to fight the urge to succumb, she cannot in the end resist the persuasiveness of Lloyd's message, which comes "sneaking up on her" (27):

> And who had given it to her? [Doree muses,] Not Mrs. Sands—that was for sure. Not in all those hours sitting by the desk with the Kleenex discreetly handy. Lloyd had given it to her. Lloyd that terrible person, that isolated and insane person.... Insane if you wanted to call it that. But wasn't it possible that what he said was true ...? (27)

This idea "worm[s] its way into her head and stay[s] there" (28), resulting in her conviction that "Lloyd, of all people, might be the person she should be with now. What other use could she be in the world ...?" (28) Rendering Doree's point of view, the phrase "to be of use" deserves particular attention with regard to the story's finale.

As one may have expected, Doree boards the bus to London to be with Lloyd—but then something extraordinary happens: the bus is made to stop as an accident occurs on the road. Doree leaves the bus and miraculously manages to resuscitate a severely injured, unconscious motorist, thereby saving his life. An epiphanic moment, this also saves her own life as she comes to realize that she can *be of use* in the world—and that *to be of use* in the world means more than *to be of use* for Lloyd. When the bus driver urges her to come on board again after another witness has volunteered to stay with the injured man, "[h]e had to bend to hear her. She spoke dismissively, without raising her head, as if she were the one whose breath was precious" (31).

Reanimating the young man reflects Doree's own revival: both, in some way, have to learn to breathe again. It would not be Munro, however, if the reader were to be left with this prospect of "healing." After all, Doree is able to save the young man only because she remembers

Lloyd's instructions in case of an accident involving one of their children. Even though the story ends upon Doree's assuring the bus driver that she does not have to go to London anymore, we cannot be certain if this is really a final decision to stop visiting Lloyd altogether—and thus also liberate herself from her prison of submissive dependence. And although the persuasiveness of Lloyd's letters is shown, in the story, to have worked on Doree, inviting the extra-textual reader to adopt a critical distance, that very reader, too, may not have proved entirely immune to the appeal of the epistolary. In other words, the actual reader may in the meantime also have been induced, at times, to form a more conciliatory opinion of the murderer. Maybe Lloyd has indeed changed? Maybe it is indeed Doree's duty to stay by his side? Again, we must be aware that one of the functions of the letters in "Dimensions" is to include an additional point of view.

With Doree as focalizer, Lloyd's perspective enters the story only via his letters. Doree's growing psychological re-attachment to the murderer of her children can be followed as the reader witnesses the act of persuasion and manipulation effected by the letters. Altman's observation that "[w]hat is . . . striking in epistolary narrative is its emphatic portrayal of the art of close reading, the art of analysis and explication" (92) is of particular relevance regarding Doree's interpretation and re-interpretation of Lloyd's letters, the second one in particular. Here, the reading process is inextricably interwoven into the narrative fabric, doubling our own reading of the letter and, additionally, offering Doree's assumptions about the therapist's evaluation of it. The persuasive effect of Lloyd's letter becomes stronger the longer she reflects on it, an effect which seems to derive from the continuing (pseudo-) validity inherent in the epistolary, as has been mentioned above. While the negative memories of Doree's actual contact with Lloyd fade with time and spatial distance, the power of his words, as materialized in the letter, not only remains stable but even assumes an increasingly positive aura.

This degree of plausibility of Doree's manipulation by Lloyd would have been difficult to achieve had Munro not used the intrinsic power of the letters to "carry away" her female protagonist. Similarly, for the letter writer, the outrageous can more easily be communicated via the more distanced form of the letter. This is confirmed by Lloyd's following remark in his letter: "*I can write to you after all better than I can talk*" (25). "The idea of the *letter*," as Koepke notes, "is based on an urgent need for communication and on a distance between the correspondents which makes a direct dialogue impossible. Such isolation and distance . . . does not have to be geographical. It can be an isolation in the same house, be it an imprisonment or as a psychological or social barrier which precludes speech" (265). By capturing Lloyd's disturbed psyche in the first-person voice of his letters and Doree's precarious emotional state by narrativizing her reception of these letters, Munro has found a congenial tool for the impactful mediation of the psychological wasteland that underlies this story. And even if, as Isla Duncan puts it, "[t]here is some vestige of hope offered at the end of 'Dimensions'," I heartily agree with her that "the road toward the ending is unbearably bleak" (152).

* * *

As she has expressed in an interview, Alice Munro is fascinated by "the way people fall in and out of love, the way people twist things around, things that are ways that we all contrive our lives, I think . . . to me they seem really extraordinary and things I want to explore" (Gzowski F4). For the critic, in turn, it is an ongoing challenge to explore the intricate strategies the author employs to translate these twists into a narrative form that makes them comprehensible for her readership. As Howells has appropriately stated, "[t]he critical question is how Munro's stories manage to represent these dislocations and multiplicities within individual identity without her characters becoming estranged from the material spaces of their everyday worlds" (170).

In the present essay, I have focused on one such strategy that the author employs to make the extraordinary transmittable and comprehensible. Letters not only allow for a high degree of immediacy, largely resulting from a minimal distance between experiencing self and narrating self, but also involve the reader in the textual process of writing and reading. This narrativizing of the reading process (Altman 111 f.), through which the external reader is not only offered the content of the letter but also its intradiegetic reception, as with the letters contained in "Carried Away," "Hateship, Friendship, Courtship, Loveship, Marriage," and "Dimensions," significantly increases the plausibility of the extraordinary plotlines that characterize these stories. The temporal and spatial displacement of the correspondents proves to be another feature which, as I have shown, engenders ideal prerequisites for the construction of fantasies. While the lack of face-to-face contact opens up ample room for imaginary conceptions of the "other," it is the temporal delay of production and reception that promotes the illusion of emotions as stable and continuously valid. Through these features, letters become one of the most powerful textual strategies employed by

Munro to create extraordinary imaginaries and to render them in a most forceful and intriguing manner.

Works Cited

Altman, Janet Gurkin. *Epistolarity. Approaches to a Form.* Columbus: Ohio State UP, 1982.

Bray, Joe. *The Epistolary Novel. Representations of Consciousness.* London: Routledge, 2003.

Cox, Ailsa. *Alice Munro.* Tavistock: Northcote House, 2004.

Duncan, Isla. *Alice Munro's Narrative Art.* New York: Palgrave Macmillan, 2011.

Gzowski, Peter. "You're the same person at 19 that you are at 60: Interview with Alice Munro." *Globe and Mail,* 29 September 2001: Focus F4–F5.

Heble, Ajay. *The Tumble of Reason: Alice Munro's Discourse of Absence.* Toronto: U of Toronto P, 1994.

Howells, Coral Ann. "Intimate Dislocations: Alice Munro, *Hateship, Friendship, Courtship, Loveship, Marriage.*" *Alice Munro.* Ed. Harold Bloom. New York: Bloom's Literary Criticism, 2009. 167–92.

Koepke, Wulf. "Epistolary Fiction and Its Impact on Readers: Reality and Illusion." *Aesthetic Illusion. Theoretical and Historical Approaches.* Ed. Frederick Burwick and Walter Pape. Berlin: Walter de Gruyter, 1990. 263–74.

Lecker, Robert. "Machines, Readers, Gardens: Alice Munro's 'Carried Away'." *The Rest of the Story. Critical Essays on Alice Munro.* Ed. Robert Thacker. Toronto: ECW, 1999. 103–27.

Munro, Alice. *Dear Life.* London: Chatto & Windus, 2012.

———. *Too Much Happiness.* London: Chatto & Windus, 2009.

———. *Hateship, Friendship, Courtship, Loveship, Marriage.* 2001. New York: Vintage, 2002.

———. *Open Secrets.* 1994. New York: Vintage, 1995.

———. *Dance of the Happy Shades.* 1968. New York: Vintage, 2000.

Perry, Ruth. *Women, Letters, and the Novel.* New York: AMS, 1980.

Pruitt, Virginia D. "Gender Relations: Alice Munro's 'Differently' and 'Carried Away'." *Bulletin of the Menninger Clinic: A Journal for Mental Health Professionals* 64. (2000): 494–508.

Richardson, Brian. *Unnatural Voices: Extreme Narration in Modern and Contemporary Fiction.* Columbus: Ohio State UP, 2006.

Thacker, Robert. *Alice Munro. Writing Her Lives, A Biography.* Toronto: McClelland & Stewart, 2005.

Bridging the Gaps through Story Cycle: *The View from Castle Rock*

TINA TRIGG

In the current climate of re-discovering memoir and autobiography, Alice Munro's *The View from Castle Rock* (2006) seems an obvious text to support the resurgence of interest. In the foreword, Munro herself nods to the memoir-like quality of these stories, offering an account of their genesis. However, her nod of acknowledgement is immediately qualified, accompanied by a hesitation in voice and a carefully guarded description of this "special set of stories" as "not memoirs but . . . closer to my own life than the other stories I had written." In her insistence that "[t]hese are *stories*," Munro's discomfort with the label of memoir highlights the narrative space between genre boundaries—in particular, how bridging the gaps among "family history," "memoir," and "fiction" in *The View from Castle Rock* enables the discovery of what she terms "the truth of a life" (xiv). Munro's stories compellingly foreground questions of self and truth, often by exposing the rich (overlooked) potential for meaning and mystery in the ordinariness of life. Such revelations are heightened in *The View from Castle Rock*, a book that inhabits a gap between genres. Neither a miscellany of short stories nor a novel, the story cycle highlights the role of gaps through the incremental narrative structure. Munro's focus on multigenerational history establishes self in the context of community, altering ways of understanding the constructed nature of self and truth by emphasizing the vital role of gaps in individual and genealogical stories.

Far from precluding the construction of meaning, the inevitability of gaps enables a mode of discovery particular to fiction. Philosopher

Martha Nussbaum contends that a reader's willing acceptance of ambiguities, contradictions, and uncertainties—all created by gaps—uniquely positions narrative, as opposed to other discursive forms, to disclose the mystery or complexity of humanity that is part of self-knowledge; like Mikhail Bakhtin, she favours the extended form of the novel as the pinnacle of this representation. In *The View from Castle Rock*, however, Munro demonstrates the dialogical power of the short-story cycle. Both the individual and collective stories in a cycle depict craft and coherence, but the construction of the whole requires gaps in the stories to interrogate "the truth of a life" in a compressed, distinctive manner.

Munro's own ambiguous introductory remarks do nothing to dispel critical uncertainty about how to categorize *The View from Castle Rock*, an outcome not exclusive to this collection. This difficulty is similar to the fate of her early text, *Lives of Girls and Women*, about which most critics' uncertainty was apparent. Despite Munro's own description of it as "'really just a collection of linked stories'" (qtd. in Allardice), *Lives of Girls and Women* is widely labelled as her "one novel" (Anderson), "an early novel-in-stories" (Allen 858), or as a (failed) attempt: "her one 'novel' . . . [which is] really a closely linked series of stories, and after it was published in 1971, Munro would never attempt a novel again" (Valdes 87). Notably, Robert Thacker, Munro's biographer and one of her earliest critics, resists this labelling impulse and, instead, highlights the fundamental significance of the interconnectedness of her stories—the structure of her collections—thereby turning the tide of analysis from external form (to be or not to be a novel?) to a focus on internal form. He recognizes Munro's exposure to linked collections as a milestone in her development as a young writer, and recalls her absorption in Eudora Welty's *The Golden Apples* as early as 1959.[1] Thacker suggests this interest aligns with Munro's own movement toward discovering "how to evoke a world through a series of connected short stories" (Valdes 88). Established early in her career, Munro's affinity for the short-story cycle has not waned.

Nevertheless, *The View from Castle Rock* repeats this early pattern of uncertain critical reception. Like *Lives of Girls and Women*, it has been characterized variously by critics: ambivalently as "memoir-ish . . . hybrid stories" (Medwick), churlishly as "a self-indulgent project [of] fictionalized memoir . . . . A book that rambles" (Watman 60), and more generously when focused on the individual stories as "works [which are] . . . a species all their own: not quite fiction, not quite memoir" (Meacham 24). Consistent with the structure of story cycles, this latter view stresses the individual integrity of each story; it also suggests that *The View from Castle Rock* inhabits a gap between the typical categories of fiction and memoir. Critics' use of qualified descriptions (such as "fictionalized memoir" or "memoir-ish") signals an uneasiness with demarcating *The View from Castle Rock* as memoir—notwithstanding its significant incorporation of personal family history. Assessing it as a short-story cycle demonstrates the suitability of this hybrid form to investigate narrative truth and self-knowledge by foregrounding gaps, recurrence, and the insistent role of mystery in interpretive acts.

Such an argument relies to a large extent on a clear differentiation of story cycle from short-story collections generally. The subtle formal features are worth rehearsing briefly. Here, short story theorists Forrest L. Ingram and Gerald Lynch provide insight. Lynch bases his contemporary work on Ingram's pioneering definition of the short-story cycle as "'a book of short stories so linked to each other by their author that the reader's successive experience on various levels of the pattern of the whole significantly modifies his [or her] experience of each of its component parts'" (19 qtd. in Lynch 18). Ingram draws equal attention to the *author's* constructive power and the *reader's* successive experiential interpretation; both are related to the careful assembly of the individual stories into the cycle as a whole, to creating what Ingram terms "'the tension between the one and the many'" (19 qtd. in Lynch 18). One notes the crafted interdependence of stories in a cycle as well as the reader's experience of the stories—they are both individual and collective, removable but never entirely separate, and always subject to interpretive "bleed." Story cycle thus emphasizes the constructedness of narrative through the intensified and strategic use of gaps and layerings.

In addition to Ingram's emphasis on the tension between "the one and the many," short-story cycles are identifiable by their coherence. Lynch convincingly delineates the unifying factors of story cycles as character and/or place, giving particular emphasis to place (21) and to its recurrence—notably, as typically established in the opening and closing stories of the cycle (25). Munro is widely admired for her intimate, evocative account of place in all its apparent ordinariness, and *The View from Castle Rock* upholds this tradition; though the stories extend the horizons of place to Ettrick Valley, Scotland, they eventually settle in to her comfortable but complex space of small-town Ontario. Place retains a prominent role, drawing attention to the return to Wingham as more marked in this story cycle precisely because of beginning elsewhere and emphatically *away*. Rebecca Meacham contends that while "Munro's fictions are carefully designed to create tension . . . and intensity," *The View from Castle Rock* is "less invested in twists and turns, momentum, or suspense" because of its alliance with memoir (24). However, reading the text as a story cycle (rather than a qualified memoir) suggests that tension, intensity, and momentum are created by the incremental approach from Scotland to Illinois, Upper Canada, and back to Huron County, particularly to the house in Wingham. While Munro ranges outward through time and place, seeking "the truth of a life" necessarily brings her back home. Suspense is created not only by what will be revealed, but also by what will remain unknown and how the narrative will take shape around the gaps.

From the beginning of *The View from Castle Rock*, Munro draws attention to interpretation, the recording of history, and imaginative reconstruction—events that necessarily accommodate gaps. In the opening story, an epigraph from the 1799 Statistical Account of Scotland establishes place in terms of absences: "This parish possesses no advantages. Upon the hills the soil is in many places mossy and fit for nothing . . . . The nearest market town is fifteen miles away and the roads so deep as to be almost impassable." The residents are snowed in for months at a time; roads are flooded out for "want of bridges"; several crops are notably absent, and as for the parish landowners: "none of them resides in it" (3). This catalogue of what Ettrick lacks at the turn of the century hints that the story may shift from this low point to reveal some progress, that told from the vantage point of a twentieth-century Canadian descendent, perhaps "No Advantages" may reveal its title to be ironic. However, after tracing seven generations to a farm aptly named Far-Hope, Munro concludes with her great-great-grandfather as another absentee; having fled the area, he is described as "so scornful . . . of the place where he was born" that to return is "unthinkable" (26). Munro's interpretive act is revealed here as dependent upon limited historical documentation. While William Laidlaw's scornful rejection of Ettrick Valley is recorded in a letter to his fiancée, his reasoning is imputed retrospectively; Munro's narrator concludes, "[t]he poverty and the ignorance distress him, apparently. The poverty which seems to him wilful, and the ignorance which he judges to be ignorant of even its own existence. He is a modern man" (26). Since Ettrick Valley is not materially changed over these generations, Munro infers that an unfulfilled expectation of progress drives her ancestors away from Far-Hope to the Highlands and then across the sea.

As the opening story, "No Advantages" is the most far-reaching history of persons and place in the loosely chronological volume, revealing gaps within and across generations. Some silences seem palpable; when a son leaves Scotland for America without communicating his whereabouts or occupation, the expected family correspondence is noticeably absent. Retrospectively, Munro is able to trace her ancestor's relocation through other immigrant documents, speculating on the anxiety caused by the missing information (25). In other cases, letters are preserved, such as those recording the family's requests for emigration assistance, yet their outcome is unrecorded and cannot always be discovered. As Munro's narrator admits after searching related information, whether any financial assistance was forthcoming in this case is unlikely but unknown: "I do not know. Probably not . . ." (25). The existence of significant gaps despite extant documentation demonstrates the textual nature of history, including family history. As Linda Hutcheon observes, "The writing of history also involves a process of interpretation, for the facts must be given meaning in a particular context, whether they be dates in a church ledger or the complex personal interactions of the people involved" (87). Documents, gaps, and the act of documenting the past all necessarily function together. While missing facts about the material conditions of her ancestors are expected absences in a family history, Munro's method of storytelling emphasizes the interpretive act more than the factual information—existent or not. At times, her stories fill the gaps with likely outcomes while, other times, they draw attention to the absences.

Munro's variable use of gaps emphasizes that narrative coherence is a construction subject to change and error. "No Advantages" tempers unknowns and ambiguity by using place and language to create a sense of stability—an impression that Munro establishes and then undermines. A mythical gathering place from her ancestral past is cited as the "same high house" where James Hogg later gathers some male cousins, "not to get drunk and tell stories but to *read essays*" (22, emphasis in original). Initially Munro's narrator deems this act progressive and political, only to retract the definitive proclamation shortly thereafter: "I could be guessing wrong, of course. What Hogg calls essays could have been stories." A progressive political act is revealed as possibly a mysterious, fanciful act of the imagination, part of "a rash of literature, a fever of poetry [that] was breaking out in all classes" (23); in either case, her admiration remains. Suggesting a slippage between political and imaginative writings parallels Munro's own project in *The View from Castle Rock*, a chronicling of her personal and ancestral past that occupies a gap between fact and fiction. She opens the volume by claiming that "the part of this book that might be called family history has expanded into fiction, but always within the outline of a true narrative" (xiv). For Munro and her ancestor, Hogg, the historical leans into the fanciful, guided by a desire to capture and communicate truth.

Munro also emphasizes storytelling as an act of selection and creation, a self-conscious interpretation of the past. Her narrator wryly remarks on Hogg's translation of oral folk tales into written form, acknowledging that "[t]here would be some trimming and embroidering of material on Hogg's part. Some canny lying of the sort you can depend upon a writer to do" (21). Since writing is an active construction with an aim to coherence, "a true narrative" is not necessarily identical to factual truth and so readily accommodates gaps; the structural complexity and breadth of a story cycle seem to demand them. As a function of storytelling, the interpretive act of "trimming and embroidering" or "canny lying" occurs within and across generations; its shape is determined by the storyteller's objective, not by distance from the person, place, or event. Like Hogg, Munro identifies herself as a writer and in the next story her narrator flatly states, "I am surely one of the liars . . . in what I have written about the voyage [from Scotland]" (84). Through this "lying," Munro seeks narrative truth.

Since textual documents and historical gaps contribute to interpretive possibilities, Hutcheon argues that constructed meaning remains subject to change, which creates a rich potential for writers: "Of course, the past once existed. But we can *know* it today only through its documents, its traces in the present. If our knowledge of the past is something constructed (or even re-constructed), its meaning cannot be eternal and is certainly not unchangeable" (22). Writers who draw attention to the instability of meaning are "trying to unsettle our unexamined convictions about the status of fact and truth . . . [in order to] set up a new tension between the fictive and the historical" (Hutcheon 22). Indeed, Munro's narrative craftsmanship relies on indeterminacy in technique and content. Apart from a few letters and a factual journal about the ocean passage, Munro's narrator confesses that "The View from Castle Rock" is an artistic construction: "the story is full of my invention" (84). Her emphasis on fictionalizing is particularly significant here since one might expect the titular story of a family history to be most factual—an act of reclaiming the past by searching out origins and ancestors. Instead, by drawing attention to the extent of her "invention," Munro underscores the importance of gaps to the interpretive act of storytelling that dominates the volume as a whole. While incorporating letters, journals, and statistical accounts, *The View from Castle Rock* approaches "the truth of a life" through successive stories, crafted and layered to sustain the possibilities of people, place, and self-knowledge.

Shifting from ancestral story to Munro's lived experience, the second half of the volume maintains coherence through gaps, layerings, and the significance of place. "What Do You Want to Know For?," the final story before the epilogue, emphasizes Munro's use of landscape to create overlap between generations and to retain the appeal of the unknown. Munro's narrator describes her love for the geology of southwestern Ontario and the pleasure of driving about with her husband "in this part of the world looking at the countryside that we think we know so well and that is always springing some sort of surprise on us" (318). The enjoyment is thus expected, a fondly shared pastime for this older couple, and unpredictable: the landscape reveals itself in sudden glimpses of the past that do not disclose all of its secrets. Their unplanned discovery of a crypt becomes an intriguing exploration; the landmark seems to disappear from the map temporarily and when located after diligent search, the crypt remains mysterious, without visible markings and only disclosing a skeleton of its link to the past through local oral history. As Munro's narrator affirms, "[t]he landscape here is a record of ancient events," yet its temporality is also dependent on perspective; a glacial melt fifteen thousand years ago is considered to be quite recent "now that I have got used to a certain way of reckoning history" (318). While time seems to expand and contract—place is both ancient and recent—Munro also communicates an increasing sense of urgency in "What Do You Want to Know For?" The paradoxical nature of time as stable and transient, enduring yet elusive, is evidenced as the narrative alternates between place and person. The story opens with a dual focus: her initial discovery of the crypt is followed by a gap of one year, resuming the personal narrative with a threat of cancer. Munro's narrator navigates an interminable ten-day waiting period before a biopsy through distraction, busying herself with people and a search for the elusive crypt. The ancient glacial landscape, enduring over generations and filled with stories of lives, is characterized as both "vulnerable" and ever-changing (318), leaving her to conclude: "[s]o you have to keep checking, taking in the changes, seeing things while they last" (319). Seeing well requires vigilance—presumably not only of the landscape but of her self—since constant change means that gaps are unavoidable. Munro's deft handling of gaps, particularly her refusal to fill them all, reveals their narrative potential by suggesting there is always another hidden story.

Just as the Ettrick Valley statistical record in the volume's first story emphasizes absence, significant gaps in place, history, and self-knowledge recur throughout the volume. Munro consistently presents the absences as opportunities, not obstacles. In "What Do You Want to Know For?" she describes place as a site of constant change and focuses on gaps in the landscape. The common practise of selling gravel is described as an exciting childhood event characterized by heavy machinery, loud activity, and temporary warning signs. An economically driven act creates sudden and enduring change in the landscape; rather than a regrettable absence, the created depressions become interesting opportunities to witness gradual regrowth. In adulthood, the physical gaps and depressions in landscape continue to be of interest; Munro's narrator seeks evidence of crevices and describes her favourite topographical features, kame moraines, as "all wild and bumpy, unpredictable, with a look of chance and secrets" (321). Though vulnerable to destruction, the land has the potential for surprise and revelation—as do people; Munro's stories emphasize both aspects.

Through its layering of stories, *The View from Castle Rock* represents a changing relationship between place and self, a negotiation between landscape and urban space (particularly in its small-town manifestation). After returning to Wingham, Munro's narrator proposes that storytelling can expose and may impoverish a place:

> The town ... stays very much the same—nobody is renovating or changing it. Nevertheless it has changed for me. I have written about it and used it up. Here are more or less the same [public buildings], but all their secret, plentiful messages for me have drained away. (300)

Devoid of the mysteries of ordinary life, the storefronts and town hall have become two-dimensional false fronts. Restoring perspective requires re-animating the secret lives of place and persons. The narrator's quest for the mysterious crypt leads to a conversation with a stranger, affirming her desire to be connected with the past, her family, and her childhood home: "I am happy to find somebody who can see me still as part of my family, who can remember my father and the place where my parents worked and lived . . ." (332). Her homestead has become an automobile wrecking yard, but Munro's narrator confides, "that is not the only thing that deprives it of meaning for me. No. It is the fact that it *is* only twenty miles away, that I could see it every day if I wanted to. The past needs to be approached from a distance" (332). Ironically, the radical outward destruction of her childhood home is no more limiting than its physical proximity. As Munro's narrator remarks in the volume's opening story, "[t]he past is full of contradictions and complications, perhaps equal to those of the present, though we do not usually think so" (17). Telling "the truth of a life" requires seeing beneath the exterior and the expected—in part by looking past the commonplace.

Throughout *The View from Castle Rock*, Munro stresses the need for looking carefully while also acknowledging the limitations on what one can see. Distance (in space and time) can provide perspective by defamiliarizing places and people, but storytelling also involves construction. As a result, distance creates space for the imagination, which can be illuminating or distorting. Describing her ancestral place in Ettrick Valley, Scotland, Munro initially sprinkles it with mystery and magic; the valley has been home to war heroes, philosophers, wizards, and literary figures: "and there is a story of Merlin—*Merlin*—being hunted down and murdered, in the old forest, by Ettrick shepherds" (5). However, the magical allure quickly evaporates; Munro's narrator admits that "the valley disappointed me the first time I saw it. Places are apt to do that when you've set them up in your imagination" (5). The early spring valley is too brown, the river too narrow, and the stones are not "interesting remnants of Celtic worship" but ordinary sheep pens. The experience leaves her feeling dislocated, dispirited, and limited in understanding: "I was a naive North American, in spite of my stored knowledge. Past and present lumped together here made a reality that was commonplace and yet disturbing beyond anything I had imagined" (7). The volume thus begins by foregrounding gaps as historical, personal, and cultural constructs with the potential to stretch one's imagination beyond the apparent. Having established these gaps in place, the story turns to William Laidlaw, who takes up the abandoned family farm, Far-Hope, and identifies so closely with it that he becomes known as Will O'Phaup. Munro recounts his life of tall tales, fairy (or ghost) stories, and ordinary sorrows, leading up to his grandsons, including James Hogg. Throughout, her focus is on O'Phaup's storytelling—how reputations were built from them, how their supernatural claims evoked skepticism, and how they continue to preserve generational links to the past.

Glimpses of the hidden stories that fill the past and present fascinate Munro. Recounting her family history means admitting to many unknowns, the gaps where stories hide. A particularly vivid example is young James Laidlaw, a rascally, jealous toddler who animates the ocean voyage and vies for attention in "The View from Castle Rock" only to die in unknown circumstances within a month of arrival. The story closes by cataloguing the deaths and burials of the emigrants, leaving young James for last: "[h]is name is here [in the cemetery near Milton, Ontario] but surely he cannot be. They had not taken up their land when he died, they had not even seen this place" (87). After listing many possible burial sites and the likelihood of an unmarked resting place, Munro concludes his story simply but ambiguously as a common casualty: "any of the ailments, the accidents, that were the common destroyers of little children in the time" may have killed him (87). On the specifics of death, history is silent and Munro's story honours that gap. However, her fictional version of young James also reclaims him from obscurity; such is the power of story and a "true narrative."

Similar gaps exist in the lives she imagines for her ancestors and in the stories passed down about them. "The Wilds of Morris Township" begins with an excerpt from the settlement records, followed by a list of her ancestors. Munro seems to provide a comprehensive account of nine siblings, but undercuts these facts with the narrator's offhand remark that "Duncan left home early. (That name is correct, but I am not absolutely certain of the others)" (117). Interestingly, this disclosure does not undermine the credibility of the story, for these ancestors exist in a spotty version of the past sustained by rumours across generations. The narrator's familiarity with them is through both documentation and oral history. Her parents kept alive the stories of these second cousins on her paternal grandfather's side even though their own knowledge was indirect and limited. Her mother "had never actually met them" but was favourably disposed to their sibling devotion; her father had minimal contact with them as a child, but in adulthood "did not admire them, or blame them. He wondered at them" (126). As the descendants of ancestors who risked everything in emigration, they are expected to make it worthwhile; her father, though solitary himself in youth, professes to be baffled by their withdrawal from community and into what Munro's narrator terms "a life that was monastic without any visitations of grace or moments of transcendence" (118). Her father's unanswerable question resonates as the story's final line: "What was it squashed their spirits? So soon" (126). Like the mystery of young James's demise, the story opens a gap without providing resolution; in both instances, the questions continue to hang.

Such gaps are not limited to distant ancestors but characterize the narrator's interaction with her immediate family, and even herself. In "The Ticket," Aunt Charlie discloses a secret narrative about her sister's pride, morality, fortitude, and relinquished love. A plot of romantic intrigue is metered out to her niece's wondering ears, revealing an unimaginable past. Munro's narrator measures this story against her mother's characterization of the air of general annoyance between her grandparents. Aunt Charlie affords no clarification, simply remarking, "'I wouldn't know where your mother got that [idea]'" (276). Against this interpretive discrepancy, Munro's narrator affirms her assessment of Aunt Charlie's marriage to Uncle Cyril as simple and definitive, declaring that "[t]heir affection was legendary" (277). Yet, in retrospect, she wonders how much of this impression of harmony is idealized: "perhaps it's only what I've been told, what I think I remember." Realizing that her interpretation defines Aunt Charlie's marriage in contrast to her parents' and grandparents' relationships, she begins to suspect oversimplification: "I'm certain, though, that the other feelings I remember—the sense of obligation and demand . . . the stale air of irritability, of settled unease . . . —were absent from that one marriage" (278). Facing the unknowns of her own pending marriage, Munro's narrator is secretly intimidated by the prospect of "*living your life with that one person*," a fear Aunt Charlie senses (282). Most unexpectedly, she is the one to offer the narrator a way out: an emergency fund in case the young bride changes her mind. Stunned into silence, Munro's narrator refuses the money, but her thoughts betray her own hidden story and expose a limited understanding of others: "I couldn't let a soul see into me, let alone a person as simple as Aunt Charlie" (283). Munro's story subtly discloses that for each of these women, life is more complex than the visible scripts of their lives.

The mystery that Munro's stories preserve, or partially disclose, is not limited by generation or gender; the depiction of her father in "Working for a Living" is a similar combination of recognized features and unfathomable depths. Departing from his parents' ambitions for their only son and without solid goals of his own, her father seeks a life and career but initially finds only absence. Munro's narrator remarks, "[h]e was edging towards a life he probably could not clearly visualize, since he would know what he didn't want so much better than what he wanted" (132). Her father affirms the ordinariness of such gaps and the incidental nature of life much later, confiding after his wife's death, "'[y]ou get into things, you know. You sort of don't realize what you're getting into'" (154). Even though his disclosure matches the narrator's own experience (particularly of marriage), it contradicts her assumptions about her parents. As an individual, her father seems to disappear into relational roles—son, husband, father, and failed entrepreneur—but Munro's narrator questions the truthfulness of this identity: "didn't he think of himself, of the boy who had trapped along the Blyth Creek, . . . didn't he struggle for his own self? I meant, was his life now something only other people had a use for?" (166). Her alarm at his self-effacement reveals her interest in self-knowledge and the inevitability of gaps; even one's closest family members have hidden stories.

Imagining a life around these gaps, however, does not always reveal "a true narrative." The narrator's view of her parents before marriage is idealistic and oversimplified: "they seem not only touching and helpless, marvellously deceived, but more attractive than at any other time. It is as if nothing was thwarted then and life still bloomed with possibilities, as if they enjoyed all sorts of power before they bent themselves towards each other." Her perception is also admittedly false: "That can't be true, of course—they must have been anxious already— . . . They must have known failure already" (139). Nevertheless, her reconstruction of an impossible past for her parents extends to place; Munro's narrator imagines the young couple choosing their Wingham home on a day characterized by idyllic weather, easy travel, and a "luxuriant optimism" (139–40). This fiction of the past is possible only by disregarding the limitations of circumstance and the likely facts about the people involved; it is a construct fuelled by self-interest and self-deception. The narrator confesses that the romanticization of her parents derives from a need to believe she was not "born out of affection that was always stingy, or an undertaking that was always half-hearted" (139). In an intimate disclosure, Munro reveals that gaps in knowledge—about others in past and present—are often filled with fictions based on the storyteller's own desires and needs; they are stories s/he wants to believe.

Munro also investigates her quest for self-knowledge as a desire-driven narrative in *The View from Castle Rock*; as the title suggests, the quest for self-knowledge requires perspective, some distance, and awareness of one's context—in place, in time, and in relation to others. Moreover, the view of oneself is always suspect since competing stories, limited awareness, and falsifications result in contradictory and multiple selves. The goal of narrative "truth," however, is not to achieve a stable singular "I," but to acknowledge the self as complex, fragmentary, and evolving—a variability highlighted by feminist and postmodernist theories, and, in lived experience, by the coming-of-age process. To her mother's dismay, Munro's narrator is "a ringleader and a loudmouth" as a teen, but she expresses ambivalence about this singular identity in retrospect: "[i]f that was a disguise it was one that I managed easily. Or it might not have been a disguise, but just one of the entirely disjointed and dissimilar personalities I seemed to be made up of" (204). While Munro's narrator concedes a multiplicity of personalities and their incompatibility, she makes no attempt to argue for a dominant identity, suggesting that fragmentation is desirable—perhaps even necessary—and, as a measure of self-knowledge, more truthful. Even with her first boyfriend, aspects of her identity remain hidden, largely because of an absence of narrative disclosure; the narrator concedes, "I did not speak much about myself and I did not listen to him all that closely. . . . A lot of me was under cover, as it was with my friends on Saturday nights" (210). In these moments of potential intimacy, her withdrawal extends from people to the environment; the gaps in self-disclosure are a conscious defence against vulnerability, a means of protecting self-truths. Though "secretly devoted to Nature," Munro's narrator ignores it on her dates—just as she hides her "addiction" to poetry at home and at school—to avoid being "put . . . into a condition of permanent vulnerability" (198–99). Yet attempts to suppress her deep connection to poetry and nature with their inspiring and evocative characteristics has limited success; her defences are unsatisfying and exposed as false, temporary armour.

Such exposure, often originating from an unexpected encounter with place or others, is usually unwelcome since it reveals vulnerability—chinks in one's armour. Just as Aunt Charlie perceptively reads the young bride's hesitancy in "The Ticket," Munro's stories generally present self-knowledge as responsive to a moment in time, a particular environment, and a community or relationship. As in earlier volumes, "present tense is only the surface of a many-layered past, just as places bear traces of their earlier history and families accumulate forgotten rubbish in cupboards or attics" (Howells, *Alice* 152). The combination of story cycle and family history in *The View from Castle Rock* highlights a complex understanding of humanity by enacting the interpretive process while also acknowledging its limitations for knowing self or others. This postmodern contradiction is evident in how Munro depicts the mundane aspects of life. The narrator's father works at the foundry in his later years, a common place "soon to disappear" (162) and easily ignored as unimportant. She remarks on the ordinariness of this phenomenon: "places like this [exist] all over the country, in every town and city. . . . You passed them in a car or on the train and never gave a thought to what was going on inside. Something that took up the whole of people's lives. A never-ending over-and-over attention-consuming life-consuming process" (161). The possibility for a place to be utterly absorbing to one and yet virtually invisible to others hints at similar paradoxes related to people. By drawing attention to this tension, Munro challenges the complacency of any simplified interpretation of self or others.

Munro's stories offer alternatives to complacency, nudging readers to be "humble, open, active yet porous," and to exhibit "trust, the acceptance of incompleteness" in others, in stories, and in self (Nussbaum 282). Such engagement resists certainty and control, and requires vulnerability of the reader—as does Munro's incremental movement toward self-knowledge in *The View from Castle Rock*. In Nussbaum's view, literary stories are a unique means to self-knowledge largely because they require acceptance of irresolvable tensions and seek to preserve mystery (285). Significantly, Munro's stories are widely admired for her skilful use of mystery and secrets—in narrative structure, characterization, and thematic development.[2] Howells observes that Munro's narrative analysis has been the focus of recent critical attention primarily because of her craftsmanship and the appeal of complex storytelling that preserves mystery; she notes that as an outcome, "the multiple narrative strands render a story both lucid and resistant to interpretation" (*Alice* 145). Through her method of storytelling, Munro creates a place of vulnerability and potential revelation by inviting intimacy while acknowledging the impossibility of full disclosure.

While submerged secrets and hidden stories of others are appealing, these gaps in self can be discomfiting—particularly when they are pinpointed by others. In *The View from Castle Rock*, the small town's constant appraisal of the ill-suited country girl figures prominently in the stories based on Munro's lived experience. "Lying Under the Apple Tree" depicts the narrator's attempt to hide her Romantic view of nature. Having reclined under a particularly old apple tree for the aesthetic pleasure of simply "see[ing] how it rose, as if out of my own skull, rose up and lost itself in an upside-down sea of blossom," the young girl finds herself confronted by the female landowner for trespassing (199). Surrounded by male onlookers, the landowner chastises her, assuming that her flimsy excuse (her "lying") is an inexperienced cover for sexual exploits ("lying") under the tree. Significantly, Munro's narrator is more enraged by the violation of her privacy (her self) than by the unjust moral censure; she confesses that "[p]eople's thoughts about me . . . any thoughts at all, seemed to me a mysterious threat, a gross impertinence. I hated even to hear a person say something relatively harmless" (202). Her defensiveness reveals an aversion to vulnerability, a fear of self-disclosure that carries through adolescence into adulthood. Munro emphasizes this continuum in a cluster of three stories found in part two of the volume: "Lying Under the Apple Tree," "Hired Girl," and "The Ticket."

While the narrator's love of nature is exposed as a liability when emerging from under the apple tree, her private love of words and nature culminate in "Hired Girl," the account of her first job as a live-in maid. Mr. Montjoy, her employer, spies Munro's narrator reading his "very unusual" book, *Seven Gothic Tales*, and secretly gives it to her at summer's end. The narrator's response is revealing:

> I didn't feel particularly pleased, or grateful, in spite of my repeated thank-yous. I was too startled, and in some way embarrassed. The thought of having a little corner of myself come to light, and be truly understood, stirred up alarm, just as much as being taken no notice of stirred up resentment. (254)

Instead of using gossip and stories to deflect attention from herself, as "the entertainer around home" typically would (193), Munro's narrator is now in public and painfully aware that her love for books, a deeply buried part of her, has been recognized by a stranger—and an expendable one, at that. Her characterization of Mr. Montjoy as "probably the person who interested me least, whose regard meant the least to me" (254), intimates her blindness toward him as a source of self-knowledge. The narrator's defensive distancing of Mr. Montjoy is replicated in "The Ticket"—even though Aunt Charlie is among her favourite relatives. The moment they recognize her hidden self, Munro's narrator dismisses both individuals, treating them like the all-consuming yet invisible foundry: as separate from and inconsequential to herself. The realization of their insight—manifested in their offerings of the gothic book and the emergency cash—jarringly exposes her vulnerability and her unacknowledged connection to others through shared narratives. By sequencing these three stories—"Lying Under the Apple Tree," "Hired Girl," and "The Ticket"—Munro depicts self-knowledge and the limits of perception in an effective layered form.

As fictionalized family history, *The View from Castle Rock* occupies a privileged position in Munro's oeuvre. These stories are distinct from her other material and more personal because of their objective; Munro notes that they were created primarily not to "mak[e] a story," but rather to "explor[e] a life, my own life . . . as searchingly as I could" (xiv). Part of this search for self-knowledge inevitably involves unwelcome revelations, layers of self peeled back through successive layers of narrative.

Munro's proclivity for layering meanings (including contradictory and partial ones) is not only a function of narrative generally, but is directly aligned with the form of story cycle. As Lynch observes in relation to the layered meanings of *Who Do You Think You Are?* "short-story sequencing generally, and the dynamics of the short-story cycle especially, facilitate this strength of her literary art" (164). Similarly, Magdalene Redekop acknowledges the importance of multiplicity in Munro's stories, aligning them with Walter Benjamin's notion of oral tradition, a form reliant on "'that slow piling one on top of the other of thin, transparent layers . . . in which the perfect narrative is revealed through the layers of a variety of retellings'" (93 qtd. in Redekop 25). In this respect, *The View from Castle Rock* continues Munro's longstanding quest "to write stories that will adequately accommodate the indeterminacy and disparate realities observed by her increasingly self-conscious storytellers" (Howells, *Alice* 11). By layering her self on to the character/storyteller, this volume intensifies the self-consciousness to the point that author, narrator, and character are indistinguishable.[3] The volume shifts Munro's narrative position from a "persistently peripheral point of view" as an "outsider" (de Papp Carrington 210) to one of increasing complicity. By placing more emphasis on the interdependence of self and others, she is able to function more strategically as "a person who exposes not only others but also herself" (de Papp Carrington 210). To focus on the overlap of self through family history, Munro chooses a storytelling form that emphasizes reciprocity and gaps: the short-story cycle.

Moreover, Munro intensifies the interdependence through the volume's structural complexity. *The View from Castle Rock* departs from the story cycle's typical emphasis on opening and closing stories, and refuses the general expectation of "the pivotal status of the title story in each [of Munro's] collection[s]" (Thacker, "Alice Munro, Writing 'Home'"). Instead, through careful organization and multiple subtitled sections, Munro shifts emphasis to the sequencing of stories and their successive effect: a hallmark of story cycles. The layered, multipart organization suggests that the genealogical exploration is as important to self-knowledge as her own lived experience. In fact, some critics note that the stories memorializing the harsh deprivations of her ancestors are most poignant and can be considered "the book's great achievements" (Allen 858). To underscore the volume's coherence, Munro strategically positions the shift from ancestral story to her own life prior to the volume's formal break. The offset transition signals continuity between generations and emphasizes the interdependence of successive stories overall.

As Munro notes early in *The View from Castle Rock*, despite a familial distaste for "*[c]alling attention to yourself* . . . [through] any need to turn your life into a story, either for other people or for yourself," she stands alongside those who "have that need in large and irresistible measure" (20, emphasis in original). Arguably, this recent volume is her most explicit attempt to fulfill that need. Since self-knowledge is always partial, imperfect, and constructed, the successive arrangement of stories relies on layering as well as gaps, on revelation and mystery, to approach "the truth of a life." As Thacker notes, "Alice Munro is always able, often stunningly so, to take a web of human connections and, by the way *her* story is told, by finding *her* way into her material, to discover and articulate its mysteries" (*Alice Munro: Writing* 17). Her discovery and articulation of the mysteries of human stories is not to explain or to limit them, but to preserve them and, by so doing, to validate them. As Munro readily acknowledges, "I like gaps, all my stories have gaps. It seems this is the way people's lives present themselves" (qtd. in Allardice). And, presumably, based on *The View from Castle Rock*, this is the way her own life presents itself as well—subject to fictionalization, fallibility, and change; or, to quote Munro from "The Ticket": "This is the story, or as much as I know of it" (266).

As Munro hints, part of the power of gaps is their tantalizing unknowing—an absence that resonates with possibility. The first person narratives in *The View from Castle Rock* are "filled with secrets and deceptions"; Howells notes that they "retain her [Munro's] characteristic elusiveness and complexity," and finally offer "only partial explanations . . . for some secrets are destined to remain secret" ("Writing" 167). The self-knowledge attained by and through storytelling is complemented by the mystery—not just as a postmodern assumption but as a more accurate portrayal of human complexity, extending to the reader. Characterized as "inordinately respectful" of readers, the short story, Sarah Hall argues, demands an intensity of involvement that makes it "powerful and memorable." Whether attributed to her association with orality (Redekop 25), familiar structure and affirmation of "the basis of self-identity" (Lynch 165), or ability to create a readily accessible embodiment of trust (Goldblatt 23), Munro is a gifted and widely admired writer. Being honoured with the Nobel Prize for Literature is a mark not only of authorial achievement but of well-deserved popularity for stories that offer readers the pleasure of intimate disclosure abounding with hidden mysteries.

Munro closes *The View from Castle Rock* in "Messenger" by recollecting "a big mother-of-pearl seashell" from the past—from a house now forgotten (and belonging to someone else) and from a place far away—which used to enable her narrator to "discover the tremendous pounding of my own blood, and of the sea" (349). Like the story cycle itself, this memory in the epilogue is recurrent, individual and collective, tied to place and life, to change and mystery, to suggestiveness and interpretation. As a messenger herself, Munro remarks on her interconnection with her ancestors: "Their words and my words, a curious re-creation of lives, in a given setting that was as truthful as our notion of the past can ever be" (xiv). Through its individual-collectivity, *The View from Castle Rock* highlights the provisionality of self-truths, the complex nature of interpretation, and the power of narrative gaps to construct meaning through the cumulative effect of successive stories. In true Munrovian fashion, the seemingly simple prefatory statement that "[t]hese are *stories*" is, in fact, a bold declaration of the particular narrative power of the story cycle.

Notes

1. Munro's sustained interest in Welty's 1949 text is echoed by other critics; see, for example, Howells (*Alice* 8–9).
2. In 1983, for example, Lorna Irvine insightfully recognized Munro's emphasis on secrets as characteristic of women's writing in its insistence on alternate texts. The alignment is endorsed by important feminist assessments of Munro, notably by Barbara Godard (1984) and Magdalene Redekop (1992).
3. It is important to note that Munro specifically distinguishes the presentation of herself in *The View from Castle Rock* from her other material, identifying this narrator as "closer to my own life than the other stories I had written, even in the first-person. . . . [I was] exploring a life, my own life, but not in an austere or rigorously factual way. I put myself in the center and wrote about that self, as searchingly as I could" (xiv). Nonetheless, for clarity, this discussion employs the term "Munro's narrator" when quoting from the volume.

Works Cited

Allardice, Lisa. "Nobel Prizewinner Alice Munro: 'It's a wonderful thing for the short story.'" *The Guardian* [UK], 6 December 2013. https://www.theguardian.com/books/2013/dec/06/alice-munro-interview-nobel-prize-short-story-literature.

Allen, Bruce. "Some Canny Living. . ." Review of *The View from Castle Rock*, by Alice Munro. *Kirkus Reviews* 74.17 (2006): 858.

Anderson, Hephzibah. "Alice Munro profile: The mistress of all she surveys." *The Guardian* [UK], 31 May 2009. https://www.theguardian.com/books/2009/may/31/alice-munro-man-booker-prize-profile.

Bakhtin, M. M. *The Dialogic Imagination: Four Essays.* Ed. Michael Holquist. Trans. Caryl Emerson and Michael Holquist. Austin: U of Texas P, 1981.

de Papp Carrington, Ildiko. *Controlling the Uncontrollable: The Fiction of Alice Munro.* DeKalb: Northern Illinois UP, 1989.

Goldblatt, Patricia. "Reciprocity Between Life and Art: Telling Stories." *Multicultural Review* 17.3 (Fall 2008 17.3): 23–28.

Godard, Barbara. "Heirs of the Living Body: Alice Munro and the Question of Female Aesthetics." *The Art of Alice Munro: Saying the Unsayable.* Ed. J. Miller. Waterloo: U of Waterloo P, 1984. 43–71.

Hall, Sarah. "Sarah Hall on why we should have a short story laureate." *The Guardian* [UK], 11 October 2013. https://www.theguardian.com/books/2013/oct/11/sarah-hall-short-story-laureate.

Howells, Coral Ann. *Alice Munro.* Contemporary World Writers. Manchester: Manchester UP, 1998.

———. "Writing Family History." Review of *The View from Castle Rock* by Alice Munro. *Canadian Literature* 195 (December 2007): 166–68.

Hutcheon, Linda. *The Canadian Postmodern: A Study of Contemporary English-Canadian Fiction.* Oxford: Oxford UP, 1988.

Lynch, Gerald. *The One and the Many: English-Canadian Short Story Cycles.* Toronto: U of Toronto P, 2001.

Meacham, Rebecca. "Taking the Risk." Review of *The View from Castle Rock* by Alice Munro. *Women's Review of Books.* 24.4 (2007): 24–25.

Medwick, Cathleen. "Imagining the Past." *O, The Oprah Magazine* 7.11 (2006): 240.

Munro, Alice. *The View from Castle Rock: Stories.* Toronto: Penguin, 2006.

Nussbaum, Martha C. *Love's Knowledge: Essays on Philosophy and Literature.* Oxford: Oxford UP, 1990.

Redekop, Magdalene. "Alice Munro and the Scottish Nostalgic Grotesque." *Essays on Canadian Writing* 66 (1998): 21–43.

———. *Mothers and Other Clowns: The Stories of Alice Munro.* New York: Routledge, 1992.

Thacker, Robert. *Alice Munro: Writing Her Lives: A Biography.* Toronto: McClelland & Stewart, 2005.

———. "Alice Munro, Writing 'Home': 'Seeing This Trickle in Time.'" *Essays on Canadian Writing* 66 (1998): 1–20.

Valdes, Marcela. “Some Stories Have to be Told by Me: A Literary History of Alice Munro.” *Virginia Quarterly Review* 82.3 (2006): 82–90.

Watman, Max. “Severe Manners.” *New Criterion* 25.3 (2006): 59–64.

II
Themes

The Short Stories of Alice Laidlaw, 1950–51

D. M. R. Bentley

> I think every young writer starts out this way, where at first the stories are exercises. They're necessary exercises, and I don't mean they aren't felt and imagined as well as you can do them.
>
> —Alice Munro (qtd. in Struthers 21)

In the fall of 1950, Alice Laidlaw, who had entered the University of Western Ontario a year earlier intending to take a degree in journalism, changed her major to English. Primarily because of her impending marriage to James Munro and the conclusion of her two-year scholarship, she left the university in 1951 without completing her degree. Her association with Western's English Department from 1949 to 1951 was a productive one, however, for, in addition to taking first- and second-year courses with Brandon Conron, Carl Klinck, and others, she published three short stories in *Folio*, the Department's student magazine. Although "The Dimensions of a Shadow" (April 1950), "Story for Sunday" (December 1950), and "The Widower" (April 1951) have been briefly discussed by Robert Thacker and others,[1] they have been seen primarily as pale precursors of Munro's later fiction. Since the first two stories contain female protagonists and are set in urban areas, and the third focuses on the monotonous life and quiet desperation of its male protagonist, this teleological view of them as apprenticeship work is perfectly understandable. Nevertheless, it overlooks features of all three stories that set them apart in varying degrees from Munro's later work, including, as will be seen here, elements of setting and dialogue that bear the deep imprint of James Joyce and D. H. Lawrence and elements of plot and character that clearly reflect Sigmund Freud's and Carl Jung's theories of mind,[2] which had already proved attractive and useful to several Canadian writers and would become increasingly so in the future, cases in point being Sinclair Ross, A. M. Klein, Robertson Davies, and Margaret Laurence.

"The Dimensions of a Shadow"

As she emerges "alone" from church at the beginning of "The Dimensions of a Shadow" (the very title, of course, points to Jung), the protagonist, Miss Abelhart, is wearing shoes and clothes that she has "chosen for their ugliness and absurdity" and displays with "a certain defiance, as if she recognized in them a drabness closely akin to her own" (4). Even her "tightly and tastelessly curled" "straw hair" contributes to the overall impression of eccentricity, as does her makeup: "something like dust lay over her face." In Jungian terms, this is her persona, "a kind of mask, designed on the one hand to make a definite impression upon others, and, on the other, to conceal the true nature of the individual"—a "two-dimensional reality" that "*feigns individuality*, making others and oneself believe that one is individual, whereas one is simply acting a role" (Jung, *Two Essays* 192, 157–58). Apparently Miss Abelhart's persona is convincing, for "People who looked at her knew that she was old, and had always been old" (4). In fact, however, she is only "thirty-three"—the age, that is, of Christ at the time of the crucifixion and, as such, the first of a number of hints in the manner of Joyce in *Dubliners* and Lawrence in "The Horse-Dealer's Daughter" (and elsewhere) that a Christological pattern is at work in "The Dimensions of a Shadow."

If, as her spinsterhood and name (Abelhart: murdered heart) already suggest, Miss Abelhart has developed her persona at the expense of her inner self, psychological problems will soon manifest themselves, and they do. After she has reacted to an invitation to join other parishioners at a "temperance meeting" with eyes that are "cunning and afraid," she aligns herself with negation by using the word "no" and its cognate "not" seven times, the last three "under her breath." Evidence now quickly accumulates to suggest that she is a neurotic in "a state of psychic disequilibrium" that is manifesting itself in the "dissolution" or "disintegration of . . . [her] persona" and a consequent "release" from her "unconscious" mind of what Jung variously calls "involuntary fantasy" and "repressed personal fantasies" (*Two Essays* 159–61). "Often lately," states the narrator, "she found that she was talking to herself" (4). First feeling happy "to be free for a moment" and then acknowledging that it is "terrible to be endlessly alone," she continues on her way. It is early June, a time of growth and maturation, and "pale soft clouds" are "promising rain," but here, unlike in *The Waste Land*, no rain will fall. The air is filled with the "heavy sweetness" of "lilacs" that, like Miss Abelhart, are "already past their prime"; by a "garden gate" some similarly correlative "Peonies droop . . . their deep reds darkened, and their petals fallen together because they belong . . . to the day"; "Perhaps on the hills outside the town" there are "night-flowers, wild and scentless, stars buried in the long grass—but those . . . [she] would never see."

As night approaches, she moves ever closer to confrontation with (quoting Jung again) the "dark interior world" that lies beneath her persona and beneath "the penumbra of consciousness"—the "dark hinterland of the psyche" where "crepuscular figures" lurk (*Two Essays* 174, 206, 210). Walking along the street in the deepening darkness, she shows signs first of infantile regression and then of paranoiac delusion: "like a child," she avoids stepping on "the cracks in the sidewalk" and, like many a character in *Dubliners*, observes the "houses on either side of the street—"houses of brick and stone, decent with porches and steps and shutters . . . closed houses watching covertly with hooded eyes, knowing their place in the pattern. Yet some of them had lamps lit in the windows [. . .]" (5).[3] Then in "the yellow circle under a streetlight" she encounters "three girls," who greet her with the "quick bland smiles they kept for a teacher" (the first indication of her stereotypically repressed profession) and trigger a self-protective reaffirmation of her persona. Noticing "the lovely clarity of . . . [the girls'] features, and the grace of their young bodies," she "look[s] away from them . . . straighten[s] her shoulders and walk[s] more stiffly, more carefully, feeling the girls' clear eyes at her back." What happens next is the sudden and, for the reader, quite unexpected manifestation of the shadow of the story's title, which is to say, the emergence from just below the surface of her consciousness of a projection and personification of aspects of her self (ego) that are usually suppressed by parental, religious, and societal pressures:

> She thought of the boy. The thought of him was never far from the surface of her mind, always wavering, like a shadow, over her consciousness. Girls like those were for him. Their long light limbs, and their soft mouths and the tender fullness of their cheeks were only for his pleasure. They smiled at him and followed him with their eyes; they waited for him and wanted him. One of those he would choose. (5)

The sexual electricity of this passage leaves little doubt that the part of her nature that Miss Abelhart has repressed is her libido, which Jung maintains "can never be apprehended except in definite form" in "fantasy-images" (*Two Essays* 215). Immediately after her eroticized and envious response to the three girls, such a "fantasy-image" emerges further from her unconscious, couched in italics to indicate the articulation of a hitherto unexpressed aspect of her psyche: "*But he does not look at them as he looks at me. They are young and common and willing* [. . .]" (5).

Sympathy for Miss Abelhart becomes tinged with misgiving when it emerges that the boy in question is in her upper-year Latin class (Latin being an appropriately moribund language for her to teach), and as her mental picture of him is placed on view:

> his dark hair was tumbled and . . . his long legs stretched carelessly across the aisle. Then, slowly he lifted his head and smiled, his brown eyes twinkling to hazel, and his mouth twisted up at one corner, so that he looked like a roguish, beautiful little boy . . . . His slim body was too frail and graceful, his untidy curls too picturesque, and his smile too charming, but he was beautiful. When she thought of him, Miss Abelhart felt a great tenderness and anguish. (5)

"Once Sunday had been a day for forgetting" about Latin class, but now it is "an empty day, stretching and yearning" towards "Monday, when the days of meaning and possibility beg[i]n again"—namely, seeing "the boy" in class, in Assembly, in the halls . . . watch[ing] her, and hid[ing] secret things under his words." Fearing for her sanity, she nevertheless "cross[es] the street, and st[ands] in front of the school," which "h[olds] the early darkness around it, becoming shadowy and indistinct." Both psychologically and atmospherically the conditions are now ripe for an apparition of the "shadow-side of . . . [her] personality," a "fantasy-image" of her "unrecognized desires" (Jung, *Two Essays* 25). "Everyone has a shadow," writes Jung in *Modern Psychology and Religion*,

> and the less it is embodied in the individual's conscious life, the blacker and denser it is . . . [I]f it is repressed and isolated from consciousness, it . . . is liable to burst forth in a moment of unawareness . . . . If it comes to a neurosis, we have invariably . . . a considerably intensified shadow. (93)

When the "fantasy-image" duly appears in the form of the boy in her Latin class and greets her with a "'Hello, Miss Abelhart'," she "trembl[es]" and, when he tells her that the school year about to end has been "'more important'" because of her, "a deep shiver passe[s] over her whole body, and she . . . [is] happy and afraid" (6). "He was here then; he was looking at her, and telling her and he was himself, not the restless, beloved shadow that ate the substance of her mind." As a manifestation of that shadow, the "fantasy-image" also resembles and aggregates other such boys whom she has known—"the boy at college," "the boy at home" (6), and, later, "'others'" (9). When the "fantasy-image" states that he has had a crush on her and admits that initially he could not understand why this happened since she is perhaps "'as old as . . . [his] mother'" and "'not pretty,'" she takes him to mean that she is "'sexless. Like a block of wood or a husk of corn'" and concedes that to eyes other than his she appears "Barren and sterile and useless" (6–7). "The things that had lain so darkly hidden," comments the narrator, "were given sound and shape and hung in the air" (7).

Miss Abelhart's concern with how she is perceived by other people remains a central focus of the dialogue, as the "fantasy-image" continues to wonder why he has a crush on a woman about whom everyone laughs. "Maybe it wasn't anything about me," she suggests before entering a heartfelt plea for affection on behalf of all women:

> Did you ever think that once in her life, a woman has a right to have someone look at her and not see anything about her, just her, herself? Every woman has a right, no matter how old or ugly she is. Someone should love her, even because she is ugly. (7)

Having voiced this appeal, she invites the "fantasy-image" to walk with her and to tell her about his crush. As they proceed, the "town clock str[ikes] nine," the hour of the crucifixion, an allusion that brings with it a sense of imminent suffering. As they pass under a street light, her "shadow . . . [is] black and solid and clearly drawn, but . . . [his is] long and misty, curving like smoke over the sidewalk and the grass." The crush began during the fall, he recalls, when she came to watch a rehearsal of *As You Like It*, in which he was playing Orlando (not fortuitously, of course, because in the play Orlando falls in love with Rosalind at first sight). Dressed in "*tights and a homemade green suit,*" she recalls, "*Young Orlando [was] . . . [t]all and gallant and lovely, moving like a wild young animal on a bit of a wooden stage . . . smiling and shaking the curls from [his] forehead*" (7–8). In stark contrast to this image of youthful masculinity is the accompanying evidence of her age and mortality: "*the sun went down outside and the smell of burning leaves came in through the window*" (8). From the time she came to watch the rehearsal, the "fantasy-image" continues, he became obsessed with her, waiting longingly for Latin class, leaving a book in her classroom so that he could return to fetch it, playing the piano in the "Wreck Room" during midday break for her rather than "*the girls with long legs and loud voices*" who were "*dancing*," and so on. "'I don't know how it can stop'," he wails in exasperation; "'I don't know what to do'." In response to this gratifying outburst Miss Abelhart feels a rush of tenderness that makes her want "to stroke his hair . . . and hold his head gently in her hands," an urge evocative of Mary Magdalene's response to the risen Christ. She does not touch him, however, but "stare[s] at him, fascinated almost unbelieving." "'It is you, isn't it?' she whisper[s], 'You are here?'" Convinced that he loves her as none of the "others" did, she coaxes an affirmation from him—a "'You—love me,'" "'Yes, yes I do'" that is resonantly Lawrencian in wording[4] and fully in accordance with her conviction that every woman has a "right" to be loved: "'A woman has to have something, even a husk of a woman like me. I always knew a woman had to have something, and now I have [. . .]'," she says, "'I never saw anyone's face look like that, for me [. . .]'" (9). With that, she breaks Christ's command to Mary Magdalene (*noli me tangere*), takes "his face in her hands," and after he has "twisted away from her," whispering, "'Don't look at me like that,'" their interaction ends:

> "I don't care if you forget," she [says]. "I don't care if I don't have anything for the rest of my life. Oh, you don't understand, do you?"
>
> He did not answer. He did not even turn his head.
>
> "You are so young," she [says] gently. Then, "Go home now. I'll go the rest of the way by myself."
>
> "Go home . . . . It's all right now. Goodbye." (9)

Without saying goodbye, the "fantasy-image" turns and moves away. "In a moment she . . . [cannot] see him at all. His body ha[s] faded into thin darkness."

Miss Abelhart's personal shadow has manifested itself, but it has not, as Jung urges, been integrated into her self. To adapt Jung's words in *Psychology and Religion*, she has not found "a way in which . . . [her] conscious personality and . . . [her] shadow can live together:" her "mere suppression of the shadow ["Go home . . ."] is just as little of a remedy as is beheading against headache" (93–94). Because of this failure, she remains incompletely individuated and in a mental state that is potentially pathological. As she walks toward her boarding house, she is "crying, and the close, sweet night presse[s] around her, making her weak and sick. The night . . . [is] full of poisonous fragrance and whirling, dissolving shadows, and she . . . [is] dizzy, very dizzy" (9–10). It remains to the three girls whom she encountered earlier to shatter her illusions and to precipitate her psychopathological breakdown: "'She thought she was talking to somebody . . . Jesus Christ!'"[5] exclaims one horrified girl in a blasphemous fulfillment of the Christological pattern of the story; "'She thought there was somebody right their beside her!'" (9–10). For Miss Abelhart there will be no psychological resurrection, only a mental crucifixion and a descent into psychic hell. In the purple passage with which "The Dimensions of a Shadow" ends, she

> stagger[s] once, and lean[s] against a lamp-post. She press[e]s her hands to her head and stare[s] into the outer night. The night . . . [is] black, the color of madness. The laughter of the girls r[ises] crazily and scream[s] about her ears, and then f[alls] away. Miss Abelhart . . . [is] alone in a bottomless silence (10).

"Story for Sunday"

"Story for Sunday" also focuses on the sexuality of its female protagonist, this time from a perspective that is Freudian rather than Jungian. When it opens, the fifteen-year-old Evelyn, whose age places her at puberty and whose name indicates both her innocence and her susceptibility to temptation, is hurrying toward what seems to be a Catholic or Anglican church,[6] where she hopes to be of assistance to the new Sunday-school superintendent, Mr. Willens. Despite her father's caustic comment that "only kids" go to Sunday school and it is time for her "to grow up" and her mother's condescending description of Willens as a clerk "down at the factory," she is determined to go because the "glow of . . . [a] secret tremble[s] inside her" (4). Some of the attitudes and behaviours that Anna Freud sees as characteristic of puberty in her highly readable and popular *The Ego and the Mechanisms of Defence* (1946)[7]—"defiant rebellion against any and every authority," "submission to some self-chosen leader," and religious "asceticism" (149, 167)—are already evident in the opening sentences of "Story for Sunday," and more will soon appear.[8]

Before the nature of her secret is revealed, Evelyn is characterized as both religiously susceptible and fanciful. To her, "The Church . . . [is] the only building in the village which . . . [is] not squat or ugly . . . the real place. The stores and the houses and the shabby room at home" where she had left her parents "d[o] not exist anymore, nor . . . the days of the week. There . . . [is] only the Church, and only Sunday" (4). As she opens the door to the church basement, "her whole body . . . [comes] alive in a new way and tingle[s] with faint excitement. Her thoughts . . . [are] a little dizzied, and for a moment it . . . [is] hard to realize that she . . . [is] here, and not living in a daydream" (5). Once inside the basement, she transforms it in her mind's eye into the body of the church:

> The room . . . [is] very dark after the sunlight. Only two small yellow lights . . . [are] lit; they burn . . . like candle flames, one on each side of the platform. Evelyn ma[kes] the platform an altar. The worn carpet with its dirty fern-leaves, the frayed velvet curtains become rich and mysterious, blood-crimson in the shadow. (5)

Looking around the room, she notes first a text behind the "tall pulpit chair" that reads "*Blessed are the pure in heart*," then "paintings with strangely misted landscapes and men and women in loose, vivid robes," and finally "the pure and passionless face of Christ, careless silken locks rounded by white radiance." The few readers who have not already guessed Evelyn's "secret" are now given a large clue: "Today when she look[s] at the pictures it . . . [is] not quite the same; even in the depths and stillness of the moment she remember[s] Mr. Willens." "Sometimes [during puberty] the individual becomes attached . . . to an older person, whom [s]he takes as . . . [her] leader," writes Freud in what could be a commentary on what is to come; "[w]hile they last, these love-relations are passionate and exclusive, but they are of short duration" (183).

As "other people" arrive in the church basement, Evelyn pays particular attention to the flamboyantly named Myrtle Fotheringay,[9] who "seat[s] herself at the piano" and begins to "play over the hymns" that will be sung in the service (5). With her "little plumed hat," her "dainty, fur-topped boots" (surely a Freudian symbol in the popular sense), and her "small, delicate female hands," Myrtle is "so consciously and completely a woman, so vividly feminine" that, "even looking at her," Evelyn "fe[els] herself to be a neutrality, a blob of nothing and everything, without shape or color." This sense of nonentity and formlessness quickly gives way, however, to a less abstract and more searching reflection on her physique and appearance that captures brilliantly the agonizing self-doubt of many girls (and boys) her age:

> She look[s] down at her own large hands, her feet big in clumsy galoshes. Her body . . . [is] too big, in every part, too boney, and uncertain of itself; all her movements . . . [are] too indecisive, constrained. Her hair ha[s] not curled right, either, and she kn[ows] that her cheeks and forehead . . . [are] heavily flushed, with all the freckles showing. She f[eels] dampened, and a little weary; she . . . [is] only a lumpish thing, after all, not in the littlest way like the self of her imaginings. (5)

That Mr. Willens would "even notice" the plain and gangling girl that she now recognizes herself to be strikes Evelyn as unbelievable, but "it had happened," the "it" here being, first, a reference to his noticing her and then, in the succeeding sentences, the vehicle for suggestions of something more physical and portentous: "She remember[s] it now, not with her senses, as she ha[s] remembered it all week, but with her mind. It was a real thing; it had *been*, and *here* last Sunday."

What "it" turns out to be occurred "upstairs" in a little room "beside the vestry" where Evelyn "had left her gloves" prior to the "lesson." On returning to retrieve them, she found Mr. Willens alone, "standing by . . . [a] table, and "sorting out Sunday-school papers" (5–6). "[H]e was very tall, silent and somehow liquid"—the last because he is a condenser for her romantic and religious ideals, part larger-than-life man and part sacred image: "His eyes were deeper, quieter than any eyes she had ever seen, his lips full and delicately-made, and tender. He was not handsome; his face in profile was somewhat flat, almost convex, not handsome at all, but beautiful" (6). A descendant of the highly imaginative and almost fatally romantic Anne of the early chapters of *Anne of Green Gables*,[10] Evelyn projects what she later calls "the love she had read about in stories" (7) onto Mr. Willens, but with a sexual inflection alien to Montgomery's heroine: when he handed her gloves—a traditional and subsequently Freudian symbol of the female—"she saw his hand touch them" and observed that "he touched everything with the suggestion of a caress, as if his fingers had some quick and magical sensitivity." But Mr. Willens is not the sensitive soul of Evelyn's romantic imaginings; rather, he is an adept manipulator and a sexual predator. When she entered the little room he greeted her with an exclamation ("'Evelyn!'"), gave her his undivided attention ("He considered her . . . with his head to one side"), and conveyed the impression that he had her best interests at heart ("'I was . . . keeping [your gloves] to give to you, in case you didn't remember'"). Later, "When he looked at her, his eyes caught hers and held them, drawing them into depth and darkness and unreadable meaning," which she, naive as she is, interprets as a secret love in the process of being revealed. Later still, he describes her as "'very thoughtful'," "'Always helpful'," and "'very faithful'." Feigned concern, shared knowledge, and extravagant flattery are core components of Satan's temptation of Eve in *Paradise Lost*, and they are no less central to Mr. Willens' seduction of Evelyn.

Near the beginning of the seduction scene, an echo of Molly Bloom's soliloquy at the end of *Ulysses* can be heard in Evelyn's response: "'Yes,' she had said breathlessly, feeling the blood beat into her face. 'Yes.'" But in the scene as a whole the loudest and most lasting echoes are of the relationship that develops between Mabel Pervin and Dr. Ferguson in "The Horse-Dealer's Daughter." In both short stories, preliminary eye contact is followed by a sexual laying-on of hands, and eventually, by a passionate kiss. A juxtaposition of passages describing the preliminaries to and the effects of the kiss will show their similarities. Here is Lawrence:

> he felt warm inside himself.... It was as if she had the life of his body in her hands..., clutching him with a strange, convulsive certainty.... He was amazed, bewildered, and afraid.... She lifted her face to him, and he bent forward and kissed her on the mouth, gently, with the one kiss that is an eternal pledge.... He never intended to love her. But now it was over. He had crossed over the gulf to her... (425–26)

And here is Laidlaw:

> He turned her gently to face him, drew her gently into his arms, then bent to kiss her and stroke her cheek with his long soft-tipped fingers.... She was empty of everything but the sweetness of sensation. She did not even wonder at what had happened; she was not yet amazed or bewildered. She had been held by him, kissed, drawn for a moment into a strange, exquisite intimacy; now there was nothing else. She could not understand yet, but he would come and take her again, and she must wait for him. (6)

Yet there is a crucial difference between the two stories: in "The Horse-Dealer's Daughter," there are inequalities of class and gender between Mabel and Dr. Ferguson, but they are both adults. In "Story for Sunday," by contrast, Mr. Willens is in a position of power over Evelyn by virtue of his age and his position, as well as his gender. His seduction of her is thus trebly repugnant, no more jarringly so than when, after kissing her, he mutters, "'You dear child. You dear, sweet child!'" Evelyn's "lofty" adolescent "view of love" (Freud 175) dictates that she experience his actions not as exploitative but as evidence that "the things of dreams" and "stories" are "true" (7). Since reality has obeyed the rules of romance, after Mr. Willens has left the room like a true romantic hero—"without looking back"—Evelyn knows exactly how the future will unfold and how she should behave; one cliché of romance is followed by another: "he would come and take her again, and she must wait for him" (6). The dark connotations of "take her again" are lost on Evelyn, but not on the reader.

When the narrative returns to the present, the Sunday-school service becomes an occasion for Evelyn to engage in erotic communion with the "slender young priest in a black robe" who is the object of her desire. As he "kneel[s]" by the lectern, Mr. Willens's

> compassionate, musical voice flow[s] out in rhythmic phrases. Evelyn shiver[s] to hear him .... He close[s] his eyes as he s[ings], and his voice c[an] be heard over all the rest, passionate and clear. She move[s] in a clear, cold flame of love. It d[oes] not matter that she ... [is] only fifteen, and clumsy and homely, because it ... [is] not the ordinary kind of love .... This ... [is] the secret kind, that ha[s] perhaps never been before, a kind no one else would believe or understand. (7)

Despite evidence to the contrary—Mr. Willens has not even looked at her this Sunday—"when the class ... [goes] downstairs" she resolves to "go and find him," using as an excuse to go upstairs to the little room off the vestry the fiction that she has again left her gloves there. Almost needless to say, as she approaches the room she hears her dialogue with Mr. Willens on the previous Sunday replicated almost exactly with Myrtle, complete with "a long sigh," the "rustle of a silk dress," and a glimpse of their embrace. Disbelief is followed by acceptance, romantic fantasy by harsh reality: "it *was* true," "he had kissed her last Sunday ... and now he was kissing Myrtle; He [sic] would kiss others too, many others. It was all quite meaningless. There was no secret, special love for her, no clear cold flame, nothing."

But the "flame" is not extinguished: "she loved him so much that she could have nothing else in her mind, her life [...]," and when she returns downstairs she finds herself with a "hymn-book open in her hand ... singing" with the others. "Mr. Willens had come down too, and his voice, as he sang, rang through ... [her] body like fever pounding in the blood. She trie[s] not to look at him, but even with her eyes held tight to the book, she c[an] see only him, black-robed and beautiful." Then, as she "s[ings] ... fervently" "'Thou O Christ, are all I want .... More than all in thee I find'" (Charles Wesley's "Jesus, Lover of My Soul"), she has an epiphany that begins with a burst of self-recrimination—"Now she underst[ands]. She ha[s] been wrong and stupid all the time"—that recalls the boy's epiphany at the conclusion of Joyce's "Araby,"[11] but then moves in a very different direction, ending with "Pure light that ... [is] the centre of a flame around the face of the immaculate Christ." To Thacker, Evelyn's shift from adolescent rapture to religious fervour" is "forced" and "neat" but "unlikely" (100), but it is not so much a "shift" as a sublation that entails both the transcendence and the preservation of her "adolescent rapture." It is also a textbook example of three of the defense mechanisms that Freud discusses: "sublimation"—"the displacement of . . . instinctual aim in conformity with higher social values," and the "intellectualization of instinctual life"—"the attempt to lay hold on the instinctual processes by connecting them with ideas which can be dealt with in consciousness" (56, 178). "She had imagined that . . . [Mr. Willens] could love her, only her, that he could make a circle around himself where only she could come" (8). Now, however, she not only accepts that "others must love him too," that "no one love could be enough for him," but also sees him as a type of Christ: he is "so much above them all, so large in soul and wisdom and spirit, his . . . love surround[s] every one whom he cho[oses], b[ears] them all away until they . . . [are] wholly lost in it. The thing that she ha[s] discovered was greater than a mean little private love, more strange and wonderful [. . .]." Not until the final mention of "the face of the immaculate Christ" is it clear that the "he" to whom Evelyn refers is other than Mr. Willens, as, indeed, he both is and is not: "She lift[s] her head as the music fell away, and she s[ees] him [not, note, Him] as if she were seeing him for the first time. All the people in the room, the velvet curtains and the emblazoned texts, blur . . . into a jumbled mosaic, and there . . . [is] only his white still face." In the "jumbled mosaic" of Evelyn's mind and perceptions "adolescent rapture" jostles with "religious fervour," puberty with adulthood.

"The Widower"

The third of Laidlaw's three stories, "The Widower," opens with a terse and flat statement—"Mr. McManus' wife was dead" (7)—that launches a gloomy tale of the protagonist's complex response to the loss of his wife. Unobtrusively placed among the expository statements that follow—"Ella Maria Gilbank" "died in January" of a "heart attack," she was "in her sixty-fourth year," "She left only her husband and one brother; there were no children"—is the first of several triplets—"in January . . . the days were all alike, bitter and soiled and cloudy"—that individually and collectively reflect the repetitiveness of Mr. MacManus's life and lend technical unity to the story.

When the story focuses exclusively on Mr. MacManus[12] himself, the reportorial tone of its opening paragraphs is abandoned for a masterful example of the free indirect style that vividly conveys his responses to the atmosphere and awkwardness of the visitation:

> Mr. MacManus was rather awed by the funeral parlours. The soft light seemed to come right out of the pink walls, the thick carpet hushed every footstep, and there was music playing all the time, behind [a]

> curtain or beyond a hidden door. Mr. MacManus felt clumsy and nervous, and he could hardly convince himself that the funeral was real. He did not understand the soft-footed, soft-voiced man in the black coat, who slid about arranging chairs, smiling a polite mournful smile; he did not like the rich, oily tones of the young preacher. People tiptoed in and spoke to him of how very sorry they were and it was nice of them, although, of course, they were not very sorry. There were wreaths of flowers with a sick, sweet, heavy smell; these were sent by ladies' clubs and customers of long standing. (7)

What might have been a sorrowful, even traumatic event is coloured by Mr. MacManus's detachment, cynicism and revulsion—attitudes whose origin and consequences are placed on view as the story unfolds.[13]

As it does so, the focus remains unremittingly on Mr. McManus, moving back and forth between the present and past, always with an emphasis on his relationship with his wife and, within that, on his perception of his marriage as claustrophobic, constraining, emasculating, loveless, and cluttered with the trappings of femininity. On returning home from the funeral, he goes into Ella's room—the "front room" above the grocery store that they own and run—and resolves to move, throw out, or put away several things in it that he had long disliked, such as "her geraniums" and a "painted silk screen" (7–8). Only with the realization that he is free to do as he wishes with his wife's possessions does "he beg[i]n to understand that . . . [she is] dead" (8). Put perhaps too simply, the remainder of the story is a revelation of why Ella's death has given her husband a sense of freedom and what he does with that freedom.

Already a curiously sympathetic and yet unsympathetic character, Mr. McManus quickly becomes more so. In the kitchen, having made himself "some bologna sandwiches and a cup of tea," "he is lonesome," not for Ella, but for her "good warm supper and her comfortable bickering talk," but "only for a little": "he had not time to be lonesome or sorry for Ella; he was curiously excited. It seem[s] to him that some kind of change ha[s] come, a free, lonely, happy life . . . [is] about to begin for him" (8). "[H]astily," as if attempting to curtail his inappropriate thoughts, he recalls that "he and Ella . . . had been as happy as most people," but then allows his toxic bitterness over the Jamesian failure to live that was his marriage to emerge full-blown: "she had clung to him and twisted around him, and filled up his life for him. A woman was like that when she didn't have any children." Casting his mind back to "the secret guilty happiness" that he felt on "the rare evenings when Ella had gone out to Mission Circle"[14] he resolves to relive those times when he was able to sit alone in the front room enjoying the streetscape, drinking "a little glass of wine" or playing "for a while on his violin," a pastime preferable to going over his account books. As Ella had repeatedly and condescendingly said, "he was not much of a businessman . . . only a puttering small-store grocer." For a time, his plan works; he would even occasionally have "some friends up to sit and talk, but mostly he would be alone."

Despite his desire for a "free, lonely, happy life," he is haunted by Ella: "he wander[s] about the small rooms, so faintly, mustily scented" with her; he is unable to dispose of her geraniums; he puts her "painted silk screen" back where it was. Kindly women bring gifts of food to the store and speak "comfortingly" to him, but cynically he suspects them of "gloating" and imagines that they are thinking, "*How lost he is, poor man, he's just lost without his wife*" (8–9). Nor are they wrong. His grocery business deteriorates because Ella is no longer there to drive hard bargains and to ensure competitive prices, but, "without Ella to prod him, he . . . [does] not much care" (9). He has lost momentum, and inertia has set in. Earlier he had "wandered about" his apartment; now he becomes "puzzled," "bewildered," and "confused": "nothing . . . [is] working out as expected: Ella was gone . . . but there . . . [is] not much change in his life." He has "the feeling of something missed—perhaps lost"—and hopes that with "spring" there will be a "difference." "There had never been a difference before, but then Ella had been there, shutting off spring and summer and the bigger world," leaving "Only the store, the rooms upstairs, the proper walking to church [. . .]." Two parallel triplets here mirror the haunting exclusions and repetitions of his claustrophobic life of quiet desperation with Ella, and his thoughts trail off in a Joycean ellipsis of incomplete comprehension and articulation.

"On a Sunday afternoon, a fine afternoon in April" (the traditional month of renewal and rejuvenation), he sets off for a walk "in the direction of a park . . . nearer the outskirts of the city," noticing as he goes promising signs of new life and approaching summer: "birds singing in backyard apple trees," "patches of front lawns . . . coming green," "sky . . . blue as in summertime," "little girls in new bright-coloured coats" who look "scrubbed and tidy and good." Happily anticipating "the openness [and] the early greenness" of the park, he sits down on a bench just inside its gate" where he can see "right across it." There a tide of remembrance washes over him, bringing with it the memories and the feelings that will lead to his epiphany.

On a Sunday "very like this one" during the "year after he was married," when Ella was "petty and miserable" as a result of being pregnant with the baby that she would lose, he had walked to the park, and "circl[ed]" it in a "mood of . . . longing" and "tightened, helpless anger" (10). "His old instinct for contact with his surroundings" had come "gradually back to him. He could look at the clouds over the grimy city roofs . . . . He was alone again, an outside person floating in the world." As these involuntary memories of freedom and weightlessness take Mr. McManus's younger self back to his boyhood on a farm, they take the old man with them so that the distinctions between the present, the past, and the distant past are no longer clear: as the young man recalled his boyhood on a farm, where in "the long fields" he had "great dreams" of being "free and somehow splendid" that would "be made true in his life," so too does the old man. "Today" then and now, "the fine childish dreams excited"—and excite—"him again." "[H]e would go away; he would travel to "tall cities" and "to countries across the sea; he would learn to play the violin as he wanted to play; he would buy a farm . . . ; he would work hard again with his body, in the fields, in the hot sun [. . .]." None of these dreams ever "came true," of course "because he had wanted to marry Ella, and Ella's father had a store . . . . He had thought she was worth throwing out all the boy's dreaming . . . , worth the grocery store, and the stuffy rooms upstairs, church every Sunday, and dinner with her parents." Like Gabriel circling his galoshes in Joyce's "The Dead," "the young man walked around and around the park," a repetition reinforced by the stylistic repetitions that surround it: he knew that "he had to be home for supper at five, had to talk to Ella and go to Service with her in the evening," knew that "Ella would always be there, all the time. Then in a wild, baffled, angry moment, he thought that he would give anything, half the years of his life, to be free" (11).

The flashback is cathartic, for as evening descends and Mr. MacManus finds himself "getting cold," he is "actually looking forward to the hot little living-room." After feeling a muted and self-centred sense of regret at Ella's absence ("He . . . [is] sorry, in a way, that . . . [s]he would not be there to get him his supper, talk to him and keep him company"), he starts for home, and resigns himself to the fact that "nothing . . . [is] going to change in his life; it . . . [is] much too late for that." The "free, lonely, happy life" that he had imagined would come with release from Ella would not be "made true," so she "might as well not be dead; it would be better, more comfortable." As the sun disappears, the shadows lengthen and intensify the cold, and he is "still thinking" and "wondering" about "the young man and the afternoon of the young man in the park." "[N]ear home, he . . . [sees] the stealthy movement of a neighbourhood woman's curtain. *He's going home,* she would say to her husband. *He just sits at home all by himself, he's that lost without his wife.*" What the woman cannot know but the reader does is that he was as lost with Ella as he is without her.

* * *

Viewed as an ensemble, "The Dimensions of a Shadow," "Story for Sunday," and "The Widower" contain several elements and commonalities that resonate between and among them and set them apart somewhat from Munro's later work, even as they anticipate it. None of these are more evident than in the stories' descriptions of the structures and patterns of urban space and the components and characteristics of domestic space. Houses, stores, and streets are described in all three stories, sometimes with an accuracy suggestive of photography. On and behind the drawn "green blinds" of "The Widower" are "bright stickers advertising Salada Tea, and Coca Cola," "pyramids of tin cans [and] pyramids of oranges and apples" (7). At the park, Mr. McManus notices its "gravel walks laid out in a pattern" and recalls how his younger self could see the clouds "over the grimy city roofs, [and] the crazy jumbled lines of chimneys and alley fences" (10). In the "long, crooked street" along which Evelyn walks in "Story for Sunday," the "Locked and shuttered stores" seem to her to have "foolish metal signs" and an "odd look," a "queer air of stiffness and isolation" (4). Near the beginning of "The Dimensions of a Shadow," Miss Abelhart notices that the "sidewalk . . . is divided into squares, and the squares make a block, small and tight, and the blocks make a tidy pattern" and imagines that the "town is a pattern, hidden in the dark"—a pattern that, as she slips into madness, "disappears, leaving only the empty broken country, pathless in the dark" (5, 8). The interior spaces of the stories are almost invariably cluttered, shielded by lace curtains, and "stuffy," "musty" ("Story for Sunday" 4, 5), or "mustily scented" ("The Widower" 8). Indeed, scents appear in all three stories, as does Sunday, either as a day of anticipation ("The Dimensions of a Shadow," "Story for Sunday") or as a day of excursion ("Dimensions of a Shadow," "The Widower"). It is as if the Church-dominated streets, rhythms, and people of Joyce's Dublin have been transplanted, adapted, and given a local habitation but, note, not a name: none of the urban areas in any of the stories is identified and no mention is made of their geographical locations, though it is surely Ontario in the era of the Lord's Day Act.

The three stories also have in common a multifaceted indebtedness to modernism, especially, as seen here at several points, to the short stories of Joyce and Lawrence. In addition to being epiphanic in their trajectories, all three are formalistically tight and graced by motivated details and suggestive nuances; and all three focus centrally on the psychological interiors of their protagonists, all of whom are mentally disturbed and harbour thoughts that manifestly come from somewhere other than the conscious mind and, to a greater or lesser degree, elude the protagonist's capacity for understanding and articulation. Moreover, all three stories focus on feelings and relationships that do not accord with middle-class mores and expectations—a high-school teacher's attraction to one of her male pupils, a Sunday-school superintendent's sexual overtures to young girls in his charge, a widower's failure to mourn the death of his spouse of many years. "The Widower" does not display the interest in Jung and Freud that is programmatically present in "The Dimensions of a Shadow" and "Story for Sunday" but, as observed at the outset, the development and themes of all three stories reflect the growing interest in Canada from the 1930s onwards in such concepts as repression, sublimation, paranoia, infantile regression, and, more generally, psychological mechanisms and structures. In sum, the three short stores of Alice Laidlaw reveal a writer in the process of finding the themes, absorbing the ideas, and developing the techniques that would emerge fully assimilated in the work of Alice Munro, the consummate physical and psychological realist of southwestern Ontario[15]—the region that now belongs as indisputably to her as Wessex does to Thomas Hardy.

Notes

1. See Thacker's "'Clear Jelly'" (37–39) for details of Laidlaw's time at Western and, for commentaries on the three short stories, his magisterial *Alice Munro* (93–100).
2. Munro appears to have taken a course in psychology, which became a separate department at Western in 1948. Unfortunately, there is no record of what was taught and by whom in the psychology department's introductory course in 1949/50, but, in 1948, in the fledgling *Canadian Journal of Psychology*, the head of the department, R. B. Liddy, published "The Teaching of Psychology at Canadian Universities," an article presenting the results of a survey sent to fifteen English-Canadian institutions. The survey posed the question: "What are your chief aims in teaching undergraduate psychology?" Liddy summarized the survey results as follows: "Our chief aim . . . should be to make the student curious about human nature, to

create an awareness of the complexity and importance of human relations, to train him to adopt an objective attitude to himself and to others, to increase self-knowledge and healthful personal adjustment, to eradicate superstitious beliefs about things psychological, to provide as adequate a background as possible for further psychological study" (110). A year earlier, in the same journal, Liddy and his colleague in psychology at Western, Leola E. Neal, published "The First Course in Psychology at Canadian Universities," which examined the question: "In your opinion what should be the instructor's chief objective in the teaching of introductory psychology in Arts Classes?" They summarized the responses as follows: "(1) To understand what psychology is; (2) To develop a sound point of view toward the study of human affairs; (3) To lay the basis for further study; (4) To show the pertinence of valid psychological knowledge to everyday *practical affairs*" (64). According to the same survey, the most commonly used textbooks in introductory psychology courses in Canada were Norman Leslie Munn's *Psychology: The Fundamentals of Human Adjustment* (1946) and Robert Sessions Woodworth's *Psychology* (1949) (four departments each), and John Frederick Dashiell's *Fundamentals of General Psychology* (1949) (three departments). All of these books refer to a greater or lesser extent to Freud and Jung. A probable reflection of the teaching of psychology at Western is to be found in *Personality and Its Deviations: An Introduction to Abnormal and Medical Psychology* (1947, 1950), by Neal and George H. Stevenson, a professor of psychiatry at the university. Of course, Munro may well have encountered the ideas of Freud and Jung outside the classroom; indeed, in an interview with J. R. (Tim) Struthers that was published in 1983, she states that she "did not discover anything [i.e., new books] through . . . [her] courses": "I worked in the library, and I stumbled on books . . . [T]he most important work I did . . . was reading in the library" (8).

3. Ellipses in the short stories that are indicative of incomplete or inconsequential thoughts (a device perhaps gleaned from *Dubliners*) are placed in square brackets throughout the present essay. In her interview with Struthers, Munro responds to a question about the influence of *Dubliners* on her *Dance of the Happy Shades*: "I don't like *Dubliners* as much as I admire it. I've read 'The Dead'"—which contains numerous such ellipses—"a couple of times . . . I'm always unconscious of influences, though. I read for pleasure, really for intoxication" (36).

4. See the declaration of mutual love between Mabel Pervin and Jack Ferguson in "The Horse-Dealer's Daughter": "'You love me?'" she said, rather falteringly. "'Yes.'" The word cost him a painful effort . . . "'I love you! I love you!'" (425–26).

5. Thacker records that this blasphemy was "hurtful to female members of her and her future husband's family," but her father "understood why she had used the expression" (99).

6. The church has "carved wooden doors and stained glass in the windows" and Mr. Willens later wears a "black robe" (4, 7); however, the hymn sung toward the end of the story—"Jesus, Lover of My Soul"—was written by Charles Wesley and is included in Methodist and United Church as well as Anglican and Catholic hymnals.
7. By 1950 Cecil Baines's translation of *The Ego and the Mechanisms of Defence* was in its third printing.
8. It may not be fortuitous that one of the cases discussed by Ana Freud in her chapter entitled "Instinctual Anxiety during Puberty" is of a "fifteen-year-old girl" who fell "violently in love . . . with a boy rather older than herself" (186).
9. Perhaps the name is a droll indication of her destructive attractiveness: in classical mythology, myrtle is a shrub or bush sacred to Aphrodite, and Fotheringay, which is pronounced "fungee," is the castle in which Mary Queen of Scots was executed.
10. In her interview with Struthers, Munro mentions *Anne of Green Gables*, but expresses a strong preference for Montgomery's "Emily books," especially *Emily of New Moon*, commenting: "It's close, in a lot of places, to being the book she should have written—in spite of having to follow certain conventions of what an entertaining novel should be and also certain conventions of all the things that you can't mention. In many ways there's great psychological truth in it, and it's also a very powerful book" (18).
11. See Thacker's "'Clear Jelly'" for Munro's comments about "Araby" in an interview with Jill Gardiner.
12. The name McManus—man + us—and the absence of an individualizing first or Christian name suggests that in the banality of his quotidian life and the narrowness of his emotional range he is to be seen as a modern, middle-class everyman figure. That his wife's name, Ella, means "all" accords with the fact that she is stiflingly all in all to him.
13. The temptation to read "The Widower" through the lens of Sigmund Freud's "Mourning and Melancholia" was resisted because neither mourning nor a developed sense of melancholia is important to the development of the story, which focuses, rather, on old-age sadness and powerlessness, and, unlike "The Dimensions of a Shadow" and "Story for Sunday," contains (for this reader at least) no clear gestures toward psychoanalytical theory.
14. Many Presbyterian churches had a women's circle dedicated to supporting the Women's Missionary Society of the Presbyterian Church of Canada.
15. Since Carl F. Klinck was the "Staff Advisor" for *Folio* during the period when all three of Laidlaw's short stories appeared there, it is worth wondering whether he had any part in steering her toward the realism

that is increasingly apparent in the three stories and, of course, a hallmark of Munro's work. Klinck was a great admirer of Robert E. Spiller, whose monumental and enormously influential *Literary History of the United States* was first published in 1948. Not only do Spiller's volumes contain extensive commentaries on the romance-versus-realism debate of the previous century, but they also provide introductions and bibliographies for such twentieth-century writers as William Faulkner and Ernest Hemingway. (Klinck's *Literary History of Canada* [1965] bears the deep imprint of Spiller's *Literary History*, as, of course, does Richard Chase's *The American Novel and Its Tradition* [1957].) "Klinck often mentioned Spiller in my class [in 1959–60]," recalls D. S. Hair, "and I think he would have done so even more frequently when Spiller's work was 'cutting edge'."

Works Cited

Freud, Anna. *The Ego and the Mechanisms of Defence.* Trans. Cecil Baines. 1946. New York: International Universities P, 1965.

Hair, D. S. E-mail to author. 21 July 2013.

Joyce, James. *Dubliners.* Ed. Hans Walter Gabler and Walter Hettche. New York: Garland, 1993.

———. *Ulysses.* Ed. Danis Rose. London: Picador, 1997.

Jung, C. G. *Psychology and Religion.* New Haven and London: Yale UP, 1938.

———. *Two Essays on Analytical Psychology.* Vol. 7. *Collected Works.* Ed. Sir Herbert Read, Michael Fordham, and Gerhard Adler. Trans. R. F. C. Hill. Bollingen Series XX. 1953. 2nd ed. New York: Pantheon, 1966.

Laidlaw, Alice. "The Dimensions of a Shadow." *Folio* [London, ON] 4.2 (April 1950): [4–10].

———. "Story for Sunday." *Folio* [London, ON] 5.1 (December 1950): [4–8].

———. "The Widower." *Folio* [London, ON] 5.2 (April 1951): [7–11].

Lawrence, D. H. *Collected Short Stories.* London: Heinemann, 1974.

Liddy, R. B. "The Teaching of Psychology in Canadian Universities." *Canadian Journal of Psychology* 2.3 (September 1948): 104–11.

Liddy, R. B., and Leola E. Neal. "The First Course in Psychology in Canadian Universities." *Canadian Journal of Psychology* 1.2 (1947): 61–66.

Stevenson, Geoge H., and Leola E. Neal. *Personality and Its Deviations: An Introduction to Abnormal and Medical Psychology.* 1947. Toronto: Ryerson P; Springfield, IL: Charles C. Thomas, 1950.

Struthers, J. R. (Tim). "The Real Material: An Interview with Alice Munro." *Probable Fictions: Alice Munro's Narrative Acts.* Ed. Louis K. MacKendrick. Downsview, ON: ECW, 1983. 5–36.

Thacker, Robert. *Alice Munro: Writing Her Lives: A Biography.* McClelland & Stewart, 2005.

———. "'Clear Jelly': Alice Munro's Narrative Dialectics." *Probable Fictions: Alice Munro's Narrative Acts.* Ed. Louis K. MacKendrick. Downsview, ON: ECW, 1983. 37–60

Momentous Shifts and Unimagined Changes in "Jakarta"

TRACY WARE

People make momentous shifts, but not the changes they imagine.
—Georgia, "Differently"

According to Jonathan Franzen, "What makes Munro's growth as an artist so crisply and breathtakingly visible . . . is precisely the familiarity of her materials. Look what she can do with nothing but her own small story; the more she returns to it, the more she finds" ("Alice's"). Such critics as Ildikó de Papp Carrington, Dennis Duffy, and Catherine Sheldrick Ross were quick to recognize that process at work in the title story of *The Love of a Good Woman* (1998), which not only returns to the Maitland River that runs through Munro's early work, with its spring floods and occasional drownings (Carrington, "'Don't'" 159), but also reworks "Images" (1968) in surprising detail (Duffy 172). Ross argues that

> Previous experience with earlier Munro stories, where the patterns are clearer, provides a sort of scaffolding helpful in making sense of these [later] works. In the stories in this collection, I found myself digging down through layers and following threads backward through to earlier handlings of the same material. Underneath a reading of the current story are the contours of previous readings of earlier stories, in which some of the same material is handled but with variations. (786)

In addition to "Cortes Island," which in Ross's words "seems to have swallowed up 'The Office' [1962] as just one element among many (786)," "The Children Stay" reworks the theme of adulterous desire in "White Dump" (1986) and elsewhere, while "My Mother's Dream" provides a comic version of Munro's most obsessive subject, the relations between mothers and daughters, and atones for her earlier avoidance of what she calls the "great drama" of childbirth (Hancock 216). In this paper, I read "Jakarta" as a revision of "Mischief" from *Who Do You Think You Are?* (1978)[1]. Munro's return to familiar concerns is not at first clear because of the unusual structure of "Jakarta": its two protagonists alternate the focalization over two times and settings, West Vancouver around 1960 and the Oregon coast more than three decades later. As Isla Duncan writes of "Lichen," such "shifting focalization lays bare the chasm in understanding that each character has of the other" (48). Munro might have learned the technique from Katherine Mansfield, for whom she has often expressed her admiration,[2] while the subject of "Jakarta," the struggle of the sexes as evident in the relations between two couples, resembles D. H. Lawrence's in *Women in Love*. Munro's debts to her great predecessors make "Jakarta" sound late modernist (Wilde 120–21), but it adds something not to be found in either Mansfield or Lawrence: a detailed discussion of their work.

"Jakarta" begins with Kath and Sonje taking shelter from "the Monicas," a group of young mothers who are memorably but cruelly associated with what the heroine of *The Bell Jar* calls "the whole sprawling paraphernalia of suburban childhood" (Plath 122). Revising a similar passage in "Oranges and Apples" (1988),[3] Munro describes these mothers in devastating detail:

> The Monicas' encampment is made up of beach umbrellas, towels, diaper bags, picnic hampers, inflatable rafts and whales, toys, lotions, extra clothing, sun hats, thermos bottles of coffee, paper cups and plates, and thermos tubs in which they carry homemade fruit-juice Popsicles. (79)

Although Monica herself is always considerate of others in her several appearances, Kath and Sonje recoil from the collective activities of the women who have "reached a stage in life that Kath and Sonje dread. They turn the whole beach into a platform. Their burdens, their strung-out progeny and maternal poundage, their authority, can annihilate the bright water . . ." (80). As a new mother herself, Kath "feels their threat particularly," and so "When she nurses her baby she often reads a book, sometimes smokes a cigarette, so as not to sink into a sludge of animal function" (80). That reaction suggests what Elaine Showalter calls, in a discussion of Sylvia Plath, matrophobia: "Hating one's mother was the feminist enlightenment of the fifties and sixties; but it is only a metaphor for hating oneself" (135).[4]

We know nothing about Kath's mother, and little about her past, though Kent recalls that "They all scorned their parents then, for something" (87). But Kath's problem is shared with Plath and other women of her generation who had excelled at school only to find that they were expected to conform to traditional expectations. As Wini Breines writes in *Young, White, and Miserable: Growing Up Female in the Fifties*, "Women had more options than ever before but were discouraged from acting on them . . ." (41). Kath's ability to quote Matthew Arnold suggests some academic education, and she is clearly intelligent, curious, and well read, all of which make her deeply conflicted about marriage and maternity. The tension between intellectual interests and motherhood emerges when she uses the metaphor of examinations to express her sense of an identity that is starting to become stifling:

> It seemed to her that life went on, after you finished school, as a series of further examinations to be passed. The first one was getting married. If you hadn't done that by the time you were twenty-five, that examination had to all intents and purposes been failed. . . . Then you thought about having the first baby. Waiting a year before you got pregnant was a good idea. Waiting two years was a little more prudent than was necessary. And three years started people wondering. Then down the road somewhere was the second baby. After that the progression got dimmer and it was hard to be sure just when you had arrived at wherever it was you were going. (82–83)

Kath's thoughts reflect what Breines calls "the real confusion about gender that defines the period: boys and girls were formally treated as equals in the midst of a tendency toward increased differentiation of their future roles" (34). Marriage is an examination that only women sit, and passing means acquiring a new name. Until now, Kath has internalized these values to such an extent that she signs herself "'Mrs. Kent Mayberry' with a sense of relief and mild elation" (82); later, that name will have become oppressive if not intolerable.

Even in this early passage, Kath's understanding gets "dimmer" when she looks to the future, and her examination metaphor suggests the difficulties that many women faced in coordinating their lives before and after graduation. As Breines notes, the women in the Radcliffe class of 1952 (almost exactly Munro's contemporaries) addressed similar problems when they issued a critical report twenty-five years later, stating that they graduated with "misgivings, lack of confidence, uncertainty and without goals" (193).[5] And as Michael Gorra writes in a perceptive review, Munro's interest in these issues makes "Jakarta" central to a volume in which most of the stories "look back to the years around 1960. Read together, they so reinforce one another as to amount to nothing less than the portrait of a generation: a generation that came to adulthood with one set of rules and then found it could live with another; a generation of women through whom the great turn of our times first quickened into life" ("Crossing").

Munro understands these problems, but her distance from feminist politics is implicit in her depiction of "the Monicas" and the West Vancouver setting. Those suburbs, she explained in 1994, were "much more narrow and crushing than the culture I grew up in. So many things were forbidden—like taking anything seriously." For the most part, she found the women as oppressive as the men: "the men didn't like you to talk, and the women didn't like it either. So the world you had was female talk about the best kind of diet, or the best care of woolies. I was with the wives of the climbing men. I hated it so much I've never been able to write about it" (interview with McCulloch and Simpson 252). She found relief in her friendship with Daphne Cue (Thacker 128–29; Sheila Munro 75–80): as she told Beverley Rasporich, "I had a very good friend in West Vancouver and we used to spend every Tuesday afternoon together, drinking coffee and smoking until we were dizzy. . . . We read all the books by and about D. H. Lawrence, Katherine Mansfield, the Bloomsbury group, and then we'd get together and we'd talk with incredible excitement" (Rasporich 9).

Kath's friendship with Sonje involves similar literary interests. Sonje's husband, Cottar, is a radical journalist, but he is more of a domestic tyrant than Kent: whereas Kath is free to read what she likes, Cottar selects his wife's books, and he "liked Sonje to go without a brassiere, as well as without stockings or lipstick" (98). Such domination may "have something to do with Marxism" (98), as Kath thinks, but it has more to do with sexism, which Munro is too subtle to identify with conservatism. As Breines writes, and as many women discovered in the sixties, "Nonconformity was articulated within traditional gender forms; these were the last to fall even in deviant subcultures" (144). And the subculture of Cottar and his friends is certainly what sociologists would then have called deviant: when Cottar and Sonje lived with another couple, "there had been an orderly exchange of sexual partners. The older man had an outside mistress and she was in on the exchange part of the time" (96). This bohemian lifestyle attracts Kath, but the very word "mistress" alerts us to the difference between "deviant" and "progressive." Cottar selects his wife's partners as well as her reading, and he is disappointed when she fails to experience "sexual release" (97). So Sonje is at least as restricted as Kath, and both "pretty well stayed out of the conversation" (90) when Kent gets into an argument with Cottar and others. As in "Miles City, Montana," the wives have to endure the discussions in silence. It's not that they have strong views on the Cold War, but that no one is interested in their opinions.

Kath met Sonje before she had her child, a time that she now associates with "freedom" (81). Both worked at the Vancouver Public Library, though their mobility is soon curtailed: "Kath had quit in the sixth month of pregnancy as you were required to do, lest the sight of you should disturb the patrons, and Sonje had quit because of a scandal" involving Cottar's travel to China (81–82). As their friendship develops after they leave their jobs, they discuss books: Kath is reading Mansfield and Lawrence, and Sonje "has got into the habit of putting down her own book and picking up whichever book of Kath's that Kath is not reading at the moment. She limits herself to one story and then goes back to Howard Fast" (80–81), the politically correct writer whom her husband has decided she must read, "if she has to read fiction" (80).[6] The first story discussed is Mansfield's "At the Bay," and both prefer Jonathan Trout to Stanley Burnell: "He is such a boy, with his pushy love, his greed at the table, his self-satisfaction" (83). Mansfield's story supports their observations, though Linda Burnell's appreciation of Jonathan's wit is balanced by a recognition of his fecklessness (Mansfield (273–75), and Kath is secretly troubled, though "She can't mention it or think about it. Is Kent something like Stanley?" (83). Because of Kath's unspoken anxiety, the two women have "an unexpected and disturbing argument" about Lawrence's "The Fox," which ends as Kath describes it, with the narrator's remarks on March's need to submerge her identity in her husband's: "Like the reeds that wave below the surface of the water. . . . And that is how her female nature must live within his male nature. Then she will be happy and he will be strong and content. Then they will have achieved a true marriage" (84).

Calling the idea "stupid," Kath asks how Nellie March could submerge her mind if she had to look after a child, then moves from the story to the author, arguing that Lawrence was "jealous" of Frieda's children. Sonje is more taken with "The Fox" than with her friend's commentary, and

> Kath knows that something has gone wrong. . . . Why is she so angry and excited? And why did she shift over to talking about babies, about children? Because she has a baby and Sonje doesn't? Did she say that about Lawrence and Frieda because she suspects that it is partly the same story with Cottar and Sonje? (85)

Kath might have argued that the concept of marriage is not the only problem in "The Fox." March is caught between her lover and her friend, an issue decided when Henry fells a tree and kills Jill Banford: "She would never leave him again. He had won her. And he knew it and was glad, because he wanted her for his life" (66). Soon March is also "glad Jill was dead" (68). The story, one of three "novelettes" that Lawrence published in 1923 (Mehl xix), offers much for discussion, but Kath knows "that she is covering up. She can't stand that part about the reeds and the water, she feels bloated and suffocated with incoherent protest. So it is herself she is thinking of, not of any children. She herself is the very woman that Lawrence is railing about" (85). She conceals her feelings because "she didn't want Sonje to think that she was a woman who had missed out on love. Who had not considered, who had not been offered, the prostration of love" (86).[7] Like Rose in "Mischief," Isabel in "White Dump," and Pauline in "The Children Stay," Kath imagines love as a contrast with what Munro calls the "predictability" of her marriage; as she told Eleanor Wachtel, such characters "want more," and so they nurture "rather girlish hopes of finding love, finding excitement" that they do not "altogether regret" when things do not work out as they hoped (interview, CBC Radio).

In "Mischief," Rose bonds with Jocelyn at the maternity ward of the North Vancouver General Hospital when they discover their mutual love of literature and their shared exasperation with a woman who could be one of "the Monicas" in her incessant talk of cupboards and vacuum cleaner attachments. Later Rose "fell in love with" Jocelyn's husband at a party in the same area of West Vancouver in which "Jakarta" is set, a place of "summer cottages, haphazardly winterized" ("Mischief" 105). The key scene occurs when Rose hears an argument in an adjacent room:

> Rose recognized [her husband] Patrick's voice, soaring over and subduing everyone else's. She opened her mouth to say something, anything, to cover him up—she knew some disaster was on the way—but just then a tall, curly-haired, elated-looking man came through the hall . . . holding up his hands for attention.
>
> "Listen to this," he said to the whole kitchen. "There's this guy in the living room you wouldn't believe him. Listen."

> There must have been a conversation about Indians going on in the living room. Now Patrick had taken it over.
>
> "Take them away," said Patrick. "Take them away from their parents as soon as they're born and put them in a civilized environment and educate them and they will turn out just as good as whites any day." No doubt he thought he was expressing liberal views. If they thought this was amazing, they should have got him on the execution of the Rosenbergs or the trial of Alger Hiss or the necessity for nuclear testing. (114–15)

It is not just hindsight that undermines Rose's emphasis: there is nothing remarkable in Patrick's stance on the Rosenbergs, Hiss, and nuclear testing, for those views would have been almost obligatory for a supporter of the right-wing Social Credit party that governed British Columbia from 1952 to 1972. It is only because the artists and academics at the party are defiantly unconventional that the "elated-looking man" exclaims, "This has got to be a Socred politician" (115). What is remarkable is the virulent racism of Patrick's remarks on Aboriginal peoples and, even more, his delusion that "he was expressing liberal views." It was not liberal even then to argue, as Patrick does, that they "have to be dragged kicking and screaming into the twentieth century" (115). Although Rose approached the party with "no idea that her life was about to be altered" (105), a momentous change occurs when she reacts to her husband's speech by stepping outside and kissing Jocelyn's husband Clifford: "She wanted tricks, a glittering secret, tender celebrations of lust, a regular conflagration of adultery. All this after five minutes in the rain" (120). Though her attempted tryst in Powell River is not successful, Rose tells Patrick "that she had 'had an affair' with Clifford, and by the telling gave herself a dim secondhand sort of comfort, which was pierced, presently, but not really destroyed, by Patrick's look and silence" (139). She has not committed adultery, but her story has the desired effect of ending her marriage.

Something similar happens to Kath at a dinner party in "Jakarta." The incident is told twice, first from Kent's perspective more than thirty years later and then from Kath's more immediate perspective. In contrast to the external and one-dimensional representation of Patrick, the scene in "Jakarta" enables the reader to understand why Kent is uncomfortable with everything about this occasion, and so it is harder to take sides. As Munro said in 1986, "I want things to come in as many layers as possible, which means the stories have to come from as many people as possible, with their different baggage of memories" (Macfarlane 54).

Whereas "most of the men" at Jocelyn's party are dressed like Patrick (112), Kent soon realizes that his "shirt and tie were wrong" (91), and "he felt the hostility, the judgment, in the room. Just as you'd feel in a room full of gospel tracts and pictures of Jesus on a donkey, Jesus on the Sea of Galilee, a judgment passed down on you" (91). Although he "didn't know what propelled him" (92), he cannot resist defending the values that the other guests attack, and he is probably right that he has been set up: a group that regards a newspaper as a "[t]ool of the capitalist classes" (91) is unlikely to appreciate Kent's work as a pharmacist for a chain drugstore, and "Are you on the management track?" (92) is indeed a question that "suggested the others would see this as a joke but Kent wouldn't" (92). When an argument erupts, Kent is not like Patrick in arrogantly starting a political debate; instead he stands alone in defending the conventional values of the Cold War:

> Kent took it upon himself to defend capitalism, the Korean War, nuclear weapons, John Foster Dulles, the execution of the Rosenbergs—whatever the others threw at him. He scoffed at the idea that American companies were persuading African mothers to buy formula and not to nurse their babies, and that the Royal Canadian Mounted Police were behaving brutally to Indians, and above all at the notion that Cottar's phone might be tapped. He quoted *Time* magazine and announced that he was doing so. (92)

Unlike Patrick, Kent makes no pretense of "expressing liberal views:" he knows that his values derive from the North American capitalism that he admires: "That was the real world and he went out into it every day with the weight of his future and Kath's on his shoulders. He accepted that, he was even proud of it, he was not going to apologize to a roomful of groaners" (93). Some of his views seem troubling in retrospect, but he certainly has the courage of his convictions, and there is a big difference between Patrick's gratuitous racism and Kent's trust, however misplaced, in North American authorities. In both stories, a wife is caught between her sympathies with her husband and her growing affinities for her bohemian friends, and her position is rendered excruciating by an observer's surprise that anyone could hold the positions that their husbands defend: "I can't believe this guy," says a younger man in Kent's presence, "Can you believe this guy? I can't" (92). Kent does not "disagree with his younger self even now," but he "wondered about the anger in that room, all the bruising energy" (93).

Their responses to this incident reveal the growing gaps between Kent and Kath. She thinks that the others

> tied Kent up in knots and he didn't even realize it. . . . Cottar spoke with the worn patience of a teacher to a pupil. The older man was bitterly amused, and the woman was full of moral repugnance, as if she held Kent personally responsible for Hiroshima, Asian girls burned to death in locked factories, for all foul lies and trumpeted hypocrisy. And Kent was asking for most of this, as far as Kath could see. She had dreaded something of the sort, when she saw his shirt and tie and decided to put on jeans instead of her decent maternity skirt. (95)

Her embarrassment undermines Kent's belief that he won the argument: "she wished her water would break. Anything to deliver her. If she scrambled up and puddled the floor in front of them, they would have to stop" (96). But Kath also recognizes the dubious certainty of both sides: "Everybody in the room was so certain of everything. When they paused for breath it was just to draw on an everlasting stream of pure virtue, pure certainty" (95). The woman who speaks as if Kent were responsible "for all foul lies and trumpeted hypocrisy" is unlikely to have been free of those things herself, as Munro suggests in her earlier reference to Howard Fast, "the last surviving American recipient of the Stalin peace prize" (Homberger). The point is not to return to the conflicts of the Cold War, but to see that Kent's opponents are also flawed,[8] and that Kath is caught between sides, even as her sympathies shift. Aside from his breach of manners as a dinner guest, Kent's offence is simply that his views are conventional. If Rose resents Patrick for what he says, Kath resents Kent for what he is, and, given her former "mild elation" (83) at using her married name, there must be a degree of self-loathing in her resentment.

When Kath leans away from Kent, it is not clear who or what she is leaning toward. As she thinks back on the argument on the occasion of a farewell party for Cottar some months later, she "was anxious not to talk anymore about politics," changing the subject by telling Kent about the sexual exchanges among the other guests (96). He is disgusted at the idea of young men sleeping with the older woman, but she "gets a deep obscene thrill" at the idea of "those stipulated and obligatory copulations" (96). At the party, her restlessness increases though she still thinks of herself as Kent's wife: "For all the tempting thoughts that came into her mind, Kath believed that she could only, ever, sleep with Kent. . . . Trying it with somebody else would mean a change of circuits—all of her life would blow up in her face" (97). Talking to the older man from the dinner party, however, Kath "wanted right then to have a man like this kiss her. A man she hardly knew, and cared nothing about" (100–01). And he does kiss her, after "humorously" quoting

Arnold's "Dover Beach" on the retreat of the "sea of faith" (100; Arnold l. 21). When he sighs, Kath caps the quotation but stops, "because it seemed too much to go on with 'Oh love let us be true—'" (100; Arnold l. 29), the start of the proclamation of love that ends the poem. As Sara Jamieson argues elsewhere in this volume, the recitation of poetry suggests a shared culture, but Munro's recitations often reveal the differences between characters. In this instance, Kath cannot quite join the older man's mockery of Arnold.[9] She is as painfully self-conscious about quoting—or not quoting—"Dover Beach" as she is about skinny-dipping—or not skinny-dipping. She may kiss a man whom she hardly knows, but she is not about to take Matthew Arnold's words in vain. And she recoils from the older man's second wife, one of the skinny-dippers, who stands "so close that Kath was afraid of being grazed by her long dark nipples or her mop of black public hair" (101). We might well have taken the earlier reference to this woman's "low-slung breasts and graying hair" (91) as the attitude of an insensitive male, but Kath responds similarly.

Later, after Amy, the older man's mistress, applies to Kath's face an elaborate arrangement of mascara, gloss, and pink lipstick, Kath is effectively wearing a mask when dancing with a complete stranger. Although she believes that "it was all a joke," the mask enables her to assume a different identity as "They advanced and retreated and circled and dodged, putting on a show for each other, and looking into each other's eyes. Their eyes declared that this show was nothing, nothing compared to the raw tussle they could manage when they chose" (105). When her babysitter calls Kath by her married name, her unknown partner "caught her hips, turned her around, dropped to his knees, and kissed her crotch through her cotton pants" (105). Arriving to find her husband feeding her baby from "her supplemental bottle," Kath "raised a hand to her breasts to test their fullness, but the stir of the wool gave her such a shock of desire that she couldn't press further" (106). Because the word "shock" echoes the reference to the explosive "change of circuits" (97) that would follow a change of sexual partners, the story suggests that Kath's adulterous desire is aroused by the dancing partner touching "her still breasts under their electric wool" (105). Worried that her husband might have seen her dancing on the beach, she assumes that their relationship has changed: "She thought his cockiness sounded sad and faked. He must have seen her dancing. Or else he would have said, 'What have you done to your face?'" (107). Something has happened to Kath, but Kent doesn't know what it is. No one detail proves it, but the whole third section suggests that a marriage is ending without the participants fully realizing it. Changes that neither imagined have been set in motion, and Kath is as unlikely to remain "Mrs. Kent Mayberry" as she is to become one of "the Monicas."

My sense of "Jakarta" is that the focalization is shared equally between Kent and Kath, but the implied author's sympathy is not equally distributed. Unable to escape the self-criticism that distinguishes Munro's most memorable characters, Kath knows that she is projecting her own problems onto the fiction of Lawrence and Mansfield, and so she is capable of changing her life and resisting nostalgia. Kent, by contrast, "did not disagree with his younger self now" (93), more than thirty years, two wives, and two children later. He too has lived through "momentous shifts," but not the changes he imagined, to return to my epigraph from "Differently" (242). Seeing no need to reconsider his own role in these changes, he has no chance for an epiphany in the last section, his second as focalizer. He has the pathos of living through at least two operations and of aging generally, but he looks to others for insights that only he can provide: "With every visit he had made on this trip, there had come a moment of severe disappointment. The moment when he realized that the person he was talking to, the person he had made a point of seeking out, was not going to give him whatever it was he had come for" (110).

Kent's vanity makes him conceal his need to take a pill even as he hopes that "Sonje might report to Kath how well he was looking" (114). He is approaching nostalgia when he says that Cottar and Kath "got away" (115), but Sonje responds icily: "Your wife's been gone a long time. . . . It's absurd, but young people seem unimportant to me" (115–16). Instead of learning anything about Kath, he hears of Sonje's plans to travel on the chance that her husband is still alive: "it was all Cottar, and stupidity, and Jakarta" (114). The story ends with the promise of an illumination, but it is induced by Kent's medication: "Because of the pill his thoughts stretch out long and gauzy and lit up like vapor trails. He travels a thought that has to do with staying here, with listening to Sonje talk about Jakarta while the sand blows sand off the dunes" (116). Since these thoughts have nothing to do with Kent's possible future, they are a false conclusion, not an epiphany.[10] What Charles Baxter says of James Alan McPherson's "Elbow Room" is also true of "Jakarta": "It shrugs off portentous declamations and in general resists the earth-shaking masterpiece tone. . . . It sets before us, instead, the fictionality of all insight" (56). Baxter does not "believe that a character's experiences in a story have to be validated by a conclusive insight or a brilliant visionary stop-time moment" (52), and Munro appears to agree, though she still uses concluding epiphanies where appropriate, as in "Floating Bridge." Perhaps a story focalized entirely by Kath could lead to insight, but not one that uses a shared focalization ending with Kent. Readers who are unable to share his nostalgia may find themselves in the position described by Munro in relation to "Differently," a story set in 1968–74: those years, she says, and the point holds for the slightly earlier time of "Jakarta," are "Not necessarily to be regretted or deplored or hankered after, just described" ("Contributor's" 352).

Using "Mischief" as what Ross calls "a sort of scaffolding" to read "Jakarta," I have implied that these stories are similar treatments of disintegrating marriages and female adulterous desire in the context of the gender assumptions of the 1950s. The main differences are that "Jakarta" withholds the wife from the distant retrospection and offers a more expansive social background: in addition to Kath, Kent, and Sonje and Cottar and their radical friends, the story provides two temporal frameworks and looks at the lives of "the Monicas," the other women who work at the Vancouver Public Library, and various neighbours who attend Cottar's farewell party. None of them could have imagined how Kent's life has changed more than three decades later, as he travels with his third wife (who is a year younger than his daughter with Kath—88) to visit old friends and his children from previous marriages. Though he is keenly sensitive to the historical changes reflected in "Jakarta," Gorra finds that Munro "is no more interested in the lives of men than Conrad was in those of women" ("Crossing"). Her reputation is still often based on such views, but Munro makes increasing use of male protagonists and focalizers in the 1980s and after. As Carrington observes, what began with such isolated stories as "Thanks for the Ride" (1957), "Walking on Water" (1974) and "Wood" (a 1980 story not collected until *Too Much Happiness*, 2009) becomes more extensive in *The Progress of Love* (1986), which features two stories with "shared focalization" ("Lichen," "A Queer Streak"), and three focalized by male protagonists ("Fits," "The Moon in the Orange Street Skating Rink," "Monsieur les deux Chapeaux"). For Carrington, "Munro cannot be characterized as a feminist writer who programmatically limits herself to female narrators or protagonists or who presents the struggle of the sexes only from the feminine point of view. But neither does she always present her male characters sympathetically" (*Controlling* 159). "Jakarta" is more complex and more compelling than "Mischief" because Munro has learned that even a story about adulterous desire will be better for including the husband's perspective, however unsympathetically. Elsewhere in *The Love of a Good Woman*, the extraordinary look at the lives of three boys in the "Jutland" section of the title story reveals that Munro's work defeats any attempt to limit her art to her gender. Much of this volume, like much of her Nobel Prize—winning canon, concerns the lives of girls and women, but her understanding of the lives of boys and men is an essential part of the story.

Note: My thanks to three of Munro's best critics: Sara Jamieson and Tim McIntyre provided helpful responses to my questions, and Robert Thacker commented generously on earlier versions of this paper.

Notes

1. Munro had four stories ("The Children Stay," "Save the Reaper," "Before the Change," and "Cortes Island") in the *New Yorker* between December 1997 and October 1998, at a time when the magazine's new editor, Tina Brown, "cut the number of stories published by about half" (Thacker, *Writing* 475). So it was likely the sheer volume of Munro's material that caused that magazine to pass on "Jakarta," which appeared in *Saturday Night* (February 1998, 45–50).
2. Asked in 1994 by the Canadian Congress for Learning Opportunities for Women to donate a book "by or about a 'special' woman," Munro donated her high-school library's copy of the *Collected Stories of Katherine Mansfield*, with a due date of November 13, 1975, indicating that "she came to own the discard some time after her own tenure at the school" ("Celeb's" 45).
3. "Barbara began to describe . . . the beach encampment set up by the Other Mothers. Their folding chairs and umbrellas, inflatable toys and mattresses, towels and changes of clothing, lotions, oils, antiseptic, Band-Aids, home-frozen popsicles, and healthful goodies. 'Which are supposed to keep the little brutes from whining for French fries,' said Barbara. 'They never look at the lake unless one of their kids is in it. They talk about their kids' asthma or where they get the cheapest T-shirts" (128). The passage seems stranded in "Oranges and Apples," which is more concerned with a man's jealousy of his wife than with the conflicts of maternity.
4. Ailsa Cox notes that "It is difficult for those born since the woman's liberation movement to imagine how absolute the choices were in the 1950s. Muriel Spark and Doris Lessing both gave up their children" (29).
5. In *The Bell Jar*, Esther Greenwood is a top student in a similar plight: when her editor at *Ladies' Day* asks about her future plans, she responds, "'I don't really know,' I heard myself say. I felt a deep shock, hearing myself say that, because the minute I said it, I knew it was true" (Plath 34).
6. In his obituary for Fast, Eric Homberger writes that "For a decade after the Second World War, [Fast] moved in the upper strata of international

anti-fascism and communist propaganda. His historical novels, which ranged from portraits of slave revolts in antiquity, as with *Spartacus* (1953), to the American Revolution, won him a broad readership across the world. In the Soviet Union, his print runs were substantial. Having refused to cooperate with the House Un-American Activities Committee and provide records of the Joint Anti-Fascist Refugee Committee, he was convicted of contempt of Congress in 1950, and served three months in jail—it was in effect a congressional imprimatur of his leftwing credentials and integrity" ("Howard"). In fairness, we should note that Fast turned against communism after 1956. If Cottar had known of that turn, he would have been unlikely to insist that his wife read Fast's novels.

7. In her 2004 radio interview with Eleanor Wachtel, Munro revealed that she responded similarly to "The Fox": she found the passage about the wife's need to submerge her identity in her husband's "horrifying, I guess because it came from a writer whom I so admired." And she adds that she was frightened by this possibility: "What if it's true?" She refers to Lawrence in two stories from *Something I've Been Meaning To Tell You.* In "Tell Me Yes or No" (1974), the narrator "remembered from far back—from four or five years back, actually, that seemed a long time to me—how sex had seemed apocalyptic (we read Lawrence, many of us were virgins at twenty)" (107). In "Material" (1973), the narrator remembers that she and her husband "played in bed that I was Lady Chatterley and he was Mellors" (36). Chris Baldick notes that after the 1959 trial of *Lady Chatterley's Lover*, Lawrence "became one of the patron saints of 'the sixties'" (263). By that time, Cottar might have been more interested in Lawrence than Fast.
8. I am indebted to Claire Russell for this point.
9. Similarly, Kath was unable to share the older woman's playful mockery at the dinner party: "Oh, Sonje, are you going to be the tactful hostess. . . . Like somebody in Virginia Woolf?" Kath's response indicates her distance from both the older woman and from Kent: "So it seemed Virginia Woolf was at a discount too. There was so much Kath didn't understand. But at least she knew it was there; she wasn't prepared to say it was nonsense" (96).
10. In the first of two related articles, David Crouse argues that the endings in *Friend of My Youth* (1990) "should be seen as an extension of epiphanic techniques, not a reversal of them" ("Resisting" 53). In the second, he denies that the small insights in *Hateship, Friendship, Courtship, Loveship, Marriage* (2001) are epiphanies: "In fact, it would be inaccurate to call them epiphanies; they are small realizations not so much visited upon a character as generated by that person's attention to the world, his or her careful memoir-style assemblage of memories and details. Sometimes these realizations are contradicted paragraphs later, sometimes even within the same paragraph" ("Honest" 232). Crouse notes that Charles Baxter "does not mention Munro by name [in "Against Epiphanies"], but her stories

seem to act as a solution to what he sees as a relatively pervasive problem: the overuse and misuse of the epiphany in contemporary literature" (232). When Eleanor Wachtel comments, in her 1991 interview with Munro for *Brick*, that "Many traditional stories lead to a moment of insight, an epiphany, that sort of thing. Your stories have moments of insight—"Munro interrupts, "Yeah, and then they're wrong" (51–52).

Works Cited

Arnold, Matthew. "Dover Beach." *Matthew Arnold.* Ed. Miriam Allott and Robert H. Super. Oxford: Oxford UP, 1986. 135–36.

Baldick, Chris. "Post-mortem: Lawrence's Critical and Cultural Legacy." *The Cambridge Companion to D. H. Lawrence.* Ed. Anne Fernihough. Cambridge: Cambridge UP, 2001. 253–69.

Baxter, Charles. "Against Epiphanies." *Burning Down the House: Essays on Fiction.* 2nd ed. Saint Paul, MN: Graywolf, 2008. 41–61.

Breines, Wini. *Young, White, and Miserable: Growing Up in the Fifties.* Boston: Beacon, 1992.

Carrington, Ildikó de Papp. *Controlling the Uncontrollable: The Fiction of Alice Munro.* Dekalb: Northern Illinois UP, 1989.

———. "'Don't Tell (on) Daddy': Narrative Complexity in Alice Munro's 'The Love of a Good Woman.'" *Studies in Short Fiction* 34 (1997): 159–70.

"Celeb's Donations Speak Volumes." *Quill and Quire* April 1994: 45.

Cox, Ailsa. *Alice Munro.* Tavistock, UK: Northcote House, 2004.

Crouse, David. "Honest Tricks: Surrogate Authors in Alice Munro's *Hateship, Friendship, Courtship, Loveship, Marriage.*" *Critical Insights: Alice Munro.* Ed. Charles E. May. Ipswich, MA: Salem, 2013. 228–41.

———. "Resisting Reduction: Closure in Richard Ford's *Rock Springs* and Alice Munro's *Friend of My Youth.*" *Canadian Literature* 146 (1995): 51–64.

Duffy, Dennis. "'A Dark Sort of Mirror': 'The Love of a Good Woman' as Pauline Poetic." *The Rest of the Story: Critical Essays on Alice Munro.* Ed. Robert Thacker. Toronto: ECW, 1999. 169–90.

Duncan, Isla. *Alice Munro's Narrative Art.* New York: Palgrave Macmillan, 2011.

Franzen, Jonathan. "Alice's Wonderland." Review of *Runaway,* by Alice Munro. *New York Times Book Review,* 14 November 2004. http://www.nytimes.com/2004/11/14/books/review/runaway-alices-wonderland.html. 17 June 2014.

Gorra, Michael. "Crossing the Threshold." Review of *The Love of a Good Woman,* by Alice Munro. *New York Times Book Review,* 1 November 1998. https://www.nytimes.com/books/98/11/01/reviews/981101.01gorrat.html. 17 June 2014.

Hancock, Geoff. "Interview with Alice Munro." 15 September 1982. *Canadian Writers at Work.* Toronto: Oxford UP, 1987. 187–224.

Homberger, Eric. "Howard Fast: Prolific Radical Novelist Who Championed the Cause of America's Common People." *The Guardian* [UK], 14 March 2003. https://www.theguardian.com/news/2003/mar/14/guardianobituaries.books. 17 June 2014.

Jamieson, Sara. "'The stuff they put in the old readers': Remembered and Recited Poetry in the Stories of Alice Munro." *Alice Munro's Miraculous Art.* Ed. Janice Fiamengo and Gerald Lynch. Ottawa: U of Ottawa P, 2017. 80–95.

Lawrence. D. H. "The Fox." *The Fox, The Captain's Doll, The Ladybird.* Ed. Dieter Mehl. The Cambridge Edition of the Letters and Works of D.H. Lawrence. Cambridge: Cambridge UP, 1992. 7–71.

McCulloch, Jeanne, and Mona Simpson. "The Art of Fiction CXXXVII." Interview with Alice Munro. *Paris Review* 131 (1994): 227–64.

Macfarlane, David. "Writer in Residence." Review of *The Progress of Love*, by Alice Munro. *Saturday Night* (December 1986): 51–55.

Mehl, Dieter. Introduction. Lawrence. xix–xlvii.

Mansfield, Katherine. "At the Bay." *Katherine Mansfield's Selected Stories.* Ed. Vincent O'Sullivan. Norton Critical Edition. New York: Norton, 2006. 250–79.

Munro, Alice. "Contributor's Note." *The Best American Short Stories 1990.* Ed. Richard Ford and Shannon Ravenel. Boston: Houghton Mifflin, 1990. 352.

———. "Differently." *Friend* 216–43.

———. *Friend of My Youth.* New York: Knopf, 1990.

———. "Jakarta." *The Love of a Good Woman.* Toronto: McClelland & Stewart, 1998. 79–116.

———. "Material." *Something* 24–44.

———. "Mischief." *Who Do You Think You Are?* 1978. New York: Penguin, 2006. 105–41.

———. "Oranges and Apples." *Friend*, 106–36.

———. *Something I've Been Meaning to Tell You.* 1974. Toronto: Penguin, 1996.

———. "Tell Me Yes or No." *Something* 106–24.

Munro, Sheila. *Lives of Mothers and Daughters: Growing Up with Alice Munro.* Toronto: McClelland & Stewart, 2001.

Plath, Sylvia. *The Bell Jar.* 1963. London: Faber and Faber, 1982.

Rasporich, Beverly J. *Dance of the Sexes: Art and Gender in the Fiction of Alice Munro.* Edmonton: U of Alberta P, 1990.

Ross, Catherine Sheldrick. "'Too Many Things': Reading Alice Munro's 'The Love of a Good Woman.'" *University of Toronto Quarterly* 71.3 (2002): 786–810.

Showalter, Elaine. "Toward a Feminist Poetics." *Women's Writing and Writing About Women.* Ed. Mary Jacobus. London: Croom Helm, 1979. 22–41.

The New Feminist Criticism: Essays on Women, Literature, and Theory. Ed. Showalter. New York: Pantheon, 1985. 125–43.

Thacker, Robert. *Alice Munro: Writing Her Lives, A Biography.* Toronto: McClelland & Stewart, 2005.

Wachtel, Eleanor. Interview with Alice Munro. *Brick* 40 (1991): 48–53.

———. Interview with Alice Munro. "Writers and Company." CBC Radio, 7 November 2004.

Wilde, Alan. *Horizons of Assent: Modernism, Postmodernism, and the Ironic Imagination.* Philadelphia: U of Pennsylvania P, 1987.

"First and Last": The Figure of the Infant in "Dear Life" and "My Mother's Dream"

AILSA COX

We have all experienced infancy, but very few of us would claim any recollection of that early state and the first dawning of consciousness. Psychoanalytical theory regards infancy as the nexus of instinctual drives, which are necessarily repressed with the emergence of the psyche through a process of separation from the mother. Julia Kristeva refers to what she calls the semiotic *chora*, a mobile, boundless and indefinable space where the self is undifferentiated from the maternal body. She claims that "all discourse moves with and against the *chora*" (Kristeva 1984, 14), and also suggests that language acquisition is motivated by the desire to recapture the mother in her absence—to "picture her in words" (Kristeva 2002, 23).

Infancy, then, is a liminal condition, an irrecoverable state of consciousness, blurring the boundaries between self and other. In Kristeva's semiotic *chora*, time is a boundless flow. The philosopher Henri Bergson says that "real time" exists as just such a flow or "duration." In order to manage our lives, we have to measure time, we have to set our watches and draw up timetables, but when we do so we are, according to Bergson, handling time artificially, as though it were space. Bergson argues that there is no such thing as the present, only "the invisible progress of the past gnawing into the future" (150). Symbolically, then, I would argue that the figure of the infant embodies this impossible present, a temporal intersection between past and future, memory and speculation. The infant represents the inheritance of the past and its endurance into the future. But each infant is also a new beginning, with a personality and a potential that is yet to emerge and must remain unforeseeable whatever the burden of hope and expectations invested by parents and well-wishers in that fragile frame.

The title piece in Alice Munro's 2012 collection *Dear Life* brings to a close the four "final" works that she claims are "not quite stories [. . .] they are the first—and last—and the closest—things I have to say about my own life" (255). That statement may seem, at first sight, a little disingenuous; the "Finale" sequence is more complex than "the simple truth," as she describes it in an interview with Deborah Treisman for the *New Yorker*. When Munro labels her writing autobiographical, as she also does in *The View from Castle Rock* (2006), she is often searching for the origins of her own practice as a writer. When I read the avowedly autobiographical "Dear Life," I returned to my earlier reading of "My Mother's Dream," which is also positioned as the final piece in a collection (*The Love of a Good Woman*, 1998). "Dear Life" ranges throughout Munro's childhood, but it centres on an incident from infancy, which gives both the story and the collection its title. Like "My Mother's Dream," "Dear Life" reconstructs events from a homodiegetic narrator's infancy, events in which she figures, but which she is unlikely to consciously recall. Both texts use the narrators' return to personal prehistory to create ambiguities in focalization that destabilize truth in the telling.

"My Mother's Dream"

"My Mother's Dream" opens abruptly with what at first appears to be an awakening:

> During the night—or during the time she had been asleep—there had been a heavy fall of snow.
>
> My mother looked out from a big arched window such as you find in a mansion or an old-fashioned public building. She looked down on lawns and shrubs, hedges, flower gardens, trees, all covered by snow that lay in heaps and cushions, not leveled or disturbed by wind. The white of it did not hurt your eyes as it does in sunlight. The white was the white of snow under a clear sky just before dawn. Everything was still; it was like "O Little Town of Bethlehem" except that the stars had gone out. (294)

Gradually this peaceful scenario reveals itself as the disorienting landscape of the eponymous dream. The season is out of kilter, with green leaves visible under the snow. The character labeled "my mother" is in a strange place, abandoned by people she can't quite remember. All she can be sure of is that somewhere within this atemporal and indefinable space she has left a baby "overnight [. . .] and perhaps it was not last night but a week or a month ago [. . . .] She might even have travelled away from here and just returned" (ibid.).

As she searches for the mislaid child, she crosses almost imperceptibly into her waking life, where the only remnant of the snowy landscape is the white blanket half covering the real baby in its crib. The tense changes from past to present, and the indeterminacy of the dream yields to the specific space-time coordinates of July 1945 in a small town near Lake Huron. This is where the narrator's father grew up, and where her mother, Jill, has joined the in-laws after his death in the Second World War. The story details Jill's struggle to cope with the demands of a young baby in the judgmental atmosphere of the family home. This situation is exacerbated by her musical vocation. Pregnancy has kept her away from her instrument, the violin, by thickening her fingers, and now the baby starts screaming if she tries to pick it up again.

The temporal and spatial fluidity introduced by the dream recurs throughout the narrative. These shifts back and forth between memories, perceptions, and fantasy, this constant reconfiguration of reality, are defining features in Munro's aesthetic, familiar to her regular readers and equally apparent in the other stories in *The Love of a Good Woman*, not least the long title story. What is especially innovative about "My Mother's Dream" is the split in identities signaled by the variations in names and pronouns—"a baby," "her baby," "me," "my mother," "Jill." While the unnamed narrator identifies herself as Jill's child, looking back to the period around the time she was born, the narrative is focalized mostly through Jill. The narrator comments retrospectively on these past events, even guessing at her own motives, refraining from any attempt to directly represent her own consciousness in its earliest prelinguistic state. The amount of physical detail in the story, including the precise character descriptions, might be taken to imply that the first-person narrator is elaborating on a family story, fictionalizing her own mother's memories.

As Deborah Heller points out, the narrator describes these events "with a more detached, ironic point of view than Jill could be expected to have recounted" (13). Heller relates this detachment to the story's theatricality, expressed through the parodic presentation of Jill's sister-in-law, Iona, which I discuss below. The frequent excursions from past tense into present tense are another aspect of this theatricality, staging the past in minute detail:

> Haul the mess out, wash off my scalded parts, pin on a clean diaper, and take the dirty diaper and sheet into the bathroom to be scrubbed off in the toilet. Put them in the pail of disinfectant which is already full to the brim because the usual baby wash has not been done today. Then get to me with the bottle. I quiet again enough to suck. It's a wonder I have the energy left to do that [...]. (325)

This passage, of course, also implies repetition, the timeless drudgery of a maternal routine which—at least until the advent of disposable diapers—endured across generations.

Many critics have applied the Bakhtinian concept of double-voiced discourse to their analysis of Munro's work—the interplay of character voices with an overt or implicit authorial voice, producing multiple layers of meaning within every utterance. In the passage above, as elsewhere, the narrator's voice and viewpoint seem to fuse with the mother's: "It's a wonder I have the energy left." When motives are attributed to the child, voice and viewpoint are even more slippery: "I refused to take my mother's breast. I screamed blue murder. The big stiff breast might just as well have been a snouted beast rummaging in my face" (314). Like that other phrase, "it's a wonder . . . ," the colloquial "blue murder" evokes the mother's speech, but what about the image of the "snouted beast"? Bakhtin defines double-voiced discourse as "*another's speech in another's language*, serving to express authorial intentions but in a refracted way" (Bakhtin 1992, 324, original emphasis). This refracting discourse of the narrator approximates and hyperbolizes impressions she attributes to her re-imagined self.

The phrase "blue murder" could be attributed to Jill, and also to her neurasthenic sister-in-law Iona, who placates the newborn with a bottle, and whose ministrations she much prefers to her mother's. Thus the constant shifting of positions between mother and daughter extends beyond the biological mother/daughter dyad. There is at least one other voice embedded in this text, that of the maternal substitute, Iona herself. Munro describes the satisfaction Iona takes in her indispensability from a variety of contrasting viewpoints, including the comments of Ailsa, the eldest sister-in-law, whose voice is also implicated in the telling of this story. In some passages the focalization shifts briefly to Iona, as filtered through the observing consciousness of the narrator:

> She knew herself to be the only person who didn't wince, who didn't feel the distant threat of annihilation, when I sent up my first signal

> wail. Instead, she was the one whose heart jumped into double time, who felt like dancing, just from the sense of power she had, and gratitude. (316)

The story's tragicomic climax is reached when the in-laws leave Jill and the baby alone in the house. With Iona gone, the child proves impossible to soothe. Previously, she has reacted badly when Jill tries to practice; but, with nothing to lose, Jill fetches the violin out anyway. The violin also refuses to cooperate, its screeching merely augmenting the screams of the infant. In desperation, she shares a sleeping pill with the child; Jill's dream could be narcotically induced. When Iona returns, finding the child preternaturally quiet, she assumes Jill has smothered her and hides the supposed corpse under the sofa, where, co-incidentally, Jill has stowed the violin.

Iona's hysterical refusal to reveal the "dead" child's whereabouts is followed by Jill's assumption of the maternal role appropriated by her husband's sister. Above all the hullaballoo, she hears a faint cry that leads her to the baby:

> During that short trip from the hall to the living room, Jill has remembered everything, and it seems as if her breath stops and horror crowds in at her mouth, then a flash of joy sets her life going again, when just as in the dream she comes upon a live baby, not a little desiccated nutmeg-headed corpse. (333)

The "flash of joy" that "sets her life going again" echoes Iona's response to the baby's cry—the "double-time" rhythms of her dancing heart. Jill's sensitivity to these faint sounds, together with the recapitulation of the dream, validates the concept of the maternal bond as ultimately instinctual. Before too long, the infant is finally accepting a bottle from her mother.

However, as Naomi Morgenstern has said, "Motherhood is never a simple fact in Munro's fiction. Motherhood is not what comes 'first,' not simply what is essential and established before being called into crisis" (Morgenstern 2012, 75). The reconciliation between mother and child, or more specifically mother and daughter, is, as we shall see, a work in progress. After her almost farcical humiliation, Iona gives up child-care, resuming her job at a bakery, but she is not entirely divested, symbolically at least, of her maternal role. The snowy imagery from Jill's dream is reprised in "the great white mass of dough that shifted and bubbled like something alive" at the bakery where the narrator, as a child, watches Iona working; and again in Iona's apron, the bright white kitchen, and the icing on the wedding cakes (338). Like the snow and the white blanket covering the baby, the dough, "bubbling like something alive," contains a life below the surface. The dazzling whiteness suggests the enchantment the bakery holds for a child; the parallels with the imagery of the dream also realign Iona with the maternal and the atemporal *chora*.

In contrast to the events reconstructed from a prelinguistic past, these recollections are salvaged from direct experience, and present more benign versions of both Jill's sisters-in-law than we have seen in the preceding pages. After all, we have been told that "Jill took on loving me, because the alternative to loving was disaster" (337); but Iona's love for the baby is "the most wholehearted love I will ever receive" (336–37).

Magdalene Redekop has observed that "Munro shows people surviving by means of a story; it is what enables them to go on with their lives" (xi). In "My Mother's Dream," survival itself is the story. Even before the episode with the sleeping pill, the posthumous child embodies the family's survival, even acting as a surrogate for her dead father. The pictures of her father, George, displayed throughout the house include several from childhood. A need to repossess the dead George may be one of the factors driving Iona's rivalry with the baby's biological mother.

The choice of survival initiates the child into the narrative of femininity, a narrative constructed through a fierce battle of wills:

> To me it seems that it was only then that I became female. I know that the matter was decided long before I was born and was plain to everybody else since the beginning of my life, but I believe that it was only at the moment when I decided to come back, when I gave up the fight against my mother (which must have been a fight for something like her total surrender) and when in fact I chose survival over victory (death would have been victory) that I took on my female nature. (337)

Morgenstern gives a very clear reading of this turning point in the story, showing how "mother and daughter mutually become female in their choice to give up, to lose out, which is also the choice of survival" (87). She argues that only by using the "impossible baby narrator" (ibid.) can Munro present this psychic process, demonstrating that "the 'feminine' 'choice' of loss or lack is a choice akin to a life drive, a will to survive" (82).

The phrase "I took on my female nature" echoes between the figures of mother and daughter: "to some extent Jill took on hers. [. . .] she took on loving me, because the alternative to loving was disaster" (337).

This repetition exploits the various connotations of "taking on"—the tackling of an onerous task; the assumption of a new role; and, although this notion is suppressed by the context, ideas of confrontation. Jill takes on her role only "to some extent"; the narrator's own ambivalence is enacted in the closing paragraph, as she describes herself at twelve, watching older girls messing about with their boyfriends at a local swimming pool. Here gendered identity clearly is being contested:

> I despised their antics because I took life seriously and had a much more lofty and tender notion of romance. But I would have liked to get their attention just the same. I would have liked for one of them to see my pale pajamas moving in the dark, and to scream out in earnest, thinking that I was a ghost. (340)

There is, then, still, something of the revenant about her. Iona may not have been entirely mistaken when she took her for dead:

> I don't believe that I was dead, or that I came back from the dead, but I do think that I was at a distance, from which I might or might not have come back. I think that the outcome was not certain and that will was involved. It was up to me, I mean, to go one way or the other. (336)

Perhaps we should see femininity itself as an ongoing process, rather than a fixed identity, something that is "taken on" subject to negotiation. This twelve-year-old ghost watching from beyond the fence re-enacts the earlier battle for death or survival, a battle that will help determine who she will become in the unknowable future that lies beyond the text.

"Dear Life"

One difference between a fictive text and one that declares itself autobiographical is that fiction is not obliged to account for its own telling. While there are references to the narrator, in adolescence, eavesdropping on her mother's conversations, no source is given for the events in "My Mother's Dream." "Dear Life" is more overtly self-reflexive, comparing different versions of an incident described by Munro's mother, and re-interpreting the anecdote through hindsight. In an interview with the *Virginia Quarterly Review*, Munro explains what, for her, is special in the "Finale" sequence:

> Certainly the "Finale" stories are a conscious working with memory, and I haven't done that very often because I think if you're really going to write seriously about your parents, your childhood, you have to be as honest as you can, you have to think about what really happened, rather than what story your memory dishes up to you. But of course

> you never can do that, so at least you've got to say, "Well, this is my side of the story—this is what I remember." (Awano)

The central incident in "Dear Life" recapitulates many of the tropes in "My Mother's Dream"—the fragility of the infant, her exposure to peril, the intervention of a mentally unstable older woman, the inexperience of the young mother, panic and hysteria, farce and melodrama. It is this incident which gives the story, and the collection, its title; when "Dear Life" was first published in the *New Yorker*, its importance was underlined by the subtitle, "a childhood visitation." (The text is illustrated with a photograph of the author as a toddler, and categorized as "personal history.") The text is circumlocutory and anecdotal, only reaching the story of the "visitation" at the halfway point. It opens with another mapping of the local landscape that situates the narrator's younger self in a peripheral space at the edge of town—a space very familiar to readers of the fiction. This topographical mapping and the establishment of geographical borders transmutes into a mapping of social boundaries as the narrator describes a friendship with a girl whose mother, she has since realized, worked as a prostitute. The friend's house becomes out of bounds when Munro's own mother forbids her to visit. Later, Munro relates geographic to social mobility in her account of her mother's thwarted aspirations:

> She must have thought that she and my father were going to transform themselves into a different sort of people, people who enjoyed a degree of leisure. Golf. Dinner parties. Perhaps she had convinced herself that certain boundaries were not there. She had managed to get herself off a farm on the bare Canadian Shield—a farm much more hopeless than the one my father came from—and she had become a schoolteacher, who spoke in such a way that her own relatives were not easy around her. (304)

As the piece makes clear, both the narrator and her mother are, in their different ways, resistant to the borders erected by social conformity. The story of an encounter with an elderly eccentric who is perceived as a threat to the infant Munro shows how we are limited by, but may also transcend, these socially imposed limitations.

Munro reconstructs her childhood home just as she maps the surrounding landscape; the house's precise configuration plays an important part in the movements of the three participants in the central trauma—her mother as a young woman; the mad Mrs. Netterfield; and the author as an infant, inside a baby carriage on the lawn. Chancing to look through a window, the mother spots Mrs. Netterfield heading down the driveway, rushes out, grabs the baby, and hides indoors.

Mrs. Netterfield has a reputation for unpredictability, even violence, even though Munro's mother has previously felt compassionate towards her: "Mrs. Netterfield was said to be quite a lady when she was younger" (311); the visit is a parody of the refined social calls Munro's mother might have aspired to making and receiving. In most versions of this family anecdote, Mrs. Netterfield inspects the empty pram, peers through the windows and disappears without a word. Even when the tale is embellished with the banging of windows and rattling of doors, she remains speechless.

Windows, spectatorship, and visibility are crucial elements in this encounter, which begins with the mother washing baby clothes at a sink. The narrator speculates about what might have prompted her mother to move away from her chores to look through the window, wondering if she might have been anticipating her husband's return with fabric for a dress or ingredients for a fancy recipe—both of these markers of what is regarded locally as ridiculous pretension. She hides with her child where she cannot be seen; it is summer, the blinds are up and the unwelcome visitor "could press her face against every pane of glass" (314). I shall return to these windows later.

As in "My Mother's Dream," subtle shifts in focalization mark the overlapping, even merging, of identities within the mother/daughter dyad. Once again, an adult narrator is re-assembling a tale in which she herself figures as a child too young to retain a conscious impression, based on memories of a story told, in this case, by a woman who has been dead for fifty years. Munro unpicks the narrative at every turn, asking the obvious question about the face at the window: "How did my mother know this? It was not as if she were running around with me in her arms, hiding between one piece of furniture after another, peering out, distraught with terror, to meet the staring eyes and maybe a wild grin" (314).

She also emphasizes that the story was not repeated often; "the visitation of old Mrs. Netterfield" (315) was not one of the classics in what she describes as her mother's "repertoire" (315). Redekop's study, *Mothers and Other Clowns*, gives a full analysis of parody and clowning in Munro's handling of mother figures, including the interplay between autobiographical source material and the fiction-making process. In "Dear Life," the parodic "staring eyes and maybe a wild grin" might be taken from some horror movie—perhaps the well-known image of

Jack Nicholson terrifying his wife and child in Stanley Kubrick's film *The Shining.*

The narrator associates the more graphic versions of the visitation story, the ones including "the rattling and the banging" (315), with the onset of her mother's Parkinson's disease. She also refers to her mother's difficulty in making her stories understood because of the disease, adding the proviso that she herself was always able to interpret on her behalf. The voiceless Mrs. Netterfield is in this respect an avatar of what the young mother will later become—misunderstood, bereft of speech, interpreted through another viewpoint. In the *New Yorker*, the parallels between the two women are underlined by a concluding paragraph that has been cut from the final version:

> When my mother was dying, she got out of the hospital somehow, at night, and wandered around town until someone who didn't know her at all spotted her and took her in. If this were fiction, as I said, it would be too much, but it is true.

"They took her away"—to repeat the phrase used by the narrator's mother to describe what eventually became of Mrs. Netterfield (316). That last sentence in the *New Yorker* version is something of a tease for anyone who recognizes the incident from "The Peace of Utrecht" (*Dance of the Happy Shades*, 1968). "The Peace of Utrecht" marks a turning point in Munro's aesthetic practice; it is with this story's struggle to reconcile contradictory memories of the mother that Munro begins to develop what Adrian Hunter has called her "anti-narratives" (176)—texts that question their own attempts to contain a complex and contradictory reality within conventional narrative patterns. The phrase "too much," as it is used at an earlier point in "Dear Life," indicates a resistance to tragedy or self-dramatization:

> You would think that this was just too much. The business gone, my mother's health going. It wouldn't do in fiction. But the strange thing is that I don't remember that time as unhappy. There wasn't a particularly despairing mood around the house. (309)

In the passage that follows, the narrator describes the father making a living as best he could, and her younger self taking over the cooking—the family surviving adversity.

Yet, as suggested by Redekop, dramatizing the past as fiction is itself a mechanism for survival. The tales her mother tells, including several about Mrs. Netterfield, become increasingly colourful during the mother's illness—a time when the narrator is also reading novels avidly—but the older Munro resists the seductions of fiction-making in the text generated by her own memories. Toward the end of "Dear Life," she reveals that the house had once been in the old woman's family, and that the "visitation" may have been prompted by nothing more threatening than a simple desire to see her own home.

Robert McGill's article "Where Do You Think You Are? Alice Munro's Open Houses" examines the well-known analogy in Munro's essay "What is Real?" between the spaces of a house and the reading and writing of fiction: "Everyone knows what a house does, how it encloses space and makes connections between one enclosed space and another and presents what is outside in a new way" (Munro, "What is Real?" 224). McGill investigates the "open houses," which serve as a repository of hidden knowledge, concluding that "Munro's house-fiction comparison insists on a relationship in which each co-constituent both defines itself in opposition to and shares characteristics with the other" (2).[1]

In "Dear Life," Munro turns again to the metonym of the open house, the house of fiction and the place of storytelling. The house is unsecured, with a back door that can't be locked; but it is the windows that offer points of ingress (or egress) in both this story and "My Mother's Dream." In "My Mother's Dream," the fictional landscape of the dream is framed by "a big arched window" (293). Freudian dream analysis usually interprets a house as a body, a window as a cavity; it stands at the boundary of inside and outside, the self and the world. You are on the inside looking out, but you are also exposed to the gaze of the outer world.

In "Dear Life," Munro is writing from a blind corner where the story cannot be firmly attributed or verified, that corner next to the dumbwaiter where the mother hides with her child. This child is invisible and silent. Unlike the perverse infant in "My Mother's Dream," this child sleeps in her pram without a murmur, allowing her mother to wash out her ribbons and knitwear undisturbed. She does not cry even when she is snatched up so abruptly "for dear life" (318). She is not there when the old woman rummages in the pram, flinging the blanket to the ground (an event which is surmised but not described directly).

I have already referred earlier to Kristeva's theory that speech and representation compensate for the absence of the maternal body, and to the significance of the maternal in the development of Munro's practice. The ellipses and indeterminacy of her work contribute to a poetics of absence that is especially suited to the short-story form. In a perceptive review of *Dear Life*, the Irish writer Anne Enright observes that "Munro makes fiction from her anxiety about making fiction, that mixture of distraction and attention, absence and desire" (Enright 2012). Enright links a "sense of withholding" in the fiction to remarks Munro made in her *Paris Review* interview about the distractions of motherhood when her children were young:

> Some part of me was absent for those children, and children detect things like that. Not that I neglected them, but I wasn't wholly absorbed. When my oldest daughter was about two, she'd come to where I was sitting at the typewriter, and I would bat her away with one hand and type with the other.

The irresolvable battle between artistic frustration and maternal guilt is acted out in "My Mother's Dream" and again in the opening story in *Dear Life*, "To Reach Japan." In the *Paris Review* interview, Munro describes unsuccessful attempts to take her writing to a dedicated space, including the one that is fictionalized in "The Office" (*Dance of the Happy Shades*). In "The Office," a busybody landlord disrupts all the writer's attempts to get on with her work; paradoxically the tale of these disruptions becomes a story in itself. In more ideal surroundings, as a writer in residence in an Australian university, Munro describes herself as "paralyzed"; she is no more absorbed in her writing than in her maternal duties, and we might deduce that a state of distraction is, despite its obvious limitations, in some way necessary to her practice. The implied author in these texts is "absent-minded"; the text is generated from lapses of attention and failures of memory, as the narrative slips back and forth between past and present.

One of the properties of autobiographical writing is the foregrounding of an embodied author. The fluid exchange of identities between mother and daughter, also seen at work in the fictional "My Mother's Dream," is made especially poignant by the reader's awareness that this is a story composed in old age. As the narrator testifies, she herself was a young mother when her own mother died. Munro, the narrator, is the young woman inside the house, but she also identifies imaginatively with the outsider, the misfit, "old Mrs. Netterfield" (she is always "old Mrs. Netterfield," "the old woman"); and the figure of the old woman, in turn, is a phantom from the past of the house, but also from a future as yet unknown, foreshadowing what lies ahead for its socially ambitious and clever young inhabitant.

The shortened ending of "Dear Life," of the autobiographical "Finale" sequence, and hence, if Munro is to be believed, of the last words in her career, concludes on a note of absence. This is the narrator's absence from her mother's funeral—an absence she now questions, just as she interrogates the choices and the motivations of the other characters in this text. The concluding passage follows the coda concerning Mrs. Netterfield's connection to the family house, which emerges through some poems published by a stranger who turns out to be Mrs. Netterfield's own daughter. Here we have another doubling and redoubling, the whimsical verses a parodic echo of the narrator's own lost and abandoned attempts to memorialize the landscape round the Maitland River:

> The daughter lived not so far away from me for a while in my adult life. I could have written to her, maybe visited. If I had not been so busy with my own young family and my own invariably unsatisfactory writing. But the person I would really have liked to talk to then was my mother, who was no longer available. (318)

Munro made the right decision when she chose to end "Dear Life" with this paragraph. As Bakhtin says, "There is neither a first nor a last word and there are no limits to the dialogic context (it extends into the boundless past and the boundless future)" (1986, 170). These "final" words from Munro take us full circle to the zero point of the text, a point of invisibility and silence where oppositions collapse and the act of writing begins.

Note

1. The British critic Nicholas Royle also interprets Munro's house analogy as the starting point for his analysis of short-story form. Royle is especially interested in the conflation of inside and outside, and the destabilization of viewpoint this confers on the narrative. "The model," Royle says "is always cryptic, haunted [. . .] and, in crucial ways, blind" (156).

Works Cited

Awano, Lisa Dickler. "An Interview with Alice Munro." *Virginia Quarterly Review* (Spring 2013). http://vqronline.org/vqr-portfolio/interview-alice-munro. 30 August 2014.

Bakhtin, M. M. "Discourse in the Novel." *The Dialogic Imagination: Four Essays by M.M. Bakhtin.* Trans. Caryl Emerson and Michael Holquist. Ed. Michael Holquist. Austin Texas: U of Texas P, 1992. 259–422.

———. *Speech Genres and Other Late Essays.* Trans. Vern. W. McGee. Ed. Caryl Emerson and Michael Holquist, Austin: U of Texas P, 1986.

Bergson, Henri. *Matter and Memory.* Trans. Nancy Margaret Paul and W. Scott Palmer. New York: Zone Books, 1996.

Enright, Anne. "*Dear Life* by Alice Munro—Review." *The Guardian* [UK], 8 Nov. 2012. https://www.theguardian.com/books/2012/nov/08/dear-life-alice-munro-review. 15 August 2015.

Heller, Deborah. *Daughters and Mothers in Alice Munro's Later Stories.* Seattle: Workwoman's, 2009.

Hunter, Adrian. *The Cambridge Introduction to the Short Story in English.* Cambridge: Cambridge UP, 2007.

Kristeva, Julia. *Intimate Revolt: The Powers and Limits of Psychoanalysis.* Trans. Jeanine Herman. Vol. 2. New York: Columbia UP, 1984.

———. *Revolution in Poetic Language.* Trans. Margaret Waller. New York: Columbia UP, 1984.

McCulloch, Jeanne, and Mona Simpson. "The Art of Fiction 137: Alice Munro." *Paris Review* (Summer 1994). http://theparisreview.org/interviews/1791/the-art-of-fiction-no-137-alice-munro. 30 August 2014.

McGill, Robert. "Where Do You Think You Are? Alice Munro's Open Houses." *Mosaic* 35.4 (2002): 103–20.

Morgenstern, Naomi. "Seduction and Subjectivity: Psychonalysis and the Fiction of Alice Munro." *Critical Insights: Alice Munro.* Ed. Charles E. May. Ipswich, MA: Salem, 2012. 68–86.

———. "The Baby or the Violin? Ethics and Femininity in the Fiction of Alice Munro." *Literature Interpretation Theory* 14 (2003): 69–97.

Munro, Alice. *Dance of the Happy Shades.* 1968. Rpt. London: Penguin, 1983.

———. "Dear Life." *New Yorker*, 19 September 2011. http://www.newyorker.com/magazine/2011/09/19/dear-life. 30 August 2014.

———. *Dear Life.* London: Chatto and Windus, 2012.

———. *The Love of a Good Woman.* London: Chatto and Windus, 1998.

———. *The View from Castle Rock.* London: Chatto and Windus, 2006.

———. "What is Real?" *Making it New: Contemporary Canadian Stories.* Ed. John Metcalf. Auckland: Methuen, 1982. 223–226.

Redekop, Magdalene. *Mothers and Other Clowns: The Stories of Alice Munro.* London: Routledge, 1992.

Royle, Nicholas. "Spooking Forms." *Oxford Literary Review 26* (2004). 154–72.

Treisman, Deborah. "On 'Dear Life': An Interview with Alice Munro." *New Yorker* 20 November 2012. http://www.newyorker.com/books/page-turner/on-dear-life-an-interview-with-alice-munro. 30 August 2014.

Invasion Narratives: Alice Munro's "Free Radicals" and Joyce Carol Oates's "Where Are You Going, Where Have You Been?"

Carol L. Beran

The solitude of a woman home alone is invaded by a threatening male. This story goes back to preliterate times and continues into the present in urban legends.[1] Forty-two years after Joyce Carol Oates published a version of this story, "Where Are You Going, Where Have You Been?" (1966, in *Epoch Magazine*), Alice Munro published her version, "Free Radicals" (2008, in the *New Yorker*). How each writer clothes the naked story reveals that the vision of these two major writers overlaps to some extent, but also diverges in ways that can only partly be attributed to social changes over the intervening decades.

For Roy R. Male, invasion stories form a recurring motif in American literature: "If one major strain of American fiction does indeed deal with the person on the run, there is an important minor strain that dramatizes in one form or another the decision to stand firm and confront invasion" (7). Strangers, Male asserts, can be "potential saviors, potential destroyers, or ambiguous combinations of both" (10). The conventions of invasion stories include an "isolated, circumscribed setting" (15) in which the stranger is "by definition incongruous" (20). Nevertheless, the stranger "comes as if in answer to some unuttered call" (21). "With the entrance of the stranger, the mythic impinges upon the normal human world" (19), for even if the intruding stranger is presented realistically, he signifies the entrance of God or the Devil (21).[2]

Gothic and Grotesque

Although the basic invasion plot is familiar to readers of gothic romance, neither story takes place in a sinister crumbling castle. Oates presents a new ranch house in an upscale area where houses are some distance apart, probably suburban, since Connie visits a mall,[3] while Munro's setting is a remodeled "weekend place," "half a mile from the village" (120), an area that might be sparsely populated except in summer, with a cellar full of random items left over from rebuilding the house that evokes a slightly gothic atmosphere (123).[4] Since both houses are near a town, the protagonists isolate themselves by choice rather than necessity, Connie staying home from a family gathering to dry her hair and Nita refusing invitations to social activities from friends, presumably due to grieving for her recently deceased husband, although she explains to herself that she can't even read her favorite books anymore: "Too busy paying attention. . . . I mean thinking" (124).

Because the home and the body are symbolically equivalent as sites of invasion, either may substitute for the other. Male asserts that rape and castration may be the ultimate invasions of privacy (72). Both Connie and Nita fear rape by the invaders, but Nita's unnamed antagonist deflects that fear—leaving the question one of life or death—whereas Connie's intruder, Arnold Friend, demands she imagine a sexual encounter: "I'm always nice at first, the first time. I'll hold you so tight you won't think you have to try to get away or pretend anything because you'll know you can't. And I'll come inside you where it's all secret and you'll give in to me and you'll love me" (591).[5] As Christina Mardsen Gillis writes, Oates makes us aware that "seduction involves the invasion of personal, interior space" (133).

Because both Oates and Munro imagine normal, non-threatening settings, evil seems to enter the everyday world suddenly with the arrival of the intruders, both in disguise: Connie's invader having "shaggy, shabby black hair that looked crazy as a wig" and sunglasses that "mirrored everything in miniature" (587), Nita's claiming to be a fuse-box inspector. Yet in retrospect, clearly evil is already impending before the invasion, coming, as Male says, in response to "some unuttered call" (21). Oates's fifteen-year-old Connie lies to her mother about where she goes and what she does at night; she seeks male attention and kisses, enjoying her experience of something "sweet, gentle, the way it was in movies and promised in songs" (587).

While one critic believes that Connie has already lost her virginity (Coultard 507), others see her as merely flirting with sex and therefore especially vulnerable to shock on hearing Arnold's graphic description of invading her body while promising not to invade her home, a situation that Munro's story reverses. Larry Rubin, affirming Connie's virginity, writes of her fear, but also asserts her complicity: "The episode with Arnold Friend, then, may be viewed as the vehicle for fulfillment of Connie's deep-rooted desire for ultimate sexual gratification, a fearsome business which, for the uninitiated female, may involve destruction of the person" (59). Connie's mixed attraction/repulsion to seeing Arnold through the windshield of his car the night before—or possibly to "her own distorted reflection" in the glass, as Mike Tierce and John Michael Crafton write (222)—implicates her own fantasies and desires in Arnold's arrival in her yard when she is home alone (Tierce and Crafton 222). This point is substantiated by the fact that when Arnold arrives, he and Connie are listening to the same music on the radio (587). Descriptions of Arnold invoke demonic imagery, giving readers reason to fear that Connie's Edenic world has been invaded by Satan himself. Joyce M. Wegs describes these images not as gothic but as grotesque, asserting that Oates is here "drawing upon both its traditional or demonic and its contemporary or psychological manifestations," and using the grotesque "to suggest a transcendent reality which reaches beyond surface realism to evoke the simultaneous mystery and reality of the contradictions of the human heart" (87).

Munro's narrator emphasizes that Nita's body has already been invaded sexually by mentioning a particularly risky outdoor sexual encounter by the railroad tracks that leaves Nita and Rich "inordinately pleased with themselves" (122). Because her body has also been invaded by cancer, she is already dealing with the threat of death before her home invader arrives. Her home has been invaded previously, by herself as the other woman whose sunglasses (her disguise?) left in the house under reconstruction bring about discovery by Rich's first wife, Bett (121). Nita's invasion of Bett's marriage leads to an invasion of Nita's body by a pastry apparently contaminated by Bett with poison, presumably from "the little red veins of the big rhubarb leaves" (135)—which, we can extrapolate, precipitated Rich's divorce from Bett, which freed him to marry Nita. With Rich dead, Nita thinks of his study as a secret chamber, another site of invasion, repeating the term: "One of these days she would have to enter. She thought of it as invading. She would have to invade her husband's dead mind" (122).

The invasion tale provides both authors with an opportunity to present the feminist theme of a male/female struggle for supremacy.

Although readers generally don't find Arnold Friend charming or charismatic, he seems to hypnotize Connie with "a simple lilting voice, exactly as if he were reciting the words to a song" (589). In contrast, the self-acknowledged killer who invades Nita's home is clearly repulsive to Nita as well as readers, having murdered his family, which includes a mentally disabled sister. He is anything but charming to Nita when he laughs at her foolishness in believing his lie about checking her fuse box, and taunts her about her fear, saying he won't rape her because he prefers sex with "some nice lady I like and what likes me" (127).

However, both authors complicate the story of a male invader intimidating an innocent female with a female/female conflict. Connie's power struggle is not so much the battle of the sexes as the war she wages with her mother for control of her life. One result of Arnold's entry into her life is that her attitude toward her mother and family changes: she not only wants to see her mother again at the end, in spite of previous struggles for freedom, she is also willing to sacrifice herself to save her family from Arnold's threat: "You don't want them to get hurt" (594); "you're better than them because not a one of them would have done this for you," Arnold announces (595). Nita's rivalry with her husband's first wife is attenuated by her imagining herself as Bett to save her life; she even thinks of writing Bett to tell her—an overture of forgiveness and friendship or of female solidarity.

Nita's struggle has progressed beyond female rivalry to the point where her most important conflict is with death. Her solitude, her "paying attention," "thinking" (124), suggests she may be contemplating death. Her epiphany that "[t]he fact that she was going to die within a year refused to cancel out the fact that she might die now" (133) indicates that she wins this struggle with death in one of the few ways possible. Some critics see Connie's final acquiescence to Arnold's insistence that she come out of the house to him as an indication that she has transcended her earlier selfishness and can now think in terms of her family: as Stephen Slimp puts it, Connie has "in a moment, developed the spiritual life lacking in her former existence" (n.p.). In contrast, Nita's lack of involvement in her community, evident in her withdrawal from friends and the minimal arrangements she makes for her husband's funeral, is emphasized in the ending when she lies to the police about her car, possibly because telling about the invader would provoke an interrogation that would interrupt her solitude.

Ambiguities

Both stories contain troubling ambiguities that leave readers with unanswered questions. Oates's story, much anthologized since 1966, has been deemed significant for long enough to have evoked many articles, including a whole book of essays devoted to interpreting it—long enough, in fact, for Oates herself to respond to many of the critical controversies the story has generated. Yes, she did read about the Tucson murders and did find inspiration there, but, she said, "I do recall deliberately not reading the full article because I didn't want to be distracted by too much detail" ("'Where' . . . and *Smooth Talk*" 68). The dedication to Bob Dylan means that "It's All Over Now, Baby Blue" is the Dylan song that helped spark the story ("'Where'. . . and *Smooth Talk*" 68), and is alluded to by Arnold in the final paragraph of the story, not "Mr. Tambourine Man" or "Like a Rolling Stone" or "The Times, They Are A-Changin'."[6] Yes, Oates acknowledges, "Connie is shallow, vain, silly, hopeful, doomed—but capable nonetheless of an unexpected gesture of heroism at the story's end," when she is "generous enough" to sacrifice herself ("'Where' . . . and *Smooth Talk*" 69).

Yet readers' questions continue to point to ambiguities: Is Connie raped during the story (SparkNotes Editors)? Will she be raped after the story ends (see Easterly)? Does Connie's body want Arnold even as her mind judges him repulsive (Wegs 91)? Is her terrifying experience a dream or a dream vision (Rubin 58; Hurley n.p.)? Is the story a "pointed criticism" of the American dream (Quirk 81)? Is Arnold Bob Dylan, accompanied by Ellie as Elvis (Petry 155)? Does the story critique pop culture (Petry 157; Showalter, Introduction 7)? Announce an end to American innocence (Showalter, Introduction 7)? Is Arnold realistic rather than supernatural (Coulthard 505)? A satyr, "half-man and half-beast" (Easterly n.p.)? Is Arnold Satan (see Coulthard)? Is Arnold the "catalyst" for Connie's "inevitable realization of her insignificance and powerlessness" (Urbanski 78–79)? Does Connie grow spiritually through her experience of evil (see Slimp)? Given Connie's "claustrophobic world," is her experience "both terrifying and liberatory" (Showalter, Introduction 16)?

Similar ambiguities dot exchanges on Internet blogs concerning "Free Radicals." Is the killer, who emerges from Rich's cellar workshop more sinister than when he went down into it, a double for Nita's husband? (I'd add, does he come up from the depths of Nita's unconscious?) Does Nita poison the invader? With herbal tea? With red wine, a traditional poisoned drink of folklore (Thompson lists murder with poisoned wine as folk motif K929.1 [631])? (I'd add, or with scrambled eggs or ketchup? Did she perhaps also poison her husband? Did Rich turn evil toward Nita in some way?) Why does she lie to the police? (I'd add, or does she tell the police the truth, which would make the invasion a fantasy?) And I'd add more questions: Why does she take a drink of wine with the invader when she says she isn't allowed to drink, and she hasn't felt compelled to share other food and drink she has given him? Why does she say that she doesn't drive, and then tell of driving to town when she tells Bett's story as her own? Does she just miss the contradiction, since she's now telling the story of another in her own voice? Isn't telling the story of someone else in one's own voice what fiction writers do? Are the various discrepancies an indication she is fantasizing, that the invader is purely in her imagination? Is the whole story of the invader a fiction? Why does Munro entitle the story "Free Radicals"? Free radicals invade bodily cells and can cause cancer; antioxidants combat them ("Coenzyme"). Could the title, then, point toward a symbolic level of the story in which the killer is a free radical invading, while the herbal tea, ketchup, and red wine provide the antioxidants, along with Nita's storytelling, that defeat him?

Are the protagonists of both stories initiated into evil? If Connie's sexuality prepares her for Arnold's entrance into her life, does Nita's contemplation of death—or possibly her poisoning of her husband—indicate that the evil is within as well as without her? Or is there irony as she pretends she is the evil woman to save herself? Good women traditionally save themselves and others through their virtue, but Nita may save herself through her complicity with evil. In addition, we should ask of these two stories what Male asserts is true of invasion stories in general: has the stranger intruded or has the character projected the scenario (33)?

I believe that with both of these stories, we should read both/and or all/and rather than either/or because so many ambiguities that are so evident to readers, from literary critics to bloggers, must be intentionally set up for readers to puzzle over, to keep thinking about long after they have finished reading. Stories, as Male suggests, invade readers' consciousness (95). As readers try to solve a story's mysteries, just as they do constantly in real life, they try to make a story that incorporates enough of the details—the clues—to be satisfying. But as in real life, not all the details will fit into the story they compose. Alternatively, readers can avoid the lack of full closure by turning to a standard narrative to collect and organize the details, not questioning discrepancies.

Folk Tales

In clothing the naked home-invasion story, these two writers juxtapose myths and folk tales in ways that both revise the traditional tales and add new meanings to the stories of Connie and Nita. Each is a pastiche of other stories, and each is a story about storytelling.

Oates terms her story "an allegory of the fatal attractions of death (or the devil)" ("'Where' . . . and *Smooth Talk*" 68).[7] Oates's story also reflects folk tales featuring the Big Bad Wolf coming to the door, such as the Brothers Grimm's "Little Red Cap" or "The Wolf and the Kids." Connie saw Arnold in the car, and dallied a bit, like Little Red Riding Hood on the path to her grandmother's house—Eden invaded in both cases. Oates describes Arnold "sniffing as if she were a treat he was going to gobble up" (588); "his teeth were big and white" (590). Connie is smart enough not to let the wolf in, but in the long run that doesn't matter. He has eaten the family—metaphorically, by making her envision them having fun without her, and by his comments about her neighbor being dead, and perhaps a reflection of "The Three Little Pigs," since Arnold tells her, "This place you are now—inside your daddy's house—is nothing but a cardboard box I can knock down any time" (594). Psychologist Bruno Bettelheim says that the "wolf is an externalization, a projection of the child's badness" (44); "the wolf is not just the male seducer, he also represents all the asocial, animalistic tendencies within ourselves" (172). He explains, "If there were not something in us that likes the big bad wolf, he would have no power over us" (172). We like him since he is part of ourselves. Gretchen Schulz and R. J. R. Rockwood see Arnold as "the Woodcutter as well as the Wolf," the one who liberates as well as the one who destroys (125).[8]

Munro's story revises the folk tale "Snow White," a tale that focuses on the rivalry between older and younger women. Rich's first wife is the wicked queen offering poisoned food to the younger rival; Nita later apparently offers poisoned food after "becoming" Bett—that is, after growing older. Killing the male rather than the female rival, she has progressed beyond the point of female rivalry and is in a combat with death, represented by the killer, who is male, and the other killer, the disease. Biology is destiny, not merely for young women but ironically for the older woman. Like Snow White, Nita falls asleep near the end of the story, wakened not by a prince's kiss but by the knock of a policeman, her would-be modern-day rescuer. Bettelheim analyzes the sleeping motif in folk tales: "Each reawakening or rebirth symbolizes the reaching of a higher stage of maturity or understanding" (214). The ending of Nita's story, then, may be hopeful, may suggest she has reached a new level, and that her struggle with Death has ended with the death of Death as a threat to her.

Munro also evokes the Bluebeard stories that the Brothers Grimm tell: "The Robber Bridegroom" and "Fitcher's Bird." These stories tell of a young woman given to a rich man who has a secret room where the chopped up pieces of his former wives are hidden. In "The Robber Bridegroom," when the clever young woman discovers the secret, she waits until the wedding day and then tells the story, saying she "must have been dreaming" (Grimm 153); when the man is exposed by her story, he is punished by the community. Rich's cellar workshop with odd pieces of lumber strewn about evokes the secret room of folk tales; it is from the cellar that the murderer emerges as a threat to Nita.

The use of folk-tale motifs in both stories heightens readers' sense of familiarity as they read these strange stories, but it also sharply contrasts the endings of the ancient stories and the more recent ones: the joyous happy endings of the earlier stories are replaced by appropriate endings that leave much untold while making it clear that whatever happens won't provide happiness ever after.

Fiction and Reality

Reading "Where Are You Going, Where Have You Been" and "Free Radicals" together calls attention to the ways each story insists we think about the nature of reality and its relationship to fiction.

Connie composes fictions in her lies to family and, if Arnold's visit isn't real, in her fantasy or dream. Tierce and Crafton assert, "Both Ellie's and Arnold's existences seem to depend completely on the 'perpetual music'; consequently, Oates appears to be suggesting that they are not literally present," but rather "part of Connie's musically induced fantasy" (221); they note that "the fact that the phrase 'as if' is used over thirty times suggests that there is something dubious about Connie's experience" (222). Joan D. Winslow elaborates: the encounter can be seen as a dream, or it "can be read as a fantasy about a supernatural encounter and as a psychological analysis of the emotional state which could create such a dream" (96). However, D. F. Hurley writes of Oates's story, "The troubling possibility that no part of the story is a dream accompanies the more benign possibility, and this interpretive competition and uncertainty may be a partial explanation for the story's power and lasting popularity" (n.p.).

Whether reality or fantasy, Connie confronts what she doesn't acknowledge in daily life—that her town adventures with boys involve great risk that she might get raped there just as easily as in the scenario with which the story ends. This anti-American dream offers coercion, violence, and death rather than life, liberty, and the pursuit of happiness. Connie can't save herself by telling a story, because her story (like Nita's) is the same as that of her intruder: she already has the desires that Arnold Friend externalizes. Furthermore, she has no story of her own to tell because she lets popular music tell it for her. When Arnold alludes to Bob Dylan's song "It's All Over Now, Baby Blue" (595), inappropriately about this brown-eyed girl, it becomes even clearer that Connie is walking into a story not of her own making, even if it may reflect some of her desires; Dylan's lyrics in that song speak of the end of relationships rather than the sweet love celebrated in the songs Connie likes. Like her creator, Connie is a maker of fictions, and like readers, is enticed by fictions.

Nita's reimagining the scenario of poisoning suggests she is a creator of stories too, like Munro building from life events and altering them for her purposes. Telling one's own story and survival are linked in Margaret Atwood's concept of the "creative non-victim," who transcends victimization by accepting her "own experience for what it is, rather than having to distort it to make it correspond with others' versions of it" (39). In telling her predecessor's story as if her own, thereby acknowledging that she and the intruder harbor the same murderous impulses, she joins a small community of murderers: Bett, the invader, and Alice Munro, who has, as author, murdered all those in her stories who are killed. Unlike Connie, Nita can envision her own complicity in murder.

Munro presents Nita as a fiction reader: "Always fiction. She hated to hear the word 'escape' used about fiction. She might have argued, not just playfully, that it was real life that was the escape. But this was too important to argue about" (124). After asserting the primacy of fiction, and Nita's current inability to concentrate on reading it, a blank space initiates the next part of the story, which begins, "One morning" (124), reflecting the familiar "Once upon a time" of the folk or fairy tale beginning. Is Nita telling herself a story, which Munro is then telling us? Is Nita working out in her fantasy some of the problems to which she has been "too busy paying attention" (124)? After the sequence with the invader, Nita falls asleep, awakened by the policeman's knock on her door (138–39). Is his visit a fantasy too, or has her car been stolen? If the latter, what does the story suggest about how mysteriously fiction and reality blend into each other?

Male asserts that "if the quest is one of several analogies for the act of reading fiction, the intrusion is another"; characters "'read' the stranger the way we size up any new acquaintance" (95); so do readers. Like Nita and Connie, readers try to read each invader's intentions. The invader is also the reader: the writer invades lives to write of them, and by going along with the writer, readers similarly invade the story, telling it in ways that seem most appropriate to them. Stories invite readers to "penetrate" private spaces (Gillis 134). As Oates says, "We want so desperately to know—what? Others' lives are forever veiled from us, we can only hope to honor them in their complexity and remoteness" ("On the Composition" 357). The invasion narrative, therefore, is of particular interest to writers and readers alike because of the ways it raises questions about the nature of fantasy, the nature of reality, and the nature of our curiosity about others.

Cultures

Reading each story in the context of the other not only calls attention to similarities in their use of the gothic, in showing a female–female struggle within the context of a female–male one, in calling attention to the functions of folk-tale intertexts, and in highlighting ways the stories demand attention to the relationship of fiction and reality, but also contributes to readers' experiences of both narratives by highlighting differences. The forty-two years separating the stories facilitate Munro's selection of a sixty-two-year-old heroine rather than a young heroine on the verge of sexual initiation. The choice elicits a different reaction to the sexual threat and the death threat posed by the invader. Traditionally, virginity enhances the horror of rape, just as extreme youth enhances the horror of death; Oates uses these cultural constructs to increase our sense of revulsion at the likely outcome of Arnold's invasion. If, as Ailsa Cox writes, Munro's story is "a testimony to the fierceness of the will to live, even, or perhaps especially, in a character on the brink of death" (287), the age and health of the protagonist heighten rather than diminish the power of the death threat: "Death has come to the door, and has been, at least temporarily, repelled" (Cox 287–88).

While the age of the heroines may be connected to changes feminism has wrought in asserting that the sexual initiation of the young girl is not the only part of a woman's life that is interesting to tellers and readers of stories, feminism probably is not the major cause of another difference in focus: that related to concepts that have been seen to distinguish Canadian and American thinking.[9] Oates evokes a suburban Eden—a strong postwar myth in the United States—in which characters are pursuing happiness, but in which the American dream becomes ultimately a nightmare as a symbolic Satan enters the Edenic place. For Oates's Connie, the popular myth of the tender happily-ever-after romance is undercut by Arnold Friend's threatening narrative of rape. By staying home when her family goes out, Connie asserts her independence, her freedom to pursue happiness in her own way, reading her life by a master narrative central to American culture. Arnold invites her further into the American dream of land in some lovely place she has never been, thus offering her knowledge of sex and a chance to be a pioneer on a new frontier rather than offering her the knowledge of good and evil that Satan offers Eve: the narrator says he is thinking of "the vast sunlit reaches of the land behind him and on all sides of him, so much land that Connie had never seen before and did not recognize except to know that she was going to it" (595).[10] Oates's presentation of horror entering the everyday world unexpectedly echoes an additional core American myth: the image of a human as a spider hanging from a thin filament over the flames of hell, the condition of "Sinners in the Hands of an Angry God" from the famous sermon from 1781 by Jonathan Edwards:

> You hang by a slender thread, with the flames of divine wrath flashing about it, and ready every moment to singe it, and burn it asunder; you have no interest in any Mediator, and nothing to lay hold of to save yourself, nothing to keep off the flames of wrath, nothing of your own, nothing that you ever have done, nothing that you can do, to induce God to spare you one moment. (647)

In terms of Edwards's image, Connie experiences that sudden and shocking moment of being dropped into the flames of hell in the middle of a sunny afternoon.

In contrast, Munro uses Atwood's identification of survival as the quintessential Canadian theme (33), as Nita realizes her desire to survive not solely in the context of her cancer but in her dialogue with the invader, reimagining a story out of materials from her life to save her life.[11] If Connie discovers, in the words of the ancient Latin antiphon, that "in the midst of life we are in death" ("Media Vite"), Nita discovers the opposite: that in the midst of death we are in life, and that her life has value to her. To survive, she becomes a storyteller, an inventor of short fiction like her creator, Alice Munro. As we speculate on the ambiguities of the story, we may consider Nita to be telling lies to the invader and the police, reinventing herself as her enemy to save herself, and reinventing herself yet again to save herself. In "Free Radicals," life consists of one remission after another from death, which stalks constantly.

Notes

1. In Antti Aarne's classification of folk tales, tale type 956B, "*The Clever Maiden Alone at Home Kills the Robbers*" (339), is the story of a "solitary woman" who "realizes the presence of a disguised robber in the house and contrives to wound him, kill him, or put him to flight" (Simpson, qtd. in Brunvard 39). A related tale is 956D, "*How the Girl Saves Herself when she Discovers a Robber under her Bed*" (Aarne 339). In Oates's variant, however, Connie doesn't kill the invader, which juxtaposes Connie's story with those of her more clever predecessors. In *The Choking Doberman*, Jan Harold Brunvard surveys some of the contemporary urban legends that use this motif. Many thanks to Dr. Rita Ross of Canadian Studies at the University of California, Berkeley, for calling my attention to the earlier and persisting folk stories behind the stories by Munro and Oates.
2. Male specifically mentions "Where Are You Going" with regard to young girls being expected to stay under the protection of father and family, and notes that Oates's story is "rendered through Connie's acute but disordered senses" (71–72). Tierce and Crafton discuss Male's ideas about mysterious strangers being "saviors, destroyers, or ambiguous combinations of both" with respect to Oates's story (Tierce and Crofton 220; Male 10).
3. Some critics believe the house is on a ranch in Arizona, extrapolating from the story's connection to the well-publicized Tucson murders of young girls (see Quirk 86). The Tucson murderer, Charles Schmidt, was called "The Pied Piper of Tucson" in *Life* magazine (cited in Hurley n.p. 2; see also Showalter, Introduction 7–8, and Don Moser's article reprinted from *Life* in Showalter 51–66).
4. Citations to "Free Radicals" are to the version in Munro's collection *Too Much Happiness.*
5. Citations to Oates's much anthologized story are to the anthology *Literature*, edited by X. J. Kennedy and Dana Gioia.
6. See Tierce and Crafton on "Mr. Tambourine Man" and "Like a Rolling Stone" (223–24), and Petry on "The Times, They Are A-Changin'" (157). Oates also acknowledges the ancient ballads of "The Demon Lover," who spirits women away from home and family, as a source of the story, and used the folk motif "Death and the Maiden" as an early title of the story ("'Where' . . . and *Smooth Talk*" 68).

7. Marie Mitchell Oleson Urbanski writes that Oates "presents an allegory which applies existential initiation rites to the Biblical seduction myth to represent *Everyman's* transition from the illusion of free will to the realization of externally determined fate" (79).
8. Schulz and Rockwood find in Oates's story "motifs from such tales as 'The Spirit in the Bottle,' 'Snow White,' 'Cinderella,' 'Sleeping Beauty,' 'Rapunzel,' 'Little Red Riding Hood,' and 'The Three Little Pigs.' The Pied Piper is the "'frame device' that contains all the other tales" (116). Urbanski adds the biblical story of the seduction of Eve to the intertexts (75; see also n7 above).
9. Oates taught in Windsor, Ontario, from 1967 to 1978 (Showalter, Introduction 5); in short, after she wrote and published "Where Are You Going, Where Have You Been." None of the themes I discuss in this section are confined to any one culture, though some have more emphasis in the master narratives of one culture than another.
10. Margaret Atwood (following Frederick Jackson Turner among others) identifies the frontier as the defining American myth in contrast with survival as the core Canadian myth (31–32).
11. Cox sees the "theme of survival" as central to several stories in *Too Much Happiness* (287).

Works Cited

Aarne, Antti. *The Types of the Folktale: A Classification and Bibliography.* Trans. and enlarged by Stith Thompson. 1961. Second revision. Helsinki: Academia Scientiarum Fennica, 1987.

Atwood, Margaret. *Survival: A Thematic Guide to Canadian Literature.* Toronto: Anansi, 1972.

Bettelheim, Bruno. *The Uses of Enchantment: The Meaning and Importance of Fairy Tales.* 1975. New York: Vintage, 1977.

Brunvard, Jan Harold. *The Choking Doberman and other "New" Urban Legends.* New York: Norton, 1984.

Coulthard, A. R. "Joyce Carol Oates's 'Where Are You Going, Where Have You Been?' As Pure Realism." *Studies in Short Fiction* 26 (Fall 1989): 505–10. 10 July 2013. http://connection.ebscohost.com/c/literary-criticism/7135813/

Cox, Ailsa. "'Age Could Be Her Ally': Late Style in Alice Munro's *Too Much Happiness.*" *Critical Insights: Alice Munro.* Ed. Charles E. May. Ipswich MA: Salem, 2013. 276–90.

Easterly, Joan. "The Shadow of A Satyr in Oates's 'Where Are You Going, Where Have You Been?'" *Studies in Short Fiction* 27 (1990). 537–43. Omnifile Full Text Mega (H.W. Wilson). 10 July 2013.

Edwards, Jonathan. "Sinners in the Hands of an Angry God." *The Heath Anthology of American Literature, vol. 1.* Ed. Paul Lauter et al. New York: Houghton, 2002. 641–52.

Gillis, Christina Mardsen. "'Where Are You Going, Where Have You Been?': Seduction, Space, and a Fictional Mode." Showalter 133–40.

Grimm Brothers. "Little Red Cap." Tatar 13–16.

———. "The Robber Bridegroom." Tatar 151–54.

Hurley, D. F. "Impure Realism: Joyce Carol Oates's 'Where Are You Going, Where Have You Been?" *Studies in Short Fiction* 28.3 (1991): 371ff. OmniFile Full Text Mega (H.W. Wilson). 10 July 2013.

Male, Roy R. *Enter, Mysterious Stranger: American Cloistral Fiction.* Norman: U of Oklahoma P, 1979.

"Media vita in morte sumus" *Wikipedia.* http://en.wikipedia.org/wiki/Media_vita_in_morte_sumus. 23 March 2014.

Moser, Don. "The Pied Piper of Tucson: He Cruised in a Golden Car, Looking for the Action." Showalter 51–66.

Munro, Alice. "Free Radicals." *Too Much Happiness.* New York: Knopf, 2009. Print.

Oates, Joyce Carol. "On the Composition of *I Lock the Door Upon Myself.*" *Uncensored: Views and (Re)Views.* New York: Harper, 2005. 355–58.

———. "Where Are You Going, Where Have You Been." *Literature: An Introduction to Fiction, Poetry, Drama, and Writing.* Ed. X. J. Kennedy and Dana Gioia. Eleventh Edition. New York: Longman, 2010. 584–95.

———. "'Where Are You Going, Where Have You Been?' and *Smooth Talk:* Short Story into Film." Showalter 67–72.

Petry, Alice Hall. "'Who is Ellie? Oates' 'Where Are You Going, Where Have You Been?'" *Studies in Short Fiction* 25 (Spring 1988): 155–57. 10 July 2013. EBSCO. http://connection.ebscohost.com/c/book-reviews/7685126/who-ellie-oates-where-are-you-going-where-have-you-been.

Quirk, Tom. "A Source for 'Where Are You Going, Where Have You Been?'" Showalter 81–99.

Rubin, Larry. "Oates's 'Where Are You Going, Where Have You Been?'" *Explicator* 42 (Summer 1984): 57–60.

Schultz, Gretchen and R. J. R. Rockwood. "In Fairyland, and without a Map: Connie's Exploration Inward in Joyce Carol Oates's 'Where Are You Going, Where Have You Been." Showalter 113–31.

Showalter, Elaine, ed. *"Where Are You Going, Where Have You Been?": Joyce Carol Oates.* 1994. New Brunswick: Rutgers UP, 2002.

———. Introduction. Showalter 3–21.

Slimp, Stephen. "Oates's 'Where Are You Going, Where Have you Been?'" *Explicator* 57.3 (1999): 179. OmniFile Full Text Mega (H.W. Wilson). 10 July 2013.

SparkNotes Editors. "SparkNote on 'Where Are You Going, Where Have You Been?.'" SparkNotes.com, 2007. http://www.sparknotes.com/short-stories/where-are-you-going-where-have-you-been/. 23 Feb. 2015.

Tatar, Maria, ed. *The Classic Fairy Tales.* New York: Norton, 1999.

Thompson, Stith. *Motif-Index of Folk-Literature.* Vol 6. Indiana University Studies vol. XXIII, Studies nos. 111, 112. Bloomington: Indiana UP, 1936.

Tierce, Mike, and John Michael Crafton. "Connie's Tambourine Man: A New Reading of Arnold Friend." *Studies in Short Fiction* 22 (Spring 1985): 219–24. 27 March 2014.

Urbanski, Marie Mitchell Oleson. "Existential Allegory: Joyce Carol Oates's 'Where Are You Going, Where Have You Been?'" Showalter 75–79.

Wegs, Joyce M. "'Don't You Know Who I Am?' The Grotesque in Oates's 'Where Are You Going, Where Have You Been?'" *Critical Essays on Joyce Carol Oates.* Ed. Linda W. Wagner. Boston: GK Hall, 1979. 87–92.

Winslow, Joan D. "The Stranger Within: Two Stories by Oates and Hawthorne." Showalter 91–98.

Religion in Alice Munro's *Lives of Girls and Women* and *Who Do You Think You Are?*

JOSEPHENE KEALEY

In *Who Do You Think You Are?*, "Wild Swans" stands out for its religious component. In this story (the fourth of ten), alone on a train to Toronto, Rose has a sexual encounter involving a man dressed as a clergyman. Except for this instance, and in the retrospective final story, religion is not a strong feature of Alice Munro's story collection. This fact is significant for a few reasons. First, Munro is generally interested in Christianity. As Margaret Atwood explains, "The society Munro writes about is a Christian one. This Christianity is not often overt; it's merely the general background" (Atwood, "Alice Munro"). For example, Munro's collection *Lives of Girls and Women* (published in 1971, seven years earlier than *Who?*) is much interested in the Christian religion, and of different denominations—Evangelical, Baptist, Catholic. The chapter titles of this book alternate with religious and Christian vocabulary: "Heirs of the Living Body," "Age of Faith," "Changes and Ceremonies," "Baptizing." Furthermore, as Munro's *Who?* is bookended by a small-town setting—and much of the author's oeuvre is based on small-town experience—the depiction of Hanratty with little reference to a church or to the practice of churchgoing stands out. In the tradition of Canadian literary representations of small towns, the community parish or congregation is as much a mainstay as Main Street, the department store, and the barbershop. The small-town fictions of Stephen Leacock, Robertson Davies, and Margaret Laurence readily come to mind as being engaged with Christians and their churches. It is then conspicuous that Christian faith does not remain a determining force in Rose's life.

As a writer known for reworking thematic concerns—women's lives, sex, art, religion, education—from one collection to the next, Munro obviously was not obligated to reappraise religion in *Who?* as directly and heavily as she had in *Lives*. Indeed, if we were to imagine a trajectory from Del's small-town childhood in *Lives* to Rose's life following her move out of small-town Hanratty to a major city, it is appropriate, according to Munro's treatment of religion and religious faith in *Lives*, that religion would cease to be an element in Rose's story. In *Lives*, Del Jordan makes a circuit of Christian churches in her hometown Jubilee that culminates in her sexual relationship with the Baptist Garnet French. Garnet tries to force her into baptism, but Del rejects and fights Garnet's violent and religious insistence: "He pushed me down again but this time I was expecting it. I held my breath and fought him" (*Lives* 222). Del turns her focus away from religion as a medium for exploring and understanding identity and toward sex, and then to writing. While the first four stories are set in Hanratty, *Who* also develops its protagonist's adventures in the city after she leaves home, taking off, as it were, from *Lives*'s epilogue. Rose's explorations involve identity, art, sex, relationships, and home, and not religion or religious faith. Del's concluding rejection of religion—by ending her relationship with Garnet—presents religious exploration and faith as a part of maturation that one ultimately outgrows. *Who?* is not bothered by religion past Rose's childhood; sex and art, in contrast, are mainstays of adulthood.[1] Religion and its offerings are finally no longer useful to the Munrovian young woman on the brink of adulthood and artistic maturation.

This is not to say that sex and art are themselves not fraught with complications. Indeed, sex and art intertwine with religion in the coming-of-age moments experienced by Del and Rose. For example, it is at a Baptist church meeting that Garnet French laces his fingers with Del's, prompting an eager response from Del (*Lives* 199), who then takes Garnet as a sexual partner. After accepting Garnet's advances, Del's attendance at religious meetings is prompted by her desire to be with her new boyfriend. She is eager for sex now, and less for religious exploration (202–03). In *Who?*, Rose's most intense experience with religion is with a clergyman on the train and her experience, as stated, involves inappropriate sex. However, Rose is leaving her small-town home for the first time to visit Toronto, and the sex she receives at the hands of the clergyman initiates Rose's transition out of girlhood. Religion thus seems necessarily present at the turning points of both young women's lives, suggesting that the move toward maturity, adulthood, and art entails a final meeting with religion.

It would be too simple to characterize Del and Rose as mere victims of Garnet and the clergyman, respectively. Although their interactions with religion are finally violating, violent at some level, marking a significant moment for each young woman, consent is a vexed issue in both stories. The extent to which the characters consent to, and therefore are responsible for, what happens to them fills out our reading of how religion is used in the stories. For instance, Del is initially an eager partner, attending Garnet's religious meetings as a way to stay close to him (*Lives* 201). In "Baptizing," Del surprises herself by admitting her desire to be married to Garnet and to have children: "'Yes,' I said [to Garnet's question, "Would you like to have a baby?"]. . . . Where would such a lie come from? It was not a lie" (221). But she refuses his insistence that she be baptized: "I don't want to be baptized. It's not good if I don't want to be baptized" (221). Garnet attempts a perverse form of baptism, forcing Del underwater until she will relent: "He kept saying, 'Baptize you!' and bobbing me up and down, with less and less gentleness, and I kept refusing . . . " (221). Her willingness to attend religious functions as a means to remain Garnet's sexual partner is in contrast to Garnet's need for her to be baptized in order for her to become his lifelong partner.

As Del correctly understands, consent to baptism is crucial; Garnet's violence at the river is therefore offensive also because of the religious element of the event. Consent to a future of domesticity frightens Del much less than Garnet's request that she be baptized. Del's unequivocal refusal to be baptized and her fierce physical struggle against Garnet seem to align religious affiliation with the intellectual poverty that Garnet and his family represent:

> I had thought I wanted to know about him but I hadn't really, I had never really wanted his secret or his violence or himself taken out of the context of that peculiar and magical, and it seemed now, possibly fatal game. (222–23)

For Del, the consent to being officially Christian, and not merely an observer of religious life, would gravely alter her future as a writer. Del takes religion seriously, it appears, at least the official religious affiliation that baptism would confirm.

Rose's contact with religion is less personal. Her stepmother's disdain for religion exempts Rose from attending church in Hanratty

(*Who?* 30); thus, that the man who molests her on the train is dressed as a clergyman, if he's not indeed one, is a religious non-issue for Rose. That is, she seems intrigued by the possibility that the man is in a religious disguise but not disturbed by the fact that a clergyman might be gravely betraying his vocation. We, as readers, might be scandalized, but Rose is not. We might feel repulsion toward the clergyman, but it is not clear that Munro insists that we do. In Rose's story, sex is often, if not always, disturbing. In the stories before "Wild Swans," school-age children explore sex with mockery and disgust (30); school-age boys rape a vulnerable girl (30–33); adults are generally ill-equipped to educate children about sex in healthy ways. In comparison, we might understand Rose's experience on the train as less repellent. The childhood sexual aggression that Rose witnesses culminates in the confusion she feels about the sex that the clergyman insists on *and* offers her. Indeed, Rose is greedy for the experience, caught in a situation that offers her sexual excitement and pleasure even as she struggles to understand the nature of the violation: "But there was more to it than that. Curiosity. More constant, more imperious, than any lust. . . . Invasion, and welcome . . . " (75, 76–77).

Rose, we would be justified to argue, is incapable of resisting the clergyman's advances. She is, after all, an adolescent. But the adult narrative voice of the story wants us to understand that Rose is embarking on adulthood, an obviously positive life stage. The clergyman's molestation[2] sets Rose at a transitioning moment, as mentioned above. Leaving the constricted Hanratty for the expansiveness and independence that city life momentarily offers, Rose, at the hands of the clergyman (literally), awakens to her own sexual desires as a woman. For someone whose original understanding of sex largely entailed cruelty and assault, Rose elicits sympathy for succumbing to the meager, vile sex the clergyman provides. It is thus (perversely) fitting that a clergyman, whose religious duties include performing initiating rituals, takes advantage of the ambivalent Rose.

Thus, religion, in a state of arrogance and disingenuousness, enables sex but then is finally shrugged off. Writing about Canadian fiction, including that of Munro, William Closson James helpfully generalizes about the literary use of Protestantism:

> The search for something larger is a religious quest. . . . This quest or search for something larger than the self may be launched by Protestantism, or even encouraged by Protestantism's religious ethos and engaged in those terms, but the God of traditional Protestant

> Christianity is no longer available to serve that "something larger" to which they might belong. (37)

It would be hard to argue that either Del or Rose needs a religious figure to stand in for the transition each girl experiences, but religion fits Munro's purposes. For Del, it is in rejecting religion via Garnet French (and all that it is associated with in the stories) that enables her movement into art, as we see in the final story, "Epilogue." For Rose, the sexually initiating experience on the train signals her move away from home and (as she sees it) all that it entails. The clergyman on the train is a useful prop to initiate a carnal experience while simultaneously performing a sending-off function. A process is in order here in which either girl must progress from childhood through an experience that involves religion (and sex), and then proceed to adulthood, leaving religion behind (sex, of course, remains). The suggestion seems to be that religion is a part of childhood interests that initiates mature sex, religion being an explainer of the meaning and significance of sex. But then done away with, religion is ultimately a short-term and dubious contender in the lives of maturing young women.

As an enabler of sex, religion possesses a threatening quality. As we know, religion in *Lives* and "Wild Swans" is physically violating: Garnet French attempts to force Del into baptism by nearly drowning her, and the clergyman on the train takes advantage of his status to molest Rose. Garnet's religion also threatens Del's intellectuality and future as a writer, and the possibility of the clergyman's disguise reinforces the book's agonizing question, "who do you think you are?" An effect of this threatening quality is that it serves to relieve us, as readers, when Del escapes Garnet and his religious insistence, and to underscore the uncertainty Rose feels about herself—the book's central concern. After having experienced the sex enabled by either story's religious manifestation, the characters are not bothered by religion again. We are not supposed to be worried, of course, over Del's abnegation of religion and Rose's once and final involvement with a religious affiliate.[3] Tied to their respective hometowns, which are short on cultural enlightenment, religion is a temporary influence that gives way to mature adult imagination and creativity. Del's and Rose's responses to religion are also ironically tied to their anti-religious mothers.

For example, Del's hometown, Jubilee, impresses upon her and all girls that they are expected eventually to marry and bear children. Del is not impressed with that future based on the examples of marriage and childrearing she sees. Her mother, an atheist, makes efforts to rise above conventionality and appears to be a model to emulate. Addie sells encyclopaedias door to door to improve life generally in Jubilee (*Lives* 62), joins a reading and discussion group (69), and writes letters to the newspaper (76–77). But because of her difference from everyone else in Jubilee, she falls short of Del's aspirations and is subject to her daughter's criticisms:

> I hated her selling encyclopaedias and making speeches. . . . I hated her writing letters to the newspapers. Her letters about local problems, or those in which she promoted education and the rights of women and opposed compulsory religious education in the school. . . . (76–77)

Del's early investigation into sex and religion is, in large part, a way to distance herself from her mother, finding both, as stated, entwined in Garnet French. Near the end of her relationship with Garnet, Del surprises herself by accepting Garnet's proposal of a domestic future resembling her mother's but wants to avoid—as did her mother—religious affiliation. Garnet's insistence on baptism unwittingly forecloses what could have been a life of maternal imitation for Del, and which propels Del's flight from religion *and* domesticity. Del's future, as suggested in "Epilogue: The Photographer," the final story of *Lives*, is non-religious and non-domestic, and creative and artistic: "this female *bildungsroman* ends in authorship and exile not in love and marriage" (Beer 128). She finds salvation in art, as it were.

In *Who?*, Rose is also affected by her stepmother and seeks to disassociate herself from her. In "Wild Swans," we are told that Flo, Rose's stepmother, warns her stepdaughter of men who disguise themselves as ministers in order to disarm girls whom they intend to molest (67–68). Flo is a storyteller, a gossip who takes pleasure in the salacious details of sordid acts. As a young girl, Rose indulges her stepmother with grim stories about her school, of classmates and teachers involved in shameful events (49). Embarking for Toronto for the first time, and thus, hopefully, on a superior life, Rose physically and psychologically distances herself from Flo when she boards the train to Toronto. Amazed that the clergyman might be, after all, a molester in disguise as described by Flo, she is not prepared to challenge his authority, nor is she sure she wants to. In her youthfulness, Rose is inexperienced and hence at a disadvantage; but her youthfulness also makes her desire experience. Rose's sexual experience on the train is, in a way, a practical affair. By succumbing to the clergyman's molestation, Rose takes advantage of the opportunity to participate in sex, obviously, but also to take a role in a sordid tale, thereby countering her stepmother's influence. The poetic language that parallels Rose's sexual pleasure prevents us from taking a tragic approach to the scene: "You could have had such a flock of birds, wild swans, even, wakened under one big dome together, exploding from it, taking to the sky" (77). Her orgasm is a heightened, aesthetic experience. Rose commits her transition in a transformative, albeit offensive way by rewriting, as it were, Flo's tale of the molesting clergyman in disguise. Rose becomes a story writer and can tell her own tales.

What then about Del and Rose's artistic achievements in light of their interaction with religion? *Lives*'s final story, "Epilogue: The Photographer," opens with Del discussing her mother's exaggerations about the number of suicides that have occurred in Jubilee: "'This town is rife with suicides,' was one of the things my mother would say . . . " (*Lives* 227). Del admits having once believed her mother, carrying "this mysterious, dogmatic statement around with me . . . —that is, believing that Jubilee had many more suicides than other places . . . " (227). She later develops an attitude of "skepticism and disdain" "towards everything my mother said" (227). The language here is religious, and then anti-religious, the latter attitude taking final hold: "I was probably closer to the truth than [my mother] was" (227). If official religion has been put aside, Del solicits truth (and meaning) in the "real" story of Jubilee.

The penultimate story, "Baptizing," ends with the italicized line "*Real life*," which reads like a resolution following the mantra "*Garnet French, Garnet French, Garnet French*" (226). In the language Del uses to describe her loss of faith in her mother, we are not surprised that she, through acting, turns to storytelling to explain real life. Indeed, Del imaginatively composes a story based on the lives of a Jubilee family—the Sherriffs—which had been the subject of much local gossip: "what had happened to them isolated them, splendidly, doomed them to fiction" (228). Although she uses local gossip to embellish the events in her ridiculous gothic novel, Del explains the difference between reality and truth in her storification of Jubilee: the events in her imaginative novel "seemed true to me, not real but true, as if I had discovered, not made up, such people and such a story, as if that town was lying close behind the one I walked through every day" (231). Here, Del adopts "truth," a philosophical and theological concept, to describe her desire to understand Jubilee, turning art into a matter of faithfulness to her hometown. To say that the Sherriffs are "doomed" and, in a later reflection, in "danger" (232) of her fictional rendering of them suggests a strong correlation between the belief in art to explain reality and the failure of religion as depicted in *Lives*. As practices that attempt explanation, both fail to reveal adequately life's experiences.

As an adult, Del later recognizes the immaturity of the art that was her gothic novel:

> I never said to myself that I had lost it, I believed that it was carefully stored away, to be brought out some time in the future. The truth was that some damage had been done to it that I knew could not be put right. Damage had been done; Caroline [her imaginative character] and the other Halloways and their town had lost authority; I had lost faith. (234)

Again Del uses religious language to describe her artistic process. Her loss of faith in her representation of Jubilee and its inhabitants results from greater perspicacity. She realizes that her Halloways are poor manifestations of what she really wants to do with Jubilee, what she wants from her writing:

> It did not occur to me then [at the time of her gothic novel] that one day I would be so greedy for Jubilee. . . . [N]o list could hold what I wanted, for what I wanted was every last thing, every layer of speech and thought, stroke of light on bark or walls, every smell, pothole, pain, crack, delusion, held still and held together—radiant, everlasting. (236)

The reality of Jubilee, she exclaims, mocks her attempts to aestheticize it:

> And what happened, I asked myself, to Marion [the inspiration for her character Caroline]? Not to Caroline. *What happened to Marion?* What happened to Bobby Sherriff when he has to stop baking cakes and go back to the Asylum? Such questions persist, in spite of novels. (234)

I find it very interesting that Munro chooses "in spite" instead of "despite" to mark the power of reality over art/fiction. Del loses faith in trying to depict Jubilee because any attempt to do so, she is arguing, falls short of the strange beauty of reality.

In the final story of *Who?*, also titled "Who Do You Think You Are?," Christianity is again mentioned in flashbacks of Rose's childhood. The character of Milton Homer, the catalyst for Rose's lifelong mimicry of Hanratty, is said to have "baptized" local babies with a comic ritual (236); he had disrupted parades with cruel mockery (238); his aunts were members of the socially powerful Methodist church, whose influence eventually dies (244–46). And the passing influence of that church seems to have gone hand in hand with Milton Homer's garish antics: "In short, he had made himself so comical a sight [that] the power of the Milton sisters, the flax-mill Methodists, could be seen as a leftover dribble" (246). The class and social power of the church dissipates through the comedic powers of one of their own.

The theme of performance is heavily played out in each of *Who?*'s ten stories, and the case of Milton Homer recalls the performance of the clergyman (or disguised clergyman) in "Wild Swans." As Homer's antics undermine the gravity and legitimacy of his aunts' affluent and influential church, the suggested religious front of Rose's molester removes religion (in this case, specifically Christianity) from any status of importance. Although Milton's behaviour embarrasses his aunts' pride and propriety, we already understand from "Wild Swans" that Christianity is not a spiritually commanding institution in Hanratty. It is performed and uses the art of display to control or manipulate others. Flo's final comment about the aunts underscores this: "'That was the end of them thinking they could run things,' Flo said. It was hard to tell, as always, what particular defeat—was it that of religion or pretension—she was glad to see" (246). Both, of course, are defeated: religious pretension and pretentious religion.

The significance of Milton Homer is a serious issue for Rose because in this final story that introduces the garish comedian, Rose comes to a critical understanding about herself. Upon visiting Hanratty, she meets an old friend, "Ralph Gillespie," whom she remembers imitating Milton Homer when they were school mates (236–37). Rose here reveals that her own adult imitations of Milton Homer—in particular, the scenes of Milton's self-authorized baptisms—are in fact borrowed from Ralph's imitations: "'I didn't see (Milton) [perform].What I saw was Ralph Gillespie *doing* Milton Homer'" (236–37). It seems to me that here we see the ghost of the clergyman of "Wild Swans." Milton's mock religiosity reflects back on Rose's sexual initiation by the disguised clergyman, which in turn clarifies Rose's attraction to men who disguise, perform, and imitate roles: her husband who wishes to be the worshipper of his white goddess; her theatrical, deceiving lover Clifford; and another lover, Simon, who playfully pretends various characters (and eventually performs a true disappearing act). Indeed, upon meeting Ralph again, encountering him in the legion hall, Rose attempts to bond with him by reminding him of his school-age mimicry of Milton Homer (Ralph remains introverted) (253–54). To sum up this mix of questionable religion, performative behaviour, and relationships, *Who?* suggests that mock performance of those behaviours and beliefs held (too?) dear dismantles the power these elements hold over the person, but we are left bereft when the performance comes to an end:

> The thing she was ashamed of, in acting, was that she might have been paying attention to the wrong things, reporting antics, when there was always something further, a tone, a depth, a light, that she couldn't get and wouldn't get. And it wasn't just about acting she suspected this. Everything she had done could sometimes be seen as a mistake. (254–55)[4]

Munro's conclusions in both stories do not leave us content, of course, because even as her characters come to some revelation about themselves, the wisdom they achieve teaches that they do not know themselves. At the end of *Lives* and of *Who?*, Del and Rose, respectively, engage with the disparities between life, self, and the attempt to articulate both in art. We leave them facing this significant dilemma and challenge. Therefore, it is expected that Munro's characters cannot use their hometown religion as a guide when they become adults. The religion of their childhood and adolescence is depicted as more interested in itself than in the "other." Garnet French, as the strongest religious manifestation in *Lives*, requires Del's conversion for his own sake; and obviously the clergyman of "Wild Swans" is an unholy and abject depiction of Christianity. Religion is ultimately separated from these characters' search for identity and meaning but remains a part of their critical survey of home and the past. Religion might be a characteristic of home and history, but in Munro's fiction, it has no active role in the protagonist's future.

Notes

1. In Robert Thacker's biography of Alice Munro, the author describes how she wished to sectionalize *Lives:* "I wanted each section to cover *an area of growing-up*—Religion, Sex, etc. . . . " (211, emphasis mine).
2. There is no doubt in my mind that the clergyman molests Rose. He is absolutely morally guilty. Rose's conflicted feelings do not positively qualify the clergyman's act in any way.
3. We find the rhetoric of religion in *Who?* after "Wild Swans," used in secular and pagan terms. As a new university student, for example, Rose observes the tense reverence for academia projected by other female students: "Rose did not care for the look of them, for their soft-focused meekly smiling gratitude, their large teeth and maidenly rolls of hair. They seemed to be urging on her some deadly secular piety" (85). Again, her new boyfriend Patrick worships her, thinking of her as a maidenly goddess (95–97). As Atwood explains for us, in the quote above, religion is in Munro's background.

4. Compare these lines with a quote from *Lives*, above: "And no list could hold what I wanted, for what I wanted was every last thing, every layer of speech and thought, stroke of light on bark or walls, every smell, pothole, pain, crack, delusion, held still and held together—radiant, everlasting" (236).

Works Cited

Atwood, Margaret. "Alice Munro: An Appreciation." *The Guardian* [UK]. Culture/Books, 11 October 2008. https://www.theguardian.com/books/2008/oct/11/alice-munro. 24 June 2014.

Beer, Janet. "Short Fiction with Attitude: The Lives of Boys and Men in the 'Lives of Girls and Women.'" *The Yearbook of English Studies* 31 (2001): 125–32.

Munro, Alice. *Lives of Girls and Women.* 1971. Toronto: Penguin, 2005.

———. *Who Do You Think You Are?* 1978. Toronto: Penguin, 1996.

James, William Closson. *Locations of the Sacred: Essays on Religion, Literature, and Canadian Culture.* Waterloo, ON: Wilfrid Laurier UP, 1998.

Stovel, Nora Foster. "Temples and tabernacles: alternative religions in the fictional microcosms of Roberston Davies, Margaret Laurence, and Alice Munro." *International Fiction Review* 31.1–2 (January 2004): 65.

Thacker, Robert. *Alice Munro: Writing Her Lives, A Biography.* Toronto: McClelland & Stewart, 2005.

III
Effects

"Something": The "Dark Sides" of Alice Munro's Story-Telling in Its American Context

DAVID R. JARRAWAY

There is always in this life something to discover.
—Alice Munro, "The Albanian Virgin"

. . . we live amongst riddles and mysteries—the most obvious things, which come in our way, have dark sides, which the quickest sight cannot penetrate into . . . in almost every cranny of nature's works . . .
—Laurence Sterne (qtd. in Alice Munro "Introduction," *Selected Stories*)

. . . it is part of morality not to be at home in one's home.
—Theodor Adorno, *Minima Moralia*

In "A Conversation with Alice Munro," which took place around the time that *The Love of a Good Woman* was published, in 1998, the editors at Knopf Doubleday posed the inevitable interview question: "What writers have most influenced you and who do you like to read?" Munro's immediate response is instructive since all of the writers in the first instance are American: "Eudora Welty, Carson McCullers, Katherine Anne Porter, Flannery O'Connor, James Agee. Then Updike, Cheever, Joyce Carol Oates, Peter Taylor." But then she adds William Maxwell, and with a significant qualification: ". . . and especially and forever, William Maxwell."[1] The "especially and forever" thus anticipates six years later a glowing tribute Munro will pay to Maxwell, the long-time fiction editor at the *New Yorker* magazine who had done so much to solidify Munro's own reputation in the United States (and elsewhere) over the years. But it's also a rare moment of artistic apology for Munro, and highlights the "something" alluded to in my title.

Commenting on Maxwell's novel *They Came Like Swallows* (1937), Munro writes, ". . . there is something new with each telling, some new action at the periphery or revelation near the centre, a different light or shading, a discovery, as there must be in the stories at the heart of our lives," and goes on to link this moment to a similar one in Maxwell's later novel, *The Folded Leaf* (1945), when Munro further observes that "the friendship between [two adolescent boys growing into men] is turning into something they cannot bear" ("Maxwell" 40, 41). Wistfully reflecting on such moments in Maxwell's fiction, Munro then speculates about a rhetorical means for retrospectively renovating her entire narrative canon: "If only I could go back and write again every single thing that I have written" ("Maxwell" 35). More precisely revolving that "something" at the centre of her work two years later, Munro offers a formulation that might strike some as distinctly postmodern when she further observes: "It's not the story—it's more like the spirit, the centre of the story, *something there's no word for*, that can only come into life . . . when words are wrapped around it" ("Writing. Or, Giving Up Writing" 300, emphasis added).

In the decade previously, it's arguably Munro's story collection entitled *Open Secrets* (or *OS* in citations below) that comes closest, I would argue, to that unspeakable Maxwellian crux that conceivably offers the author a quite radically new purchase on her narrative art. For this is the volume that also promises something like a paradigmatic shift to a whole new counterfactual reality, as Munro discloses to Peter Gzowski in a CBC *Morningside* interview, broadcast hard on the heels of the publication of *Open Secrets*, in 1994:

> I want to move away from what happened, to the possibility of this happening, or that happening, and a kind of idea that life is not just made up of the facts, the things that happened . . . . But all the things that happen in fantasy, the things that might have happened, the kind of alternative life that can almost seem to be accompanying what we call our real lives. I wanted to get all that, sort of, working together. (qtd. in Thacker 450)[2]

The speculation here about an "alternative life" shadowing some more plausibly factual or real dimension of human experience is provoked, for Gzowski at any rate, in the opening story of *Open Secrets* entitled "Carried Away" by the reappearance in Toronto of Jack Agnew in the female protagonist Louisa's itinerant life some years after his ghastly death via decapitation in the Doud piano factory back in Carstairs. As Louisa divulges to either a fictive or a real Jack Agnew near the end of the story, "[I]t turned out to be something else I wanted entirely" (*OS* 40). Yet that enigmatic "it," or *lapse* in realism, forms a vital thread linking almost all of the stories in the volume to follow: the mysterious disappearance of Heather Bell in "Open Secrets," for example, or the riddling cause of Simon Herron's death in "A Wilderness Station," or Eunie's problematic alien abduction in the penultimate "Spaceships Have Landed," to mention only three. As Maureen Stephens revolves all such phantasmatic alternatives in her own fraught life—"But suppose you did see something? Not along the lines of Jesus, but something?" (*OS* 132)—she stumbles onto a rhetorical formulation that just might be the long held "open secret" of American literature much before the novel writing of William Maxwell last century: in Maureen's words once again, "something not startling until you think of trying to tell it" (*OS* 134).

Repeatedly trying to tell or talk down that which intractably lies hidden to plain sight is the "open secret" that Richard Poirier, for one, refers to in American literature as the achievement of a certain "vagueness." As Poirier quite precisely explains that term (in a borrowing from William James's *Principles of Psychology*), "the reinstatement of the vague" in American pragmatism has everything to do with "efforts to create the gel of human relationships even as the gel is forever melting away" (274, 275). Such vagueness (in a further borrowing of James's *The Will to Believe*) approximates "[t]he bottom of being [that] is left logically opaque to us, as *something* which we simply come upon and find, and about which (if we wish to act) we should pause and wonder about as little as possible . . . [as] the ungraspable phantom of life" (279, emphasis added). And it's Poirier's further association of that opaque selfhood or phantom being with the image of an abyss—"a gap or an abyss [as] an invitation simply to get moving and keep moving, to make a transition" (279, 280)—that perhaps best establishes Munro's own connection to vagueness by means of a character like Annie McKillop, say, in "A Wilderness Station." For Annie, the gaping wilderness provides her the opportunity not so much to "station" her identity, to go with the story's title, but rather the momentum "*to get our station changed*" since as one letter writer states, "*the move will be out of one wilderness station unto another*" (*OS* 171), and never more so than when Annie, very much on in years, takes to her Stanley Steamer in search of her brother-in-law, George Herron, in the story's fourth and final part: "People were still in church when [she] started, but later on the roads were full of horses and buggies making the journey home . . . . But it turned out Old Annie did not want to be so sedate . . ." (*OS* 184).

Annie's highly mobile surrender to open space, then, conceivably reinstates at a pivotal point in Munro's own storytelling more generally the vagueness of America's modernist subjectivity, an airy or phantom nothing whose "burden of obscurity" will baffle readers "in the very process of the [text's] delivery to us," as Poirier notes (287). Here, one perhaps might recall the punning "waywardness about [Annie's] one eye that does not interfere with her vision and her excellent sewing" (*OS* 161), or maybe even more baffling, her refusal to remain in her house, finding in the bites of flies and mosquitoes "another sign that in the outside [she] was protected" (*OS* 180). As Poirier further observes, "there is a mixture here of directness with exploratory uncertainty, of forthrightness with confusion, a compulsion to speak along with a fear that there may be nothing to say" (287)—precisely Maureen Stephens's "open secret" conundrum observed previously.

That combination of "forthrightness and confusion," of course, rehearses once again the problematic of realism alluded to earlier with Munro's Maxwellian insistence upon interposing some kind of alternative as an accompaniment to "what we call our *real* lives"—in Annie McKillop's case, a certain relaxation of the "order imposed on her days" with the removal of the Herron brothers from her life, and symbolized by her "open door" and the animals "[coming and going] in her house" at once (*OS* 167). Joyce Carol Oates, a longtime reader of Munro (and vice versa, as noted earlier), characterizes this problematic as "an elliptical and poetic sort of vernacular realism" (43), much in the spirit of Annie's allergy to "the monotony of life or the drudgery [she] may have been born to" (*OS* 172), hence another reinstatement of the vague.[3] But as Oates goes on to relate, the vagaries of such an elliptical realism can also serve as a salutary stay against "the deep suspicion[ing] of people who seem to deviate from the norm, who threaten the protocol of narrow domesticity"—characters, that is, viewed as "lesions in the carapace of uniformity that provide the writer [like Munro] with the most extraordinary material" (43, 42). Hence, a character like Maureen, once again from "Open Secrets," wistfully reflects upon the disappearance of Heather Bell from her Canadian Girls in Training (C.G.I.T.) summer outing:

> Sometimes when [Maureen] is just going to sleep but not quite asleep, not dreaming yet, she has caught something. Or even in the daytime during what she thinks of as her normal life. She might catch herself

> sitting on stone steps eating cherries and watching a man coming up the steps carrying a parcel. She has never seen those steps or that man, but for an instant they seem to be part of another life that she is leading, a life just as complicated and strange and dull as this one. And she isn't surprised. It's just a fluke, a speedily corrected error, that she knows about both lives at the same time. (*OS* 132)

Could it be that in the "Open Secrets" narrative, Heather Bell has indeed bounded past the carapace of uniformity and sided with the vagaries of that "other" life, just as Maureen describes?

With the sharp contrast presented in the preceding passage between a "normal life" associated with daytime and "another life" just short of sleeping and dreaming, this important meditation on "both lives at the same time" contains another significant intersection with Oates and American literature more generally. In a hypnotic reflection on Edward Hopper's justly famous painting entitled *Nighthawks*, novelist Oates, like the character Maureen, finds "another life" in the form of a "night-self" calling out to her from the dark "interiority" of Hopper's canvas. As a young teenager, Oates remarks that she found this vaguely aberrant notion of subjectivity descending upon her, as in Hopper's *Nighthawks*, during "[t]hose long, lonely stretches of time when no one else in the house was awake (as far as I knew); the romance of solitude and self-sufficiency in which time seems not to pass or passes so slowly it will never bring dawn" (*Where* 346). In clear contrast to the night-self's "mystery in the insomniac night" under the influence of the enigmatic Hopper, Oates pits the very conventional and the very house-bound "day-self": "a self that was obliged to accommodate others' expectations, and was, indeed, defined by others, predominantly adults." The stark juxtaposition of day and night here, rather like the "light or shading" for Munro of "something" in Maxwell, thus provokes Oates ultimately to proclaim: "*Yes, but you don't know me* . . . in adolescent secrecy and defiance. You really don't know me!" (346, emphasis retained).

In a further meditation on contemporary art, this time on Charles Sheeler, Oates discloses her being overtaken by variations of her very own night-self while perusing Sheeler's painting *Upstairs* (1938):

> simple geometric figures are so arranged to suggest stairs leading up from a well-lighted room into the darkness of an unseen upstairs—an ominous unknowable future . . . [where] All is still, silent, utterly mysterious. One seems to be gazing upon one's own future. (*Where* 353)

The self's disappearance into a futural darkness similarly underscores for Maureen in "Open Secrets" the true significance of Heather Bell's disappearance, and perhaps Maureen's own longing to elude containment in the same way:

> *I dare you to run away.* Was it possible? There are times when girls are inspired, when they want the risks to go on and on .... From the chintz-covered hassock at her husband's side [Maureen] looked out at the old copper-beech trees, seeing behind them not the sunny lawn but the unruly trees along the river—the dense cedars and shiny-leaved oaks and glittery poplars. A ragged sort of wall with hidden doorways, and hidden paths behind it where animals went, and lone humans sometimes, becoming different from what they were outside, charged with different responsibilities, certainties, intentions. She could imagine vanishing. (*OS* 117)[4]

"But of course you didn't vanish," the passage concludes, "[for] there was always the other person on a path to intersect yours and his head was full of plans for you even before you met" (*OS* 117). In Munro's reading of Maxwell, that ghastly intersection for the female protagonist in Maxwell's novel significantly titled *Time Will Darken It* (1948) perhaps takes the form of her husband's arm "whose hand settled on her heart, and she let it stay there for a moment, thinking how hard and heavy it was . . . how importunate, how demanding; how it was not part of her and never would be, insisting on a satisfaction, even in sleep, that she could not give" (qtd. in "Maxwell" 39). And so for Maureen back in "Open Secrets," when her husband "first put his arm around her waist, in the office, [and] she thought he must believe that she was headed for the wrong door and was redirecting her . . . because of his propriety, not because she hadn't longed to feel his arm there" (*OS* 129).[5]

It therefore should not surprise us to discover that Hopper holds an important attraction for Munro as well.[6] In an "Open Letter" from 1974, she renders one painting in particular by Hopper this way:

> A barber-shop, not yet open; the clock says seven and it must be seven in the morning, yes, a cool light, fresh morning light of a summer day. Beside the barber-shop a summer-heavy darkness of trees. The plain white slight shabby barber-shop, so commonplace and so familiar, yet everything about it, in the mild light, is full of a distant murmuring, almost tender foreboding, full of mystery like the trees. (qtd. in Thacker 88–89)

Like Oates's attraction to Hopper and Sheeler, Munro's initial daytime response to the interiority of the "commonplace" and the "familiar" inevitably gives place to its opposite, as the "darkness" and "mystery" of the exterior come to take its place. In such moments, clearly, we are in the vicinity of that mysterious "something" in Hopper to which Munro is intuitively responsive. "Silently in [Hopper's] pictures," Wells likewise responds, "*something* is happening. And if it isn't happening at the moment, it has just happened, or is about to. We are brought to some existential threshold." Concludes Wells: "Near the end of his life, Hopper said that each of his pictures represented 'an instant in time arrested—and acutely realized with the utmost intensity,' *something* akin to those epiphanous moments in Joyce or Proust" (11–12, emphases added, and further in Wells on 82, 86, 95, 150, 174, and 274n4).

For Munro, then, the Hopper painting thus becomes the very emblem of the "open secret," quite like a poem by Emily Dickinson, according to Diana Fuss. "[T]hrough the mimetic act of unlocking [an Emily Dickinson] poem," so Fuss contends, "readers are invited to discover their [own] unbounded interiority . . . . For Dickinson, the most private spaces are the most public, and hiding is simply the best way to be seen" (60). The open-endedness of the secret arguably forges the clearest link between Munro and Hopper, one surmises. For as Gail Levin, Hopper's most important biographer, records, "the one important feature" shared between Hopper's artist studio in New York City and his summer home in Truro, Massachusetts, was their "treasured sense of openness—of openness that he could look out on, no matter how small his own interior space might be," that is, "the kind of view [Hopper] had as a boy in the family house at Nyack [New York] with its unobstructed view of the river down the hill" (258–59). What is more, as Fuss further remarks, "the door in Dickinson's poetry is a completely indeterminate figure" like the "instability" of the human subject itself, and finds further corroboration in the work of German philosopher Georg Simmel "that the door is far superior to the dead geometric form of the wall [since] to Simmel, a wall is 'mute,' but a door 'speaks'" (43). And because "a door more successfully transcends the divide between the inner and the outer[,] a door [being] where the finite borders on the infinite" (Fuss 43), little wonder then that in the "ragged sort of wall" that we recall drawing Maureen Stephens outside her own private space into something more public, she should set such great store by "the hidden doorways, and hidden paths behind it"—doorways egressing into that "big bulging awful mysterious entity called THE TRUTH," as Munro phrases it (see n1 below) for "becoming different" (*OS* 117).

After the publication of *Open Secrets* in 1994, Munro moved on to a volume of *Selected Stories* in 1996, which may be thought of as a kind of portal to all of her later work, particularly in light of the quotation she carefully chooses to round out her own "Introduction" to that mammoth collection—a passage from Laurence Sterne's *The Life and Opinions of Tristram Shandy, Gentleman*—which rehearses all over again something of the darker opacities of "THE TRUTH" about selfhood just scanned:

> *But mark, madam, we live amongst riddles and mysteries—the most obvious things, which come in our way, have dark sides, which the quickest sight cannot penetrate into; and even the clearest and most exalted understandings amongst us find our selves puzzled and at a loss in almost every cranny of nature's works: so that . . . we cannot reason upon it . . .* (qtd. on xvii, italics retained)

Interestingly, Oates is prepared to view Munro's treatment of the "dark sides" of the phantom subject right from the beginning of her publishing career, citing a passage in "Walker Brothers Cowboy" from *Dance of the Happy Shades* (1968) about the father's life "turn[ing] into something you will never know, with all kinds of weathers, and distances you cannot imagine" (qtd. in "Who Do" 42). So with John Updike, who views that very same passage as a specific reflection on the "the wooing of distant parts" of selfhood in *Selected Stories*, and quite likely all of Munro's writing to follow.[7] And perhaps, via a work like *Something I've Been Meaning to Tell You* (1974), we catch the darker sides of that mysterious "something" extending into Munro's much later work as well, into a work like *Hateship, Friendship, Courtship, Loveship, Marriage* (2001), for example, where we might hypothesize a possible raison d'être for the storytelling art itself—"I did not think of the story I would make . . . in particular—but of the work I wanted to do, which seemed more like grabbing *something* out of the air than [of] constructing stories" (119)—or even into a more recent story collection like *Too Much Happiness* (2009): "There is *something*, anyway, in having got through the day without it being an absolute disaster. It wasn't, was it? She said maybe. He hadn't corrected her" ("Deep-Holes" 117).

In his *Edmonton Journal* review of *Hateship, Friendship, Courtship, Loveship, Marriage*, Thomas Wharton observes, "Reading Alice Munro is a quiet reminder that, amid the big ideas, the big important books always in a rush to sum up 'society as a whole,' it is always the solitary, observing, *ultimately unknowable self*, to whom life, and death, happen" (qtd. in Thacker 503, emphasis added). Robert Fulford, dates this preoccupation in Munro to much earlier, remarking with reference to *Something I've Been Meaning to Tell You* that "You can't really understand anyone, you can only nibble at the edges of comprehension, . . . a truth Alice Munro has been telling us, in one way or another, for two decades" (qtd. in Thacker 269). Alison Lurie, however, finds this particular preoccupation especially evident in a later work like *The View from Castle Rock* (2006), underscoring there "Alice Munro's commitment to indeterminacy and the essential confusion and mystery of life" (qtd. in Thacker 545). But to go back to that "something you will never know," from Munro's very much earlier *Dance of the Happy Shades*, my own inclination is to view that hypnotically charged "something" as the repeated occasion, as I argue elsewhere, for a kind of subjective "avoidance" within the larger interrogation of "house and home" underwriting much of American literary discourse almost from its inception (see Jarraway 2010), hence a final context for revolving Munro's storytelling art with which I shall briefly conclude.

The significant placement of characters like Annie McKillop and Maureen Stephens in *Open Secrets* with respect to doors and doorways, along with their ultimate extrusion, either real or imagined, into some secret but wide open space—such eventualities offer readers of Munro something of a placeless sense of mystery surrounding the human personality that accords rather well with David Macey's psychoanalytic view of subjectivity as something "non-known" (in a bow also to Maurice Blanchot)—something rather like "an absence" or "a void," an "always-already [] lost object," and hence "a mirage of totality" (77, 75). Dorrie Beck, for instance, who fails to show up at her engagement dinner in "A Real Life," or even at the "open door" (hence her name) of her own house as Millicent discovers—"the evil silence and indifference of a house lately vacated by *somebody*" (*OS* 61, emphasis added)—thus becomes yet another vague or void subject in a rather long litany. "Caught between the imperatives of the super-ego and the instinctual demands of the id," Macey further observes, "the ego is not, however, *master* in its own house, and cannot aspire to Cartesian certainties" any longer (74, emphasis added). Instead, Macey concludes (bowing to Michel Leiris this time), "the ego is a collage of identifications, the work of a psychic bricolage," and Macey underscores his houseless characterization by emphasizing the ego's inability to exist "in situation," an "abstraction," therefore, "that becomes an opaque obstacle to the understanding of concrete subjectivity" (75, 81).

Macy thus nudges us toward the notion of a Jamesian dismantled self in Deleuze and Guattari's *A Thousand Plateaus*, whose veritable "becoming" lies precisely in "one who knows how to be nobody, to no longer be anybody. To paint oneself gray on gray" (197). "From Hardy to Lawrence, from Melville to Miller," write Deleuze and Guattari firmly in the American literary context, "the same cry rings out: Go across, get out, break through, make a beeline, don't get stuck on a point . . . *break through the wall* of the signifier . . . toward the realms of the asignifying, asubjective, and faceless" (186, 187, emphasis added). How else to explain, in the concluding story of *Open Secrets*, entitled "Vandals," Liz's wanton trashing of the Ladner country house in light of Bea Doud's own capitulation to a controlled (and controlling) egotism—one "insanity" who is "living inside [another's] insanity," as she refers to it (*OS* 225). Nor is Liz's horrific refusal of the claustral domestication of subjective space necessarily a feminist stance as Warren, Liz's partner in crime, reflects about a similar experience from his boyhood:

> But then something took over. They dumped a bottle of ketchup on the tablecloth and dipped their fingers in, and wrote on the wallpaper, *"Beware blood!"* They broke plates and threw some food around . . . . Nobody had seen them getting into the house and nobody saw them leaving. (*OS* 236–37)

Precisely at the point, therefore, when Dorrie reappears in "A Real Life"—"in the dim window light . . . a most mysterious and maddening person whom Millicent seemed now to have conquered" (*OS* 64)—Ralph Waldo Emerson is there in American literature perhaps to warn us about the strict demarcations of domestic space. "The experience of creativeness," Emerson importantly remarks in an essay on Plato, "is not found in staying at home, nor yet travelling, but in transitions from one to the other" (qtd. in Jarraway *Wallace Stevens*, 30n10), as Annie McKillop proves only too well in her own transit from one wilderness station to another.

Taking Emerson at his word, therefore, readers casting Munro's storytelling within its American context offer themselves several opportunities to explore the deep sense of irony attached to the troping of house and home generally in contemporary fiction, if according to Adorno, ". . . it is part of morality not to be at home in one's home" (39). And it is a sense of irony, following Deleuze and Guattari further, that Dorothy's repeated invocation of "No Place Like Home" from *The Wizard of Oz* suggestively endeavours to impart in her own traumatic states of transition, like those of Annie and Dorrie and perhaps

Munro herself, throughout much of Victor Herbert's 1939 film adaptation. Yet much before Munro's fiction and Herbert's film, the writing of Herman Melville in American literature serves as the provocation for Deleuze and Guattari elsewhere to remark that "Everything begins with Houses," and additionally to suggest that the ironization of the house in American fiction is part and parcel of "a kind of deframing following certain lines of flight . . . in order to dissolve the identity of the place"—and, by implication, human identity—"through variation with earth" (*What Is Philosophy?* 189, 187). The promise of freedom and agency signalled by such ironization and such dissolution is "something" at least held out to a character like Rhea in "Spaceships Have Landed": "Outside was the night with the river washing out of sight . . . [and] the dirt roads faintly shining on their way to nowhere . . ." (*OS* 205). But "[knowing] all this was there" (*OS* 205), something tells Rhea she may not be up to the challenge of its "darker sides," at least not yet:

> she couldn't pay attention to it . . . Billy Doud had chosen her, an engaged girl was confiding in her, her life was turning out perhaps better than anybody might have predicted. But at a time like this she could feel cut off and bewildered, as if she had lost *something* instead of gaining it. As if she had suffered a banishment. From what? (*OS* 205, emphasis added)

Fortunately for Rhea, she retains the memory of a former time when she and Eunie might "cut from Eunie's yard down to the riverbank [where] they became different people . . . . The Two Toms . . . not male or female . . . [but] somebody exceptionally brave and clever . . . and—just barely—indestructible" (*OS* 197). In reflecting upon "the way people's different memories deal with the same (shared) experience," Munro is persuaded that "The more disconcerting the differences are, the more the writer in me feels an odd exhilaration" (see n1 below)—which is perhaps the best invitation for readers to revisit the Munro "House of Fiction" for "something" further, since, in her words, "You go back again and again, and the house the story, always contains more than you saw the last time" (*Selected Stories* xvii).

Notes

1. For the full text of the conversation, see http://knopfdoubleday.com/2010/01/08/alice-munro-interview/ (accessed March 16, 2014). Frequent reference is also made to the work of William Maxwell in the McCulloch and Simpson *Paris Review* interview from 1994.

2. In the *Paris Review* interview from the same year, Munro once again gives voice to the Maxwellian importance of making a place for "alternate realities" in her story writing: "Changing your perceptions of what is possible, of what happened—not just what *can* happen but what really *has* happened. I have all these disconnected realities in my own life, and I see them in other people's lives" (244). Hence, if there is something of an "alternative" to our "real lives" recorded here, then, as Julia O'Faolain remarks in the 1994 *Times Literary Supplement* review of *Open Secrets*, "realism can only be a convention and a willed distortion" since Munro's "new stories pivot [now] on reality's slipperiness" (qtd. in Thacker 460–61). The problematic of "reality" in Munro's fiction is thus taken up in what follows, but I shall return specifically to the issue of the "disconnected realities" seen in "other people's lives," especially in the conclusion here.
3. In the *Paris Review* interview, Munro talks about her new life as a young mother in West Vancouver in the early 1960s very much in the same terms: "Life was very tightly managed as a series of permitted recreations, permitted opinions, and permitted ways of being a woman. The only outlet, I thought, was flirting with other people's husbands at parties; that was really the only time anything came up that you could feel was real." Accordingly, Munro divulges, ". . . something I'd like to write about and haven't [is] that subversive society of young women, all keeping each other alive" (242), and it's interesting to speculate that a character like Annie McKillop might just be a move in that direction, as I argue in what follows.
4. If the "dare . . . to run away" in this citation's opening line is motored by a flight toward "something," it seems possible to imagine how Munro's later collection of stories entitled *Runaway* (2004) might want to enlarge exponentially this motivational dynamic in several of the narratives contained therein; hence, in "Chance," for example: "I thought something was going to happen . . . ." "Then something happened that was as sudden and unbidden as her tears" (60, 68); or, in "Soon": "My faith isn't so simple . . . I can't describe it. But it's—all I can say—it's *something*. It's a—wonderful—*something*" (124, italics retained); or, in "Trespasses": "[Delphine] spoke about herself—her tastes, her physical workings—as about a monumental mystery, something unique and final" (210, and elsewhere on 131, 158, 265, and passim). A further gloss on this entire dark passage might be provided by Munro herself in a brief commentary entitled "On Writing 'The Office,'" from 1978: "A woman who sits staring into space, into a country that is not her husband's or her children's is likewise known to be an offense against nature. So a house is not the same for a woman. She is not someone who walks into the house, to make use of it, and will walk out again. She *is* the house; there is no separation possible" (qtd. in Thacker 174). The problematic relationship between the house and identity, particularly the "night-self" aspect of that identity implicit in Oates's previous remarks, I therefore take up as a final "American context" for Munro's storytelling further down.

5. Cf. a quite similar moment later in the *Open Secrets* sequence with the narrative entitled "Spaceships Have Landed": "When they parked, and sometimes even when they drove, Billy put an arm around Rhea's shoulders, he squeezed her. A promise . . . . He tapped his fingers on her, on her knees, and just at the top of her breasts, murmuring appreciatively and then scolding himself, or scolding Rhea, saying that he had to keep the lid on her" (203).
6. In his majestic *Silent Theater: The Art of Edward Hopper* (2007), Walter Wells cites a passage in Clement Greenberg's *The Collected Essays and Criticism* (1986) where the claim is made that although "[the] best of Hopper's images are 'literary,'" according to Greenberg, "they convey 'insight into the present nature of American life for which there is no parallel in literature'" (qtd. on 12). Both Oates and Munro would undoubtedly beg to differ with this assessment.
7. For an extended reflection on the "distant parts" of selfhood specifically in the American literary context, see my *Going the Distance* (2003).

Works Cited

Adorno, Theodor W. *Minima Moralia: Reflections from Damaged Life.* 1974. Trans. E. F. N. Jephcott. London: Verso Editions-NLB, 1978.

Deleuze, Gilles and Félix Guattari. *A Thousand Plateaus: Capitalism and Schizophrenia.* Trans. and foreword by Brian Massumi. Minneapolis: U of Minnesota P, 1987.

———. *What Is Philosophy?* Trans. Hugh Tomlinson and Graham Burchel. New York: Columbia UP, 1994.

Fuss, Diana. *The Sense of an Interior: Four Writers and the Rooms That Shaped Them.* New York: Routledge, 2004.

Jarraway, David R. "Future Interior: Subjective (A)Voidance in John Updike's 'Rabbit' Novels." *Canadian Review of American Studies* 40.1 (2010): 45–62.

———. *"Going the Distance": Dissident Subjectivity in Modernist American Literature.* Baton Rouge: Louisiana State UP, 2003.

———. *Wallace Stevens and the Question of Belief: "Metaphysician in the Dark."* Baton Rouge: Louisiana State UP, 1993.

Levin, Gail. *Edward Hopper: An Intimate Biography, Updated and Expanded Edition.* New York: Rizzoli, 2007.

Macey, David. "On the Subject of Lacan." *Psychoanalysis in Contexts: Paths Between Theory and Modern Culture.* Ed. Anthony Elliott and Stephen Frosh. London and New York: Routledge, 1995. 72–86.

McCulloch, Jeanne and Mona Simpson. "Alice Munro: The Art of Fiction." *Paris Review* 87.1317 (1994): 226–64.

Munro, Alice. *Alice Munro: Selected Stories.* Toronto: Penguin Canada, 1998.

———. *Dance of the Happy Shades*. Toronto: Ryerson, 1968.

———. "Maxwell." *A William Maxwell Portrait: Memories and Appreciations*. Ed. Charles Baxter, Michael Collier, and Edward Hirsch. New York and London: Norton, 2004. 34–47.

———. *Open Secrets*. Toronto: Penguin Canada, 1995.

———. *Hateship, Friendship, Courtship, Loveship, Marriage*. New York: Vintage Contemporaries, 2001.

———. *Runaway: Stories*. Toronto: Penguin Canada, 2004.

———. *Too Much Happiness*. Toronto: McClelland & Stewart, 2009.

———. "Writing. Or, Giving up Writing." *Writing Life: Celebrated Canadian and International Authors on Writing and Life*. Ed. Constance Rooke. Toronto: McClelland & Stewart, 2006. 297–300.

Oates, Joyce Carol. *Where I've Been, and Where I'm Going*. New York: Plume, 1999.

———. "Who Do You Think You Are?" *The New York Review of Books*, 3 December 2009: 42–44.

Poirier, Richard. "The Reinstatement of the Vague." *Pragmatism: A Contemporary Reader*. Ed. Russell B. Goodman. New York and London: Routledge, 1995. 269–92.

Thacker, Robert. *Alice Munro: Writing Her Lives, A Biography*. Toronto: McClelland & Stewart, 2005.

Updike, John. "Magnetic North." *New York Times Book Review*, 27 October 1996: 11, 13.

Wells, Walter. *Silent Theater: The Art of Edward Hopper*. London and New York: Phaidon, 2007.

Desire and Deferral: "Royal Beatings"

Ian Dennis

It has frequently been observed that Alice Munro's stories resist closure. Adrian Hunter identifies a story's "refusal" to "take possession of its subject" ("Taking Possession" 127);[1] John Gerlach, a "teas[ing] . . . rhythm of delay" (155). Numerous voices have invoked the creation and sustenance of "mystery." The author herself has said she "wanted to challenge what people wanted to know" (Howells 120), which both makes her practice explicitly a matter of thwarting or gratifying readerly and indeed authorial desire, and expands the provocation well beyond the question of what happens next, or last.

Here too there is considerable consensus on the result. For Ildikó de Papp Carrington "one of the most characteristic patterns in her fiction [is] the ironic reversal of both the characters' and the readers' expectations" (14). It is thus, for Carrington, "often intensely uncomfortable to read. The final emotional residue that many of her stories leave behind . . . is a lingering sense of unresolved ambiguity and dismayed unease" (5). Others, in various terms, have concurred.

Clearly, though, desires of some kind have been satisfied, or there would be no books, no conference, no Nobel Prize.

This essay will investigate how Munro's fiction works—how it evokes, defers, and satisfies desire—in the instance of one notable story, "Royal Beatings." I will proceed from what might be called an anthropologically inflected position of inquiry, making occasional reference to ideas of human desire and culture developed by Eric Gans and René Girard. But we will not require familiarity with or full acceptance of these theorists' larger hypotheses.[2] Commonplace understandings of desire and aesthetic pleasure, perhaps not finally at odds with their thinking, should mostly serve our purposes.

In narrative, of course, the desire to know what happens next is indeed primary. It is not exclusive. There are other consummations, offered, delayed, sometimes provided. Resentments, too, furies of thwarted desire, mobilized, gratified or not gratified. Still, readers really and probably firstly do read to satisfy narrative desire. Or, they read *on*, once that desire has been awakened, and the short-story form, especially in magazine publication, has a particularly urgent imperative to awaken it. The pressure this puts on the first sentence or two is as obvious as the clichés of enigmatic promise to which even competent writers are often reduced. "Royal Beatings" begins with such a promise, indeed a threat, of violence—"You are going to get one Royal Beating" (1)—issued by Flo to her stepdaughter Rose (or Nadine in the *New Yorker* version), and to the reader by the narrator. So our first, most enabling, and easiest to detect deferral is of that menaced—expected, feared, desired—outcome.

Following immediately, exploiting as it were the energy of desire the promise generates, we have Rose musing about the phrase itself, "the word 'Royal'" and how it "lolled on Flo's tongue," imagining the "occasion both savage and splendid" called forth by the adjective, a thread picked up by the narrative voice when, confirming the promise, we are told that "her father was the king of the royal beatings" (1). Punning, wordplay, has the effect of temporarily directing attention back to signs and away from their imagined referents, a deferral that depends in this and most cases upon the momentum established by other means. (A quibble, complained Dr. Johnson, was to Shakespeare a fatal Cleopatra—but then, Shakespeare at the same time demonstrated considerable ability to awaken narrative desire.[3]) All language that draws attention to its own form, for its richness, aptness, or suggestiveness as much as for its puzzlements or incongruities, defers the primary satisfaction of image consumption to some degree, and may defer it too long or not well enough. But the first paragraphs of "Royal Beatings" are managed with sufficient tact to allow most of us—or from the perspective of *New Yorker* editor Charles McGrath and his colleagues in 1976 (Thacker 11), enough of us—that crucial comfort, that confidence, that we are in hands that will neither tease nor brutalize. At least, not beyond endurance. Any shocks, surprises or epiphanies we subsequently achieve will occur under, and depend upon, the horizon of expectations thus far generated.

But we still have desires, and some of these are now briskly serviced, with a sequence of short, cumulative sentences providing context, the details of Rose's life history. "They lived behind a store in Hanratty, Ontario. . . . Her mother had died" (1–2). We want to know such things and are told them. Another form of deferral is also quite absent here: periodic sentence structure. Delays in grammatical resolution are rarely risked. A grammar of Hemingwayesque straight talk prevails, with all that such a style promises.

But distraction and redirection of desire certainly occur in other ways. Predictable detail, that satisfies immediate wants, is interrupted at carefully judged intervals with the strange, grotesque, or paradoxical. Yes, her mother died, but before doing so she says she has a feeling like having a "boiled egg" in her chest, with the shell on (2). This is rationalized immediately—a blood clot—but the physicality of it, the floating particularity of the egg, remains, indeed, is re-emphasized. The meaning and significance of the event—our heroine's mother has died—must contend with the lingering oddness of the detail. Still, authorial judgement forestalls travesty, or leavens tragedy.

The operation of such judgement has sometimes been accounted a kind of superior insight into reality, or into the reality of human feelings and experience at any rate. Lorraine McMullen, for example, cites Rose's mother's comparison when making the plausible point that such verbal manoeuvres, paradoxes, or "startling metaphors and similes, [all] reveal the unusual, the complex, and the contradictory in events and the mixed and contradictory in emotions aroused by events" (146). Perhaps such a revelation was aspired to, but it is probably worth reminding ourselves that not all fatal pulmonary embolisms produce such a simile, and that the human experience of mortality is diverse, very much encompassing the alternatives carefully avoided by the story's approach.

There clearly were at least two other options here. Perhaps I can summon them up, somewhat in the same way historians deploy "counterfactuals" to better understand the actual course of events. (I mean, of course, "counterfactual" in the sense of counter to the known facts of the words on the published page.[4]) There could have been no egg, a mother dying, a child bereft or hardened. Tears. Pathos could have been evoked, with its very obvious (and justified!) mobilization of reader sympathy. This is not merely a question of reflecting real-life statistical likelihood. Stories, good stories, but of a somewhat different character and effect, have also proceeded this way. Alternatively, there could have been an egg, and travesty more fully embraced. Mordant puns, darkly ironic egg-and-chicken jokes, even. While there might have been risks of an off-putting cleverness, if properly handled the conveyed attitude might successfully have appealed to another kind of desire. It could have provided a model. Readers too could have felt clever, original in their shared appreciation of the absurdity of a world unimagined by the generality of the sincere, the naïve, the—anyway, other people. Such works also are to be found, and satisfactory in their own way.

Now, it might be suggested that in the version actually offered us by "Royal Beatings," we have some measure of both sorts of satisfaction. But it would be more accurate to say that gratification of either kind of desire is deferred. Both remain possible as we read on. Both, to the end, are potential resolutions of a tension of deferred significance. Critics sometimes speak instead of the establishment of "distance," but such phrasing does not adequately reflect the vividness achieved. Rather, by delaying or deferring the discharge of desire or resentment, the passage leaves the image to linger, attention privileging form, for the while. Distance from imagined cathartic resolution, that is, becomes proximity to beguiling form. Similar choices present themselves and are deferred at almost every point in the story:

> On the bench outside Flo's store several old men from the neighbourhood sat gossiping, drowsing in the warm weather, and some of these old men coughed all the time too. The fact is they were dying, slowly and discreetly, of what was called, without any particular sense of grievance, "the foundry disease." They had worked all their lives at the foundry in town, and now they sat still, with their wasted yellow faces, coughing, chuckling, drifting into aimless obscenity on the subject of women walking by, or any young girl on a bicycle. (3)

Most obviously, incipient sympathy, or resentment at the damage inflicted by industrial capitalism on these victims, is undercut by their violation of another of our sensitivities with their presumably sexist—if "aimless"—commentary on passing women. Every detail of this exquisitely tuned passage works to carefully balanced purposes. Comfortably drowsy old men in warm weather, dying. The lack of grievance, the discretion, the yellowing sickness. Coughing, chuckling. Just when we might have been able to recover a kind of aged innocence—and the carnal desires of the old are of course always potentially to be treated with a degree of indulgence—we are required to accommodate an imagined assault, vague, verbal, but unquestionably sexual, on children:

> Among the people [Flo] listened to were Mrs. Lawyer Davies, Mrs. Anglican Rector Henley-Smith, and Mrs. Horse-Doctor McKay.

> She came home and imitated them at supper: their high-flown remarks, their flibberty voices. Monsters she made them seem; of foolishness, and showiness, and self-approbation. (10)

Fiction about small town life, from Stendhal and Flaubert through George Eliot and Mark Twain, has of course concerned itself very much with class—or more precisely, with the resentment of social distinctions and privileges—a resentment usually, but not always, shared by characters within and writers beyond the works in question. There is in Munro's fiction perhaps no systematic diagnosis of imitative desire and the resentments it generates, as found in Stendhal and memorably analysed by René Girard.[5] But in the passage above we can certainly see in operation the aesthetic tactic by which class resentment is deferred. Not only is Flo unreliable in the (never directly quoted) representations she offers of her ostensible social betters, but her own complex of (un)attractive qualities so thoroughly mediates any feelings we might have about the other ladies that we are left distrusting not just her view of them, but even, more quietly, such views in general. Mrs. Horse-Doctor McKay might well merit our scorn—she has not been rendered reflexively virtuous by this minimal account—but all we really have is the remarkable Flo, and she is all we may ever have in the world of *Who Do You Think You Are?*, despite that book's ostensibly central focus, starting with its (Canadian) title, on social status and the iniquities of its assertion.

Or, we may contemplate the treatment of the potentially comic, potentially grotesque, or potentially pathetic dwarf Becky Tyde, "town oddity and public pet," who is both "harmless and malicious" (8). Both alternatives are made present as she and her behaviour are described, and each cancelled or modified, deferring focussed emotional responses, and leaving us confronted with the carefully odd portrait itself, whose seemingly independent life—independent that is, of our desires and expectations—is thus a product of its incongruities.

The most salient challenge, though, must certainly be the management of the story's central episode, the Royal Beating itself.

With violence, we enter into a particularly intense field of desire and resentment. And here, more clearly than with Becky, alternative versions are discerned even as they are skirted. Indeed, one such version is explicitly presented: the beating of old man Tyde.

Preceding and shadowing Rose's beating by her father, this is a slow-motion lynching, whose details shuttle through the pathetic, the fearful, the ridiculous and comic, and, again, the odd, incongruous. At any lynching—a moment of contagious or imitative desire par excellence—human choices are actually quite stark, and even to a representation thereof only deferrals or distractions of considerable cunning can diversify our responses. The choices boil down, in *reality*, to fight or flight, participation or equally forceful rejection—before a *representation*, to resentment of the victim, or of the perpetrators (among whom may or may not be listed the narrator, the purveyor, or creator of the scene).

Those who attack old man Tyde are "useless young men," whom the narrator dryly mocks in their motivation to give him "a horsewhipping in the interest of public morality" (7). This story within the story is once again mediated through its apparent teller, Flo, but only variably so, as the last-quoted words are clearly those of the mature narrator, who may or may not also be Rose. The juices of resentment, at any rate, are made to flow: Flo's resentment, Rose's, the narrator's—and almost inescapably, ours. But then they are also comical, foolish young men, and we are given details of their essentially innocent preoccupations: baseball, horse racing, hat-wearing. If this is an indictment of a masculine culture of violence, it could certainly be more pointed. They bring guns but waste their ammunition in boyishly exuberant firing to no effect. Their victim, already established as unattractive, behaves badly, sending out his daughter, then hiding under the bed, and this of course interrupts the simpler forms of compassion or outrage at his fate. We are distracted from the pathos of his child watching her father's violent humiliation by *her* typically odd and unappealing behaviour—she doesn't open the door to him afterward because she doesn't want to let the cold in. The victim then rushes fearfully and selfishly off with his money, leaving his children unprotected, and dies later, at a distance both geographical and affective, a deferred result with a deferred or diminished emotional charge.

Everything that happens—that Flo says happens—is shadowed, however, by other possibilities, other stories. Nothing is odd if nothing is normal, and readers who have been engaged by the account necessarily experience the superimposition, or subliminal suggestion, of other, more sympathetic children in similar straits, other more noble victims, other more resentable perpetrators and their backstage manipulators (who, in Flo's account, may or may not have put them up to it). Imagination peers hungrily through Hanratty and its denizens, odd and opaque as they are, to a more unambiguously vicious community, to a brutal and brutalized human race—present company always excepted—as a whole.[6] As constantly as this alterity is summoned, however, it is dismissed, undercut, parodied, by the stream of disconcerting detail.

Even so, and even if the ethically tangential outcomes include the establishment of Becky and her brother in apparent prosperity for life (and centrality: she is as close to a celebrity as the town will permit). Even if one of the convicted attackers is incongruously lionized in old age in the story's coda, still, for all this, old man Tyde *is* apparently murdered. This has registered, and inflects the promised but much-deferred beating of our protagonist.

The royal beating is not a lynching, but one on one, male on female, adult on child, taking us into the territory of resentments and desires of a somewhat different caste, if almost as inescapable. Much could be said about the subtlety of the story's representational strategy here—worth a study in itself. But we may trace key manoeuvres.

"Suppose a Saturday" (10) we are asked—deferring our desire for the certainty even of fictional assertion, "It *was* a Saturday." Despite the brilliant clarity of the description that follows, we are to be in the territory of one memory out of many, perhaps assembled from disparate parts, the royal beatings in the plural, not merely this one. Delays, then, for picturesque and telling detail: typical Saturdays with Flo, the grotesquery of a boy exposing himself despite the cold, above all the vivid provocation of Rose's nonsense rhyme, taught to her younger stepbrother:

> *Two Vancouvers fried in snot*
> *Two pickled arseholes tied in a knot.* (12)

Faced with such distraction, such imperious form—as nonsense verse is almost by definition an exercise in almost pure form—how on earth is resentment to gain a foothold, and toward what can it be directed? How pity or compassion? Our frustration doubles that of the father with his daughter. It can only be exorcized, the foothold gained, of course, through a commensurately monstrous violence, and that is provided. Belt whipping, blows, kicks, hatred-filled vehemence, a parent attacking his own child at the behest of her wicked stepmother.

But . . . and this fiction proceeds, as we have been developing its methods, always in the form of *x but y* . . . but, this violence is provided, memorably, under the sign of inauthenticity, theatricality. Mere performance—violence as the sign of violence. Rose and Flo are compelled to their fight as actors are by their script, making use of the father to fulfill this necessity. Above all, the telling of it over and over insists, these are roles played *self-consciously* by all concerned, the provoking acts, the anger, the suffering, the humiliated and craven begging for forgiveness, the violated feelings and alienation afterward. Rose's very stumbling as she scrambles for safety upstairs is deliberate, part of the pathetic scene played for an imagined audience.

Rose's father too is "like a bad actor, who turns a part grotesque" (16). Bad acting, generally, is acting whose designs upon us are visible. And in a theatre or out of it, it is difficult for us to feel those things which we are too openly being asked to feel. Acting, that is, operates or fails to operate, in much the same way as do other potential inducements to desire. Desire is contagious, imitative. We want what other people want. But desire only works this way when it is perceived to be authentically directed toward its object. If the desire is a pretense, a detectable attempt to attract our imitation, it loses all power. It is inauthentic.

One of Girard's most significant contributions to our understanding of this familiar process is his insistence that what imitative desire ultimately or most deeply desires is *being*, or identity. The desirable person, the "model" in Girard's terminology, possesses such solidity. Those less or more strongly attracted to this solidity, the "subjects" of desire, are to the same degree emptied out, denied identity.[7] Self-consciousness is the indicator of this emptiness, of an absence of mere being. Self-consciousness, finally, is the consciousness of the self as observed by others. It implies a desire to be desired, rather than the achievement of desirability. It implies doubt. People detectably attempting to attract our desires, that is, betray their lack of autonomy, of identity. The unselfconscious, the autonomous, lack nothing and actually attract us. These are the stakes in the "Royal Beating," perhaps for Rose and her father, but even more for the readers of the story. Who is the model and who the subject? Whose authenticity is established? Who is real? And thus, whose suffering or anger evokes our resentments and desires? In the end, neither Rose nor her father can do it. Theatricality—steadily, stealthily—undermines their claims. We are left contemplating mere signs, forms of bad acting.

Mind you, there does remain in the inauthentic, in bad acting, the possibility of pathos, of the *unintended* evocation of pity and allied modes of desire or resentment. For example, of that more elaborately intellectualized response, whereby we inquire into the causes which brought the inauthentic behaviour about, and feel compassion or indignation concerning them. One might compare, for example, the spectacle of "stage-Irishness," into which intellectuals, if not lay audiences, can read the colonial oppressions of the English consumers thereof. Not perhaps as potent a source of resentment as the potato famines, and made somewhat uncomfortable to inhabit by the sheer awfulness of some of the evidence, but operable.

Steps are taken in "Royal Beatings," however, to defer or make rough this route to justified resentment as well. The blows really do land, and we are told at the pivotal moment that the father "is acting, and he means it" (16). But afterward, no one is really hurt. Rose cannot sustain her martyrdom, fails to defer eating Flo's proffered peace offering. Above all, more distraction: the old codgers imagining they see an airship on the other side of Lake Huron, and Flo's bizarre parlour trick, a deliberate if unacknowledged distraction, lying across two chairs and rotating herself like that airship. Rose laughing.

Even if there is some of both, as we are assuming there must always be in any work of art, in the end it seems we do have more cake here than we eat.

To support such a claim, it might again be useful to look directly at the other version of this second scene of violence, its spectral double one might say, that Munro's story has so assiduously both distanced itself from and called to mind. This is not the lynching of old man Tyde, which as we saw was similarly shadowed, but the family melodrama taken on its own terms, the authentic one, the emotionally lurid scene, that the characters we have both inauthentically perform and, by watching themselves perform, empty of power. That the story "Royal Beatings," in a parallel operation and to the same effect, turns to parody.

It is everywhere through the three or four pages of the beating, this other scene, this melodrama. To say it haunts the "actual" events is an understatement—it implies and inhabits them, is part of them. If one "constantly" flouts stereotypes and clichés, as W. R. Martin accurately enough contends Munro does (11), then one is constantly in their presence, constantly defining oneself against them, revealing their contours. The other story is an art work, too, but *its* emphasis is on desire and resentment, on mobilizing them, giving them things upon which to feast. It has a form, of course—the difference is a matter of degree, or the location on a spectrum. It tells of more sincere and well-intentioned daughters, who suffer more undeservingly, whose whole souls are engulfed in the horrific assault and who are not at the same time watching it from a distance, who are braver and more stoic, who protest their ill treatment more effectually, or who learn something they are able to articulate or act upon. Who may indeed "never forgive"—as the

Rose we have vows but promptly fails to do (18)—or, better still, will *never be the same again*. As our Rose immediately, repeatedly, demonstrates she is. The indeterminate number of beatings in the story, of final tableaux of domestic peace, needless to say, deliberately thwarts this aspiration—that is the point—but melodrama, like meaning itself, always fashions singularities, cleaves to them heroically. All *its* actors are authentic. So are its designs upon us, upon our passions. Surely such things have been! Bloodied bodies, bruised souls, the very earth crying out. It does not reach for an inoculating absurdity at every approach to desire or resentment. It does not turn the morally significant into a spectacle for contemplation, a mere sign.

And actually, this other story, had it been allowed to establish its claims, might have done some very good things. One might wish for a better, less prejudicial general term. But call it melodrama. Here, perhaps, of a feminist-victimary colouration. Because melodrama mobilizes desires and resentments, it is the art form of politics, of causes and civic participation. It is the art form of justice and injustice, of moral expression. It prefers a plausible impossibility to the possible implausibilities of fathers who quote Spinoza and Shakespeare and yet repeatedly and sadistically beat their daughters on second-hand evidence. Melodrama directs passions, and its knowledge is the kind of knowledge upon which human beings may *act*.

High art trades in the prejudice that that which defies our desires is more real, more likely to be true, an attitude one finds reflected everywhere in criticism of Munro. Such criticism, that is, applies the principle of authenticity as defined above to the aesthetics of fiction—direct appeals to desire must be inauthentic. And what desire—the simplifier, the organiser of passions—most abjures and thus high art most delivers, is paradox, "complexity," or again, mystery. For Martin, Munro's art is "a complex counterpointing of opposed truths in a memorable model of life and reality" (1). John Orange stresses "the sense of hidden mysteries" (90), the "ironic distance" (92), and the way stories like "Royal Beatings" can "juxtapose the secret and public lives of characters in order to expose the illusory nature of 'ordinary' life" (94). Gerald Noonan is perhaps most absolute:

> There is about real life a paradoxical, contradictory quality which pits one verity against another. . . . Her later work repeatedly presents the view that paradox is not a planing above the common level of life—it *is* the common level; it is reality. . . . Every story is framed in retrospection, and the narrator uses the distancing to counter some

> conventional expectation—which is triggered by the initial part of the fiction—with what does actually 'happen' later. . . . the later 'happenings' cannot be entirely dismissed as just more fiction since the actuality of what occurs later often abolishes, in effect, the plot conflicts of the earlier parts of the story. (164)

To all this, one may imagine, perhaps, melodrama's indignant responses. A mystery is only such as long as it *is* "hidden," and a paradox only paradoxical until it is recognized, and valued, as such. After which, it becomes an object of desire like others, just as likely to be conventional and no more likely to be "true." And, to speak of truth, a pair of opposed truths is not *my* truth! My life, ordinary as it may be, *matters*, is no illusion, to *me*! Desire and resentment don't see less clearly, they see other things or in another way, and the resentments of resentment, the desires to escape desire, are finally just as beholden to desire. Maybe most importantly, nothing, no object or person or place, is seen with such clarity, in such detail, with such vividness as that which is loved or hated, desired, or resented. This vaunted high-art realism is constructed of negations, the not-melodramatic above all, rather than of more clearly seen facts. Its mysteries are mystifications. This cherished sense of life is a kind of distracting parlour trick, at the expense of those who want to keep feeling something to the purpose, who want to keep the beaten daughters in view. Who want such beatings to end!

To take up melodrama's cause, using the anthropological tools we're wielding here, we might add that the point really is not the truth or accuracy of seeing or representation. The point is deferral. Paradox is, almost by definition, the deferral of a meaning that might in principle finally be resolved and appropriated. Desire and resentment comprehend, divide, delineate, *make* real. Deferral contemplates, desire consumes. But humanity must eat, and both phases of aesthetic experience are inevitable. Your high-art gastronome may prefer daintier fare, but cannot live, even as he or she peruses the latest *New Yorker*, on paradox itself. And if the claim is to be made that such art merely skirts the obviously manipulative in order to deliver the more authentic and thus usable truth—shuns, in effect, bad melodrama for better—the response is to point to a demonstrable and proportionate falling off of purposeful energy, the stuff of engagement, the propulsion for action. Barricades are not mounted under banners paradoxical.

Many readers will rightfully object, however, that there are other purposes, which Munro's "high art," her art of deferral, must surely serve. That lead us to anticipate, to desire its own pleasures. What such art provides, to take up this side of the question, is of another order, and need, in the longer term, neither advance nor retard social knowledge or action. The best general term for what it provides, let us suggest, is simply peace. Temporary, relative peace. Respite, or distance, from desire or resentment. This is the aesthetic dimension of what Gans calls the most fundamental purpose of representation, at its momentous invention at the origin of the human and ever after, namely, the deferral of violence. Language, form, in this telling, create a crucial interval of non-appropriation, non-rivalry, of deferral, in which the human and human culture can emerge. The first manifestation of such a culture is a degree of cooperation in consumption, a feast or collective sacrifice—*sparagmos*—in which the object of desire may be shared in an at least minimally less violent manner than in the pre-cultural context, the frustrations and resentments of delayed desire discharged upon the object itself, rather than on rival participants. Aesthetic deferral extends the time and space in which such peace may be recreated in individual human consciousness: distraction from desire, attention to form, from which we may perhaps return to the purposes and incitements of the world more calmly, stably.

Paradox is certainly fundamental to such a process. But it is the "pragmatic paradox" that is finally implied in all representation, rather than the revelation of a paradoxical quality inhering in reality. Put most simply, it is the paradox that in the sign, which each human experiences in individual consciousness, one both possesses and does not possess the object of desire. Humanity came into being with this paradox, in Gans's hypothesis, and cannot live without it.[8]

Gans variously uses "art" and "popular art," "entertainment," or indeed "melodrama"—terms he stresses are historical, dating to the Romantic era—to mark out the different emphases in aesthetic experience, which he conceptualizes as part of a human "scene" created by joint attention:

> In the context of the contemplation of the central object of the scene, the moment of art looks back to the renunciation of appetite implicit in the sign, whereas that of entertainment looks forward to the appetitive satisfaction of the communal feast that will follow (*Originary Thinking* 171).

For our purposes, perhaps "high art" and "melodrama" will suffice. While both modes of art do finally perform the same broad function, prolongation of the high-art moment creates a human interval of peace and contemplation whose final effect, at least as we attempt to gauge it in individual readers, we might judge to be *the modelling of an aesthetic experience of life*.

To inhabit the best of Munro's stories is to richly appreciate the forms of human life, their unmotivated specificities, peculiarities, ironies. Indeed, it is to see them as forms at all, and capable of possessing such qualities. It is to find them beautiful—which is to say, capable of creating a space of deferral in which contemplation and desire are experienced together, held in temporary balance. Desire is evoked sufficiently to carry us into the world of these stories, but in the artfully regulated deferral of every kind of immediate gratification of that desire—for meaning or information, clarity of understanding, imagined alimentary or sexual possession, for justice, revenge, the flattery of our resentments, the comforting of our fears—a condition of engaged attention to form is made available. The degree to which we carry that posture into our own worlds after we close the magazine is, of course, variable. But it is hard not to believe that high art fosters in all its consumers some greater capacity to contemplate the strangeness and beauty of direct human experience, to *see* it as strange and beautiful. Call it a lengthened span of joint attention, before we plunge, as we must, back into the satisfaction of our various individual "needs."

Human needs, of course, despite the scientism of some of the discourses that use the term, are relative to context, are historical, created by changing cultural conditions, the tides and eddies of imitated desire washing across the human world. Gans and the other theorists working with the hypothesis I have been referencing here have attempted to articulate a history of this desire, of its generation, deferral, redirection and intensification in the ethical systems humanity has needed constantly to develop and modify. With new desires, new risks of violence have emerged constantly, requiring new responses, a process moving at an accelerated pace in the "open societies" of our era, in which Karl Popper, who coined the phrase, saw operating just such a process: the solving of problems caused by the previous set of solutions. For this way of thinking, the crucial, large-scale shift is from a *ritual* ordering and containment of desire, to a *market*, broadly conceived. Gradually supplementing and then replacing the singular centrality of the earlier phase of culture are many individual centralities, created dynamically around the imagined periphery of the old public locus. Identities rooted in the quasi-sacral differences of geography, history, class, even gender, are increasingly to be seen as non-renewable resources, needing synthetic substitutes, self-created, negotiated in a market of other identities, all jostling for the precious human attention which creates and sustains them. (Gans memorably defines identity as "a local monopoly of attention" [*Originary Thinking* 128], by which we may understand limited both spatially and temporally. Attention, love even, is *exchanged* in the myriad forms and contexts of human interaction across an increasingly connected world.)

High art has particular value and particular functions in this historical context. The peace it proffers may most importantly be respite precisely from the need—real and finally inexorable as it is—to establish and maintain identity. This respite, of course, is once again only a deferral, or a relative escape from the importunities of such desire. It is not, finally, something that can be consciously and consistently desired in itself—to desire the cessation of desire is not the pragmatic paradox by which humanity lives, but only a particular posture assumed in relation to the rest of the human scene. But the temporary calm—or call it security—in which to contemplate the very processes by which identity is achieved, the ironies and beauties too of that process, is surely precious.

High art may create this peace in many ways, but one of the most familiar and, by the evidence of its persistence in different forms, most effective modern aesthetic vehicles is the pastoral. It is in this category or genre that the remainder of this essay will attempt to place Munro's "Royal Beatings," in order better to identify the story's ultimate, if skillfully deferred, gratifications.

Such a project might seem rather implausible, what with the pickled arseholes and bathroom noises and so forth. It might be objected that a "golden world" is one of the outcomes Munro's persistent ironies and incongruities most deliberately resists. Pastoral, though, as William Empson influentially demonstrated, is a capacious mode, and our anthropological approach may enable us to apply fairly fundamental, and thus flexible, criteria.

> They lived in a poor part of town.... Across the road from them was a blacksmith shop, boarded up about the time the war started, and a house that had been another store at one time. The Salada Tea sign had never been taken out of the front window; it remained as a proud and interesting decoration though there was no Salada Tea for sale inside. There was just a bit of sidewalk, too cracked and tilted for roller-skating... (4–5)

The authentic, as noted, is that which makes no detectable appeal to our desires, and is thus desirable. Old advertising, with its now naïve appeals to vanished desire, its outmoded tactics for peddling outmoded objects, possesses a related charm. There is nothing really for sale, nothing to need to want or reject wanting, and the unguarded obviousness of earlier marketing techniques is so easily discerned and deflected as to produce a feeling almost of relaxation. In somewhat the same way, many of the best tourist attractions—Colonial Williamsburg, Bruges, Angkor Wat—are formerly commanding social and economic centralities which have, through the vagaries of history, been prevented from developing, been left suspended in the amber of their archaic strategies.[9] They no longer dominate living desires, nor provoke the concomitant resentments, and yet they once did, and our immunity to their furies and complexities can induce a pleasing experience of security, freedom, even self-possessed superiority. The pastoral peace of Hanratty operates in a similar way.

Empson acutely noted that the pastoral is "about" the people, but not "for" or "by" them (6), a distinction easily extended to that between the high-art gaze over human desires and passions, and the melodramatic mobilization of them. Melodrama is emphatically by and for desire and resentment, privileging their evocation and imaginative satisfaction. High art is about them, providing an interval in which they can be deferred and contemplated. To say this is not necessarily to attribute class distinctions to these phases of experience. Any human being may in principle be, in different moments of either aesthetic or other kinds of experience, of "the people" or transcendent—distantly evaluative—of them and their concerns.

The pastoral is driven, in Peter Marinelli's resonant phrase, by "the desire of the weary soul to escape" (12), and it is into this desire we must inquire most closely. Escape from what? Not merely and simply from the present, from modernity per se. Munro's Hanratty/Jubilee/Wingham is observed in history, and the precision of that observation's detail is of course one of these stories' pleasures. But it is also "an Other Place that seems all we could desire" (Carscallen 132), whose most important, underlying difference from our own world is its earlier stage in the shift from ritual to market structure. The madding demands of the desires hailing us in a modern, market-based world are escaped from into the relative tranquillity of a golden domain where such desires, and the obligation to respond to them, are still under partial interdict. For all its studied oddity, it is a conventional, formal place, ceremonial even in its innocence.

It is innocent, indeed, in one particularly salient way, and that is the relative modesty of its desires, and the commensurate mildness of its resentments. Certainly, desires for more, aspirations, resentments of things as they are, are disapproved of, rebuffed, subjected to scandalized critique, the most expressive of which is, again, Flo's familiar accusation: "who do you think you are?" But such attempts to maintain what is ultimately a system of ritually sanctioned differences, identities rooted in place and caste and genetics, are not finally very formidable, very dangerous—at least not to *us*. And perhaps not to Rose either.

This relative lack of true menace, ineffectiveness at oppression, matters most for the project of identity creation, the very issue addressed by Flo's question and the title of the story cycle in which "Royal Beatings" features. Synthetic identities have to be built tentatively, in pretences and guesses, through market testing and leaps into the mimetic dark. Irony, or more forcefully, satire, are their natural enemies, weapons for the destruction of others' attempts to attain centrality; weapons, that is, in a (zero-sum) battle for selfhood, a struggle for the high ground of the model's position, from which others are subjected. But the irony, the satire of someone like Flo is weak, turns back upon her own grotesque and peculiar self, offers up easy victories, or easily managed defeats—nominal defeats, indeed, in which victory is implied. The blows of Rose's father are likewise impotent, betraying in their own inarticulate helplessness and inauthenticity the immunity of their supposed victim. Here is no patriarchal god, no king, no true tyrant over anyone's desires. How can he even be resented? Rose doesn't, not for long.[10]

But the battle underway everywhere in a more mature market world, and every day more fiercely, is much less manageable, much less easily turned to account. Children and adolescents—as Empson also points out, now among the standard inhabitants of pastoral (260)—perhaps experience it most directly, although their therefore beleaguered elders can hardly be neutral bystanders. But the struggle is general, strategies evolve rapidly and with bewildering complexity, outcomes are everywhere uncertain. For every celebrity, not Becky Tyde curiosities but hegemonic plutocrats of human attention, masses huddle in the apparent darkness of an anonymity unknown to the small-town pastoral world. Or, so it often feels. Little wonder even the youngest souls—or perhaps the youngest souls most particularly—wearily desire escape into imaginative consummations, be they triumphs of recognized centrality or flamingly unjust victimhoods, superheroic digital exploits or implausibly sparagmatic " hunger games."

And here, perhaps, we may see the end of all the deferrals, Munro's story delivering, as all art finally does, its edible cake, its own satisfaction of desire or gratification of resentment, at least to souls susceptible to its particularly deft, ostensibly anti-melodramatic technique. Because, how much easier (and more plausible) is it to imagine "rebellion"—or call it self-creation—in such a place as her vividly realized Hanratty, inoculated as it may thus seem against mere wish-fulfillment, than in one where no one actually *cares* who you think you are? Where the path from pretence to identity is being blazed with such disconcerting ease by one's rivals, one's models, on every side? Where the beatings are not "royal," but in fact entirely democratic?

Notes

1. The idea is more fully developed in the same author's "Story into History: Alice Munro's Minor Literature."
2. Readers interested in exploring these might begin with Girard's *Things Hidden Since the Foundation of the World* (1987) and Gans's *Originary Thinking* (1993). The online journal Anthropoetics would also be a good starting place for the latter.
3. See Johnson.
4. I am bolstered in this strategy by the innovative work using counterfactual techniques for literary analysis currently being done by Amir Khan.
5. Most notably in his classic study, *Deceit, Desire and Novel* (1961).
6. The operatic alternative to the approach taken by "Royal Beatings" is to be seen with great clarity in *Peter Grimes* (1945). About the scapegoating of its inherited protagonist, the composer Benjamin Britten confidently pronounced, "the more vicious the society, the more vicious the individual," even though the individual in his opera is hardly vicious at all, in sharp contrast to his original in the poetry of George Crabbe (1812), while the society is relentlessly, even rather incomprehensibly, oppressive and cruel. The quotation is from an interview in 1948, quoted in Brett (13–14). For a further discussion of these works, interested readers might consult my own article in Works Cited.
7. This topic is most thoroughly discussed in the second section of *Things Hidden Since the Foundation of the World*, on "Interdividual Psychology." For Girard, the desire for being, or what he calls "metaphysical desire," inevitably emerges after imitative desire reaches a certain degree of intensity.
8. For an extended development of this topic, see *Signs of Paradox* (1997).
9. A colonial capital, Williamsburg was left behind by the American Revolution; Bruges was a great power in the Flemish golden age of trade and early capitalism, but fell into tourist-ready oblivion about 1500 when its sea channel silted up; the largest religious complex in the world, Angkor Wat experienced a helpfully benign neglect—as opposed

to total abandonment or repeated sack—after the thirteenth century. Many more examples of the paradigm could of course be cited; indeed, it is almost a touristical truism.

10. For Gerald Lynch, "what gets confirmed at the end of "Who Do You Think You Are?" is a middle-aged woman's acceptance of self-identity as connected intimately to an unattractive place of origin" (180). Were this place attractive to desire, the task of self-acceptance might be considerably more difficult.

Works Cited

Brett, Philip. "'The More Vicious the Society, the More Vicious the Individual': *Peter Grimes* and its Message." Decca, CD insert, 2006.

Carrington, Ildikó de Papp. *Controlling the Uncontrollable: The Fiction of Alice Munro.* Dekalb: Northern Illinois UP, 1989.

Carscallen, James. *The Other Country: Patterns in the Writings of Alice Munro.* Toronto: ECW, 1980.

Dennis, Ian. "The Pastoral Victim's Progress: Crabbe to Britten." *Anthropoetics* 14.2 (Winter 2009). http://www.anthropoetics.ucla.edu/ap1402/1402dennis.htm.

Empson, William. *Some Versions of Pastoral.* Norfolk, CT: New Directions, 1960.

Gans, Eric. *Originary Thinking: Elements of Generative Anthropology.* Stanford, CA: Stanford UP, 1993.

———. *Signs of Paradox: Irony, Resentment and Other Mimetic Structures.* Stanford, CA: Stanford UP, 1997.

Gerlach, John. "To Close or Not to Close: Alice Munro's 'The Love of a Good Woman'." *JNT: Journal of Narrative Theory* 37.1 (Winter 2007): 146–58. 10.1353/jnt.2007.0017.

Girard, René. *Deceit, Desire and the Novel: Self and Other in Literary Structure.* Trans. Yvonne Freccero. Baltimore: Johns Hopkins UP, 1965.

———. *Things Hidden Since the Foundation of the World.* Stanford, CA: Stanford UP, 1987.

Howells, Coral Ann. *Alice Munro.* Manchester: Manchester UP, 1998.

Hunter, Adrian. "Story into History: Alice Munro's Minor Literature." *English* 53 (Autumn 2004): 219–38. DOI: http://dx.doi.org/10.1093/english/53.207.219.

———. "Taking Possession: Alice Munro and James Hogg." *Studies in Canadian Literature* 35.2 (2010): 114–28. https://journals.lib.unb.ca/index.php/SCL/article/view/18326.

Johnson, Samuel. *Preface to Shakespeare.* 1765. Project Gutenberg. http://www.gutenberg.org/ebooks/5429.

Khan, Amir. *Shakespeare in Hindsight: Counterfactual Thinking and Shakespearean Tragedy.* Edinburgh: Edinburgh UP, 2016.

Lynch, Gerald. *The One and the Many: English-Canadian Short Story Cycles.* U of Toronto P, 2001.

Marinelli, Peter V. *Pastoral.* London: Methuen, 1971.

Martin, W. R. *Alice Munro: Paradox and Parallel.* Edmonton: U of Alberta P, 1987.

McMullen, Lorraine. "'Shameless, Marvellous, Shattering Absurdity': The Humour of Paradox in Alice Munro." *Probable Fictions: Alice Munro's Narrative Acts.* Ed. Louis K. MacKendrick. Downsview, ON: ECW, 1983. 144–62.

Munro, Alice. *Who Do You Think You Are?* Toronto: Macmillan, 1978.

Noonan, Gerald. "The Structure of Style in Alice Munro's Fiction." *Probable Fictions: Alice Munro's Narrative Acts.* Ed. Louis K. MacKendrick. Downsview, ON: ECW, 1983. 162–80.

Orange, John. "Alice Munro and A Maze of Time." *Probable Fictions: Alice Munro's Narrative Acts.* Ed. Louis K. MacKendrick. Downsview, ON: ECW, 1983. 83–98.

Popper, Karl. *The Open Society and Its Enemies.* London: Routledge, 1945.

Thacker, Robert. *Alice Munro: Writing Her Lives, A Biography.* Toronto: McClelland & Stewart, 2005.

"Don't Take Her Word For It": Autobiographical Approximation and Shame in Munro's *The View from Castle Rock*

Linda M. Morra

A cursory glance at both the academic scholarship on and popular appraisals of Alice Munro's literary corpus would quickly register the critical fascination with the proximity between the facts of her life and her literary representation of those facts, a fascination that Robert McGill might refer to as a form of "biographical desire" (4).[1] In "Not Quite Stories—Alice Munro's Almost Autobiography," a review of *Dear Life* that appeared in the *New Republic* in November 2012, Chloe Schama confines Munro's tendency to blur fact and fiction to this collection of stories; she argues that Munro offers a "distinct turn to autobiography and a revealing window into the workings of her mind," although she concedes in Munro-like fashion that the stories therein are ultimately "more like mediations on memory and analyses of the act of storytelling than biographical sketches" (n.p.).[2] Critic and biographer Robert Thacker sees this tendency as having much broader application to the entirety of her oeuvre, and has thus observed in *Alice Munro: Writing Her Lives* that

> Autobiography is imbedded in Alice Munro's work, autobiography always resonant with fictional imaginings ("grafted on from some other reality"), and she can be seen as always "writing her lives," the lives she has both lived and imagined. (18–19)

As Thacker observes elsewhere, "by returning again and again to the subjects of autobiographical obsession, Munro is, as she has said, editing her life as she goes along," in addition to "creating a broader fictional world" (1999, 14).[3] McGill posits that the connection between fact and fiction is actually related to "Munro's anxiety about the real in her fiction": "it bespeaks a poetics in which fiction and nonfiction are vitally connected to one another, in which each is held to the same standards of verisimilitude, if not of referentiality, and in which each has a fraught relationship to reality" (128).

Munro herself does little to disentangle fact from fiction and even less to dissuade critics from seeing the autobiographical possibilities in her work. Instead, she nourishes this fascination. As one example, she identifies "The Peace of Utrecht," a much earlier story published in *The Tamarack Review* more than a year after her mother died, in the spring of 1960, as her "first really painful autobiographical story," the story in which she "first tackled personal material" (qtd. in Thacker 2011, 150).[4] In *Dear Life*, as yet another example, she argues that the final four works of the book are "not quite stories. I believe they are the first and last—and the *closest*—things I have to say about my own life" (255). By such comments, it is clear she also cultivates this fascination with the autobiographical detail she includes and a deliberate—I would say, strategic—ambiguity in terms of the factual and fictional elements in her narratives and in terms of what she allows us to know.[5]

In *The View from Castle Rock*, the focus of this essay, Munro has considerably more to say about perhaps one of the most "close" renderings of autobiographical detail of all her books:

> These stories were not included in the books of fiction I put together at intervals. Why not? I felt they didn't belong. They were *not memoirs* but they *were closer to my own life* than the other stories I had written, even in the first person. In other first-person stories I had drawn on personal material, but then I did anything I wanted to with the material. Because the chief thing I was doing was making a story. In the stories I hadn't collected I was not doing exactly that. I was doing something *closer to what a memoir does*—exploring a life, my own life, but not in an austere or rigorously factual way. But the figures around this self took on their own life and color and did things they had not done in reality. [. . .]
>
> These are *stories*.
>
> You could say that such stories pay more attention to the truth of a life than fiction usually does. But not enough to swear on. (n.p., italics mine)

Here and elsewhere, she identifies her stories in relation to their *proximity* to the facts of her life—close, closer, closest—without ever declaring outright that these or other stories are autobiographical (much less autobiography).[6] Perhaps for this reason, Thacker refers to this collection as "a hybrid of family history, fiction, memoir, and closely made autobiographical stories" (2011, 367). Both parts of the collection confirm this assessment, although the first part of *The View from Castle Rock* might be regarded as less autobiographical. In the first part, Munro calls upon surviving historical journals, accounts, and letters, such as the Laidlaw diary describing the crossing to Canada in 1818; however, the narrative primarily focuses on the narrator's ruminations on her family ancestry and presence in the Scottish area of Ettrick Valley, and her reconstruction of the characters and lives that form part of her paternal ancestry, which is "full of [her] invention" (2006, 84). The second part deals more closely with the narrator's personal life, thereby also suggesting that one's identity is connected to an understanding of one's past and a sense of connection to familial lineage.

Thus, in its focus and interest, *The View from Castle Rock* is set apart and distinct from her other collections of stories, something "closer to a memoir"[7]; by these terms, the book might thus seem to lend itself to the terms of the "autobiographical pact," what Philippe Lejeune identifies as a contract of identity between the narrator, reader, and publisher such that the text is "sealed by the proper name" applied to an autobiographical text (19). By this pact, the reader comes to believe that the author, narrator, and protagonist of an autobiography are conjoined and that the literary representation of the protagonist, therefore, imparts factual accounts about the author in question. However, Munro time and again refuses to identify her stories—here and elsewhere—fully as memoir or autobiography. Notwithstanding the claim that she shares a habit with her father of "often saying to people more or less what we think they'd like to hear" (2006, 311), she often denies people the satisfaction related to "biographical desire" by bypassing what they may want to hear, by withholding certain autobiographical details or, as the foreword to *Castle Rock* makes plain, by withdrawing from any strict adherence to fact: "there is not enough truth in [the stories] to 'swear on.'" In so doing, she stages a necessary ambiguity, and offers contradictions and undermines easy certainties—"not one of them is as close as people seem to think"—the very literary techniques she calls upon elsewhere and repeatedly in her literary corpus. The narratives she offers therein may be "closer" to representing Munro's life, but, as she elsewhere observes in her preface, not in "an austere or rigorously factual way" (n.p.).

Critics have also offered several reasons for this subversion of claims to strict autobiographical fact or to the evasion of these facts. Thacker observes her interest in the art of the story itself—she may be "seen shaping, adjusting, honing and sharpening her articulation until she finds it satisfactory" (12). McGill argues in a similar vein by not only emphasizing her literary practice but also asserting that her writing "insists that reality is more complex than positivist accounts recognize": "Her fiction gestures toward what is unknown or only dreamed; her stories open a seam in the everyday to explore the 'deep caves paved with kitchen linoleum' that are people's lives" (128). He adds that, "because fiction is not bound by juridical standards of verification, it can explore more fully than nonfiction the presence of fantasy in the real" (129).

I do not dispute these critical responses, nor that the blurring between fact and fiction in her work register both Munro's craft and the possibilities that fiction allows her. I would add, however, that the deliberate evasion of or withdrawal from claims to strict adherence to autobiographical fact and the resulting ambiguity accomplishes something more: in *The View from Castle Rock*, that ambiguous line between her life and its representation becomes a part of a dual strategy by which to honour not any such pact about truth telling, but rather the dignity of those about whom she writes. Such ambiguity, especially when allied with the deployment of shame, becomes the device by which to impose limits, and question both the right to know and the proximity between reader and autobiographical text. Intimate disclosures are at times offered and at others denied the reader, who is implicitly challenged about the right to access the private details of a life—any life. Munro's assertions, then, about the closeness of her stories to autobiographical fact, that not one of them "is as close as people seem to think," suggest not only the ambiguity between fact and fiction, but also the necessary *distance* between the autobiographical text and the reader or witness to that text.

Eliciting a sense of shame is crucial to generating that necessary distance. Critic Elspeth Probyn notes that "writing shame," a phrase she uses both to "capture the affective bodily feeling of betraying interest" and to suggest how "we might envision writing shame as part of an ethical practice" (73), "is a visceral reminder to be true to interest, to be honest about why or how certain things are of interest" (73). But, she adds, "getting too close" can also serve as "a source of shame," which implies that shame is not an inherently personal capacity that is "possessed by only individuals," but rather one of proximity between persons—or, for example, in this instance between the reader and the narrator of Munro's texts (73). Ambiguity, I would argue, is used by Munro to create an appropriate and even ethical distance between her audience and her narrator, while still allowing for some proximity: her readers are drawn in to the autobiographical text, but never too deeply. Approximation is thus not just about the "estimate" of how close the representation is to the life being represented, but also about "proximity," to call upon the root of the word, between the reader and the narrative.

For this paper, I call on two moments within *The View from Castle Rock* from different parts of the collection to make this point. Rather than set up a relationship between reader and narrator, "Illinois," in the first part of the book, establishes a relation in the narrative between those who tell stories and those who are set up as the audience to these stories, in this instance, the young boy Jamie and Uncle Andrew, respectively. The narrator recounts how William Laidlaw's wife, Mary, gives birth to her fifth child, a girl, on the same day that her husband, William, dies. William's brother, Andrew, arrives shortly thereafter with a team of oxen and a cart to bring her children back to Ontario, where she and her family would be taken care of by William's extended family. Mary's son, Jamie, is both resentful of and resistant to leaving their home and starting elsewhere, an idea that Mary claims "most falsely, most despicably" was "such a thing . . . his father would have wanted" (92): "He understood, when they left home, that his father—who was not under that stone but in the air or walking along the road invisibly and making his views known as well as if they had been talking together—*his father* was against their going" (103). In spite of his frustration, they are uprooted and begin the journey to Ontario; en route, they stop at the Indiana border, at a crossroads inn when, most unexpectedly, Mary's baby disappears and is assumed to have been kidnapped. Mary levels this charge at Becky Johnson, the Indigenous woman who was both her neighbour and caregiver to the children, and whom she believes followed them to take the baby back with her to her home in Joliet. She clings to this belief after Jamie tells her that he saw Becky on the road as they approached the Indiana border and whom Jamie claims might "have been following along trying for a chance to sneak away the baby whom she loved unreasonably" (105).

But, of course, it is Jamie who initially kidnaps his baby sister in the vain hope that his family will return home to look for both the baby and Becky. At this point, the story takes another unexpected turn and his baby sister actually disappears from where Jamie left her: in other words, his baby sister really *is* kidnapped. It is Uncle Andrew who is both privy to the story Jamie tells and then participant when, first, he discovers the baby in the barn and then returns her safely into Mary's arms. In spite of the story about Becky Johnson in circulation (and also another about a stable boy related to the discovery of the barn), Uncle Andrew does not "believe that the stable boy was in any way involved, and he did believe that James was, but *he left the matter uninvestigated*" (109, italics mine). Mary too is so "glad to have the baby back that she didn't much question what had happened" (109). Positioned as audience to Jamie's story, Uncle Andrew offers the reader one approach to a story that is suspect, whose facts hang together so loosely as to render the truth of the narrative tenuous at best. Even if he doesn't take Jamie's word for it—that is, his version of the story—he understands that the boy experiences shame, that he "might have learned his lesson" from the turmoil engendered by his actions (109), and that no good would come from pursuing the facts of the situation. So he does not pursue them: Uncle Andrew's refusal to investigate further thus provides enough distance that Jamie's sense of dignity is preserved, even if the reader in this instance is sufficiently privileged by having access to a different set of facts.

The story's conclusion offers yet another reason for Uncle Andrew's decision not to question or investigate further the facts of a story, which is related to his brother, Will, his decision to separate himself from his family, and his eventual and early demise:

> There was something about all this rushing away, loosing oneself entirely from family and past, there was something rash and self-trusting about it that might not help a man, that might put him more in the way of such an accident, such a fate. Poor Will. (110)

The passage seems to suggest that honour and the dignity of self are located within the network of stories that are generated about the family, and that disengaging from such a network or a familial context is thus not only rash but destructive, for one's self and for those by whom one is surrounded—even if those stories are only at best known partially. Whether or not these stories happened, and whether or not James has told the truth, thus become irrelevant in relation to the roles the stories perform and how they function: dignity of the individual is privileged above factual reliability.

We might see how to apply the same principle more largely to the reader when Munro shifts the focus of her stories to the present day, to the situation with the narrator's own father. In "Home," she recounts her father's increasing physical decline such that he is placed in intensive care in the hospital. The reasons for his decline in health are vague and mysterious, even to the narrator, and apparently to the medical practitioner as well: "Why do you think he is running this temperature?" she asks the doctor, who responds, "He has an infection *somewhere*" (311, italics mine). Upon the narrator's probing further, he finally replies that he believes the "main trouble" is the heart (312). Directly thereafter, this story concludes with "the scene of the first clear memory of [her] life," one that involves her father "sitting on a three-legged milking stool" (315). Recalling the details of that moment, she concludes the story by reflecting upon "the cold, which even then must have been gathering, building into the cold of that extraordinary winter which killed all the chestnut trees, and many orchards" (315).

In reading this story the first time, I wondered—and what happened to her father who lay in the hospital with a mysterious heart condition? Did he die? If he did die, how did he die? Immediately, I turned the page, and was confronted by the title of the next story that challenged the presumptuous nature of my questions: "What Do You Want to Know For?" The story begins, however, not with her father's imminent death or his funeral, as I anticipated, but rather with the narrator and her husband's identification of a crypt they notice in the vicinity of Georgian Bay (316). The leap in the narrative creates an occlusion, one that Isla Duncan observes as a kind of strategy Munro adopts elsewhere: an ellipses is placed after an admission, which Duncan observes as "arresting the narrative progress so abruptly" that it "marks the occlusion in the narrator's knowledge, as well as in her empathetic understanding" (22). In this instance, however, it is not a question of Munro's knowledge, nor her empathetic understanding. Munro claims that "gaps" have another particular function in her narratives: "All my stories have gaps. It seems this is the way people's lives present themselves" ("Nobel prizewinner" n.p.). This reason seems more appropriate; however, to this assertion, I would add that such a gap also marks, in this instance, the limit to the right or privilege to know, as the narrator also acknowledges of herself.

What indeed do we as readers want to know for? Why is it important to know? I experienced a sense of uneasiness and shame at my desire, my curiosity to know more: surely the privacy of both the narrator and her father ought to be privileged. Yet, unlike Uncle Andrew, I desired to carry my investigation further, in which instance I would have come against another obstacle, such as scholar JoAnn McCaig discovered when researching in Munro's archives and when she received a "lawyer writing on Munro's behalf" warning her against probing too far (x); indeed, McCaig herself asks, "what is the utility" of knowing certain facts, "beyond personal interest, beyond gossip, beyond the cult of personality?" (xii). It was my own sense of shame, rather than a lawyer's injunction, that marked the limit to the right to intimacy generated by personal knowledge.

Yet this experience too might be contextualized within the "watermarks of shame and guilt" that, as Lisa Allardice notes, run "through each collection" and that mark the relationships between characters (Munro, "Nobel Prizewinner"), for Munro empathetically reminds the reader that such fascination is not beyond the scope of most persons: the narrator in this particular story also possesses a form of curiosity, of the same nature that spurs her readers to raise questions and to probe into matters that position them as intrusive. Indeed, "What Do You Want to Know For?" is *not* directed toward the reader, or at least, not entirely: the narrator locates herself as the interloper, the person who, with her husband, comes across "something strange" as they are driving on a narrow, bumpy road in Sullivan Township, an "unnatural mound" that draws her attention and that elicits a series of her own questions (316). She and her husband have little time to indulge their curiosity, yet they stop to inspect the mound because, like readers in relation to Munro's texts, they are "possessive about this country, and try not to let anything get by us" (316). The mound is unyielding: at its lower end, "some big protruding stones, probably set there to hold the earth in place. No markings on them, either—no clues as to who or what might be hidden inside" (316).

This discovery prompts her to visit a college's reference room in the same city where she has a medical appointment so that she can further her research about Grey County and Sullivan Township and perhaps discover the significance of the mound. It is at this moment, in the library, that the narrator suggests the limits of what she herself can know and ask, in particular about her current source of fascination:

> It is difficult to make such requests in reference libraries because you will often be asked what it is, exactly, that you want to know, and what do you want to know it for? Sometimes it is even necessary to write your reason down. If you are doing a paper, a study, you will of course have a good reason, but what if you are *just interested?* The best thing, probably, is to say you are doing a family history. Librarians are used to people doing that . . . and it is generally thought to be a reasonable way of spending one's time . . . I thought of my writing on my form: *research for paper concerning survival of mound burial in pioneer Ontario*. (326)

She might as easily have asked, what if you are Alice Munro, for whom most librarians, I believe, would be most obliging? Still, she here maintains that human curiosity, unless contextualized within the proper authority, logic, and justification of a "research paper" or the intimacies generated by family dynamics, will not answer to protocols about what we have the right to ask. Her own response to her queries to librarians, she admits, "sounds apologetic, if not shifty, and makes you run the risk of being seen as an idler lounging around in the library, a person at loose ends, with no proper direction in life, *nothing better to do*" (326). The shame the narrator experiences at probing too far is thus shared with the reader.

My response to this passage was evidently to link the reader's fascination—my fascination—with that of the narrator, and with the reader's reading of her books with the narrator's own reading of the landscape and speculation about the mound's significance: *research for paper concerning obsession with Alice Munro and all aspects of her life and career*. However, the implications extend beyond these correspondences. Directly before this passage, she comments on a visit to the doctor to consult with him about an equally unyielding and mysterious lump "deep in my left breast, which neither my doctor nor I had been able to feel" and for which her medical practitioner sets up an appointment with "a city doctor" to do an invasive "biopsy" (317). The narrator's own mortality, in other words, becomes a source of her exploration here, and she contextualizes her ruminations within and makes remarks about her health that are analogous to the "countryside that we think we know so well and that is always springing some sort of surprise on us" (318). Thus, when she comments upon the changes to a landscape with which she was so familiar, and remarks that "you have to keep checking, taking in the changes, seeing things while they last," her observation is equally applicable to the regular visits to her doctor to consult further about the results of her mammogram (319). She, too, must necessarily be curious about her own body and "keep checking" to see if any of the discernable changes require further investigation.

Within proper confines and contexts, she seems to suggest, human curiosity is not shameful and not a means of generating limits between persons but rather its opposite: some probing is necessary, for one's own well being and that of a larger community. Learning and investigating to acquire knowledge is not always or necessarily a shameful or "shifty" enterprise. In her search for more information about the crypt, when she and her husband approach the minister of St. Peter's Church, located outside of Williamsford, the narrator learns not only about Mannerow Cemetery but also about her own family. She notes that the minister "invites us into her house" and "does not seem at all surprised by our curiosity or put out by our visit" (329). Clearly, she is aware of the potential for intrusiveness or for inappropriate curiosity, and the limits thereof, but, as she converses with the minister, she also makes plain that there are protocols that govern such conversations, which she knows about and heeds. Indeed, she claims to understand these protocols because of her own origins in the place.

At the same moment the narrator speaks to the minister, her husband takes the opportunity to speak to the minister's husband: "That is the proper way for conversations to go in our part of the country" (329–30). She is also able to ask about his knowledge about her family—"any Laidlaws from around that area"—and adds that her removal of "the" before the proper noun is "another rule in *our* part of the country" (330, italics added): "you never say *the* so-and-so's, just the name" (330). The narrator makes the point that it is a shared context they occupy, which lends some legitimacy to the nature of her questions. Curiosity does some good in this instance, since the minister's husband comes to recognize both who her father is and who the narrator herself is, and they consequently "explore the connection as far as it will go" (331): curiosity generates an appropriate intimate connection. She is indeed pleased that "somebody" is able to "see me still as part of my family" and "remember my father and the place where my parents worked and lived for all of their married lives" (332), a fact that is particularly important in view of how the landscape of her upbringing has "changed utterly," which "deprives it of meaning for me" (332). In other words, there are appropriate contexts and circumstances for one's curiosity about other's personal lives, for which the narrator herself serves as a model, and these contexts and circumstances bring coherence and significance to her life.

Still, Munro does not discount the curiosity of the outsider who wishes to know about personal matters that have no particular relevance to his or her own life outright; in fact, the narrator herself poses as such an outsider, a "city person," in a later exchange when she approaches a descendent of the Mannerow crypt. Upon being asked questions, Mrs. Mannerow, the narrator observes, does not "seem to find it strange that anybody should wish to know about things that are of no particular benefit or practical importance" (337). Still, she locates her own desire to know as perhaps verging on the inappropriate:

> When I was growing up an appetite for impractical knowledge of any kind did not get encouragement. It was all right to know which field would suit certain crops, but not all right to know anything about the glacial geography I have mentioned. (337)

Local and practical knowledge was privileged, such that it was shameful to pursue matters that had no application to daily life. Munro has made such observations about her own upbringing elsewhere: in interview with Allardice, for example, she noted that, "I was brought up in a community where there was shame" ("Nobel prizewinner") and in interview with Deborah Treisman that, "I was brought up to believe that the worst thing you could do was 'call attention to yourself' or 'think you were smart'" (n.p.). Shame is thus located in the desire for "impractical knowledge," which was discouraged because it made one "stand out" as an individual rather than as a participant in the community, an outcome that "was not a good idea" (337); an understanding of tacit codes of conduct would be violated in "wanting to know" about personal matters that would be deemed irrelevant. The question Munro raises at the outset of the story thus has relevance in a completely different way: what end will be achieved in knowing about the personal details of someone else's life, an "impractical" subject? How would it facilitate one's sense of being or position *within* a community?

The fact that Munro locates these questions in her observations about glacial geography extends the nature and implication of the question: it is not only local in its repercussions. She situates human curiosity within larger existential questions about why knowing is important and what ends it will serve. She does so by locating her own investigative questions within a geographical landscape that extends well beyond her own lifetime:

> The landscape here is a record of ancient events. It was formed by the advancing, stationary, and retreating ice. The ice has staged its conquest and retreats here several times, withdrawing for the last time about fifteen thousand years ago.
>
> Quite recently, you might say. Quite recently now that I have got used to a certain way of reckoning history. (318)

The narrator here invites contemplation and understanding that calls upon another "way of reckoning history" that is *other* than personal. As Caitlin Charman notes, "in this piece [. . .] Munro is still connecting her personal experience of the landscape to the 'larger processes of society and environment' . . . [She] discovers that when you consider history from a geological perspective, the human presence is but a small blip on the radar" (272–73). Curiosity, in this sense, serves as a humbling reminder of the narrator's mortality—and of that of the reader: it underscores the existential nature of human existence and, perhaps, the futility of knowing.

Such curiosity, asking and knowing about the personal lives of others, has its uses and its contexts, Munro suggests, but an absolute adherence to the facts less so. As she has elsewhere noted, she desires "to write in a way that both honours her subject and treats it honestly" (qtd. in Thacker 2011, 493). If she is ambiguous in such disclosures related to autobiographical detail, these disclosures have less to do with adherence to the facts than with dignity and honesty: such ambiguity serves as a reminder of the limits to intimacy and an invitation to the reader to consider what purpose such intimacy would serve. In the last few lines of "What Do You Want to Know For?," therefore, the narrator remarks upon how the biopsy was one of a series of frights that "come and go," until "there'll be one that won't. One that won't go" (339). The reader is not provided with other details—another reminder, I believe, of the appropriate limit of knowing, of the limits to intimacy. By staging a necessary ambiguity between fact and fiction, and using shame as a device to guard against readers who may probe too deeply, Munro reminds readers of "who we think we are" and invites us to consider "what we want to know for."

Notes

1. By "biographical desire," McGill refers to both the contemporary fascination with confession and autobiographical detail, and the simultaneous impulse to "tell all."
2. See also, as another example, Tanja Cvetkovic, who argues that in Munro's work, "the distinction between fact and fiction becomes blurred; and, after closing the last page of the book, readers remain pondering the ways fact is turned into fiction. No doubt, the stories in *The View from Castle Rock* have an autobiographical dimension" (102). She adds that, ultimately, Munro "leaves her readers puzzled to determine on their own the truth of the events in the past." As yet another example, Val Ross, in an interview with Munro, claimed that "[t]he 12 stories in *Castle Rock* are as close as [she] has come to turning her family's life into stories" and calls upon her primary source material as evidence of the factual basis of her work: "She uses author James Hogg's late 18th-century account of her folk, the Laidlaws, of the Ettrick Valley, south of Edinburgh. She quotes a Laidlaw

diary describing the crossing to Canada in 1818, and selections from her father's novel *The Macgregors*" (n.p.).

Critics make similar observations about her other work, not only *The View from Castle Rock*. Robert Thacker, for example, argues that many of the stories from *Something I've Been Meaning to Tell You* are "among her most transparently autobiographical stories" (1999, 253). When *Lives of Girls and Women* first appeared, as another example, Denise Levertov noted that "we cannot but believe Del and Alice Munro to be one and the same" and that the reader would be thus assured of Del's success in finding "her own path out of Jubilee into the rest of her life" (qtd. in Thacker 2011, 250).

3. Critics also identify the degree to which her stories are "autobiographical." Thacker, for example, notes that it is "Miles City, Montana," based on a visit the Munro family made back home to Ontario during the summer of 1961, that is "one of Munro's most autobiographical stories" (2011, 172).

4. Of "Privilege," as yet another example, the short story that appears in *Who Do You Think You Are?*, she notes that the details of the school described therein are predicated on her experience at the Lower Town School: the school, she observes, is "the most autobiographical thing in the book. One of the more autobiographical things I have written" (qtd. in Thacker 2011, 56). The disclaimer to *Lives of Girls and Women*, what was suggestively titled *Real Life*, indicated that the "novel" was "autobiographical in form but not in fact" (qtd. in Thacker 2011, 250). The early identification of the manuscript as a novel would indeed indicate its fictional qualities, however autobiographical the form might be. Of "The Office," Munro claims that it was "the most straightforward autobiographical story I have ever written" (qtd. in Thacker 2011, 172). In her introduction to *The Moons of Jupiter* (1985), as yet another example, she argues that "[s]ome of these stories *are closer* to my own life than others are, but not one of them is as close as people seem to think."

5. See for example her interview with Deborah Triesman, in which she claims, "I have used bits and pieces of my own life always, but the last things in the new book were all simple truth. As was—I should have said this—*The View from Castle Rock*—the story of my family, as much as I could tell."

6. Thacker also claims that "Home" and "What Do You Want to Know For" have been emphasized as key texts because "of the autobiographical detail they offer" (2011, 528).

7. As A. O. Scott observes, Munro's insistence that "these are *stories*" in *The View from Castle Rock* "may seem a little odd. What else would they be?" Yet, he adds, "when Munro emphasizes that 'these are stories,' she is, at least in part, defending the prerogative of fiction as a vehicle for truth-telling against the literal-minded incursions of genealogy and memoir": "Whether they are the literal truth is beyond irrelevant. The point of storytelling, as Munro practices it, is to rescue the literal facts

from banality, from oblivion, and to preserve—to create—some sense of continuity in the hectic ebb and flow of experience" (n.p.). "We can't resist this rifling around in the past," she writes in an epilogue, "sifting the untrustworthy evidence, linking stray names and questionable dates and anecdotes together, hanging on to threads, insisting on being joined to dead people and therefore to life" (n.p.).

Works Cited

Allardice, Lisa. "Nobel Prizewinner Alice Munro: 'It's a Wonderful Thing for the Short Story.'" Interview with Alice Munro. *The Guardian* [UK], 6 December 2013. https://www.theguardian.com/books/2013/dec/06/alice-munro-interview-nobel-prize-short-story-literature.

Charman, Caitlin. "'Secretly Devoted to Nature: Place Sense in Alice Munro's *The View from Castle Rock*." *Critical Insights: Alice Munro*. Ed. Charles May. Ipswich, MA: Salem Press, 2013. 259–75.

Cvetkovic, Tanja. "Reinventing Lives Into Stories: Historical Autobiography in Alice Munro's *The View from Castle Rock*." *Theory & Practice in English Studies* 5.2 (2012): 101–110. http://www.phil.muni.cz/plonedata/wkaa/The%20PES/2012_Vol5_2/THEPES_Vol%20V%20issue%202_article%203_Czetkovic.pdf.

Duncan, Isla. *Alice Munro's Narrative Art*. Basingstoke, UK: Palgrave Macmillan, 2011.

Lejeune, Phillipe. *On Autobiography* Ed. Paul John Eakin. Trans. Katherine Leary. Minneapolis: U of Minnesota P, 1989.

McCaig, JoAnn. *Reading In: Alice Munro's Archives*. Waterloo, ON: Wilfrid Laurier UP, 2002.

McGill, Robert. *The Treacherous Imagination: Intimacy, Ethics and Autobiographical Fiction*. Columbus: Ohio State UP, 2013.

Munro, Alice. *The View from Castle Rock: Stories*. Toronto: Penguin, 2006.

———. *Dear Life: Stories*. Toronto: McClelland & Stewart, 2012.

———. *The Moons of Jupiter: Stories*. Toronto: Macmillan, 1982.

———. Probyn, Elspeth. "Writing Shame." *The Affect Theory Reader*. Ed. Melissa Gregg and Gregory J. Seitworth. Durham and London: Duke UP, 2010. 71–92.

Ross, Val. "Eating and Talking at Alice's Restaurant." *Globe and Mail*, 28 October 2006. http://www.theglobeandmail.com/arts/books-and-media/eating-and-talking-at-alices-restaurant/article12674739/?page=all.

Schama, Chloe. "Not Quite Stories—Alice Munro's Almost Autobiography." Review of *Dear Life*. *New Republic*, November 2012.

Scott, A. O. "Native Ground." Review of *The View from Castle Rock. New York Times*, 10 December 2006. http://www.nytimes.com/2006/12/10/books/review/Scott.t.html.

Thacker, Robert. Introduction. *Critical Essays on Alice Munro: The Rest of My Story.* Ed Robert Thacker. Toronto: ECW, 1999.

———. *Alice Munro: Writing Her Lives, A Biography.* 2005. Toronto: McClelland & Stewart, 2011.

Triesman, Deborah. "On *Dear Life*": An Interview with Alice Munro. *New Yorker*, 20 November 2012. http://www.newyorker.com/books/page-turner/on-dear-life-an-interview-with-alice-munro.

Once Upon a Time: Temporality in the Narration of Alice Munro

E. D. Blodgett

The past needs to be approached from a distance.
—Alice Munro (*The View from Castle Rock* 332)

Among the few reviewers who have had the temerity to argue against the validity of Alice Munro's stature in the world of contemporary English literature, Christian Lorentzen, a senior editor of the *London Review of Books*, stands out not only because of his own stature but also because of the articulate and highly persuasive character of his review of *Dear Life*. It is so powerful that one doubts if he would have modified it had he written after Munro's acquisition of the Nobel Prize. His opening remarks all but disarm most critics of Munro by observing that "her critics begin by asserting her goodness, her greatness, her majorness or her bestness, and then quickly adopt a defensive tone, instructing us in ways of seeing as virtues the many things about her writing that might be considered shortcomings" ("Poor Rose" 11). Incisive as this statement is in its desire to reduce all critical commentary to defensive stances, it is only preparatory to gathering most of Munro's themes through which Lorentzen begins to see "everyone heading toward cancer, or a case of dementia that would rob them of the memories of the little adulteries they'd probably committed and must have spent their whole lives thinking about" (11). By the time he reaches her fourth collection, he concludes that:

> Munro's incessant reworking of the material in *The Beggar Maid* [*Who Do You Think You Are?*] has had the odd effect of diluting the original; later versions of the first sexual encounter [...], or the adultery story, or the stale marriage story, or the lonely single mother story, don't so much enhance the originals as point up their flaws, making them seem even more schematic. ("Poor Rose" 12)

An effort to suggest that Munro's later stories tend toward a greater use of fictionality as opposed to her earlier realism returns, however, to the preoccupation with cancer and dementia (which may account for her contemporary acclaim). It is still the same story in *Dear Life*, but made to look lighter, less sad, more full of "*le plaisir du texte.*"

Limited as Lorentzen's critique may be, he comments at least on structure and form. Jonathan Franzen, whose fame as a writer is certainly greater than that of Lorentzen, chooses reasons that have prevented Munro from becoming famous and then argues against them. Franzen's is, in effect, the reverse of Lorentzen's approach, but it is one that prompts him to resort to summaries—and often long ones—to make his point. Despite telling the same story in various ways for fifty years, Munro still finds more in it to develop. For Franzen, "the familiarity of her materials" is the basis of her artistic achievement ("Runaway"). Of course, his injunction "Read Munro" is a fine idea, but is it enough to discover that "the only adequate summary of the text is the text itself" (Franzen). Taken together, these two extremes of approaches to Munro, both full of praise and full of vilification, fail to assist the reader. Both are interested in what the text says, but they are insufficient in leading the reader to see how she says it; in other words, in moving from the text to its pleasures.

Although it may be bad form, I want to pick up where my book on Alice Munro, in which I addressed the function of narration, left off. I chose such a point of departure because I was unsure of how to approach her as a realist, as she is commonly read. I stepped away from such a reading for two reasons. First of all, it was and remains difficult for me to find shared ground between my experiences and those depicted in Munro's stories. Second, even if that were possible, I always responded to the theatrical, hyperbolic side of Munro's writing and especially to the sense, frequently expressed by her narrators, of failure to recapture, in Leopold von Ranke's famous phrase, "wie es eigentlich gewesen" [how it really was] (see Stern 57). Hence, my sympathetic response to the narrator's desperate remark at the end of *Lives of Girls and Women*, namely that the "hope of accuracy" that would restore "every smell, pothole, pain, crack, delusion" prompted efforts that could only be "heartbreaking" in the end (253). The anxiety that such efforts produce is already anticipated in the collection's earlier story in which the younger Del seeks the reality of God and declares, "If God could be discovered, or recalled, everything would be safe" (*Lives* 100). In other words, there would be no heartbreak. Del makes the provisory assumption that if everything is held in God's mind, then everyone could go on "breathing and existing" (100). By the end of "Age of Faith," Del and her brother become sadly aware that God is so distant that safety cannot be assured.

The conclusion of *Lives* can thus be read as an *ars poetica* in the sense that one can only return rather hopelessly to the same situations in order to seize the smell and pain. Thus, Munro unwittingly anticipates Lorentzen's circumscribed reading of a writing growing weaker, always struggling with the same material. My reading was designed to suggest, however, that the primary material was heartbreak; the rest was secondary. That heartbreak, I argued, drawing upon Jacques Derrida, was in fact *différance.* To say as much is to point to the space between a discursive practice and what is narrated, or discourse and story. Once this has been done, it might be said that the discussion of narrative kind becomes secondary, that is, it does not matter whether Munro's stories are realistic. It matters how they are told, and Derrida's notion of *différance* matters because it is a technique to which Munro's narrators always have recourse to make sense of their lives. To cite my earlier comments,

> Its bearing on writing springs from the fact that nothing can be said all at once; and it is a mark of the act of writing, as Derrida distinguishes it from speaking, to separate the narrator from the narrated, to create a kind of distance that differs and defers. Thus what the writer wants to recapture is continually put off with each word that would make an effort to seize it. The real, then, that one has known, and experienced, once it enters language, enters a system of signs that depend in their sound and sense on difference. Furthermore, once it enters discourse, it is inhabited by time as we move through the statement. At what moment can we say that the object of our quest is made present again, that is, re-presented? The object as it becomes written is entrapped by deferral. . . (*Alice Munro* 8–9)

So powerful are such entrapments that Munro's narrators appear to operate in a feedback loop, partly because of the familiarity of the material and partly because of the conditions in which that materiality is continually deployed. Deferral is at once removal and return.

Not all acts of deferral are marked by the withholding of discovery or insight. They can often occur as a move to another level of understanding. This is exactly how the narrator introduces the royal beatings in the story of the same name: "The word Royal lolled on Flo's tongue, took on trappings" (*Who* 1). The moment it is spoken it is personified, opening an initial space between signified and signifier. Rose, the protagonist of the story, becomes immediately a vehicle for the narrator's desire to distort the representation of the real: "Rose had a need to picture things, to pursue absurdities, that was stronger than the need to stay out of trouble, and instead of taking this threat to heart, she pondered: how is a beating royal?" (*Who* 1). How often one finds both narrators and protagonists making such a move, destabilizing the notion of a consensual event and making it idiosyncratic. One might say it is Munro's manner of bestowing a certain reality on her characters, by which one means that this is how characters become imaginatively realized. The reader, however, is reminded of Rose's imagination and how self-protective it is:

> She came up with a tree-lined avenue, a crowd of formal spectators, some white horses and black slaves, Someone knelt and the blood came leaping out like banners. An occasion both savage and splendid. In real life they didn't approach such dignity, and it was only Flo who tried to supply the event with some high air of necessity and regret. Rose and her father soon got beyond anything presentable. (1)

The imaginative leap is clearly distinguished from "real life." The two worlds only coincide discursively; the possibility of overlaying "real life" with deceit, concealment, pretension and disguise recurs frequently in the collection, culminating in Rose's friend Ralph imitating Milton Homer, the village idiot. Nothing acquires significance, it seems, unless it can be reshaped or translated, to use another term recurring in the story. A village idiot Milton may be, but his attraction for Rose and Ralph is creative. He is the arch "mimic of ferocious gifts and terrible energy. [Entering parades], he could take the step-dancers' tidy show and turn it into an idiot's prance, and still keep the beat" (*Who* 192). He enacts a kind of carnivalesque parody, the translation of an event that displaces emphasis and, like translation, places the reader in front of two inimical language systems, one of which, at least in literary translation, is asked to recreate, sacrifice, and imitate within various constraints. If the reader believes that the original text, by being original, is near a certain reality, the reader knows that in the translated text, the certainties of "origin" cannot be recovered. A second, uncertain reality is presented that the reader has no way of personally verifying if unfamiliar with the translated language. Hence it is that Rose, with Ralph, prefers to remain silent about many things, if only because "translation is dubious. Dangerous as well" (*Who* 206). It lies at the heart of difference.

But what is heartbreak if not a catalyst of change, of profound difference? Heartbreak, of course, happens in many ways, as most, if not all, of Munro's stories attest: relationships dissolve, families collapse, people are abandoned, and living happily ever after is practically unheard of. The essential syllable of "heartbreak," however, is not heart but break, at least on the level of writing fiction. Breaking is not necessarily, as one might assume, an ending, but is more akin to translation, that process by which one sees the familiar as other. As anyone knows who has tried translating one's own work into another language, especially a poem, it becomes quickly apparent that such handy oppositions as self and other become rather useless.[1] Otherness becomes dominant, and, as in heartbreak, the self appears so unsettled as to be other than what it was before the break: not absolutely other, and no longer wholly self. Leaving aside the tricks of translation, the self is always other to the other, a condition that heartbreak underscores. Identity can be deeply shaken; it finds itself in a dangerous and risky situation. In this sense it is consonant with what we have already discussed as deferral, that moment when difference appears inexorable. To be in such a situation appears close to apocalyptic, as in the moment when the protagonist of "A Trip to the Coast" agonizes over a decision of her grandmother: "If her grandmother capitulated it would be as unsettling an event as an earthquake or a flood; it would crack the foundations of her life and set her terrifyingly free" (*Dance* 188). It would cause a kind of break of being too difficult to bear.

Nevertheless, this otherness is the common lot of Munro's characters, and is what makes them difficult to seize as finished characters, well rounded, with clear beginnings and endings. Textual interruptions—the stylistic echoes of her approach to character formation—are already apparent in her earliest stories. Such is the effect of the narrator's reminder in "The Office" about her understanding of the building owner where she is about to rent an office: "How much of this I saw at first, how much decided on later is of course impossible to tell" (*Dance* 62). Of course, it is not impossible to tell, but the narrator's self-insertion intentionally interrupts the story, making a little discursive skip that underscores the difference between narration and discourse. The same is true of Munro's fondness for words that invariably interrupt the story. Thus, as the protagonist muses discursively in "Boys and Girls," the differences between *child* and *girl* are not simple but heavily invested both psychologically and ideologically. *Child* signifies a state of being, but *girl* is a status that one grows into, "always touched with emphasis, with reproach and disappointment," a status confirmed by the final paragraphs of the story, a confirmation belonging to the narrative level, becoming closure without interruption (*Dance* 119 and 127).

Larger interruptions are caused by the many moments of epiphany that conclude her stories, as critics have frequently noted. Probably her most dramatic epiphany is the moment at the end of *Lives of Girls and Women* when Bobby Sherriff

> did the only special thing he ever did for me . . . he rose on his toes like a dancer, like a plump ballerina. This action, accompanied by his delicate smile, appeared to be a joke not shared with me so much as displayed for me, and it seemed also to have a concise meaning, a stylized meaning—to be a letter, or a whole word, in an alphabet I did not know.
>
> People's wishes, and their other offerings, were what I took naturally, a bit distractedly, as if they were never anything more than my due. (253–54)

The reception of the young Del to Bobby's moment of self-display is in keeping with Del's generally narcissistic[2] behaviour throughout, implicitly criticized by the narrator. And so the coda is somewhat more complex than it may appear. First, it emphasizes the difference between Del as a teenager and Del as an adult. Second, it steps away from the narration to the point where it hypostatizes the signifying function of a text, as opposed to its referential role, in which a text is a code that must be translated to reach an approximate sense of the story. We are further reminded of the double role of the word "Del" in the story, namely, one who acts and one who interprets or reads. It is a double role, finally, that is repeated in the idea of theatre that occurs elsewhere: the annual school operetta and the "performance" of Mr. Chamberlain's display (*Lives* 170), and which is later developed in *Who Do You Think You Are?*

As a double role, it echoes another preoccupation of Del and other narrators. She is certain that, parallel to her world, there is another that connotes not only the exotic, but also the dangerous, the risky, the lurid, the grotesque; in other words, a romantic, secondary space, "a town lying close to the one I walked through every day" (*Lives* 248), a town that becomes the setting of the text Del embarks on toward the end of *Lives*. It is also the point of departure of all the stories in the collection, in which "lying alongside our world was Uncle Benny's world like a troubling, distorted reflection, the same but never at all the same. In that world people would go down in quicksand, be vanquished by ghosts or terrible ordinary cities; luck and wickedness were gigantic and unpredictable. . ." (*Lives* 25). Indeed, *Lives* itself is structured around the continuous interplay of two worlds—"the same, but never the same" (25)—designed to destabilize Del's initial impressions. Her desire is to hold them together by continually trying to seize the key or code by which she might do so. Everything is presented to be decoded and re-coded, read and written.

The most developed example of this aspect of Munro's writing is "Fiction." The ostensible fiction is a text discovered by the protagonist in which she is a main figure. She is presented as a character who requires decoding, and the reader over her shoulder is naturally drawn into mimicking, interpreting, or reinterpreting her. The main character is, consequently, written, at least, twice. The technique is wonderfully deceptive, for trained as the reader is to seek, to use Roland Barthes phrase, the "*effet de réel*," another dimension of the character is constructed that allows the reader to question her reality. Dividing the story into two parts assists in the process of revision. The first provides all the details and psychological insights needed to know that one is confronted with a frequent situation in Munro, in this instance, the breakdown of a marriage. At the conclusion of the section, the narrator clearly sees the world from Joyce's perspective: the anxious music instructor whose pupil, the daughter of her ex-husband's new partner, is performing. Deftly, the narrator asks, while Joyce scans the audience for Jon, "What does she see? God knows." The narrator continues: "She did not, in any sane moment, think of impressing Jon . . ." (*Too Much Happiness* 42). The section ends with the dry comment that she searched in vain: Jon did not attend. The next section follows with the observation that Joyce and Matt were giving a party to celebrate Matt's sixty-fifth birthday. This is so abrupt that for a moment the reader needs to take a moment to reorient. Much time has passed without comment, other than to remark that Matt is a good violinist and that that is how he met Joyce. And then we are informed that Joyce "is a lean, eager-looking woman with a mop of pewter-coloured hair and a slight stoop. . . " (42). It is a moment that constitutes a shift of point of view, embedding Joyce into another narrative that seems initially unconnected to the previous one. It is sufficient for the reader to begin to see the real for what it so often is in Munro: an effect of narration.

Thus, when one arrives at her former student's story (another narration about Joyce), we are prepared for the fact that "Joyce" is a floating signifier, capable of being in many fictions. But Joyce does not merely *read*, she enters the story as a figure that blurs the line between whatever the real is and fiction, challenging any notion we might have that Munro is a realist. Implying that Munro is looking over *her* shoulder, she begins to think about the tendencies of fiction in which "the writer would graft her ugly invention onto the people and the situation she had gotten out of real life" (56). One is prompted to ask what the relationship is between the narrator and author (Joyce's student and Munro), and how Joyce, who is not the writer, knows this so authoritatively. The whole interaction of Joyce's reading in "Fiction" raises with acuity how the multiple realities of character, narrator and author are under siege in Munro. This is particularly underlined at the end of the whole story in which the author, Joyce's student, abdicates any responsibility (60–61), as if the story just came out of the blue, without any necessary connection to a matrix of reality. In the final paragraph we see that Joyce, as narrator and author, will most likely spin the tale into a humorous anecdote, suggesting that the only real is fiction.

Clearly, one of the powerful effects of Munro's narrators is that they are not content with mere narration. They want to be readers in such a way as to stand in for the actual reader. Our role is to be a reader of the narrator reading, rather than of her writing; the narrator has the advantage of seeming to know how her story will unfold, an advantage we cannot share. The difficulty a reader-narrator poses is that she is capable of modifying herself as she pieces together what she is in the act of telling, as part of the process of discovery. Narrating for Munro is often a form of self-discovery, but it is not always possible to say who the narrator is behind the mask of her name or the pronoun "I," particularly as she lays out the more complex montages of what she is narrating. She constantly represents herself as a sign of change—a kind of figure of Chaucerian mutability—as if she were an echo of the effect of time itself.

Casting glances about almost at random through Munro's initial paragraphs, one cannot help but be struck by the preoccupation with the temporality of situations. The opening sentences of "Save the Reaper" read: "The game they played was almost the same one that Eve had played with Sophie on long dull car trips when Sophie was a little girl. Then it was spies—now it was aliens" (*Love* 146). Before knowing anything, we know that we are faced with at least two moments in time that relate only to each other. And how tantalizingly "Haven" begins: "All this happened in the seventies, though in that town and other small towns like it, the seventies were not as we picture them now, or even as I had known them in Vancouver" (*Dear Life* 110). While the opening phrase marks a time, it is followed by a kind of conditional warning that easily helps us understand, by the end of the sentence, that space is subject to the way time is construed. As time changes, so does the way we see a city, and vice versa, and as we know from photographs; a photograph, for example, marked 1943 will have different look and ambiance than the same space marked 2012. For sheer verve one might choose the beginning of "Dance of the Happy Shades," from the beginning of Munro's career. The narrator announces that Miss Marsalles is throwing another party at an inconvenient moment for the narrator's mother, who informs us in a moment of energetic free indirect discourse: "Oh, but won't that be too much trouble, *now? Now* being weighted with several troublesome meanings," and the meanings are each punctuated by emphatic anaphora, namely, "Now that Miss Marsalles," "now that Miss Marsalles' older sister" and "now that Miss Marsalles herself." The second paragraph begins with a further outcry: "*Now?* asks Miss Marsalles" (*Dance* 210). Although it is not clear in the absence of quotation marks whether the protagonist's mother actually expressed her worries, Miss Marsalles knows what was thought and tellingly sums up the central issue of the first paragraph by raising "now," a highly complex moment in time, as a matter of larger importance than its seeming immediacy.

In contrast, the first part of *The View from Castle Rock*, in both its structure and narrative, is remarkably linear. Commenting on this section, Munro distinguishes two types of narration in the last paragraph of her foreword: it is closer to the "truth of a life than fiction (n.p.)." One might add that the use of journals and memoirs suggests an affinity with chronicle, and when the narrator and her parents enter in the second section, it comes closer to life writing. The two conjoin in an almost startling fashion when the two registers seem to blend in her father's own chronicle of one of his grandfathers. Two kinds of time appear to confront each other. This is because chronicle foregrounds time as the constant element in which the family is rooted, and it inscribes a beginning, a middle, and an end. Life writing, which Munro here calls fiction, foregrounds time as alive in different ways in different characters, each "a live memory" (*Dear Life* 348). Linearity suffers continuous displacement, and endings give way, rather, to suspensions in time.

Although such a technique is an indelible mark of Munro's style, it is exemplary in "The Progress of Love," which begins: "I got a call at work, and it was my father. This was not long after I was divorced. . ." (3). Everything begins *in medias res* or, more accurately, *in media vita.* We begin with a kind of juncture with, and departure from, the past. A second departure is announced in her father's strange remark: "'I think your mother is gone'" (3). The uncertainty is remarkable, and instead of registering an emotional response, the narrator performs a little but not infrequent riff in Munro on language, in which certain psychological levels of "gone" are played with. The paragraph continues until it ends with the father's willingness to go to a nursing home. In the next paragraph he relates the immediate circumstances of the mother's death. Then a gap is inserted, separating what seems to have been a preface from a new section recounting her mother's way of life, her meeting and marrying the narrator's father, and her carefulness in money matters, which is later contradicted. One is prompted to ask: Where is the story going, and who will the central characters be?

Any answer is, of course, provisory and subject to constant modification. The structure of the initial pages reinforces a sense of the provisory by adding bits of information in a random fashion, hinting at a theme of knowledge as it bears on what is not known, even concealed. The narrator herself is constructed as someone from whom certain things are concealed or require discovery. Hence, "When my father was old, I figured out" (5), revealing the fact that the narrator is subject to various ages, even while telling the story. Time, as a result, has no chronological order. It is always being reconfigured, conjoined in the several "nows" that come and go in the mind.[3] The events that are used to compose a past are deliberately shaped in a kind of helter-skelter fashion that constructs a narrator who appears either overwhelmed by too much material or not capable of knowing how to sort it. In fact, the narrator appears breathless as she sketches her mother's past, leaping from the mother's decision to remain in Ramsay after her mother's death and her sister Beryl's departure with her father and stepmother, to Beryl's visit, to the narrator's entrance examinations. After a pause, the narrative resumes with her mother's childhood and her grandmother's faked suicide, all interrupted by little asides, for example, concerning her mother's German neighbour who made strudel. Her mother confides that the staged suicide broke her heart, leaving the narrator in a quandary, wishing they might stop, her mother's "stories and griefs, the old puzzles you can't resist or solve" (14).

At such moments the reader begins to ask: What does the narrator know, and when did she know it? The question is prompted by the way almost anything is seized upon to construct a past—pasts of several characters, including the narrator's, all groping toward a kind of insight, many fragments of which are shared. The insight can only be found in time, and until it is reached the narrator's function is to perform, so to speak, the ways the narration leads to it. The way is only possible through time in a kind of maze where all the characters move, none more significant than any other, including the narrator. At the centre of the maze is the narrator's shifting notion of her mother, whose stories are taken as truth until later revealed as fabrications. The story of the grandmother's faked suicide when first told makes it fairly clear she was unharmed, afterward laughing and drinking coffee. Later, when Beryl disabuses the protagonist, she still finds it hard to accept. The other story that collapses is that of her apparently frugal mother burning her inheritance with her father's consent. The protagonist also allows her current boyfriend to believe that the main-floor bedroom was hers.

Most evident in the story of the suicide and its recurrence is the fact that the protagonist invests a great deal of truth in it in order to follow her mother's version. Such willingness to invest implies that the truth, had she wished to accept it, would have been known all along. The past, then, and the various moments in time that give it structure is continually manipulated by the narrator to suggest to the reader that something concealed will come to light. Nothing prevents the reader from surmising at the end that the narrator knew what happened all along, and, consequently, time is emptied of its function of bringing things to light. The obdurate paradox of the story appears to be that stories and characters are textured by the interweaving of moments of time, and that we are at once subject to temporality but equally able to dispense with it.

It might be said that Munro's style is a continuous critique of the plot and narrator of the kind of story that Joseph Conrad's *Heart of Darkness* represents. The narrator is clear at the beginning that his narrative starts at a point when he knows nothing, unlike Munro's narrator. And the plot is shaped to carry him to a kind of knowledge, which, nevertheless, is shrouded in darkness. In a sense, Marlowe becomes complicit with the darkness, refusing to give Mr. Kurtz's fiancée his final words. The darkness is also shrouded in mystery, enhancing the variety of symbolic experience the story constructs. The plot, which moves steadily through the time of the journey, is finally designed to lead the reader to an understanding of things that escape clear articulation by evoking a transcendent plane of existence. Such a plane is notably absent in Munro. Even more troubling is that time itself is perceived as increasingly elusive as a means of locating character. Such elusiveness recalls, in fact, Gertrude Stein's casual dismissal of Oakland, where "there is no there there" (289). One is often tempted to say that in Munro there is no then, then.

Such an absence has its own problems that cannot be resolved by any referential appeal, inasmuch as the boundary between author and narrator is often blurred, as it is between fiction and the real. The real is a dimension of the fictional. At a certain moment, the narrator of "Winter Wind" interrupts her story to remark, "Whether my grandmother had disappointed [her husband] or not . . . nobody could know" (201). And then she continues, in a manner most readers of Munro would recognize as a signature of her style, that no one could know. The narrator's explanation suggests, if not avows, that she is almost speaking as the author, especially in her manner of constructing characters, implying that she did know: "I have used these people. . . . I have tricked them out and altered them any way at all, to suit my purposes." Then she denies doing this in this instance, in fact, as she hastens to remark, "I am being as careful as I can, but I stop and wonder, I feel compunction." Despite such second thoughts, "I am only doing in a large and public way what has always been done, what my mother did, and other people did, who mentioned to me my grandmother's story." Dissatisfied with such an explanation, she claims in the following paragraph to have invented nothing: "Without any proof I believe it, and so I must believe that we get messages another way, that we have connections that cannot be investigated, but have to be relied on" (*Something* 201). Interesting as this meditation is, it does not clarify the issue. If she believes she is correct, and if her intuition supports her, which is what she seems to be confessing, then to assert a lack of knowledge about the character is not quite believable. It is a curious abdication that allows the narrator (and author) to have it both ways, recalling the play with authorial responsibility toward the end of "Fiction." It is a fine illustration of how a story can be interrupted and suspended for the sake of discussing the narrator's problems with constructing character and telling a story that undermines any believable layer of the real.

A large element of pathos is often evident in Munro's stories, as a result, and frequently readers are prompted to suggest that Munro is another Chekhov. Other than the fact that he is one of the greatest writers of short stories and thus worthy of placing beside Munro, I have always felt the comparison attractive, but strangely inapt. It is appropriate only if read within the context of the classical tradition, of which Chekhov is a late member. By "classical" I do not mean an Aristotelean attention to form, which Munro happily ignores, in any case. I mean rather a sense of what I have called transcendence and which includes a notion of destiny.[4] On the one hand, limits are imposed on a character's freedom and, on the other, events that occur in time cannot be overcome. Time becomes a sign for both. Limits are imposed also on comedy, and certainly time and timeliness are necessary, but Munro is not exactly a comic writer, despite her sense of humour.

Munro's characters have a predilection for "flimsy choices, arbitrary days," "rather than a destiny to submit to" (*Open Secrets* 127), for whom, nevertheless, clarity is frequent but shaped as accidental (cf. "Differently," *Friend* 243). The narrator moves effortlessly from moment to moment, fragmenting chronologies, and seemingly overcoming the manifold constraints of the classical tradition, notably those of a mythological, theological, and cultural character. No character rashly tries to challenge a foreseen fate, as in Greek tragedy, no character is summoned by an other-worldly figure as Dante is, to witness the eternal horrors of other figures recounting the unavoidable scope of their chosen destinies, and no character is repeatedly defeated by political and cultural constraints, as they are in Chekhov. How clearly, for example, Gurov and Anna Sergeyevna perform their fate at the end of "Lady and the Lapdog," held apart by "their intolerable chains" (281). Chekhov's world is closed, like that of his predecessors, framed by the closure that composes the classical tradition. The pathos emerging from his fiction is only sentimental in appearance. It endures in the condition of the peasants, the class system, the taboos of society, the general poverty. No matter how many social barriers and historical entanglements Munro's characters encounter, the method of narration places them in a web of temporality whose texture is continually subject to change. The past appears to explain, to be indeed the necessary condition for understanding a character, until replaced by another past or version of it. The pathos that emerges from Munro's stories is of an entirely different order than that of Chekhov—in some ways more desolate, more existentially unaccommodated. It belongs to the special kind of terror that rises in the protagonist's imagination in "Oh, What Avails" as she contemplates the problems of change: "The threat is of a change, but it's not the sort of change one has been warned about" (*Friend* 208). Her image of such change is rubble: one can look down a street and see all the ordinary things "Or you can see rubble. Passing states, a useless variety of passing states. Rubble. " This is where her characters very frequently find themselves, in such passing states. Within the classical context it calls to mind the rubble of T. S. Eliot's "The Wasteland," but in Munro the ghostly presence of rubble is without a classical reference and without footnotes. The rubble appears naked and unsupported, with rarely the slightest breath of the melancholic nostalgia that runs through Chekhov. For Munro, however, nostalgia is not an option in a world where transience is all that is given, a disordered transience that often has no clear chronology, and where disaster is always imminent.

It may be thought that if Munro is not in the classical tradition, then she must be somewhere we can locate with respect to that tradition. I have shied away from placing her because I'm not sure that some other oppositional term would illuminate her fiction. One thinks of classical-romantic, which are hardly in opposition, or, as the German literary critic Ernst Robert Curtius suggested, classical vs. mannered. I read Munro as entirely apart from that tradition, and I have mentioned the tradition primarily to argue that a false picture of her work can be made by referring to it, especially through the work of Chekhov. It is too early, however, to place her in any other specific tradition, and she is not sufficiently postmodern to place her there. What new world she anticipates is not possible to predict, but it is one that confronts the reader with all the power of the ephemeral, a world without the illusion of chronological order, and without the hope that another plane of existence affords. Human temporality and fragility are so foregrounded that the reader can only take comfort in the manner in which language can evoke a recounting, if only for the moment and of the moment.

Notes

1. Cf. Blodgett, "A Note on Self-Translation."
2. It is instructive to compare this epiphany with that of the grandmother in Flannery O'Connor's story "A Good Man is Hard to Find," in which confronted with psychotic killer known as The Misfit, whose men have just shot and killed her family, she suddenly touches his shoulder and declares that he was one her own children. The asservation of kinship is scarcely to be believed, but its inscrutability adds to the transcendent power of the event. At the moment of her own death the grandmother reaches out in a gesture of humanity that Del is incapable of.
3. Cf. the epiphany at the end of *The View from Castle Rock:* "Now all these names I have been recording are joined to the living people in my mind" (348).

4. Munro rarely mentions destiny, but see "Family Furnishings" (*Hateship, Friendship, Courtship, Loveship, Marriage* 96) with reference to the mother's illness. It is hinted at in the last paragraph of "White Dump" (*The Progress of Love* 309).

Works Cited

Blodgett, E. D. *Alice Munro.* Boston: G.K. Hall, 1988.

———. "A Note on Self-Translation." *La Traductière* 23 (2005): 126–30.

Chekhov, Anton. *Lady with a Lapdog and Other Stories.* Trans. David Magarshack. London: Penguin, 1964.

Franzen, Jonathan. "'Runaway': Alice's Wonderland." *New York Times,* 14 November 2004. http://www.nytimes.com/2004/11/14/books/review/runaway-alices-wonderland.html.

Lorentzen, Christian. "Poor Rose." *London Review of Books* 35.11 (6 June 2013): 11–12.

Munro, Alice: *Dance of the Happy Shades.* Toronto: Ryerson, 1968.

———. *Dear Life.* Toronto: McClelland & Stewart, 2012.

———. *Friend of My Youth.* Toronto: McClelland & Stewart, 1990.

———. *Hateship, Friendship, Courtship, Loveship, Marriage.* Toronto: McClelland & Stewart, 2001.

———. *Lives of Girls and Women.* Toronto: McGraw-Hill Ryerson, 1971.

———. *Open Secrets.* Toronto: McClelland & Stewart, 1994.

———. *Something I've Been Meaning To Tell You.* Toronto: McGraw-Hill Ryerson, 1974.

———. *The Love of a Good Woman.* Toronto: McClelland & Stewart, 1998.

———. *The Progress of Love.* Toronto: McClelland & Stewart, 1986.

———. *The View from Castle Rock.* Toronto: McClelland & Stewart, 2006.

———. *Too Much Happiness.* Toronto: McClelland & Stewart, 2009.

———. *Who Do You Think You Are?* Toronto: Macmillan Canada, 1978.

O'Connor, Flannery. "A Good Man Is Hard to Find." *Collected Works.* The Library of America. New York: Literary Classics of the United States, 1988.

Stein, Gertrude. *Everybody's Autobiography.* 1937. New York: Cooper Square, 1971.

Stern, Fritz Richard, ed. *The Varieties of History: From Voltaire to the Present.* New York: Meridian, 1956.

L'Envoi

On Sitting Down to Read "Lichen" Once Again

MAGDALENE REDEKOP

ON REREADING AND THE PASSAGE OF TIME

Once upon a time I went out on a limb and called Munro's compassion Shakespearean (*Mothers* 233). More than two decades later, Shakespeare was on my mind again when I came up with a title that echoes a sonnet by John Keats: "On Sitting Down to Read 'King Lear' Once Again." I know very well, of course, that Alice Munro herself questions such literary hierarchies. "Who Do You Think You Are?," for example, contains an allusion to yet another sonnet by Keats about rereading.[1] In that story, a boy sitting behind Rose in school taps her on the shoulder and shows her his alteration of a text: "He had stroked out the word *Chapman's* in the title of a poem and inked in the word *Milton* so that the title now read: *On First Looking into Milton Homer*" (*Who* 240). The joke refers "rather weakly" to Milton Homer's habit of exposing himself to the people behind him in a line-up. The scene (a boy sitting behind a girl and both reading the same text) is one of many in Munro's fiction which stage the act of reading. Like Milton Homer, Munro is "a mimic of ferocious gifts" (238). It would be a mistake, however, to assume that her popularity results from her skill at deploying some antiquated notion of "realism." I begin here with a contrary presupposition—that our love affair with Alice Munro has as much to do with what we hear as what we see in her fiction. Her densely allusive stories reward an open ear and a quality in readers that John Keats called "*Negative Capability*," the ability to be "in uncertainties, Mysteries, doubts, without any irritable reaching after fact &

reason." It is the quality "which Shakespeare possessed so enormously" (Keats 261).

Munro's playful allusions to ancient oral stories are often missed because she so thoroughly updates them. One paradigm that is nevertheless clearly visible in many stories is the rhythm of departure and return that forms the quest pattern made famous by that other Homer. It often appears in Munro's stories in the inverted form of a visit. Indeed, Munro herself has likened the act of reading to a visit and suggested that a story is like a house:

> You go inside and stay there for a while, wandering back and forth and settling where you like and discovering how the room and corridors relate to each other, how the world outside is altered by being viewed from these windows. And you, the visitor, the reader, are altered as well . . . . You can go back again and again, and the house, the story, always contains more than you saw the last time. It has also a sturdy sense of itself, of being built out of its own necessity, no [sic] just to shelter or beguile you. To deliver a story like that, durable and freestanding, is what I'm always hoping for. ("Introduction" xvii)

The passage captures the experience of rereading—the return to a text and the departure. By itself, however, the analogy is inadequate to account for the impact of Munro's stories because she has left out the importance of what the visitor hears. Imagine that, like Milton and Homer, you are blind. Or else imagine the lights turned off in Munro's house of fiction. You hear voices talking and singing and you are not always sure whether they are coming from inside or outside the house. It is not only what you view from the windows of the house, but also what you hear while wandering in it that will leave "you, the visitor, the reader" altered.

All the stories Munro has "delivered" are "durable and freestanding." Visit any one of them and you will come away altered. Why, given this embarrassment of riches, did I pick "Lichen"? To some degree my initial choice was random. I didn't exactly take a book and let it fall open (as we were encouraged to do with the Bible when I was growing up, just to see what the Lord had to say to us on that particular day), but it was more of an intuitive leap than a reasoned process. It helped that, like *King Lear*, "Lichen" has two syllables. I wasn't about to propose: "On Sitting Down to Read 'The Moon in the Orange Street Skating Rink' Once Again." As happens to those of us who teach, the self-assigned text came to seem the ideal text once I sat down to reread it. What better story to choose for my purpose—which is to persuade readers to listen while they look—than one in which the allusions create echoes around an image that is the detritus of a visit. Munro's choice of an obsolete camera technology in "Lichen" comes without even a hint of nostalgia, but the movement—a few steps backward in time—slows down the reproductive processes. An Instagram would not have done the trick, would not have so richly rewarded "negative capability" in the reader.

"Lichen" is a mystery story. As the Munrovian lightness of the pun in the title shows, it is about the mystery of a process that literary critics describe with words such as representation, mimesis, imitation, and simulacrum—a version of an old Latin word meaning "likeness." A likeness is an image. Munro's early seminal story "Images" anticipates this theme with an exploration of mysterious images in the stories we tell each other. Where do these images come from "in the first place" (*Dance* 38)? In that story a young girl accompanies her father to an underground house. One of the images she remembers is from a story her mother told about "a queen getting her head chopped off while a little dog was hiding under her dress" (33). Not surprisingly, the girl pays attention to the warning that Joe Phippen gives his visitors as they enter: "Mind your head here" (39). Both "Images" and "Lichen" could be seen as parables, but both demand a wary reader.

As Frank Kermode notes, the German word for parable is *Gleichnis*—meaning likeness and a parable is "a similitude," an analogy, a "placing of one thing beside another." It is also a riddle or (in Greek) a "dark saying" (23). Liken! The title can be read as an imperative. To be invited to a process of likening opens a wide door for readers, almost as if we are being invited to make up our own parables. The kingdom of heaven, Jesus said, is "like to a grain of mustard seed," or "like unto leaven," or "like unto treasure hid in a field," or "like unto a merchant man seeking a goodly pearl" (Matthew 13:31, 33, 44, 45). "To divine the true, the latent sense" of such "dark sayings," writes Kermode, "you need to be of the elect, of the institution" (3). When the disciples asked why he taught in parables, Jesus explained that the multitude have ears and hear not. They have eyes and see not (Matthew 13:13). In Mark's version, Jesus speaks in parables *so that* the masses will not understand (Mark 4:12). Just here is where Munro's stories part company, if not with parable form, then at least with assumptions about how parables should be heard. What many have heard Jesus saying is that those who are saved no longer need the help of figurative language—a conclusion all too familiar to those of us brought up in fundamentalist communities. By contrast, Munro's stories show the experience of reading and likening to be a shared and interactive process—more like the pleasure of gossip than like disciples listening to a master.

Let me concede at the outset that in any discussion of figurative language, my response will inevitably be inflected by my Mennonite experience with an angst about representation that goes back to the Reformation. If you grow up in a conservative Mennonite community, as I did, you are part of "a people apart" who try to embody a plain style of living that rejects modernity and defines itself as being outside of history. A to-sudden entry into the modern world can feel like time warp. Although references to Mennonites are rare in Munro's fiction, when they occur they come with an awareness of temporal dislocation. This context is bound to colour my rereading of "Lichen." I have chosen to tell it as a personal story in order to dramatize an idea stated clearly by Richard Poirier: "The passage of time distorts any shapes proposed by art" (37). This distortion does not happen only for Mennonites, but my experience may have given me a heightened awareness of it. As time passes through the Polaroid snapshot in "Lichen," so also does time pass through my rereadings of the story "Lichen." Like the camera in the epilogue to *Lives of Girls and Women*, the snapshot in "Lichen" fails to keep up with "Real Life" and such failures are at the heart of Munro's comedy.

I treasure my memory of the day Alice Munro told me how much she appreciated that I had written about her as a comic writer. "I'm sick of being treated as a grim realist," she said. I responded by asking: "Do you think of yourself as a clown then?" She replied: "Always, Maggie! Always!" As I know from my training in the Pochinko clowning tradition, different clowns use different masks. Munro's masks often involve self-parody. Del, in *Lives of Girls and Women*, and Almeda Joynt Roth, in "Meneseteung," are only the most conspicuous examples of this tendency. Self-parody, as Poirier notes "is bound by its allegiance, minute by minute, to the passage of time." It does "what Griffith thought of doing with his camera: of holding it on a scene so long that the scene would have to break up. Hold the camera, that is, on the noble rider until he climbs down" (36–37). I have noted previously that Poirier's analogy "brings to mind the Polaroid picture that disintegrates after being left in the sun in 'Lichen'" ("Scottish" 39). Here my aim is to follow through on the implications of this for the reader. I seek to emulate Munro by showing how the literary critic's response is similarly vulnerable to the passage of time. As Terry Eagleton notes, "even the intellectuals—hard though it sometimes is to credit them—share a common humanity with others .... The critic who recognizes all this is the critic as clown" (627).

To self-identify as a clown does not mean that you can avoid moral questions. On the contrary. Munro's clowning raises questions that Margaret Atwood identifies as recurring in Munro's stories. "What is fakery, what is authenticity? [. . .] How much of art is genuine, how much just a bag of cheap tricks—imitating people, manipulating their emotions, making faces?" (xv–vi). Because I am a Mennonite, these questions resonate with my own culture of plain speaking. Reading Munro, however, makes me aware of how such questions are also complicated by class issues. Like Munro, I grew up on a farm. There are times when I hear her being interviewed that I feel a class connection on such a visceral level that all the differences seem beside the point. The differences are there, however, and they have to do with religion and ethnicity. The aspect of my experience that is most important for my approach to Munro is oral culture, but unlike Munro I did not learn English until I was seven. That was when I started attending a one-room school. As I think about questions related to rereading, I remember the small collection in a bookcase that stood at the back of Roseville School. I lost track of how many times I reread *Jean Val Jean* during the nine years of my education in that room. The seasons and the days just kept going round and round, as they do on a farm, but stories from the Bible were told both at home and in church and these kept reminding us (often in ominous tones) of eternity. Every day, however, was filled with Low German sayings and stories and jokes. This oral repertoire has remained available to me over the years and has influenced my focus on comedy, but I can now see that self-identifying as a clown may just be a way of affirming imbalance as the default position.

It is surely not surprising, since retrospective reflections are an inherent part of all rereading, that an aging literary critic would be inclined to reflect about the process of rereading. I think it no coincidence that Patricia Spacks wrote *On Rereading* after she retired. When I look backward, I am aware that one constant for me has been a repeated return to the stability of individual texts that offer new rewards each time they are reread. Trained as a New Critic when I was an undergraduate, I am still happiest when I permit myself the luxury of staying with a single story or poem. I follow the advice of Seneca: "We should imitate the bees," he advised, "which wander and pluck suitable flowers to make honey, then carry whatever, they arrange and distribute through the honeycomb" (Epistle 84). "[S]ince you cannot read all the books which you may possess," Seneca writes," it is enough to possess only as many books as you can read" (Epistle I). In other words, you must downsize—as we all do when we age. My own downsizing has left me with a small collection of books—mostly collections of poetry. And Alice Munro. I carry passages from Munro's stories in my head the way I remember favourite poems. Wai Chee Dimock is right that it is resonance that makes us go back to a great work of art, that a text is not a self-contained vessel holding timeless truths but more like an "echo chamber" (1062). Texts endure, Dimock argues, because they are "touched" as they travel, "causing unexpected vibrations in unexpected places" in "readers on different wavelengths" (1061).

On Rereading "Lichen" While Time Passed

These are the words from "Lichen" that resonate for me. I know them by heart. "She said it was lichen. No, she said it looked like lichen . . . . She said, 'Lichen.' And now, look, her words have come true" (*Progress* 73). Never mind truth. Never mind looking. *Listen* to the sound of the words—the alliteration that is like waves lapping as we overhear Stella hearing an echo of her own voice. Each time I read "Lichen," new voices resonate along with the ones I remember from before. The allusions are sometimes explicit—Hercules, Balm of Gilead, Book of Kells—and sometimes faint echoes that I can barely hear. Shakespeare's madrigal, once quoted, whispers over every line: "What's to come is still unsure." I did reread "Lichen" at one sitting—and then again—but in between I let it simmer—marinate—sit in the sun. Take your pick of metaphors. The point is that time passed. People died. I went for walks with my husband. Often when I started to read I would stop because of some interruption. In the meantime, the words of the story reverberated in my head. My aim here is to be open to interruptions in order to mime the way events constantly destabilize all our readings. Although the inevitable result will be a somewhat meandering and anecdotal account, there is nevertheless a selective process at work. The moments I choose to highlight will be those that illuminate the issues I have raised in my prefatory comments.

Coming back to any work of art after a passage of time is a reminder of what has changed. Nobody steps into the same river twice, as Heraclitus pointed out. No reader reads the same story twice. But it is not the story that changes. The experience of rereading is not unlike encountering a friend you have not seen for a long time. The difference is that the friend has not aged. When I first met Stella, back in the

1980s, she was older than I was then. This time, when she steps out of the bushes in the first paragraph, a "short, fat, white-haired woman, wearing jeans and a dirty T-shirt," she is closer to my age. When David fumes and says his ex-wife has "turned into a troll," Catherine "says decently, 'Well. She's older.'" In response to which David scoffs: "'Older than what, Catherine? Older than the house? Older than Lake Huron? Older than the cat?'" (43). David, of course, is a walking cliché—the man bogged down in a midlife crisis—and his joking is a defence. Most readers of "Lichen" will want to maintain an ironic distance from him, but the compassion in the story keeps us close to his feelings, to the anxiety about death that is, after all, universal. To a large extent we see him through the eyes of Stella. Her name sets up numerous echoes including an association with an important star, the sun. The sentence with which I concluded my previous close reading of "Lichen" reflected my wariness of her power: "It is oddly comforting to be reminded that the power of the sunlight on the Polaroid shot is greater than that of the 'little sunbeam' who acts as a mock mother at the 'Balm of Gilead Home'" (*Mothers* 191). My response to Stella now is more forgiving, for lack of a better word. As a housekeeper, she acts out a deep desire in all of us that Wallace Stevens refers to as our "Blessed rage for order" (130). I now hear in her name an echo that I don't remember ever hearing before: the German word *Stelle*—meaning "place" or "to place." She is a kind of placeholder for the reader. Like any other *Stelle*, "Stella's domain" is subject to the ravages of time and, like all of us, Stella has her defences.

Although the story is mostly focalized through her, there are places where a camera eye takes over (as it does, for example, when David is on the telephone trying to call Dina), and these places help to distance us from Stella. For the most part, however, her power is palpable. It can be felt in passages such as the following, which contains a satiric edge: "When David first met Catherine, about eighteen months ago, he thought she was a little over thirty . . . . She has aged since then. And she was older than he thought to start with—she is nearing forty" (44). I feel Stella nudging me to do the uncomfortable arithmetic that David avoids. At the same time, I am grateful for the fact that Munro does not leave the naked truth unclothed. Like Shakespeare in the opening scenes of *King Lear*, she rejects the language of numbers in favour of images. The title of this story is deictic. It points to a particular image in the story. In my earlier reading I described the story's sections as layered webbing, noting that the Greek word for web, *erion*, is also the word for pubic hair (*Mothers* 184). I saw the title as a veil and the search for meaning as the striptease that Patricia Parker associates with "inescapable romance."

I still think this puts an interesting spin on one of the funniest moments in *Lives of Girls and Women*, Del Jordan's lament: "Love is not for the undepilated" (196).

As I began my rereading of "Lichen" I found myself lingering over the title again. It is a tantalizing sign that floats over the story as if in search of signification. Is it simile, metonymy, or metaphor? Briefly I considered the possibility that it could be metalepsis, a trope that would allow for indirection. The daunting theoretical complexities of that possibility left me wondering if perhaps the title is a practical joke on literary critics—designed to anticipate the kind of excess for which we are now notorious. Did I say the title points to a picture? That is not the whole truth. It also points away from the text to a particular kind of plant. All theory aside, simple curiosity led me to wonder if "lichen" is an edible plant. Back in the early 1990s I would have turned to my tattered set of the *Encyclopaedia Britannica* (11th edition). This time I googled and read the Wikipedia article on *lichen*. It was accompanied by a photograph that did look a bit like pubic hair but was otherwise unhelpful. Eventually I chose to hear the title as Munro's invitation to ponder the ways in which art can be likened to an organic process. For the Romantics, this metaphor was part of an affirmation of the redemptive power of the imagination, but Munro's is a more muted response. I hear her asking some of the same questions that Shakespeare explores in act IV, scene 4 of *The Winter's Tale*. Does art "mend nature?" Or is it that "art itself is nature?" I visualize the title as a moss-covered door, perhaps like the one at the threshold of the underground house in "Images." It could conceal traps for the unwary, as the girl in that story fears, so it behooves us to be active as we listen to the story.

It is a simple story on the face of it—a story about a dinner party. The visitors (Stella's ex-husband David and his girlfriend Catherine) arrive at Stella's "high bare wooden house [. . .] on the clay bluffs overlooking Lake Huron" (42). Stella and David go to visit her father in the Balm of Gilead nursing home. They return for dinner, after which David absents himself to phone Dina while the women do the dishes. Then David and Catherine leave. The next morning Stella finishes the post-party cleanup.

The story may be simple, but underneath or behind or through the surface of it you can pick up the vibrations of multiple allusions that mix with the talk of the people at the dinner party. Other readers may be on different wavelengths, but I always hear Virginia Woolf. Fragments of Woolf float in and out of "Lichen" as I read—the image of Mrs. Ramsay sitting at the window in *To the Lighthouse*, that famous dinner party, and through it all the waves and time passing. Countless other echoes, however, are mixed in with those. Indeed, there are so many echoes that it would be overwhelming if the story were not so firmly grounded in a particular location—summer house and garden, lake and beach. On the shore near the house stands an old lighthouse. If you extrapolated it from "Lichen," it could stand as an illustration for this passage in John Berger's *Ways of Seeing:* "The convention of perspective . . . centres everything on the eye of the beholder. It is like a beam from a lighthouse [. . . .] The conventions called those appearances *reality*. Perspective makes the single eye the centre of the visible world" (16). But of course you cannot extrapolate the lighthouse. You can only see it if you stand in one particular spot in Stella's house and "squeeze right down to the end" (47) of the window. The next viewer will shove you aside to get a look and, like as not, the result will be conversation and a wave of laughter.

Stella's discovery of the Polaroid shot on the windowsill draws the reader backward into the story and downward into deeper thinking. The picture is a reminder of Dina, the person who was not invited to the dinner party and who has no voice. In this absence can be felt, if you think about it, the presence of other women who have no voice. To me, Dina appears as a shadowy version of the child in the "old negative," in "Images," the one "with blazing hair and burned-out Orphan Annie eyes (*Dance* 38). If the grouping at the dinner party in "Lichen" is seen as a parody of a family, then Dina plays the part of a child "exiled from the family," perhaps even a molested child (*Mothers* 20). While trying to reach her on the phone, David pictures her with an "assortment of windup toys," watching as they "lurch and clatter" across her floor, "spitting sparks out of their mouths" while she "squeals, and even screams with excitement" (62). In his photograph, by contrast, she appears as the "other woman" spreading her legs for his camera. These images cannot be reconciled and for that very reason go counter to the notorious rigidity of pornographic images.

Feminist debates on the topic of pornography keep foundering on issues related to agency, and my rereading of "Lichen" has brought me full circle back to the questions that obsessed me many years ago. Who is the man with the axe in "Images?" Who is "The Photographer" in *Lives of Girls and Women*? Who is the king of the royal beatings in *Who Do You Think You Are?* And where, in all this, is the reader? A voyeur? An eavesdropper? What part do we play in the development of the images from the negatives? In this story David appears to be a predator, but to what extent does he control the image? When he puts it in his pocket, there may be a sly allusion to a "pocket Venus," a term that is sometimes used to refer to a small, beautiful woman. If so, it would convey, in this context, the sinister suggestion of ownership that Susan Sontag explores with relation to photography. David, however, is a pathetic failure as a bogeyman. We know from *King Lear* that it is a shock when a king is dethroned because it means we have to confront our own power. That confrontation comes with awareness of the inescapable fact that inequality is a part of the collective human condition. There may be moments, to be sure, when we have the illusion of equality. It happens in "The Moon in the Orange Street Skating Rink" when Callie's power briefly seems to be "generously distributed." But this, as the storyteller reminds us, "was just happiness. It was really just happiness" (*Progress* 214).

Happy moments there are in Munro's fiction, but at no point in any of her stories does she offer solutions to the moral dilemmas she presents with such heartbreaking clarity. What she does do, repeatedly, is to ask questions about what it is that art—including her own—can offer in the face of them. If art does not transcend and should not evade, then of what use is it? She starts by capitulating, by admitting that all art fails. She is a clown. "Always, Maggie! Always!" Even as art fails—indeed, *because* it fails to transcend—art is transformed into something that affirms life and a common humanity. This is the deep satisfaction of metamorphosis. The way Munro achieves it in "Lichen" is by means of a subtle and layered use of *ekphrasis*, the rhetorical device that presents a work of art in one medium as a response to a work of art in another medium. The moment when Stella is alone, looking at the photograph, overlaps with the previous moment in the story when David coerces her into looking at it. The result is a doubled *ekphrastic* scene that creates a frisson, drawing the reader in. We cannot, of course, see the picture to which the title points. What we see are the filters through which the picture is seen. The two layers implicitly overlap with the long history of visual art in which naked women play an important role as the objects of a mostly male gaze. As Stella "squints obediently" (55), a camera eye seems to take over. The words reflect a conscious straining to see the image as "great art," but the feeling is that of the kind of dissociation described by victims of sexual abuse. "The legs are spread wide—smooth, golden, monumental: fallen columns" (55). As I reread this passage I heard, for the first time, an echo from Shelley's "Ozymandias." Like the "vast and trunkless legs of stone" in Shelley's "colossal wreck," these legs communicate ruin and desolation (550). Munro rejects the ideal human body of classic realism and opts instead for what Bakhtin called "grotesque realism" (19–21). Like countless other critics, I have been tempted to follow Bakhtin in associating this with folk laughter. As I read Munro's lines now, however, it seems to me that somewhere a clown is weeping. What comes to mind is that scene of *ekphrasis* in Virgil's *Aeneid*, where Aeneas (his face wet with tears) looks at a painting of the Trojan War and speaks these words: *sunt lacrimae rerum et mentem mortalia tangent* (1.462). "Tears are at the heart of things, and mortality touches us."

Lacrimae rerum. The words feel just right for the closing of "Lichen." Stella looks at the picture through the pain of her "old cavity" and through the scar tissue of her divorce. That doesn't stop the reader from reaching out to connect with Dina. It would be wrong to sentimentalize the story but also wrong to deny the depth of the feelings evoked. The comfort that can be found in Munro's art goes along with a feeling of having been stretched somehow. We are "altered," to use her word, by the visit to this story partly because of this reaching out, however partial, toward compassion. The layering of *ekphrastic* scenes in "Lichen" left me with an awareness of history—of the inheritance of the past that comes to us via allusion, as Christopher Ricks has often pointed out. Standing here with Stella I could feel the presence of countless others who have stood in some place, some *Stelle*, in front of countless other images. Have stood there and have laughed and cried.

I was reminded of how both laughter and tears are at the heart of things when, in between rereadings of "Lichen," I spent a weekend in New York in April 2014, and went to see an exhibition at the Neue Galerie. Entitled "Degenerate Art: The Attack on Modern Art in Nazi German, 1937," it is a show that might as well have been headlined: See this and weep. So why did I hear myself laughing as I stood in front of the three enormous paintings of pseudo-classical naked women that hung over Adolf Hitler's fireplace? They were painted by Adolf Ziegler, who has come down in history as "the master of German pubic hair." I thought of how this kind of realism is about as far from "Lichen" as you can get. Henri Bergson was right, I believe, that we laugh at mechanical rigidities (such as Nazi thinking) because laughter restores the plasticity of life itself. At the same time, as Munro shows repeatedly, jokes happen within social settings and offer no easy escape from moral dilemmas. David's leaving the picture on the windowsill could be a practical joke on Stella. But who gets the last laugh? He complains to Stella that Catherine makes him want to hurt her. "Sometimes I think the best thing to do would be to give her the big chop. Coup de grace. Coup de grace, Catherine. Here you are. Big chop" (57). The word *chop* echoes Stella's earlier description of Dina's pubic hair—"the dark blot she called moss, or lichen. But it's really more like the dark pelt of an animal, with the head and tail and feet chopped off. Dark silky pelt of some unlucky rodent" (55). Chop. Somewhere in some other story by Munro, somebody makes a savage joke with the term "chop suey." I could not remember which story. And then, all of a sudden, it did not matter.

It was at about this time that my sister Mary telephoned with the news that my sister Sarah had died unexpectedly—at the youthful age of eighty-three. Sarah was a storyteller, all her stories punctuated with her distinctive merry laugh. When I returned to Toronto from her funeral in Manitoba, I read at random and aimlessly as you do when you have gone through a hard time. I came across a review of Marina Warner's latest book: a study of *The Arabian Nights*. The reviewer quotes Warner: "The power of stories to forge destinies has never been so memorably and sharply put as it is in this cycle, in which the blade of the executioner's sword lies on the storyteller's neck" (Warner 5). As I read these words I heard an echo: "Big chop." It was one of those small eureka moments. Suddenly it struck me that I had missed what may well be the most important intertext in "Lichen" and that David can be seen as a domesticated version of what Warner calls the "prototype serial killer, an ogre, a Bluebeard." The series of women who get the chop—Stella, Rosemary, Catherine, Dina—are like those murdered by the Sultan in the frame story of *The Thousand and One Nights*.

Once I had registered this echo, the larger implications for Munro's fiction seemed obvious. Of course Munro (who once spoke of how she reread Proust repeatedly while writing *Lives of Girls and Women*) would be drawn, as Proust was, to think of herself as Shahrazad. And of course, like Proust, she would focus on stories about everyday events. David's attachment to Stella is to the stories she shaped "out of their life—the children's daily mishaps and provocations, the cat's visit to the vet . . . the papering of the upstairs hall" (70–1) And of course Munro, unlike Rushdie and Calvino and Marquez, would stay with the realism of the frame story, never straying from what is believable. David does not actually kill those women, but Munro takes liberties in the stories within stories. There, as in *The Arabian Nights*, heads (or trunks) are chopped off and no shape stays constant.

The most alarming shape shifting in "Lichen" is simply that of the aging human body, which is always in the process of being absorbed back into the land. Mary's chin, for example, is described as having "collapsed into a series of terraces flowing into her neck" (50). In an inversion of that trope, Stella looks at the lakeshore from the kitchen while preparing supper (52–53) and comments: "Those groins are going to have to be rewired entirely." *Groin* (sometimes spelled groyne) is a term used by coastal engineers to describe barriers that are built to prevent erosion of the shore. Stella's use of the word, however, takes on a more disturbing implication because it immediately follows a crude comment by David about how women get a smell "when they know you don't want them anymore. Stale." The sentence that follows could be read as a response of sorts: "Stella slaps the meat over." The dialogue, however, is deliberately elliptical and we know Stella is looking out the window and not at David. Ignoring his comment, she makes the observation about the groins, adding: "The wire is just worn to cobwebs in some places." (53). The scene is all the more disturbing because it is anchored by the domesticity of Stella's actions as she prepares dinner. Here, as elsewhere in the story, the sound of the words and the repetition of imagery results in a poetic effect. Reading of how the water has worn the wires to cobwebs, the reader hears an echo from a preceding passage in which Catherine's dress is described as made of a "cobwebby cotton" (43). In these tropes of disintegrating land and body, I hear an echo of Emily Dickinson's "crumbling," which is "first a Cobweb on the Soul" (230).

Deep down we know very well that what's to come is not unsure at all. Like the Sultan, we keep on listening because we want to know how the story ends. Closure is the boundary defined by genre. In "On Sitting down to Read 'King Lear' Once Again," Keats begins with Petrarchan sonnet form and then switches to Elizabethan—which allows him to end with a couplet: "But when I am consumed in the fire, / Give me new Phoenix wings to fly at my desire" (133). No such metaphor is to be found in the ending of "Lichen." As the story ends, Stella is alone in the house: "The day is perfect. The windows are open, her house is pleasantly in order, and a good fish soup is simmering on the stove" (73). Into this everyday scene Munro inserts a piece of found art. As I hope my rereading has shown, it asks ancient questions about art in a fresh new way. You could liken it to Keats's "Ode on a Grecian Urn" but it is closer to Wallace Stevens's "Anecdote of the Jar." The Polaroid shot is "like nothing else" in Huron County (76). The black of the pubic hair has "turned to gray, to the soft, dry color of a plant mysteriously nourished on the rocks" (73). Point of view is briefly focused clearly on Stella: "This is David's doing. He left it there, in the sun"—but the question of agency is up in the air. The rinky dinks control the moon in the Orange Street skating rink. Who controls the sun in "Lichen"? The ending is both comforting and discomforting because it is clear that trying to answer such questions simply generates more stories. Warner writes of the "dot dot dot which intervenes between one break of day and the next night" of the thousand and one Arabian nights (5). Listen to the echo of this in the very last lines of "Lichen": "Stella's words have come true. This thought will keep coming back to her—a pause, a lost heartbeat, a harsh little break in the flow of the days and nights as she keeps them going" (74).

We can keep the days and nights going if we keep telling each other stories (in between making some more love) but nothing can avert that "big chop." Munro's closing compassionate gesture is not an epiphany but a shared awareness that although we long for epiphany, we settle for enigma. The reward of recognizing this is an increase in "negative capability." In her introduction to *Selected Stories*, Munro ends with a quotation from *Tristram Shandy* about how we "live amongst riddles and mysteries . . . and yet we find the good of it . . . and that's enough for us" (xvii). "Lichen" is a mystery without solution that catches a reader in the act of searching for analogies. In "On First Looking into Chapman's Homer," Keats posits a series of these: "Then felt I *like* some watcher of the skies" (emphasis added) and concludes with the men staring at each other "with a wild surmise . . . silent upon a peak in Darien" (18).

As I leave this durable house of fiction, closing the lichen-covered door behind me, the voices recede. When I have left, Stella may well tidy up by tossing the picture in the garbage before returning to the writing of her book about the lighthouse. I am free to meditate on the found artifact, to express my "wild surmise" at Munro's magic but at the same time to take something away with me. This may account for the way we love "our Alice." You can take her stories to heart, so to speak, and make them part of your life. Not in the sense that they offer tangible advice for living and not in the way that David, the photographer as predator, puts the photograph in his pocket. It's rather something provisional—fallible but my own—something that I make of the story after it has changed me and that I may then pass on to you—a kind of gift. Nothing too fancy, as we Mennonites like to say. In Low German we would call it *toupjekaubelt*. Cobbled together. The failure of "the critic as clown" mimes that of the artist as clown. Munro stages failure in many and unpredictable ways. It is what clowns do and Munro is a brilliant clown. The body of her work draws readers into participation in one long "comedy of errors."

Here, in closing, is what I cobbled together one day while walking with my husband on the High Line in New York. It has become my favourite place in that city—an abandoned railway track turned into a walking path that is also an open-air art gallery. Here gardeners have created a space where nature has a chance to mend the damage done by technology. We came upon a sculpture by Gavin Kenyon entitled *Realism Marching Triumphantly Into the City*. The accompanying literature described it as one of Kenyon's biomorphic "vaguely bestial shapes"—the result of a "chance-laden process of filling fur-lined bags with plaster and then constraining them with rope." The caption helpfully suggested that it was like a "crumbling equestrian monument from a distant past." But I thought to myself: "No, she said it looks like lichen." It was one of those moments when a work of art reminds me that the earth will still be beautiful even when our species is extinct and we are not there to see it. Perched on a blossoming tree behind us, a bird—some kind of thrush—was singing like crazy. Here is what the thrush said to me:

> When old age shall this generation waste, "Lichen" shall remain, a friend to man and woman, to whom it says (in the words of James Baldwin): "Life is more important than art. That's why art is so important."

Note

1. On questions related to allusion I am particularly indebted to John Hollander's *The Figure of Echo*. Hollander's taxonomy is useful because it allows for a range of effects, some of them the result of intention and involving quotation, others arising from involuntary echoes.

Works Cited

Atwood, Margaret. "Introduction." Alice Munro. *Carried Away: A Personal Selection of Stories*. New York: Knopf, 2006. ix–xxi.

Bakhtin, M. M. *Rabelais and His World*. Trans. H. Iswolsky. Bloomington.: Indiana UP, 1968.

Berger, John. *Ways of Seeing*. London: British Broadcasting Corporation, 1972.

Bergson, Henri. *Laughter: An Essay on the Meaning of the Comic*. Trans. Cloudesley Brereton and Fred Rothwell. New York: Macmillan, 1911.

Dickinson, Emily. *Final Harvest: Emily Dickinson's Poems*. Ed. Thomas H. Johnson. Boston, Toronto: Little, Brown, 1890.

Dimock, Wai Chee. "A Theory of Resonance." *PMLA* 112.5 (1997):1060–71.

Eagleton, Terry. "The Critic as Clown." *Marxism and the Interpretation of Culture*. Ed. Cary Nelson and Lawrence Grossberg. Urbana: U of Illinois P, 1988, 619–31.

Hollander, John. *The Figure of Echo: A Mode of Allusion in Milton and After*. Berkeley: U of California P, 1981.

Keats, John. *Selected Poems and Letters.* Boston: Houghton Mifflin, 1959.

Kermode, Frank. *The Genesis of Secrecy: On the Interpretation of Narrative.* Cambridge, MA.: Harvard UP, 1979.

Munro, Alice. *Dance of the Happy Shades.* 1968. Rpt. Toronto: McGraw-Hill Ryerson, 1988.

———. "Introduction." *Selected Stories.* Toronto: Penguin, 1998, ix–xvii.

———. *Lives of Girls and Women.* 1971. Toronto: Penguin, 1996.

———. *The Moons of Jupiter.* 1982. Toronto: Penguin, 1986.

———. *The Progress of Love.* 1986. Toronto: Penguin, 1987.

———. *Who Do You Think You Are?* 1978. Toronto: Penguin, 1996.

Parker, Patricia A. *Inescapable Romance: Studies in the Poetics of a Mode.* Princeton, NJ.: Princeton UP, 1979.

Poirier, Richard. *The Performing Self: Compositions and Decompositions in the Languages of Contemporary Life.* New Brunswick, NJ: Rutgers UP, 1992.

Redekop, Magdalene. "Alice Munro's Tilting Fields." In *New Worlds: Discovering and Constructing the Unknown in Anglophone Literature* (Festschrift for Walter Pache). Ed. Martin Kuester, Gabriele Christ, and Rudolf Beck. Munich: Verlag Ernst Vögel, 2000. 343–62.

———. "Alice Munro and the Scottish Nostalgic Grotesque." In *The Rest of the Story: Critical Essays on Alice Munro.* Ed. Robert Thacker. Toronto: ECW, 1999. 21–43.

———. *Mothers and Other Clowns: The Stories of Alice Munro.* London: Routledge, 1992.

Ricks, Christopher. *Allusion to the Poets.* Oxford: Oxford UP, 2002.

Seneca [Lucius Annaeus]. *Moral Epistles.* 3 vols. Trans. Richard M. Gummere. Loeb Classical Library. Cambridge, MA: Harvard UP, 1917–25.

Shakespeare, William. *The Winter's Tale.* Oxford: Oxford UP, 1996.

Shelley, Percy Bysshe. *The Complete Poetical Works of Percy Bysshe Shelley.* Ed. Thomas Hutchinson. London: Oxford UP, 1905.

Sontag, Susan. *On Photography.* New York: Dell, 1973.

Spacks, Patricia. *On Rereading.* Cambridge, MA: Belknap-Harvard UP, 2011.

Stevens, Wallace. *The Collected Poems of Wallace Stevens.* New York: Random House, 1990.

Storace, Patricia. "Queens of the Night." Review of *Stranger Magic: Charmed States and the Arabian Nights,* by Marina Warner. Cambridge, MA: Belknap-Harvard UP, 2012.

———. Review of *One thousand and One Nights.* A retelling by Hanan al-Shaykh, with a foreword by Mary Gaitskill, New York: Pantheon, 2013.

New York Review of Books, 20 March 2014. http://www.nybooks.com/articles/archives/2014/mar/20/queens-night/. 15 August 2015.

Virgil. *The Aeneid.* Ed. J. W. Mackall. Oxford, UK: Clarendon, 1930.

Warner, Marina. *Stranger Magic: Charmed States and the Arabian Nights.* Cambridge, MA: Belknap-Harvard UP, 2012.

Woolf, Virginia. *To The Lighthouse.* 1927. London: Penguin, 2000.

Contributors

D. M. R. BENTLEY is Distinguished University Professor and the Carl F. Klinck Professor in Canadian Literature at Western University. He received his PhD in English from King's College, University of London, in 1974, and specializes in Canadian and Victorian literatures. He is founder of both the periodical *Canadian Poetry: Studies, Documents, Reviews* and Canadian Poetry Press, and the author of such comprehensive studies as 2004's *The Confederation Group of Canadian Poets, 1880–1897.*

CAROL BERAN received her PhD in English in 1977 from UC Berkeley. Since 1995 she has been Professor of English at Saint Mary's College of California. She has published widely in Canadian and American literatures.

E. D. BLODGETT received his PhD in Comparative Literature from Rutgers University in 1969 and is Professor Emeritus at the University of Alberta. Among a highly distinguished resume of publications in Canadian and Comparative literatures is his early monograph on Munro's writings, 1988's *Alice Munro.*

AILSA COX received her PhD in English from Loughborough University in 1999 and is currently Reader in English and Writing at Edge Hill University in England. Her scholarly work focuses on the short story, and she has published on Munro and edited 2011's *Teaching the Short Story.*

IAN DENNIS received his PhD in 1995 from the University of Toronto. Since 2010 he has been Professor of English at the University of Ottawa, where he currently chairs the department. He has published widely in the British Romantics and in the field of generative Anthropology developed by Eric Gans and others.

SARA JAMIESON received her PhD in English from Queen's University in 2002, and is Assistant Professor in the Department of English at Carleton University. She has published critical studies of Canadian writers such as Joan Barfoot, P. K Page, and Munro.

DAVID JARRAWAY received his PhD in English and American Literatures from Brown University in 1990. Since 2000 he has been Professor of English at the University of Ottawa. He publishes in literary history, criticism, and theory, in books and essays on subjects such as Canadian literature and film, Wallace Stevens, and Northrop Frye.

JOSEPHENE KEALEY received her PhD in English from the University of Ottawa in 2011. She is an independent scholar living in Ottawa and the mother of five young children. She has published critical studies of Sherwood Anderson and Alice Munro.

LAURIE KRUK received her PhD in English from the University of Western Ontario (now Western University) in 1992 and has been Associate Professor of English at Nipissing University since 2005. A specialist in the Canadian short story, she is most recently author of 2016's *Double-Voicing the Canadian Short Story.*

MARIA LÖSCHNIGG received her DPhil [PhD] from Graz University of Technology (Austria) in 1988, where she has been Associate Professor of English since 2012. Her research and publishing has focused on Canadian prairie and multicultural writings.

CHARLES E. MAY received his PhD in English from Ohio University in 1966, and since 2006 he has been Professor Emeritus at California State University, in Long Beach. As author of 1994's *The New Short Story Theories* and *The Short Story: Reality as Artifice*, and as editor of 2012's *Critical Insights: Alice Munro*, he is the English-speaking world's leading authority on the short story.

LINDA M. MORRA received her PhD in English from the University of Ottawa in 2002, and is currently Professor of English at Bishop's University. She has authored and edited numerous articles and books, most recently the monograph *Unarrested Archives: Case Studies in Canadian Women's Authorship*.

MAGDALENE REDEKOP received her PhD in English from the University of Toronto in 1976, where she has been Professor Emerita since 2009. She is author of one of the most influential books on Munro's writing, 1992's *Mothers and Other Clowns: The Stories of Alice Munro*.

ROBERT THACKER received his PhD in English from the University of Manitoba in 1981. He has been the Charles A. Dana Professor of Canadian Studies at St. Lawrence University since 2009. Among much else on Munro's writings and career, he is author of the monumental literary biography *Alice Munro: Writing Her Lives*.

TINA TRIGG received her PhD from the University of Ottawa in 2003. Since 2010 she has been Associate Professor of English at The King's University College in Edmonton. She has published widely on Canadian literature, with special attention to the writings of Margaret Atwood.

TRACY WARE received his PhD in English from the University of Western Ontario (now Western University) in 1984. Since 2001 he has been Professor of English at Queen's University. He has published widely in Canadian literature and British Romanticism, including articles and edited books ranging from Wordsworth to the Confederation poets, and from Susan Francis Harrison to Munro.

Reappraisals: Canadian Writers

Series editor: Janice Fiamengo

Reappraisal: Canadian Writers was begun in 1973 in response to a need for single volumes of essays on Canadian authors who had not received the critical attention they deserved or who warranted extensive and intensive reconsideration. It is the longest running series dedicated to the study of Canadian literary subjects. The annual symposium, hosted by the Department of English at the University of Ottawa, began in 1972 and the following year University of Ottawa Press published the first title in the series, *The Grove Symposium*. Since then our editorial policy has remained straightforward: each year to make permanently available in a single volume the best of the criticism and evaluation presented at our symposia on Canadian literature, thereby creating a body of work on and a critical base for the study of Canadian writers and literary subjects.

Previous titles in this collection

David Staines (ed.), *The Worlds of Carol Shields*, 2014

Janice Fiamengo (ed.), *Home Ground and Foreign Territory: Essays on Early Canadian Literature*, 2014

David R. Jarraway (ed.), *Double-Takes: Intersections between Canadian Literature and Film*, 2013

Robert David Stacey (ed.), *Reading the Postmodern: Canadian Literature and Criticism after Modernism*, 2011

David Rampton (ed.), *Northrop Frye: New Directions from Old*, 2010

For a complete list of our titles in this series, see:

www.press.uottawa.ca/series/french-and-canadian-studies/reappraisals-canadian-writers

www.ingramcontent.com/pod-product-compliance
Lightning Source LLC
LaVergne TN
LVHW010602100826
845148LV00014B/2818

* 9 7 8 0 7 7 6 6 2 4 3 3 4 *